CW00750031

Messianic Jewish
ORTHODOXY

The Essence of Our Faith,
History and Best Practices

General Editor
Dr. Jeffrey Seif

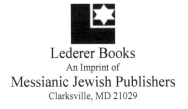

Lederer Books
An Imprint of
Messianic Jewish Publishers
Clarksville, MD 21029

Unless otherwise noted, all Scripture quotations are from the *Complete Jewish Bible* © David H. Stern, Jewish New Testament Publications, Inc., 1998 and the *Complete Jewish Bible*, updated version, 2016.

Also quoted is the NASB, used by permission of The Lockman Foundation and the Tree of Life Version (TLV), used by permission.

Printed in the United States of America

Cover design by Lisa Rubin,
Messianic Jewish Publishers
Graphic Design by Yvonne Vermillion,
Magic Graphix, Westfork, Arkansas

2019   1

ISBN 978-1733935425

Library of Congress Control Number: 2019942900

Published by:
Lederer Books
An imprint of Messianic Jewish Publishers
6120 Day Long Lane
Clarksville, MD 21029

Distributed by:
Messianic Jewish Publishers & Resources
Order line: (800) 410-7367
lederer@messianicjewish.net
www.MessianicJewish.net

This book is dedicated to my deceased wife, Patti, who encouraged me to compile a book such as this. She also designed and created the cover. May she rest in peace.

Table of Contents

Introduction

Twenty-five years ago, I had a lunch conversation with David Bricker, leader of Jews for Jesus, that left an indelible mark on me. David was lamenting how all sorts of self-taught and self-ordained teachers were out and about, peddling their fringe teachings in the marketplace of religious ideas. Though these people weren't vetted or trained by anyone, their ideas were unfortunately considered representative of Messianic Jewish or Jewish-Christian understandings. It seemed then, as now, that just about anyone could call himself a rabbi, throw around a few Hebrew words, claim to be a theologian, self-publish a book, perhaps get a TV spot and, by means of the above, become a self-appointed ambassador of things Jewish to the Christian world.

Rather than just lament the fact, my thinking then, as now, was that if those of us who *were* formally trained in theology, philosophy and ministry, and who possessed moderate theological sensibilities, didn't speak up about the essence and substance of Messianic Jewish theology and practice collectively, we by default abrogated our responsibility and gave our message and its meaning over to the crazies at the fringes. During the aforementioned lunch, David Bricker challenged me to use my influence and connections as a Bible college professor to forge a collective telling. Eventually I did, many years later... This is the result.

It sounded like a good idea, but, quite frankly, I was skeptical. I believed it was impossible to get a variety of Jews together, never mind Jewish scholars. I'd long critically reflected on the image of a shepherd leading sheep and questioned its appropriateness for ministry. For me, ministry is more like trying to herd cats. It's a messy business. I thought, *Leading a collection of Jewish scholars—no way!* But, after I later accepted Daniah Greenberg's invitation to serve as the Project Manager for the *Tree of Life Bible*, I discovered that scholars really did want to work together.

While engaged with that project, Rabbi Barry Rubin, president of Messianic Jewish Publishers, asked me to contribute to a then-forthcoming Messianic study Bible, using Dr. David Stern's *Complete Jewish Bible* for the Bible text. Published in 2016, in a partnership between Messianic Jewish Publishers and Hendrickson Bible Publishers, the *Complete Jewish Study Bible* includes a wealth of material from various sources, predominantly Jewish, to provide *Insights for Jews and Christians*, its subtitle. I discovered I really wanted to contribute to it, and so did others. Much to my surprise, I discovered I wanted to work with others, and others wanted to work with me.

This fact was further attested to when I later inquired of over 50 Messianic-minded scholars what they thought were some of the key issues worth addressing in theology and ministry today. I received around 40 responses. I assimilated those reflections, put my assessments in writing, titled them and sent summaries back to those who'd responded—so they could hear our collective response to the question. Scholars seemed genuinely interested.

Responses to the draft were received by me and further considered, and a template for a book project was organized, whereby our seasoned scholars could reflect on and give voice to what they considered some of the best understandings and practices among us. The joint-venture Messianic Jewish book you have in hand contains the results. It is bookended by two Christian theologians, associates of mine at Kings University, who explain how Jewish voice, though helpful, is both lacking and needed in Christian understanding today.

This book has been in process for quite some time. I started this when my late wife, Patricia Lynn, was dying of cancer. She eventually succumbed to the disease. The dark tunnel I walked through then, with death, grief and readjustment, slowed me down; the bright tunnel I eventually walked toward, when I found new love and new life with Barri Cae, slowed me down too. I wasn't as attuned to the intellectual life as I might otherwise have been. Eventually, however, equilibrium was restored.

The pieces came together when a rabbi's wife, Daniah Greenberg, and Rabbi Barry Rubin afforded me the opportunity to bring this work to term. Contributors make free use of the *Tree of Life* (*TLV*) version of the Bible and the *Complete Jewish Bible* (*CJB*), the two most popular Messianic Jewish versions.

A book of this nature is long overdue, though its forerunner, *Voices of Messianic Judaism: Confronting Critical Issues Facing a Maturing Movement* (also published by Messianic Jewish Publishers in 2001), tackled some of the more-challenging issues in this movement. The present book exists today because, unlike yesterday, there exist even more scholars interested in maintaining intellectual residence in two distinct-yet-related cultures: Jewish and Christian. Jews have come to faith in Jesus/Yeshua in modernity. Pride of place is naturally given to our Jewish culture of origin, on the one hand, as with membership in Christian experience and culture, on the other. Naturally, these confluences and tensions produce some new and interesting ways of seeing, thinking and being—all of which are reflected in the book.

Itself a joint-venture work from the moderate conservative center of the Messianic Jewish revival, this book also speaks to the interests the Church has in Jews, Israel and eschatology, with a balanced Jewish perspective on faith, theology, and practice and for the many tens of thousands of Jews who have come to faith and who participate in Messianic Jewish experience and who frequent churches. Our non-Jewish friends who associate with the movement will find this beneficial as well. It represents some of our best understandings and practices.

An associate of mine at The King's University, Dr. William Bjoraker (who is of non-Jewish extract), also a professor and missiologist at William Cary International University, offers the opening chapter, wherein he extols the virtues of Jewish narrative. He begins with a telling of the long-abiding Jewish premium on storytelling in theology, as opposed to attempting to make God's will and ways known through excessive theological abstractions—as is the tradition in Christian theology. Professor Bjoraker recognizes Jews think and talk about God a bit differently, with the aforementioned difference being the main one. He explains. You'll love it.

An Israeli and a Jewish believer in Yeshua/Jesus, Dr. Dan Juster, a premier Messianic Jewish scholar with intellectual roots at McCormick Seminary, gives an example of Jewish approaches to narrative theology, in his easy-to-read introductory chapter. Prof. Hellene Dallaire of Denver Seminary, an evangelical who took her doctorate in Semitic languages from Hebrew Union College, weighed in on it as well. Rabbi Juster's introductory piece is then followed by another Israeli professor, Dr. Seth Postell. Seth took a doctoral degree from Golden Gate Seminary and is a current professor at Israel College of the Bible. He responsibly walks through the Hebrew Bible and, with laser precision, creatively considers the Messianism embedded in the story's narrative. He approaches Messianism in the Old Testament with the metanarrative in mind, as opposed to, say, simply arguing the case for Jesus by lifting out and fussing over the word "virgin" in Isaiah 7:14, or by tendering a conventional rendering of Isaiah 53. For him, Messianism is in the whole story, not just pieces lifted out of it. An Israeli named John Taylor, who moved to the country after finishing at Dallas Theological Seminary, responded. These scholars all generally draw the same conclusions as evangelicals, but they get there from different angles—from decidedly Jewish ways of reckoning. You're going to appreciate what they serve up. It won't let you down.

Drawing upon her doctoral degree from Hebrew University in Jerusalem, Dr. Vered Hillel, another Messianic Jewish scholar from Israel, farms ancient post-biblical primary sources that attest to early Jewish thought processes before Jesus, and give voice to how Jews understood Messianism before Yeshua/Jesus made his entrance onto the stage of the human drama. I then follow her work on the Second Temple Period with a chapter on century one and the early Messianic movement that emerged in it. Dr. Hillel gave voice to the principal thought processes that informed the thinking of the actors who appeared on the stage of the New Testament's drama; for my part, I, a Jewish believer and former Yeshiva student who later took a doctorate from Southern Methodist University (with roots at Moody Bible Institute), explore the Jesus movement in light of those understandings, and consider where, when and how Jesus-beliefs penetrated into ancient Jewish and non-Jewish cultures, as the early Church got traction beyond Israel's borders. An evangelical, Dr. Jim Sibley, formerly with Criswell College and currently with Israel College of the Bible (who took his doctorate at Southwestern Baptist Theological Seminary), offered critical reflections on my section, as did my wife and biggest fan, Dr. Barri Cae Seif, herself a college professor at Grace Christian University.

Moving into the modern phenomenon of Messianic Jewish experience, a second-generation Messianic Jewish rabbi named Jacob Rosenberg, who wrote his Ph.D. dissertation at Trinity University on the story of the emergent Messianic movement, unpacks some of the congregational movement's best perspectives and practices. Rabbi Eric Tokajer, one of our more-successful rabbis, weighs in on it along with him. Speaking of modern, lest the book get bogged down by too much professorial, intellectual and historical fare, contemporary musical artist Paul Wilbur, along with a younger Messianic artist, Dr. Greg Silverman, lighten the intellectual load, and note how renewed Messianic Jewish energies produced then—and produce now—new expressions of inspiration and worship.

A Messianic Jewish missiologist and president of Chosen People Ministries, Dr. Mitch Glaser, who did his Ph.D. dissertation at Fuller Seminary on Messianic history and experience, took a look at ancient biblical theology and the modern state of Israel—something important to all Messianic Jews and a plethora of evangelicals. Support for Israel is central, and Mitch, whose work was reflected on somewhat by Dr. Jeff Johnson, gives voice to how and why.

Dr. Boyd Luder, who took his Ph.D. from the Dallas Theological Seminary and who has served as a seminary dean at Biola University, was tasked with reviewing the work and tendering a response. My wife, Dr. Barri Cae Seif, looked at and interacted with Prof. Luder's piece. Dr. Luder has his roots in evangelical experience, not Messianic Jewish experience. As he is a credible theologian with pristine pedigree and deep connections in the broader Christian world, I wanted him to take a look at the book and tender a response from his perspective—which, to my way of thinking, would be representative of many others in the broader evangelical world. His work is brilliant.

The book chapters were originally set up as follows. Titles changed through the editorial process. The chapter numbers and issues addressed are noted first, after which the principal author is identified. The principal author's name is followed by those who were asked to associate with it and serve as interlocutors. Updated titles are noted in the Table of Contents.

1. *Jews and Narrative Approaches to Theology and Story*, by William Bjorker, Ph.D., with Rabbi John Fischer, Th.D., Ph.D. asked to serve as respondent;
2. *Approaching God: The Essence of Messianic Jewish Theology*, by Dan Juster, Th.D. with Hellene Dallaire, Ph.D. as respondent;
3. *Messianism in the Hebrew Bible*, by Seth Postell, Ph.D. with John Taylor, Th.M. as respondent;
4. *Messianism in Jewish Literature Beyond the Hebrew Bible*, by Vered Hillel, Ph.D. with Seth Klayman Ph.D. as respondent;
5. *The Rise of Messianic Jewish Experience in Antiquity*, by Jeffrey Seif, D.Min. with Jim Sibley, Ph.D. and Barri Cae Seif, Ph.D. as respondents;

6. *History of, and Practices in, the Modern Messianic Jewish Movement*, by Jacob Rosenberg, Ph.D. with Eric Tokajer, Th.B. as respondent;

7. *The Revival of Messianic Jewish Worship* by Paul Wilbur, M.M. and Greg Silverman, D.M.A.;

8. *Not Rejected or Forgotten*: *God's Plan and Purpose for Israel*, by Mitch Glaser, Ph.D. with Jeff Johnson, Ph.D. reviewing; and lastly,

9. *An Evangelical Theologian Interacts With Messianic Jewish Theology: A Providential Journey Toward a Professional "Take"* by Boyd Luder, Ph.D. with Barri Cae Seif, Ph.D. as respondent. After the chapters were written, drafts were sent to Professor Elliot Klayman, who, in turn, sent them out for reviews. Richard Harvey, Ph.D., Seth Klayman, Ph.D., Erez Soref, Ph.D. and David Schiller, J.D. assisted with the review process.

This book is a *we thing* and not a *me thing*. There are a lot of people, and, as you can tell, a lot moving parts. There is variance in writing styles, given the variance in authors. I couldn't have undertaken this without the support of my deceased wife, Patty Seif (to whom the book is dedicated), and my present wife, Barri Cae. Absent the support of Daniah Greenberg and my publisher, Rabbi Barry Rubin, this book would not have seen the light of day. I thank them from the bottom of my heart. Though this is a collective enterprise, I accept responsibility for accidental omissions in credits and in content faults with the manuscript. I beg my readers' indulgence in advance. Potential problems aside, I hope this work will take its rightful place, contribute to the field and offer a responsible telling of Messianic Jewish faith, theology and best practice.

Jeffrey L. Seif
Dallas, TX 2019

Jews and Narrative Approaches to Theology and Story

Bill Bjoraker, Ph.D.

"God made man because He loves stories." (Elie Wiesel)[1]

Why include the theme of story and storytelling in a formal treatment of Messianic Jewish theology's best understandings and practices? The fact that between 60% and 70% of the canonical Scriptures are composed of stories should push storytelling to the top, should it not? The "People of the Book," that Book, the Jews, are actually the people of that story. The history and theology of Israel is story-based. The Scriptures comprise the master story of the universe by which all other smaller stories are given their meaning. The master story provides the necessary hermeneutical key for interpreting the other genre of Scripture by evoking the question: How does this passage or story follow the thread of God's Master Story?

Yeshua the Messiah used stories as his primary teaching method. He used stories to teach *both* the non-literate or semi-literate *am ha aretz* (the common folk) in Galilee, as well as the most highly literate Torah scholars of his day in Jerusalem. He is the Master Teacher and the exemplar for our teaching vocations. The influence of the Western conceptual and analytic approach to theologizing, homiletics and teaching has been strong and prevalent in modern Western Christianity as well as within the contemporary Messianic Jewish movement. This approach is not to be disregarded or devalued. However, we need to retrieve some lost treasures to restore balance, holism and a deeper

---

[1] Rosemary Horowitz, ed., *Elie Wiesel and the Art of Storytelling* (Jefferson, NC: McFarland & Company, Inc., Publishers, 2006), 208.

impact on hearts and lives in our ministry of the Word. This leads us back to Yeshua/Jesus' teaching style and to stories.

In modernity, the focus has been on the rational, scientific, analytic, logical, linear and technological. However, there is an ancient and continuous biblical and Jewish storytelling tradition—the *Aggadic/Haggadic* tradition. Its focus is on the literary-artistic, the aesthetic, the emotionally and relationally expressive, the big-picture, the holistic, and on metaphor, imagery and story. Yeshua said, "Every Torah scholar discipled for the kingdom of heaven is like the master of a household who brings out of his treasure both new things and old" (Matt. 13:52,). With a mind to retrieve these lost treasures and re-dig the wells of the main story, in this essay we shall consider ten "narratives":

Narrative 1:   Hebraic Theology Is Based on Story
Narrative 2:   The Hebraic and Jewish Roots of Story and Storytelling
Narrative 3:   "Hear O Israel": Orality Is Fundamental to Human Communication
Narrative 4:   European Enlightenment Epistemology
Narrative 5:   Hebraic Epistemology
Narrative 6:   Jewish *Midrash* and Story
Narrative 7:   The Power of Story
Narrative 8:   Yeshua the Messiah and Story
Narrative 9:   The Postmodern Moment and Its Prospects for Story
Narrative 10: Storytelling in Contemporary Jewish Ministry

Overview

The "Ten Narratives" in this chapter cohere as follows: The first eight give the theoretical grounding for the subject. The last two make application for contemporary practice. Israel's theology was formed by Israel's *storying* the acts of God, together with their meaning, in community, thus transmitting Israel's identity and mission from generation to generation. The literature of Israel and Judaism has always comprised both *Halacha* (law) and *Aggadah* (story), and they are interdependent. Oral speech is the fundamental nature of human language. God created human beings by His spoken word. Thus humans, reflecting the *Imago Dei*, are endowed with the gift of language and capable of "I-Thou" relationships (Buber). Israel was a hearing-dominant society in harmony with the way humans are made and most authentically communicate. The medium and technology of reading and writing detaches verbal discourse from its personal source.

There are three forms of the Word of God—(1) Yeshua the Messiah is the *Living Word*, who became flesh. (2) The inspired canonical *Written Word*, which is the authoritative standard for the testing of truth in teaching. (3) The *Oralized Word*, "Hear O Israel!" existed before the Written Word and completes its purpose. The purpose of the Book of the LORD is to know the LORD of the Book. The origin and study of Rabbinic literature was oral. Yeshua delivered his teaching orally and it was transmitted orally (he said his words are "spirit and life"); he did not write a book.

In contrast to the European Enlightenment epistemology of *disengaged reason*, Hebraic epistemology is receptive of divine revelation and is a *narrative epistemology* that embraces story as a way of knowing, and is testimony to the fact that "reason is the organ of truth, but imagination is the organ of meaning" (C.S. Lewis). There are lost treasures to recover in the Jewish hermeneutical tradition of *midrash aggadah* and the *imaginative reconstruction* of gaps in the Biblical stories. Story/storytelling is a more effective way to bring truth home to the heart than is the "naked truth" of propositional statements; stories and songs under the right conditions can most effectively mobilize groups to catalyze culture-change.

Yeshua is the Master Teacher and was a not a conceptual theologian; he was a *metaphorical theologian* and a storyteller. Yeshua's parables are like a house, into which people are invited and from which they can look out at the world from several different windows. Humans are *homo narrans*, and so story will always and everywhere be relevant, though styles of discourse and media may change. Our postmodern moment of history has created a search for new meta-narratives and provides an auspicious context to re-tell the master story of Scripture and for ministry of the Word through storytelling.

Jewish people have always been at the *vortex* of history- and culture-making movements. In this "Digitoral Era," a major way the Messianic Jewish movement will advance the Kingdom of God and be a "light to the nations" is through creatively re-telling the Biblical Story and stories to the current and succeeding generations.

Narrative 1: Hebraic Theology Is Based on Story

How did Israel come to know the Creator as *Adonai Elohim*, as *Avinu Malkeinu*, and how did Israel develop its theology? The Creator called Avram in Ur of the Chaldees. Avram listened to the voice of God and began the journey. God continued to speak to the other patriarchs, revealing Himself and His purposes. But contrary to the ancient far East religions, inner subjective experience was not the major means of revelation. God's objective outward acts in space-time history determined the content of inner revelation. Mystical experience was not the focus, but rather the very earthy, participatory, messy and concrete events that included Abraham's journeying to a place and a destiny as yet undisclosed to him, his learning by struggle and trial how to respect his wife, and the significance of an heir. Jacob's wrestling with God to be transformed into *Yis-ra'El*, and later Joseph's suffering at the hands of his brothers and his moral testing in Egypt, all in God's providence prepared Jacob's clan to be forged by blood, sweat and tears into a nation. This is revelation in and through the real, the tangible, and the actual.

After the patriarchal period God began to reveal Himself on a larger scale to the nation of Egypt and to the people of Israel, forming Israel into a nation by His mighty acts among them and for them. The powerful saving acts of God in the events surrounding the exodus from Egypt constitute the foundational narrative of Israel. History was the primary arena in which God revealed Himself. History is never a bare record of neutral facts. It always includes the meaning of those facts. The telling of those revelatory events and their God-given meaning produced Israel's theology. As the saying goes, history is "HisStory."

G. Ernest Wright, who studied under the great archaeologist W.F. Albright and participated in excavations in Israel (then Palestine) in the 1930s and later was professor of Old Testament at Harvard University, has fully researched and explained this theological formation process. He states,

> [Theology] is fundamentally an interpretation of history, a confessional recital of historical events as the acts of God, events which lead backward to the beginning of history and forward to its end. Inferences are constantly made from the acts and are interpreted as integral parts of the acts themselves which furnish the clue to understanding not only contemporary happenings, but those which subsequently occurred. The being

and attributes of God are nowhere systematically presented but are inferences from events.[2]

An example of this process of theologizing from history and story is Moshe Rabbeinu, who taught the people of Israel that when they came into the land promised to them, they were to bring a tithe of the first fruits of their produce in a basket to the place God designated. They were to offer it to the priest, who would set it before the altar. But then this striking practice is commanded:

> Then you are to *respond before the Adonai your God, and say*, "My father was a wandering Aramean, and he went down into Egypt and lived there as an outsider, few in number there, few in number. But there he became a nation—mighty and numerous. And the Egyptians treated *us* badly, afflicted *us* and imposed hard labor on *us*. Then *we* cried to Adonai, God of *our* fathers, and Adonai listened to our voice heard *our* voice and saw *our* affliction, *our* toil, and *our* oppression. Then Adonai brought *us* out of Egypt with a mighty hand and an outstretched arm, with great terror, and with signs and wonders. He brought *us* into this place and gave *us* this land—a land flowing with milk and honey" (Deut. 26:5-9, , emphases added).

Note that this was an oral-aural community event, not an isolated individual reading a text in a study carrel. The people are commanded to annually recite, to tell the story of their father Jacob, of his family's decent into Egypt, and then of the story of their great deliverance from slavery to Pharaoh which forged the Israelite peoplehood. The telling— or the *storying*—of the acts of God in their history formed the theology of Israel.

The stories of Genesis are archetypal and prismatic, but the identity of Israel is grounded in this bedrock story, this root story of the exodus from Egypt. This is Israel's master story. And as Michael Goldberg says, "master stories not only *inform* us, they *form* us."[3] This story runs through Jewish tradition like a river. Recall how the liturgy for Shabbat Eve Kiddush in the Siddur retells it, *"Blessed are You, HASHEM, our God, King of the Universe, Who… gave us His holy Sabbath…a memorial of the exodus from Egypt."* This master story of historical events gives

---

[2] Ernest G. Wright, *God Who Acts: Biblical Theology as Recital,* Studies in Biblical Theology (London: SCM Press, 1952), 57.

[3] Michael Goldberg, Jews and Christians: Getting Our Stories Straight: The Exodus and the Passion-Resurrection (Eugene, OR: Wipf & Stock, 1991), 13.

meaning and direction to the people in the present and hope for the future. Because God acted thus before, we trust He will so act again.

To the present time, each year at Passover, the Jewish people are commanded to tell their children the story of the nation's founding, of God's awesome deliverance from Egypt. "And you shall *tell* your son on that day…" (Exod. 13:8). The Hebrew verb is *vehiggadta*—to "tell." Hence the Passover event and the *Haggadah* is the oral "telling" and annual retelling of the story that reinforces the Jewish people's identity. And each Jewish feast or holiday provides an opportunity to recite and retell another story of God's gracious acts on behalf of His people. This was the rationale for the pilgrimage festivals. This retelling and reenacting through ritual and liturgy is how theology was created and how it is transmitted from generation to generation.

Psalm 78 is a retelling of the story of Israel. This is a model liturgy for Israel and is what is done in most Jewish feasts—telling and retelling the story and stories of Israel.

Psalm 78: A *maskil* of Asaf:

> Listen, my people, to my teaching;
> turn your ears to the words from my mouth.
> I will speak to you in *parables* [Hebrew: *mashal*, a wisdom
> saying, poem, or story]
> and explain mysteries from days of old.
>
> The things which we have heard and known,
> and which our fathers told us
> we will not hide from their descendants;
> we will tell the generation to come. (verses 1–4, CJB)

And this contemporary version translates the Hebrew "the things we have heard and knew from our ancestors" as "stories":

> O my people, listen to my instructions.
>   Open your ears to what I am saying,
>   for I will speak to you *in a parable*.
> I will teach you hidden lessons from our past—
>   *stories we have heard and known,*
>   *stories our ancestors handed down to us.*
> We will not hide these truths from our children;
>   *we will tell the next generation*
>   about the glorious deeds of the LORD,
>   about his power and his mighty wonders.
> (verses 1–4, New Living Translation)

Doctrinal formulation and a systematization of theology as propositional dogmatics was alien to the Hebrews /Israelites of the Biblical period. They favored the concrete and shunned the abstract. The theologians of Israel were narrative theologians. The modern habit of mind that reasons from axioms, principles or universals to the concrete was foreign to them. So, the Jewish formulation of doctrine during the Hellenistic and Talmudic periods was due to the influence set by the Athenian philosophical schools.[4]

Likewise, the theology of the earliest apostolic church (the early Messianic Jewish movement) grew out of the experience of practical ministry. Ministry preceded and produced theology (not vice-versa, as is so often assumed in the modern West). As we read in the Book of Acts, Luke records the practicing before the preaching, the doing before the teaching. "The former account I made, O Theophilus, of all that Yeshua began both *to do and to teach* ..." (Acts 1:1). The New Covenant epistles were written (theology was codified) ten or more years after the spiritual renewal movement and the launching of obedient efforts to fulfill Messiah's Great Commission.

Hebraism and Hellenism

There has long been dissention between Hellenism and Hebraism and between "Athens and Jerusalem." Though there are clear differences, and Hellenism must be critiqued, these counterpoints have often been wrongly framed as a black-and-white matter: Hebraism is good; Hellenism is bad. However, a reflective caveat is needed here—there was surely a providential encounter between Biblical faith and Greek thought. The pivotal story of when the Apostle Paul was barred from going further into Asia and was instead led through a vision to Macedonia, "Come over to Macedonia and help us!" (Acts 16:6–10), is perhaps symbolic. Paul's Jewish apostolic band entered the Greek world, and the developing Christian Faith was shaped for all time. We may identify this encounter as the beginnings of the synthesis between Christianity and Hellenism, which, though there are negatives, was not all bad. Jewish communities had encountered Greek thought two or three centuries earlier. Philo of Alexandria and others absorbed the Greek spirit.

Because the Greeks were created in the image of God, and because of general revelation (Rom. 1:19–20), the Greek thinkers were able to

---

[4] Raphael Patai, *The Jewish Mind* (New York: Charles Scribner's Sons, 1977), 67.

achieve a discipline of rationality or use of reason that, when used under the authority of Biblical revelation, was enriching to theological understanding. As is said, "All truth is God's truth," and rigorous use of reason to explore, investigate, hypothesize and learn as much as possible about creation and about reality was an enrichment to people of faith. The Great Commandment, "love *Adonai* Your God with all your heart, all your soul and all your mind," assumes a rigorous use of reason as part of holistic devotion to God and stewardship of His gifts. Followers of Messiah will not espouse an anti-intellectualism that devalues higher education in the liberal arts, advanced scholarship and research in the social and natural sciences. The Jewish people are known as the "People of the Book." They are also "people of books," valuing knowledge and education. That we read and write systematic theologies is due to the Greek heritage. So as we seek to recover and embrace more of the Hebraic epistemology, it is not rejection of the rigorous intellectual disciplines of learning, but a matter of bringing them under the authority of the Hebraic revelation and integrating them in practice with the "Ten Narratives" in this essay.

The Apostle John chose the word *logos* to begin his Gospel. "In the beginning was the *Logos*. The *Logos* was with God and the *Logos* was God" (John 1:1). *Logos* means both "word" and "reason." God is a God of reason, intelligible in His words and deeds. His character is intelligible. He does not act arbitrarily or inconsistently with His character. His created universe is intelligible; its principles and order can be known through the study of the natural sciences.

The New Covenant Scriptures are written in Greek, in God's providence, and they bear the imprint of the Greek spirit. There is a harmony between the best in Greek use of reason and Biblical faith. The *integration of faith and reason* has served in the successful development of Western civilization and in the university tradition. This is a gift of the synthesis between Greek and Hebrew thought. I could not write this essay without the benefit of the higher education in this tradition, which I was privileged to receive. Those who have benefited from a liberal-arts education and engaged in advanced study and research at institutes of science and technology, have greatly contributed to human flourishing. We can be grateful for this for this integration, as we have reaped the fruits of their labor. However, as modern Western secular humanism advanced, Hebraic treasures were left behind.

Narrative 2: The Hebraic and Jewish Roots of Story and Storytelling

The Hebraic roots of storytelling pre-date the Written Torah by many centuries. The archetypal stories of Adam and Eve, Cain and Abel, of Noah and the Great Flood, of the Tower of Babel, the stories of the families of Abraham, Isaac, Jacob and Joseph were transmitted orally over generations by good storytellers before ever they were written down in the form we have them in the Torah.

As the literature of Israel and Judaism developed, two broad genres of writings emerged—*Halacha* and *Haggadah*. Chaim Nahman Bialik (1873–1934), by all accounts modern Israel's most celebrated national poet, wrote in 1917 a now-classic essay titled *"Halacha and Haggadah."* He observed how often the two genres are considered antithetical—law and story—as if they are irreconcilable opposites.[5] Bialik writes,

> *Halacha* wears a frown, *Aggadah* a smile. The one pedantic, severe unbending—all justice; the other is accommodating, lenient, pliable—all mercy. The one commands and knows no half-way house; her yea is yea and her nay is nay. The other advises and takes account of human limitations; she admits something between yea and nay. The one is concerned with the shell, with the body, with actions; the other with the kernel, with the soul, with intentions. On one side there is petrified observance, duty, subjection; on the other perpetual rejuvenation, liberty, free volition. Turn from the sphere of life to that of literature, and there are further points of contrast. On the one side is the dryness of prose, a formal and heavy style, and gray and monochrome diction: reason is sovereign. On the other side is the sap of poetry, a style full of life and variety, a diction all ablaze with color: emotion is sovereign.[6]

---

[5] *Aggadah* or *Haggadah* (Heb. הַגָּדָה, אַגָּדָה; "telling," "narrative"), one of the two primary components of Rabbinic tradition, the other being *halakhah*, usually translated as "Jewish Law." The *Halacha* (literally "walking" so "how to walk") contains the legal rulings of the rabbis, law codes, customs and ethical rulings of the Talmud. Though the categories are broad with fuzzy boundaries, *Aggadah* is generally the non-legal literature of the Talmudic body of literature, the "Sea of the Talmud." Broadly, "The *aggadah* comprehends a great variety of forms and content. It includes narrative, legends. Its forms and modes of expression are as rich and colorful as its content. Parables and allegories, metaphors and terse maxims; lyrics, dirges, and prayers, biting satire and fierce polemic, idyllic tales and tense dramatic dialogues, hyperboles and plays on words..." *"Aggadah"* or *"Haggadah"* in www.jewishvirtuallibrary.org/jsource/judaica/ejud_0002_0001_0_00525.html.

[6] Chaim Nachman Bialik, *Revealment and Concealment: Five Essays*, trans. Zali Gurevitch (Jerusalem: Ibis Editions, 2000), 45.

Quite a colorful, expressive, lyrical description! You can tell Bialik is a consummate poet. And often we in the modern West have been taught to think in the dichotomy between reason (law, prose, philosophy, logic) and imagination (metaphor, poetry, story, drama). But Bialik insists that the two—*Halacha* and *Aggada*—are interdependent and in dialectic relationship. He continues,

> *Halacha* is the crystallization, the ultimate and inevitable quintessence of *Aggadah; Aggadah* is the content of *Halacha. Aggadah* is the plaintive voice of the heart's yearning as it wings its way to its haven; *Halacha* is the resting place, where for a moment the yearning is satisfied and stilled. As a dream seeks its fulfillment in interpretation, as will in action, as thought in speech, as flower in fruit—so *Aggadah* in *Halacha.*[7]

Bialik demonstrates, as only a poet could, that both these major genre of literature, both of these ways of teaching and knowing, are in Scripture and life; both are needed and need each other. He observes how in the collections of laws and manuals of instruction in the Torah (Leviticus) and Talmud, actually have "a kaleidoscope of pictures, large and small, of actual Hebrew life over a period of a thousand years or more." He notes,

> Do not open the *Mishnah* [the first major redaction of rabbinic oral law traditions, six tractates, mostly *Halacha*] with puckered brow. Tread leisurely among its chapters, like one exploring the *ruins* of ancient cities; ramble amid its rows of statutory enactments, set side by side as in a piece of masonry, flint-like in their compressed rigidity; look with a discerning eye at all the pictures, some small and some tiny, which lie scattered about promiscuously in their in their thousands: and ask yourselves whether you are not beholding the actual life of a whole people, ceased in its very progress and petrified in all the multiplicity of its detail."[8]

Bialik asserts that behind every law or statute or instruction is a story. The laws are "bits of crystallized life." If you look for the bit of life, the story, behind the law, it will be anything but boring. Will you ever look

---

[7] Bialik, *Revealment*, 46.
[8] Ibid., 75.

at a law or a precept the same way again? Theology is embedded in the stories. Stories can be found in Scripture wherein are embedded concepts that will address any given category of systematic theology such as soteriology, ecclesiology, pneumatology, eschatology, etc. Recalling the stories undergirding these more abstract concepts provides an anchor in the Hebraic narrative epistemology. Stories provide the grounded roots of the realities that are referred to or interpreted in the propositional statements. Story is always primary and primal; analytic propositions and deductions are derivative.

Narrative 3: Hear O Israel! Orality Is Fundamental to Human Communication

At the conclusion of the Fall feasts, the Jewish High Holy Days, is the feast of *Simchat Torah*. Traditional and Orthodox Jews passionately celebrate the gift of God's Word. To witness the exuberant dancing and singing while carrying the adorned Torah Scroll at the Western Wall in Jerusalem shames the paltry expression of devotion to the Word that characterizes most of us late moderns. This is exemplary affirmation of the Written Word of God. Yet it is clear that the Word of God is in three forms:

1 The Living Word (the *"Memra"* in Hebrew, comparable to the *Logos* in Greek), who became flesh (John 1:1-14);

2 The Written Word (in This Age, the final authority for faith and life);

3 The Oralized Word (Scripture brought to life through human communicators).

Oral language always embodies a personal address, the "I-Thou" dimension of personal relationship. God spoke into being all He created during the six days of Creation, including humans, thus humans came into existence by God's oralized Word. An aspect of the image of God in humans, intrinsic to our personhood, is our capacity for speech. This embodies the essence of the intrinsic social nature of humans made in the image of God—humans are a bi-unity of two genders, reflecting the tri-unity of the three persons of the Godhead.

Anthropologists and cultural historians have clarified that oral speech is the fundamental and essential nature of human language. Linguist Ferdinand de Saussure (1857–1913) developed the study of phonemics, showing the way language is nested in sound, made up not of letters but of functional sound units or phonemes.[9] Oralized, spoken language preceded writing by many millennia.

In the last decades of twentieth century, the academic world was newly awakened to the oral character of language and the deeper implications of the effects on human consciousness of orality and writing.[10] Non-literate people, who are oral learners, think and process information differently than people who are highly literate. Oral speech is primary; writing and reading are derivative. Oral expression can and has mostly existed without any writing; writing has never existed without orality.

Though it carries huge benefits, a downside of writing is that written discourse is detached from its author, the personal source of the message. The advantage of a book is that it provides the means for a speaker to be linked with a listener without being in the same room or even same century; the disadvantage is the loss of the personal dimension of a communication act.

Modern Western society is a literacy- and text-dominant society. Israel was a hearing-dominant society. Though written or printed texts became very important later in Jewish history, the Hebraic tradition involves the hearing ear more than the distancing eye. Biblically, we see God always speaking personally to His people, not writing to them. The *Shema* reads, *"Hear O Israel!"*, not *"Read O Israel!"* That Israel was a hearing-dominant society is in harmony with the way humans are made and how they most authentically communicate. There are very few times in Scripture where God or Yeshua wrote anything: The Ten Commandments, the handwriting on the wall in Daniel, and Yeshua writing in the sand in front of the woman caught in adultery. Yet the phrase "Thus *says* the LORD" is repeated over 400 times.

---

[9] Walter J. Ong, *Orality and Literacy: The Technologizing of the Word* (London and New York: Routledge, Taylor & Francis Group, 1982), 5.
[10] Ong, *Orality*, 5.

The God of Israel modeled for us how to embed something in the memory of a group or peoplehood. When God instructed Moses in matters pertaining the ongoing tutelage of Israel, He tells Moses the reason for the great "Song of Moses" that will follow in Deuteronomy 32. This song proclaimed God's ways, His honor, His judgment, and His salvation. God wanted Israel to take this to heart, to internalize it. So, He says, "I want you *to write down* this song and teach it to the children of Israel. Teach them *to sing it*, so it can be a witness for me against them" (Deut. 31:19).

They were to learn it by heart. So, the "Song of Moses" is in memorable poetry and was to be formally articulated in ways to facilitate memorization by the community. It was to be sung, oralized. But we note also that it was to be written down. The textual version of the poem was necessary for maintaining its permanence from generation to generation, to check its accuracy. Here we see the dynamic dialectic between the Written Word and the Oralized Word—the oralized word can be ephemeral, so must be preserved in writing. The written word must be oralized.

The Pauline epistles were circulated and read aloud in the churches. When the Apostle John sent the letters to the seven churches of Asia Minor, here were the instructions: "Blessed is he who *reads aloud* the words of this prophecy and blessed are those who *hear*" (Rev. 1:3). Reading the Scriptures is not exactly equal to listening to God. To do the former is not *necessarily* to do the latter. Atheists can read Scripture.

The rhetorical and homiletical arts are always central to ministry. The oralizing of the Word described through the cluster of word gifts—teaching, exhortation, prophecy—are endowed by the Holy Spirit to equip the church for ministry (Rom. 12:6, 7; 1 Cor. 12:8, 10; Eph. 4:11). Bible storytelling is an expression of the gifts of teaching and exhortation, but in a form often not recognized as real teaching due to our Western orientation to use lecture and monologue.

Why is orality (the oral-aural process) so singularly valuable? One reason is because of the interpersonal-relational contrasts highlighted by the following table.

TABLE 1 – CONTRAST BETWEEN READING AND LISTENING

Reading	Listening
Eyes	Ears
Read marks on a page.	Attend to the sound of a voice.
A lone person with a book, written by someone miles away, or dead, or both.	An interpersonal, relational act.
The book is at the reader's mercy. The book does not know if I am paying attention or not.	Listener is required to be attentive to the speaker, at speaker's mercy. The speaker knows if I am paying attention or not.
The reader initiates the process; the reader is in charge.	The speaker initiates the process; the speaker is in charge.
Images in life: The stereotype of the husband buried in the morning newspaper at breakfast, preferring to read yesterday's sports scores and opinions of columnists he will never meet, than to listen to the voice of the person who has just shared his bed, poured his coffee, and fried his eggs, even though listening to that live voice promises love and hope, emotional depth and intellectual exploration far in excess of what he can gather informationally from the *New York Times*.	*Images in life:* All Israel assembled at the foot of Mt. Sinai as Moses addresses them… A first-century Pauline congregation gathered to hear the oral reading of a letter from the Apostle Paul… A soldier standing at attention, listening to the commands of his drill sergeant… Boy Scouts around a campfire listening in rapt attention to a storyteller tell a ghost story… A family Passover Seder dinner, in which the father animatedly tells, once again, the Great Story of our Freedom, the children ask questions, the symbolic foods are eaten, and the songs are sung.

(created by Bjoraker, drawing from prose source in Eugene Peterson's *Working the Angles*[11])

Why is a joke always better told orally than when read from a page? Why is that that I can hear a song on the radio I haven't heard in thirty years, or a television advertising jingle I heard in childhood, and still sing along word-for-word, never having written out the words, or read them? There are regions of the human brain that have neurons that light up and retain memory of story and song longer and deeper than most of

---

[11] Eugene H. Peterson, *Working the Angles: The Shape of Pastoral Integrity* (Grand Rapids: Eerdmans, 1987), 88, 89.

the printed propositional prose that a person reads. God "wired" us as humans to connect at a deeper level than merely the cognitive.

We cannot reduce the Word of God to paper and ink in a book. The Messiah said to his contemporaries who revered the Book, "You search the Scriptures because you think that in them you have eternal life; and it is they that bear witness about me, yet you refuse to come to me that you may have life" (John 5:39, 40). The Written Word is the means to an end; making it an end in itself misses the point or even becomes bibliolatry. The purpose of the Book of the LORD is to know the LORD of the Book. The Written Word begs for oralizing and points beyond itself to the Living Word.

The Rabbis and Oral Learning and Teaching

The existence of the Rabbinic tradition of Oral Torah (*Torah Sh'b'al Peh*) with its expansions and explanations of the Written Torah is testimony to Jewish awareness of the need for texts to be oralized and for the Word of God to reach into and speak to the ongoing human situations that arise in the complexities of life in the succeeding time periods. The oral origins of Rabbinic literature and its study are quite clear:

> Even when put into writing, remained a record of oral discussions going on among multiple personalities. ... In a *rabbinic* work, each contribution quoted comes originally from an oral context... and even if there are intermediate written sources, none of these sources has lost its oral atmosphere or its character as a record of oral discussions.[12]

Yeshua's Oral Forms of Teaching

"In the beginning was the *Logos*" (John 1:1). In the Greek lexicon of the New Testament, the Greek word *logos* is denoted as an "utterance, chiefly oral."[13] In the modern West, we tend to think of it as a written word on a page. "The evidence from the Gospels is unanimous about the

---

[12] Hyam Maccoby, *Early Rabbinic Writings*, Cambridge Commentaries on Writings of the Jewish and Christian World 200 BC to AD 200, Vol. 3 (Cambridge: Cambridge University Press, 1988), 8.

[13] Walter Bauer and Arndt Gingrich, eds., *A Greek-English Lexicon of the New Testament and Other Early Christian Literature*, 3rd ed. (Chicago: University of Chicago Press, 2000), s.v. "Logos."

word, *word*. When the context was the ministry of Jesus, *logos* (or *rhema*) denoted speech."[14]

The oral origins of the four Gospels are evident within the Gospels. It was not until at least twenty years after Yeshua's public ministry that the first written accounts were inscribed. Yeshua's teachings were delivered and transmitted orally. His delivery system as a teacher was face-to-face and oral. His teaching methods were non-formal, mostly among the *am ha'aretz* in the villages and countryside. But it was also highly intensive, twenty-four-hours per day, life-on-life, an apprenticeship model with much coaching and personal mentoring, and therefore highly oral and without the aid of books or classroom lectures. Yeshua did not write a book; he did not need to. He stated, "The words I speak to you are spirit and life" (John 6:63b). It was sufficient for his oral texts to remain oral.

He taught using many questions and stories, with a cohort of twelve adult learners for discussion learning. His method was effective, such that at the end of the three short years of training, he was able to report to his Father, "I gave them the words you gave me and they have accepted them" (John 17:8). The young leaders he trained went on to change the world. A simple application for us today is that we need to recover the lost treasures of storytelling and the oral and relational teaching methods of Yeshua.

Narrative 4: European Enlightenment Epistemology

In order to compare and contrast the dominant modern Western epistemology (the study of how we know what we know, or the ways of knowing) with the Hebraic epistemology, I will first describe the Enlightenment epistemology. A major epistemological shift from medieval knowledge and learning to modern science (empiricism and rationalism) as the major way of knowing occurred during the European Enlightenment of the 18th century. It was a shift from reliance on authority as moral sources (Scripture, religious tradition, established venerated philosophers) to empirical observation (and application of the new rational scientific method of inquiry to interpret the data of experience) as the primary source of knowledge. The results of the new

---

[14] John H. Walton and D. Brent Sandy, The Lost World of Scripture: Ancient Literary Culture and Biblical Authority (Downers Grove: IVP Academic, 2013), 127.

science became the new dominant public source of authority in the West for several centuries, weakened only somewhat with the postmodern shift. The moral sources, in this case epistemological, become *disengaged reason [definition: The concept of reason or rationality disengaged from external, objective and transcendent verities and/or moral absolutes that had served as guideposts (touchstones, anchors, tethers) for the practice of rationality and the ascertaining knowledge]* ... and the deliverances of such reason via the highly acclaimed modern scientific method.[15]

Disengaged reason became supreme in Enlightenment thought such that all knowledge and any alleged authority had to pass the bar of this now presumed omni-competent reason. Starting from itself, this rationality was assumed to be able to ascertain certain, universally true and objective knowledge. Reason was presumed to be unconditioned and to operate from a totally neutral vantage point, as a sort of "epistemological Switzerland," as Paul Weston put it.[16] Reason could be applied instrumentally, but of course also amorally. Rationality thus becomes rationalism; science becomes scientism—both are reductionist. Paradoxically, exalting reason too highly, or making it the be-all-and-end-all, reduces the scope of reason and knowledge, rather than expands it. As modernity progressed, a dichotomy developed between *public facts* (viewed as the objective and neutral deliverances of pure reason via the scientific method), and *private values* (viewed as the subjective and relative beliefs based on religious texts or experiences, viewed pluralistically). This became the standard modern view.[17]

C.S. Lewis's Epistemology and Apologetics

C.S. Lewis (1898–1963) was a modern Western thinker who was able to critically detach himself from the dominant Enlightenment epistemology. Lewis is well-known for his great imaginative gift for storytelling, but many recognize his strength was his ability to present the Christian Faith both conceptually and imaginatively. He was a master of both reason and imagination. Michael Ward, a Lewis scholar, writes,

---

[15] William D. Bjoraker, "Faith, Freedom and Radical Individualism in Late Modern America: A Missiological Evaluation" (PhD diss., Fuller Theological Seminary, 2007), 365-66.
[16] Paul Weston, "The Making of Christendom," Zotero, accessed December 13, 2014, https://www.zotero.org/groups/westminstercam/items/itemKey/WGKTDRUI.
[17] Bjoraker, "Faith," 355-56.

His rational approach is seen in *The Abolition of Man,
Miracles*, and ... *Mere Christianity*. These works show
Lewis's ability to argue: to set forth a propositional case,
proceeding by logical steps from defined premises to carefully
drawn conclusions, everything clear, orderly, and connected.
And his imaginative side, so the argument goes, is seen in *The
Screwtape Letters, The Great Divorce,* and, at a more
accessible level, *The Lion, the Witch and the Wardrobe.* These
works show his ability to dramatize: to set forth an attractive
vision of Christian life, proceeding by means of character and
plot to narrate an engaging story, everything colorful, vibrant,
and active.[18]

Many scholars consider Lewis's conceptual works and imaginative
works to be dissimilar and distinct. They are two discrete modes in
which he presented the faith. Often the imaginative works, the stories
are considered *theology lite*, or for children only. It is understandable
that we would think this way. Ward continues,

The dichotomy between reason and imagination is how we have
been taught to think ever since the so-called Enlightenment of
the 17th and 18th centuries. Reasonable people don't need
imagination. Imaginative people don't need reasons.[19]

This is far from Lewis's views, for Lewis was far from being an
Enlightenment thinker. In fact, Lewis is quoted as saying, "A children's
story that can only be enjoyed by children is not a good children's story
in the slightest."

When I (Bjoraker) personally developed storytelling as ministry
several years ago, someone remarked to me, "Oh, how do you like doing
children's ministry?" I said, "I don't do children's ministry. I do Bible
storying with adults. The Bible is for adults. It takes a lot of
contextualization to bring it down to children's level."

Ward quotes from Lewis's *Selected Literary Essays*,

"All our truth, or all but a few fragments, is won by
metaphor," Lewis wrote in his essay "Bluspels and
Flalansferes." Similitudes, seeing one thing in terms of
another, finding meanings here which correspond with what

---

[18] Michael Ward, "How Lewis Lit the Way to Better Apologetics." *Christianity Today* 57, no. 9 (October
2013): 38.
[19] Ibid.

we want to say there, are for Lewis the essence of meaningful thought. *"For me, reason is the natural organ of truth,"* Lewis wrote, *"but imagination is the organ of meaning. Imagination ... is not the cause of truth, but its condition."* In other words, we don't grasp the meaning of a word or concept until we have a clear image to connect it with.

For Lewis, this is what the imagination is about: not just the ability to dream up fanciful fables, but the ability to identify meaning, to know when we have come upon something truly meaningful.[20]

Lewis's was closer to Hebraic man than to modern secular man. Lewis is an exemplar for us today, as we seek to retrieve the lost treasures of story, as we re-dig the wells of the Aggadic tradition and as we develop the arts of orality and right-brain proficiencies for teaching and ministry today.

Narrative 5: Hebraic Epistemology

"Language is the house of being," said philosopher Martin Heidegger.[21] If Heidegger is correct, then we can learn about the "being" of Israel from the nature of the Hebrew language. We learn about how the Hebrews knew what they knew, and how they knew the world. Language is both the means for things to materialize in historical time, as well as a testimony to their entry into being. So, the language of a people and their worldview and culture are integrally related.

The Hebrew language has at least these three characteristics relevant to story and storytelling. It is (1) concrete, 2) it is relational, and (3) it reflects experiential knowledge.

Hebrew Is Concrete. From the very beginning, in the account of Creation, God pronounced the created physical world "very good" (Gen. 1:31). This has echoed down through Jewish history in the Jewish affirmation of life, *"L'Chaim!"* Marvin Wilson quotes George Adam Smith as saying,

Hebrew may be called primarily a language of the senses. The words originally expressed concrete or material things and movements or actions which struck the senses or started the

---

[20] Ibid.

[21] Martin Heidegger, "Letter on Humanism," in *Martin Heidegger: Basic Writings*, ed. David Farrell Krell (London: Routledge, 1977), 213–66.

emotions. Only secondarily and *in metaphor* could they be used to denote abstract or metaphysical ideas.[22]

Examples of graphic, vivid use of concrete language to communicate abstract concepts include the following: to look is to "lift up the eyes" (Gen. 22:4); to be angry is to "burn in one's nostrils" (Exod. 4:14); to have no compassion is "hard-heartedness" (1 Sam. 6:6); to be stubborn is to be "stiff-necked" (2 Chron. 30:8); to be determined is "to set one's face" (Jer. 42:15; Luke 9:51). There are also the anthropomorphisms of the living God of the Hebrews. He is not a distant, ethereal deity, but "surely the arm of the LORD is not too short to save, nor His ear too dull to hear" (Isa. 59:1). Also, "the eyes of the LORD are everywhere" (Prov. 15:3). These concrete images are common in Hebrew.[23] Stories tell real events and actions relayed by the sensory experience of the storyteller. Often metaphors and similes from the vernacular are the most expressive terms at hand.

Hebrew Is Relational in Terms and Perceptions. German Jewish philosopher Martin Buber (1878–1965) in his classic work, *I and Thou,* explains that "I-Thou" encounters with persons are fundamentally different than "I-It" relationships with things.[24] Persons know other persons by encounter. A major theme of Buber's book is that human life finds its greatest meaning in relationships with other persons. Storytelling is inherently relational. A story is told *by* someone *to* someone. The hearers of the story vicariously encounter the characters in the story, identify with them, and have emotional and moral responses to them (positively or negatively), sometimes in life-changing ways.

Hebrew Reflects Experiential Knowledge. When thinking about God, Hebrews don't ask, "What is divinity?" (the philosophical essence of divine being). Rather they ask, "Who is God?" ... "Who is Yahweh? The Hebrew word *yada* refers to an experiential knowing more than to mere cerebral cognition. Genesis says, "Adam knew (*yada*) his wife Eve, and she conceived" (Gen. 4:1). "This is eternal life that you might know (experientially) God and Yeshua the Messiah whom He has sent" (John 17:3). Stories relay real-life experiences, encounters, firsthand experiences, and often eyewitness accounts.

---

[22] Marvin R. Wilson, *Our Father Abraham: Jewish Roots of the Christian Faith* (Grand Rapids: Eerdmans, 1989), 137.

[23] Wilson, *Our Father Abraham*, 137.

[24] Martin Buber, *I and Thou*, trans. Walter Kaufmann (New York: Touchstone Books, 1970).

Narrative Epistemology: Story as a Way of Knowing

A story, in its telling and hearing, in its wholeness, imparts a quality of knowledge that is greater, thicker in description, comprehending more of reality, and fuller than all the sum of lists (or bullet points) of the summary phrases, or abstracted statements, propositions or theses that could be derived from it. As someone has said, "We dream in story, not bullet points."

American Protestant scholar Walter Brueggemann (b. 1933), widely considered one of the most influential Old Testament scholars of the last few decades, recognized the importance of narrative as a way of knowing. He is known for his advocacy and practice of "rhetorical criticism" which studies how the elements of oral speech—in oral performances, texts, films, and discourse in general—work to affect and influence people through their imagery, symbols, body language, and other rhetorical elements.

This, of course, has everything to do with orality and storytelling. Brueggemann's emphasis on the importance of knowing through oral methods brought into question the categories of modernity and the Enlightenment and how the Enlightenment epistemology has become a "tyranny of positivism," generating "models of knowledge" that are thought to be objective and neutral but are actually dominating. He has championed that aspect of the postmodern critique and postmodern epistemological shift that allows for a loosening from the oppression and reductionism of the scientific method of modern rationalism (or positivism).

Psychotherapist and Brueggemann scholar Kevin M. Bradt has researched and written on story as a way of knowing. Much of his research focused on Brueggemann's work on Israel's storying. Bradt observes how that when Enlightenment thought became dominant,

> Debates raged about the historical facticity behind the biblical texts while the study of Israel's rhetorical practices, her long traditions of alternative speech, orality, and storying went into eclipse. Now all the wonderful, messy, contradictory narrative particularities of the biblical stories were seen only as intellectual embarrassments.[25]

---

[25] Kevin M. Bradt, *Story as a Way of Knowing* (Kansas City: Sheed & Ward, 1997), 127.

Brueggemann discovered how a *narrative epistemology* could sustain a community's sense of hope and history in the face of systemic repression and violence. Through Israel's tradition of storying, a defiant, shared imagination powerful enough to activate an alternative future reality had been born.[26]

He is referring to Israel's sojourn as slaves in Egypt and how their alternative story of God's relationship to them, transmitted from their patriarchs, was able to defy the dominant mythic and ideological story propounded by the Pharaohs and legitimated and absolutized by their imperial state power. That mythopoetic ideology was the official sociology of knowledge that dominated the empire. For all others in Egypt, there was no alternative story to that of the Pharaohs. But Israel had another story! It empowered their dissent. Out of their story, the Exodus was able to occur, the story of the birth of the nation that would change the world more than any other in history. It was the story—or more accurately, the true and living God of Israel's story—that not only liberated and transformed Israel, but defeated imperial Egypt, the most powerful nation on earth.

Furthermore, Bradt goes on to say,

> The story of Israel and the land could not be reduced to a thesis. Only the narrative tension of the stories could hold together the complexity of the revelation of God's relationship with Israel.[27]

> For Brueggemann, the stories of the Bible reveal a relationship between Israel and her God that is so complex, inexhaustible, and fraught with all kinds of confusion, dark mystery, and shocking tensions that to try to reconcile what must ultimately remain irreconcilable can only be an exercise in futility and madness. ... It is only narrative modes of knowing and relationship that can embrace and tolerate such ambiguity, wonder, paradox, pain, grief and surprise; it is only an alternative imagination called into existence through storying that can help us understand Israel's situation as a model of our own in this postmodern age.[28]

---

[26] Ibid., 129.
[27] Ibid., 131.
[28] Ibid., 131–32.

> Brueggemann calls story "Israel's primal mode of knowing," for it is the foundation from which come all other knowledge claims we have. ... "the story can be told as a base line."[29]

The Hebrew slaves lived out of an alternative worldview, an alternative consciousness that enabled them to defy a totalitarian state power through faith in the God of their story. Their story has since empowered other oppressed people throughout history, e.g. the African-American slaves in the United States' Antebellum South. Recall the "Negro Spirituals" that sang of that overcoming faith. Think of "We Shall Overcome," a protest song that became a key anthem of the Civil Rights Movement (1955–1968).

> What Israel knows is that if the story is not believed, nothing added to it will make any difference—not more commandments, rituals, or laws. ... Israel knows that pain like story, can never be abstract or universal, so she trusts the details of both. Israel knows that long after all the dissertations have been read, defended, and forgotten, her stories will remain. It is her mission.[30]

> Story in Israel is the bottom line. It is told and left, and not hedged about by other evidences... Israel understands them not as instruments of something else, but as castings of reality.[31]

In this vein, Michael Goldberg states, "there is no issue of theological substance detachable from the stories' substance. That is, these recounting of the Exodus and the Christ are not fables, such that once their point or moral has been gleaned, the actual narratives can then be discarded."[32] We cannot cash in the stories for some abstracted universal timeless truth that leaves the story behind.

---

[29] Ibid., 15.
[30] Bradt, *Story*, 157.
[31] Ibid., 162.
[32] Michael Goldberg, Jews and Christians: Getting Our Stories Straight: The Exodus and the Passion-Resurrection (Eugene, OR: Wipf & Stock, 1991), 15.

Narrative 6: Jewish *Midrash* and Story

The Jewish hermeneutical tradition that goes by the acronym PaRDeS (*peshat, remez, darash, sod*) has relevance to story.[33] The Hebrew word for "orchard" is *pardes*, which offers the helpful image of the Bible as a fruitful orchard, with truths to be picked from the trees. I will focus here on *peshat* and *darash* methods (or levels) of Biblical interpretation. In that Jewish parlance, in Hebrew, the practitioner of *peshat* was called a *pashtan*. The practitioner of *darash* was called a *darshan*. The interpretive product of the *darshan* is a *midrash*. *Midrash* is from the Hebrew root *drsh*, meaning "to search, to seek, to examine, to investigate."

Pashtan and Darshan

The *pashtan* and *peshat* exegesis, like the modern evangelical "historical-grammatical" exegete, aims to uncover and elucidate only what he believes to be the authorial intent and original meaning of the passage, what it meant to the first generation of its hearers. This meaning is usually thought to be a one-and-only-true, authentic meaning. The tools of the *pashtan* are technical and objective— philology, grammars and lexicons of the original languages and historical, cultural and archeological studies. The goal of the *pashtan* approach is to arrive at the accurate and final, best reading of the text.[34]

The tools of the *darshan* tend to be more subjective—he applies creative imagination to the text in order to squeeze out more meaning. As he deals with the narrative genre, he will not be limited by the strict rules of the *pashtan*. He knows that every Bible story has large holes— there are things that are not told in a sparse ten-, twenty-, or even 100-verse story. To use the anthropological term for detailed cultural description, the Biblical stories are not "thick description," they are often thin-on-the-ground. What are the features, the motives or goals of

---

[33] Peshat (פְּשַׁט)—"plain" ("simple"), literal, direct meaning; the historical-grammatical interpretation.
Remez (רֶמֶז)—"hints" at a deeper (allegoric, symbolic or typological) meaning beyond just the literal sense; type and anti-type.
Derash (דְּרַשׁ)—Hebrew *darash*: "inquire" ("seek")—the interpretation, applicational teaching (midrashic) meaning (a "darasha" is a homily or sermon).
Sod (סוֹד)—"secret" ("mystery") or the mystical, esoteric meaning. Proceed with caution at this level. The Kabbalah is rife with this approach and needs tethers, controls and discernment.

[34] Noam Zion. "The Origins of Human Violence and the Crisis of the Biblical First Family: Cain and Abel in Torah, Commentary, Midrash, Art, Poetry, Movies, and Thought." Notes from a class taught at the Shalom Hartman Institute (Jerusalem, 2014), 22.

this or that character? How does he view his fellow characters? What psychological, cultural or other factors in the biography of each character are influencing him or her in the story situation? As Israeli literary scholar Meir Sternberg, a master of the literary art of the Biblical narrative, states,

> From the viewpoint of what is directly given in the language, the literary work consists of bits and fragments to be linked together in the process of reading: it establishes as system of gaps to be filled in. This gap-filling ranges from simple linkages, which the reader performs automatically, to intricate networks that are figured out consciously, laboriously, hesitantly, and with constant modifications in the light of additional information disclosed in the later stages of reading.[35]

The *darshan* aims to bring the real people and events in the story to life for the present generation or audience. He believes it to be the right and obligation of every generation of Scripture interpreters to uncover meaning that is relevant to the hearers of any generation. He believes the threat of misinterpretation (which the *pashtan* fears) is less dangerous than that of irrelevance. He believes Scripture has a dynamism that is translatable to the needs of people of all ages and situations in life. The needs of God's people call for the manna of fresh *midrash*, applicable to present needs of hearts and lives. A good example of the kind of existential pressures of life that provoke new meanings and answers, is when the matriarch Rebecca was bewildered by her unusual pregnancy (the battling fetuses) and sought *Adonai, "v'tilech l'drosh et Adonai"*— her need moved her to inquire, search out, seek the LORD (Gen. 25: 22, note the same root *"drsh"* as for *midrash*). *Adonai* answered her and gave her meaning.[36]

Midrash Aggadah, Broadly Considered

For an example of the gap-filling, consider the story of the Great Flood. It comprises 85 verses (Gen. 6:1–9:17) that cover decades of tumultuous life as Noah is commissioned to oversee the humanly overwhelming and daunting task of God's near-genocide of the human race, the destruction of the world. For this story, as for all the others, the *darshan* seeks to fill in the

---

[35] Meir Sternberg, *The Poetics of Biblical Narrative: Ideological Literature and the Drama of Reading* (Bloomington: Indiana University Press, 1985), 186.
[36] Zion, "The Origins," 22.

gaps, through *imaginative reconstruction* of the gaps in the text. Another way to describe a *midrash* is as a *narrative commentary* (as opposed to a critical, analytic commentary, with lexical studies, etc.). Such imaginative reconstruction together, with drawing out applications and relevance to today, is called *midrash*, or a *midrash aggadah*. *Midrash halacha* is a different style, which this essay will not address.[37]

Jewish writers and producers Darren Aronofsky and Ari Handel put an example of a *midrash* on the Noah story to the big screen in 2014. Simply called *Noah*, and starring Russell Crowe in the lead role, the movie is a visual *midrash*. The Noah story is an epic, archetypal story and begs for *midrash*. In the movie, after Noah has heard from God, his wife asks him, "Noah, what did he say?" Noah says, "He is going to destroy the world." What kind of man was this, entrusted by the Creator with overseeing such a daunting, overwhelming venture? The human drama of this for Noah and his family, their relatives and neighbors would have included times of high anxiety, tension and emotion. These were real flesh and blood people, like you and me. That Noah got drunk and naked in his tent after it was all over is surely human realism. After years of high stress, Noah unwound, released his inhibitions; his inner moral restraints had collapsed. Compare this with the sanitized Sunday School versions of saintly old Noah with his long white beard, with all the gentle animals, represented by this children's song:

> "The Lord told Noah to build him an arky, arky... The Lord
> told Noah to build him an arky, arky... Build it out of gopher
> barky, barky, children of the Lord."

These are surely crafted and edited versions of the story, more distant from the way it most likely really was than is Aronofsky's and Handel's visual *midrash*. In his blog, Brad Jersak commented on the "evangelical panic" caused by *Noah* after it was released:

> I don't think anyone should be surprised at the usual course of
> Evangelical reactions decrying the movie for its "biblical
> inaccuracies." ... Of course, citing inaccuracies implies that
> the measure of faithfulness to Scripture is somehow
> photocopying Genesis 6–9 into the screenplay in a sort of word

---

[37] Other archetypal Genesis stories that have been treated in the form we may call a literary midrashic genre, broadly considered, are Genesis 3, the Fall of Man in Eden, by John Milton in his epic poem *Paradise Lost* (1667); Genesis 4, Cain and Abel, by John Steinbeck in his novel *East of Eden* (1952); and Genesis 27–50, the Joseph Story, by Thomas Mann in his massive *Joseph and His Brothers* (1943).

for word depiction. It's this paint-by-numbers mentality that keeps many an Evangelical trapped within the lines of their own assumptions—as if taking the text literally was remotely akin to taking it seriously. Not so![38]

Those who love Scripture and want to see its stories reach the broadest possible audience have cause to applaud this visual *midrash*, the "Noah" movie. In the days following its release, the *Christian Post* reported, "Two of the most popular online destinations for Bible readers reported robust increases in traffic in the first book of the Old Testament following the release of 'Noah' last week."[39] YouVersion said, "in the days after Noah hit theaters, people opening the Noah story in Genesis 6 increased about 300% in US & 245% globally on @YouVersion."[40] Bible Gateway reported, "visits to the Noah story in Genesis 6–9 at Bible Gateway saw a 223% increase over the previous weekend."[41]

The *Christian Post* reported that "in addition to YouVersion, an app of the Scriptures which hit 100 million downloads last summer, and the website, BibleGateway, Google trends also showed a spike in substantial increase in search queries for the Old Testament text" as a result of the Noah movie.[42] "Film analysts believe that 'Noah' attracted a wider audience, and not just the religious, due to Hollywood touches given to the film by Aronofsky."[43] "'It certainly feels like the "biggest" film of 2014,' Tim Briody, analyst for Box Office Prophets, told *USA Today*."[44] The movie stimulated the public interest in the story of Noah, making people wonder what the real original story is about, and why it is so compelling. It stirs people to go home and look it up in the Bible. Because this was a mainstream Hollywood film, the number of people and the demographic segment of people reached by this movie was far greater than would have been by a Christian movie about Noah. This gives Bible-believers opportunity to tell the more accurate story to those with awakened interest in the home and work places of social life. The

---

[38] Brad Jersak, "Noah: Who Are the Watchers and Why the Panic?," *Clarion: Journal of Spirituality and Justice*, Mar. 31, 2014, accessed Dec. 14, 2014, www.clarion-journal.com/clarion_journal_of_spirit/2014/03/noah-who-are-the-watchers-and-why-the-panic-by-brad-jersak.html.

[39] www.christianpost.com/news/noah-movie-sparks-massive-spike-in-global-reading-of-bible-book-of-genesis-117334.

[40] twitter.com/YouVersion/status/451415236675764224.

[41] www.biblegateway.com/blog/2014/04/noah-generates-a-flood-of-bible-readers-over-the-weekend.

[42] *Christian Post*, "Massive Spike."

[43] www.christianpost.com/news/hollywoods-noah-tops-box-office-with-44m-debut-117091/.

[44] *Christian Post*, "Massive Spike."

producer of *Noah*, Aronofsky, is not a follower of Messiah Yeshua. This begs the question—*What if Messianic Jews would produce movies, which would be even more accurate to the Biblical text than Aronofsky's production, but would have as large a public impact?*

Noah was controversial and featured much imaginative reconstruction, some of which piqued some people's sensibilities.[45] In the Jewish style of midrashic discussion, if one does not like someone else's picturing of events to fill the gaps, they can offer their own; in synergistic conversation milking the story for all its true worth. This, while always avoiding notions that flatly contradict the text of the story, or the kind of fanciful allegorizations such as those spun out from the parables by many church fathers.[46] (See **Narrative 8** below.)

Known among some in the broader guild of Bible teachers are two helpful alliterative rules-of-thumb that provide hermeneutical tethers to restrain midrashic exploration, if we want to still consider a *midrash* within the pale of an application of the inspired Scripture. A tether is a rope or leash that restrains, usually an animal. An interpretation,

---

[45] The "watchers" in the film were shocking to some. They were sort of sci-fi creatures, fallen from heaven into molten lava. When it hardened to stone, they were lumbering rocky creatures. The angelic "watchers" are mentioned in canonical Scripture in Daniel 4:13, 17, 23. They appear in the apocryphal books of 1 Enoch and Jubilees. Peter's New Testament epistles allude to angels who were disobedient in the days of Noah who had fallen (1 Pet. 3:19–20; 2 Pet. 2:4–5; Jude 6). The epistles state they are kept "in prison" and "Tartarus" (2 Pet. 2:4; a term borrowed from Greek mythology, for a place lower than Hades), whereas Aronofsky and Handel's movie has them wandering the earth, helping men, and some return to heaven in light form, escaping their stony condition. Jude cites 1 Enoch in Jude 14–15 directly (probably 1 Enoch 1:9), stating Enoch (the great-grandfather of Noah) himself had uttered these prophecies. If Peter and Jude can allude to them, surely a visual midrashic version of the Noah story can legitimately do so and imaginatively depict what they were like. There is enough mystery here to allow speculation. No one has copyright to the Biblical stories; they are public domain. And if they were thought to have ownership, they belonged to the Jewish people before ever they did to evangelical Christians.

[46] The teacher-storyteller is responsible to clarify and correct when a *midrash* or interpretation of a story is offered that clearly contradicts the authoritative inspired written text of a Bible story. In the case of the Noah movie, the most glaring dissonance with the Biblical story was the way the character of Noah was portrayed as having so badly misunderstood the Creator that he believed he and his family were also to be destroyed and only the animals were to be saved, this to the extreme point of planning to kill his two granddaughters to help the Creator exterminate every last human being. These notions clearly reach the zone of "Phiction" and the "Deniable" and the tethers apply (see alliterative "Four P's" and "Four D's" above). This confusion in Noah was perhaps because, in the movie, God never speaks audibly or in clear language to Noah. This contradicts the authoritative Biblical story that states in Genesis 6:9b, "Noah was a righteous man, blameless in his generation. Noah walked with God." (ESV) And it says God spoke clear, intelligible instructions to Noah, quoting the words of God, which included the promise of a covenant with Noah (Gen. 6:13; 7:1; 8:15; 9:1, 8, 12). However, considering the possible choices by the characters in the story, choices they could have made but did not make (such possible, hypothetical ones as portrayed in the movie), illumines on the choices they did make (as told in the Bible). Noah *could have* acted as confused as he was in this movie version but did not. God *could have* been as silent as He was in this movie, but He was not. What light does this *midrash* then throw upon the way they did speak and act in the Biblical story?

application or imaginative reconstruction of story may be tested by these "Four P's" and "Four D's":

Provable		Dogma
Probable	OR	Debatable
Possible		Doubtful
Phiction (Fiction)		Deniable

When the midrashic exploration reaches the "Phiction" and "Deniable" zone, that is to say that it clearly contradicts the Biblical text, then the storyteller-teacher must state unambiguously that this is no longer the Biblical story; it is outside the pale of the Biblical account. One is free to write fiction, but such should no longer be considered an application of the Word of God.

We will always need careful *pashtans*, the strict exegetes and their technical tools to stay loyal to the historical meaning of texts, especially for the non-narrative genres. However, Messianic Jews and evangelicals today need to recover and ply the approach of the *darshan—imaginative reconstruction* of the Bible stories, using good questions to search out and to squeeze out more and relevant meaning from the inexhaustible treasures of the Word of God. We need to fear less a misinterpretation of the historical-grammatical one-and-only true meaning (if there is such in stories) and fear more the relegation of Scripture to irrelevance. The stories are rich and deep, having multiple applications; they should not be reduced to or frozen to one exegete's one-and-only true best rendering.[47]

A good storyteller-teacher (*darshan*) will be able to guide a group's discussion if it gets way out of hand. We can trust the story itself and the work of the Holy Spirit to attend to His Word, applying it to the needs of the hearts and lives of any group who hears it, across cultures and

---

[47] In Jewish tradition there is the notion of "*Shiv'im Panim l' Torah* (לְתוֹרָה פָּנִים שִׁבְעִים)—"'The Torah has 70 faces.' This phrase is sometimes used to indicate different 'levels' of interpretation of the Torah. 'There are seventy faces to the Torah: Turn it around and around, for everything is in it' (*Bamidbar Rabba 13:15*). The Torah is a work of literary art, written by the LORD Himself, and therefore shares characteristics with all other works of art." (Parsons, John J., "Hebrew for Christians," accessed Dec. 14, 2014, www.hebrew4christians.com/Articles/Seventy_Faces/seventy_faces.html.) This should be interpreted as hyperbole for those accepting the authority of the New Covenant Scriptures. Controls and tethers must be applied so as not to fall into a Kabbalistic, esoteric mode. However, the notion of the "70 Faces of the Torah" jars us away from the only-one-true meaning literalist mode when dealing with stories and is a reminder of the depth and riches of the inspired Word of God. When interpreting the non-narrative genre, like the law codes of Deuteronomy or Pauline epistles, careful historical-grammatical exegesis must be used; but stories have multiple, many-faceted interpretations and applications.

generations, in multiple and various applications. Such formative work is divine and out of the *pashtan's* or the *darshan's* hands.[48]

Narrative 7: The Power of Story

Victor E. Frankl (1905–1997), Austrian psychiatrist and Holocaust survivor, is well-known for reporting that concentration camp inmates who maintained hope and meaning were likely to survive longer. Those who lost hope and meaning were likely to die sooner. A story is often what gives a person meaning and hope. So, there is truth to this saying,

> The stories people tell have a way of taking care of them. If stories come to you, care for them. And learn to give them away where they are needed. Sometimes a person needs a story more than food to stay alive. That is why we put these stories in each other's memory. This is how people care for themselves.[49]

Stories are innate and primal in human nature and experience. All human civilizations ever studied have had their bards and storytellers, persons who were repositories of the stories that gave meaning and identity to a people. Everyone loves a story. Every person's life is a story, with plot twists and a parade of interesting characters. Sharing stories brings people intimately together. When we hear stories, we identify with characters in the story who dealt with situations like we face. We learn vicariously through the truths we draw from the story. A story features real life, concrete situations like our own. A story touches us at deeper levels than abstract propositions or stated principles can. A story can penetrate our imagination, conscience and emotions, touching us at a deep personal level. Someone has observed, "If a picture is worth a thousand words; a good story's worth a million pictures."[50]

---

[48] A missionary to Africa tells of the African bush lady who heard the story of Joseph and Potiphar's wife and said, "I've never seen a man turn down such an opportunity. I want to know the God behind this man. This God must be very powerful to help Joseph turn down such a temptation." The storyteller reminded her this story was not evangelistic, but God used it to bring her to faith in Yeshua. The authorial intent of the Genesis story was to show God's power to preserve Joseph through the testing of Joseph's character to by resisting temptation, but the nature of story allows it to be used evangelistically. (As told to Larry Dinkins by African indigenous Christian leaders in a "Simply the Story" summit meeting. Hemet, California, 2014).

[49] Barry Lopez, *Crow and Weasel*. Illustrations by Tom Pohrt (San Francisco: North Point Press, 1990), 48.

[50] www.clickz.com/clickz/column/2216868/if-a-pictures-worth-a-thousand-words-a-good-storys-worth-a-million-pictures.

Insights From Rabbis About Story

According to a well-received Jewish tradition, it was King Solomon who, if not invented, popularized the parable, at least in Israel. "The Torah until Solomon's time," commented Rabbi Nachman in the *Aggada*, "was comparable to a labyrinth with a bewildering number of rooms. Once one entered there, one lost his way out. Then along came Solomon and invented the parable that has served as a ball of thread. When tied at the entrance to this labyrinth it serves as a secure guide through all the winding, bewildering passages."[51]

Taking up the thought, Rabbi Nachman's colleague, Rabbi Hanina, said:

> Until the time of Solomon, the Torah could have been compared to a well full of refreshing water, but because of its extraordinary depth no one could get to the bottom. What was necessary was to find a rope long enough to tie to the bucket in order to bring up the water. Solomon made up this rope with his parables and thus enables everyone to reach to the profoundest depths of the well.[52]

Indeed, Story gives us "a rope long enough" to reach the depths. So actually, re-digging the wells of Story may actually mean simply reaching the bottom of the already existing wells of salvation. Poet Emily Dickinson said it well: "Tell all the truth, but tell it slant." Often modern Western preachers and teachers think of stories as mere illustrations or "icing on the cake" of a lecture-type sermon. The real cake, the substance they think, is the more abstract, propositional truth in logical, told in bald statement-of-fact form. Rabbi Hanina knew stories are the rope that reaches to the profoundest depths of the well.

Rabbi Jacob ben Wolf Kranz of Dubno, known as the "Dubner Maggid," was a Lithuanian-born preacher who lived from 1740 to 1804. *Maggid* is Hebrew for *storyteller* (from the same Hebrew root as *Aggadah* and *Haggadah*). A contemporary of the Vilna Gaon, the "Maggid" was famous for explaining Torah concepts by using a *mashal* or parable. Moses Mendelssohn named Kranz "the Jewish Aesop."[53] The Dubner Maggid was once asked, "Why do you always tell stories? Why

---

[51] Nathan Ausubel, ed., A Treasury of Jewish Folklore: Stories, Traditions, Legends, Humor, Wisdom and Folk Songs of the Jewish People (New York: Crown Publisher's, Inc., 1948), 56.

[52] Ausubel, ed., *Treasury*, 56.

[53] Eliezer Steinbarg, ed., *The Jewish Book of Fables* (Dora Teitelboim Center for Yiddish Culture, 2003), xii.

are stories so powerful?" His legendary reply was to answer by telling the following story, about the power of stories:

> There was once a poor old woman. She was, well... ugly... very ugly. She had a bent back and hooked nose. Her chin was covered with warts and pimples. Her eyes bugged out. Her mouth was crooked and her teeth broken. She dressed in old rags that smelled. No one would listen to what she said or even look at her. If they saw her they would run away. . . slam doors in her face. So, she was very sad because all she wished for was some company, some companionship. But no one would pay attention to her or talk to her. So she wandered from place to place looking for friends.
>
> She crossed a great desert and came to a city in the middle of the desert. She thought to herself "Surely I'll find friends in this city. People in the desert know how hard life is and will take pity on me, and I'll find a friend." But, alas, this city was like all the rest. People ran away and slammed doors or closed their shutters. No one would talk to her or listen to her. She became very upset. "Why go on? What's the point? Life is too hard. I think I should just give up on life" So she wandered out of the city and sat down on the dusty road just outside the city. She waited, watching life pass her by.
>
> Before long a good-looking young man dressed in beautiful clothes arrived in the city and received a great reception. The people came out to shake his hand. Some even hugged him. They brought him food and drink and lavished him with gifts. The old woman said, "Life is so unfair. When you are young and good looking, everyone loves you, but when you are old, ugly and sick, they forget you and ignore you. It is so unfair!" After a while the young man gathered up his gifts, said "Goodbye," and headed out of the city. He stopped on the dusty road and sat down opposite the old woman to pack up his gifts.
>
> The old woman could keep her tongue no longer, "What is going on? What's with you? Is it like this everywhere you go? Do you always get treated so well?"
>
> The young man blushed and said, "Well... yes... I guess... Everywhere I go they treat me well."
>
> "Well, why? Why?! You must be someone special! Someone extraordinary," said the old woman.

The young man said, "Oh, no, Ma'am! Actually, I am quite ordinary."

"I don't believe it. You must be an emperor, a king in disguise, or a prince or a general," she said.

"Oh no... I am not like that...I am very common. You find me everywhere--me and my type," he said.

"Well then, what are you? said the old woman. "Who are you that people are so happy to see you when you come along?"

"Well, I am a Story, and I think I am a pretty good Story at that. Because people like a good story they are happy to see me. But, old woman, what are you? Who are you? Why don't people like to see you?" asked the young man.

"Ah, that is the problem. It's what I am. I am Truth, and nobody likes to hear the truth.

(Narrator: This may seem a bit strange to some of you...but when you think about it what the old woman said is really true, isn't it? ... If someone said to you, "I'm going to tell you what your friends really say behind your back. Do you really want to hear it? If you are destined to die a horrible death, or to die early, do you really want to know the truth about that? No, some truth is ugly, especially truth about ourselves. We avoid it, we resist it, we don't want to know it.)

The young man said, "I'm sorry about that." He then began to think how he could help the old woman. "I've got an idea, old woman," he said. "Let's team up...let's journey together! You and I can travel together and wherever I go, you'll go. Anything I am given, I'll share with you."

"That won't work," she said. "They'll see me. They'll take one look and run away from both of us!"

"No, you don't understand! You'll hide behind me—behind my cloak. Whatever they give me I'll share equally with you. Let's try it."

The woman agreed, and they partnered up and travelled together. Wherever they went, the old woman hid behind the young man's cloak, and anything he was given he happily shared with the old woman.

This worked out so well that their arrangement lasts to this very day. That is why to this very day *the truth always hides behind a good story.*

This story has also been put nicely into verse form by Heather Forest, in "Naked Truth and Parable."

Naked Truth and Parable

Naked Truth walked down the street one day.
People turned their eyes the other way.
Parable arrived draped in decoration.
People greeted parable with celebration.
Naked Truth sat alone, sad and unattired.
"Why are you so miserable?" Parable inquired.
Naked Truth replied, "I'm not welcome anymore.
No one wants me. They chase me from their door."
"It is hard to look at Naked Truth, "Parable explained.
"Let me dress you up a bit. Your welcome will be gained."
Parable dressed Naked Truth in Story's fine attire,
With metaphor, poignant prose, and plots to inspire.
With laughter and tears and adventure to unveil,
Together they went forth to spin a tale.
People opened their doors and served them their best.
Naked Truth dressed in Story was a welcome guest.[54]

"Let Me Write the Songs of a Nation…"

"Let me write the songs of a nation and I care not who writes their laws."
"Let me make the ballads of a nation, and I care not who makes its laws."

The above are two variations on this saying are attributed to Andrew Fletcher (1653–1716), a Scottish writer, politician and patriot. As a politician, he was a keen observer of what it takes to start a movement of social change, even revolution, in a society. Songs are surely more effective than laws to change the hearts and minds of the masses.

A good story is powerful in itself. Put it to music and verse and it heightens the power to cast vision, to inspire, and to motivate social groups. If you want to know what people hold as valuable, look to the songs.

King Saul, Israel's first monarch, found this out as the increasingly storied David was celebrated in the streets, the women dancing and singing,

"Saul has slain his thousands, David his ten thousands."

[54] Heather Forest, *Wisdom Tales From Around the World* (Little Rock: August House, 1996), ii.

The story became a ballad that permeated and mobilized the whole culture. King Saul correctly observed after this, "Now what more can he [David] have but the kingdom?" (1 Sam. 18:6–8). Saul's "law" had been overtaken by the songs of the people.

For a culture-change phenomenon from our times, consider how powerfully the music of the 1960s (the debut of rock-and-roll to the masses) both expressed and shaped the culture then and until the present time. It is often underestimated just how powerfully that music shaped late modern culture. Award-winning British documentary filmmaker Leslie Woodhead produced a documentary titled "How the Beatles Rocked the Kremlin," aired by the British Broadcasting Company (BBC).[55] In 2009, WNET produced a documentary showing how the Beatles' music was a strong factor contributing to the collapse of the USSR. The film argues persuasively that their music—banned in the USSR and bootlegged by teenagers—inspired dreams of hope and freedom of expression for a whole generation, which eventually led to the demise of communism. Little did the dour totalitarian rulers of the Union of Soviet Socialist Republics know their iron laws would be brought down (at least in part) by songs.

The Psalms are Israel's Song Book. They have been profitably put to music ever since the days of King David, by Jews and Christians. The Psalms express "an anatomy of all parts of the soul," according to John Calvin.[56] This feature of the Psalms is a major reason for their endurance and widespread popularity of the Psalms in every Jewish and Christian tradition. They help us express our souls *vertically*, to God. What if we could put the stories of Scripture into the contemporary and beloved and popular forms of music as inspired ballads, and into more dramatic visual and film media to express these stories (which reach all parts of the soul) *horizontally* to society today and to each generation?

The Nathan Principle

What follows is a Biblical example of truth hiding behind a good story. Imagine with me: Had Nathan the prophet approached King David, after his sin with Bathsheba, and told him the propositional truth—"You have committed adultery and murder, O King. You have broken four of the Ten Commandments." Would the King have readily

---

[55] www.thirteen.org/beatles/video/video-watch-how-the-beatles-rocked-the-kremlin.

[56] John Calvin, *A Commentary On the Psalms of David* (Oxford: Talboys, 1840), 1: vi.

received this truth? Likely not. He may have rid himself of this troublesome prophet. Off with his head! He did not want to hear the ugly, naked truth. But instead of presenting him with the naked truth, Nathan told him a story:

> There were two men in a certain city, the one rich and the other poor. The rich man had very many flocks and herds, but the poor man had nothing but one little ewe lamb, which he had bought. And he brought it up, and it grew up with him and with his children. It used to eat of his morsel and drink from his cup and lie in his arms, and it was like a daughter to him. Now there came a traveler to the rich man, and he was unwilling to take one of his own flock or herd to prepare for the guest who had come to him, but he took the poor man's lamb and prepared it for the man who had come to him." (2 Sam. 12:1–14, ESV)

This story brought David into a house and opened a window for him to see. He could see vividly the injustice done. David bought into the story. He was caught in the story's powerful rhetorical trap. The King became enraged and said, *"As the Lord lives, the man who has done this deserves to die! ... and he shall restore the lamb fourfold, because he did this thing, and because he had no pity"* (2 Sam. 12:5, 6). David thus judged himself. Nathan said, *"You are the man!"* He opened a window, which became a mirror to David. Herein is the power of story to bring truth home to the heart and core of a person.

A story is an oblique way of coming at truth and helpful in getting past the defenses of a hearer or audience. Bible storyteller and trainer Dorothy Miller calls this "the Nathan Principle,"[57] and adds this word as explicating its effect: "See, the Word of God is alive! It is at work and is sharper than any double-edged sword—it cuts right through to where soul meets spirit and joints meet marrow, and it is quick to judge the inner reflections and attitudes of the heart" (Heb. 4:12, CJB).[58] Direct route communication and processing uses argumentation; peripheral route processing circumvents argumentation to a deeper place in the heart. This is critically needed in Jewish evangelism because of the high resistance among Jewish people to direct communication of the Gospel. This is the "the Nathan Principle."

---

[57] http://simplythestory.org/oralbiblestories/index.php/practitioner-audio.html.
[58] Dorothy A. Miller, *Simply the Story Handbook* (Hemet, CA: The God's Story Project, 2012).

Narrative 8: Yeshua the Messiah: Master Teacher and Storyteller

In the Western tradition, especially following the Enlightenment, serious theology largely developed in the form of ideas held together by logic (linear, syllogistic logic) and reason. The more intelligent the theologian, the more abstract his writing became and difficult for the average person to understand—think of the German theologians of the 19th and 20th centuries. Whittaker Chambers commented on the deadening nature of much of this,

> Theology is jawbreakingly abstract and its mood is widely felt to be about as embracing as an unaired vestry. … God has become, at best, a fairly furtive presence, a lurking luminosity, a cozy thought.[59]

We can term these academic systematic theologians, *conceptual theologians*. This is not to say conceptual theologizing and writing is wrong or without value. But in the modern West, we have majored on the conceptual in theological education, to the neglect of the more Hebraic concrete and narrative approach. Yeshua, by contrast, was not a conceptual theologian.

> Jesus was a *metaphorical* theologian. That is, his primary method of creating meaning was through metaphor, simile, parable, and dramatic action rather than through logic and reasoning. He created meaning like a dramatist and a poet rather than like philosopher."[60]

In fact, we are told, "He did not say a thing to them without using a parable; when he was alone with his own *talmidim* he explained everything to them" (Mark 4:34, CJB).

Was Yeshua then but a simple teller of folktales for fisherman and farmers? Hardly. Could Yeshua have given the most erudite, learned, scholarly lecture of any of his contemporaries? … or ours? Of course he could have. When he was twelve years old he amazed the learned rabbis in the Temple with the profundity of his knowledge and wisdom (Luke 3:46). He of course was the most profound of theologians. But his primary teaching method was through stories, word pictures and metaphors.

---

[59] Os Guinness, *When No One Sees: The Importance of Character in an Age of Image.* Trinity Forum Study Series (Colorado Springs: Nav Press, 2000), 208.
[60] Kenneth E. Bailey, *Through Middle Eastern Eyes: Cultural Studies in the Gospels* (Downers Grove: IVP Academic, 2008), 279.

A metaphor communicates in ways a rational argument cannot. Recalling C.S. Lewis' insight here that "reason is the natural organ of truth, but imagination is the organ of meaning. Imagination, producing new metaphors or revivifying old, is not the cause of truth, but its condition"[61]—a word or concept takes on meaning when we have a clear image with which to connect it. Recent studies in brain science confirms this—parts of the brain light up when meaning happens, when words stimulate images in the brain.

And when the listener or disciple discovers the meaning himself (the "aha!" moment), he or she retains that truth much better, "owning" that truth. If facts are spoon-fed by lecture or monologue to a more passive mind or a mind that cannot connect a concept to an image (imagine it), they may "go in one ear and out the other" as the saying goes. Yeshua's use of stories as his primary teaching method was not merely due to his cultural context; story is a more universal means of communicating. Stories are what stick in hearts and minds, because they address both right and left brain; intellect and imagination. In short, stories grip the heart, and as the proverb says, "out of the heart are the issues of life" (Prov. 4:23).

Another major reason Yeshua's method of choice for teaching is the story is that a lecture often only speaks to the mind; it provides data or information that may or may not affect that person's heart or will. By contrast, a story with its characters, with which the story-hearers will identify, either positively or negatively, evokes response. The choices of the characters evoke a heart response (emotions and conscience). Thus, the story stirs and stimulates moral responses that can lead to change and character growth in the listener. Yeshua was after moral decisions and character transformation in his followers.

If theology were only a matter of intellectual conceptualization, then unbelievers could be as good at teaching theology as are people of faith and devotion to God. All one would need would be a bright mind and a will to work. But Yeshua taught that there is a moral pre-condition or prerequisite to really understanding God and His ways. He taught this truth through the masterful parable of the sower:

> When Yeshua was alone, the people around him with the Twelve asked him about the parables. He answered them, "To you the secret of the Kingdom of God has been given; but to those outside, everything is in parables, so that *they may be always looking but never seeing; always listening but never*

[61] Ward, "How Lewis Lit the Way," 38.

understanding. Otherwise, they might turn and be forgiven!'"
[quoted from Isa. 6:9-10] Then Yeshua said to them, "Don't
you understand this parable? How will you be able to
understand any parable?" (Mark 4:10–13, CJB)

Yeshua taught that this moral condition—a truth-seeking heart—is the
key to all theological understanding, light and truth.
     Yeshua did also make propositional statements and teach concepts,
but he did so with those whose hearts were inclined to the truth.
"Blessed are the pure in heart, for they shall see God," he said (Matt.
5:8). Jesus gave an example of a very clear propositional concept,
actually an axiom, when he stated to the seeker Nicodemus,

> And this is the judgment: the light has come into the world,
> and people loved the darkness rather than the light because
> their works were evil. For everyone who does wicked things
> hates the light and does not come to the light, lest his works
> should be exposed. But whoever *does what is true comes to the
> light*, so that it may be clearly seen that his works have been
> carried out in God. (John 3:19–21, emphasis added)

Only those who love the light and truth will come to see and understand
it. As Blaise Pascal (1623–1662) deftly observed, "Things human must
be known to be loved: things divine must be loved to be known."[62] And,
"The heart has its reasons which reason knows nothing of. ... We know
the truth, not only by the reason, but also by the heart."[63]

The Parable as a House

     Often in the Western preaching tradition, preachers use stories as
"illustrations" to exemplify or represent an abstract idea, principle or
proposition. As Bailey points out, however,

> A metaphor, however, is not an illustration of an idea, it is a
> mode of theological discourse. The metaphor does more than
> explain meaning, it creates meaning. A parable is an extended
> metaphor, and as such it is not a delivery system for an idea,
> but a house in which the reader/listener is invited to take up
> residence.[64]

---

[62] Philip Moxom, "The Insufficiency of Religious Toleration," *Addresses Before the New York Conference of Religion*, ed. James Whiton (New York: The New York State Conference of Religion, 1903), 93.

[63] Blaise Pascal, *Pascal's Pensees* (New York: Dutton & Co., 1958), 282.

[64] Bailey, *Through Middle Eastern Eyes*, 280.

Expanding upon Bailey's metaphor of a parable as "a house in which the listener/reader is invited to take up residence," that person is then urged by the parable to look on the world through the windows of the residence. We could say the parable creates a worldview of its own and the listener is encouraged to examine the human predicament and the worldview created by the parable (with its cultural and historical context).

In Western tradition, the parables of Yeshua have been abused in two major ways. First, in the early centuries, allegory reigned supreme. The Greek Church fathers applied allegorization to the parables. Their fancies ran wild. So, the fatted calf in the Story of the Two Sons (or "The Prodigal Son," Luke 15) came to symbolize Christ, because Christ was killed. Or look at Augustine's treatment of the Story of the Good Samaritan. Every detail of the story was given allegorical meanings by the readers; indeed, these special meanings kept accumulating over time. Here is a list of Augustine's allegorizations:

The man going down to Jericho = Adam
Jerusalem, from which he was going = City of Heavenly Peace
Jericho = The moon which signifies our mortality (This is a play on the Hebrew terms for *Jericho* and *moon*, which both look and sound alike)
Robbers = Devil and his angels
Stripping him = Taking away his immortality
Beating him = Persuading him to sin
Leaving him half dead = Because of sin, he was dead spiritually, but half alive, because of the knowledge of God
Priest = Priesthood of the Old Testament (Law)
Levite = Ministry of the Old Testament (Prophets)
Good Samaritan = Christ
Binding of wounds = Restraint of sin
Oil = Comfort of good hope
Wine = Exhortation to spirited work
Animal = Body of Christ
Inn = Church
Two denarii = Two commandments to love
Innkeeper = Apostle Paul
Return of the Good Samaritan = Resurrection of Christ[65]

---

[65] Robert H. Stein, *The Method and Message of Jesus' Teaching* (Louisville: Westminster, John Knox Press, 1994), 46.

One quickly sees the problem. How could this story have meant any of these things to the original hearers? With no hermeneutical tether or controls, it is a fanciful free-for-all. Secondly, and in reaction to allegorization, the 20th-century interpreters argued for "one point per parable." They swung too far in the other direction to protect the parable from wild allegorizations. But if a parable is "a house in which the reader/listener is invited to take up residence," then the one who takes up dwelling in that house will find there are a variety of rooms in the house, from which he or she can look out on the world from different windows.

Among the audiences who listen to the story, there will be various needs, concerns, perspectives and issues going on with and in that person. As the listener hears the story, he or she (with the aid of the Holy Spirit) will hear and apply aspects of the story that speak to his or her needs. There are rich moral and theological treasures in a Bible story or parable. Bailey calls this *"the theological cluster" of themes* in a given parable.[66] Each theme is in creative relation to the others. A hearer will latch on to that theme that resonates with his/her situation or need.

The content of the "cluster" (so as not to be wild allegorical fancy) must be controlled by: (1) what Jesus' original hearers could have understood from the story, and (2) what is consistent with the content of the whole story. In digging out the treasures in the story we should not find things that are not there (like the church fathers did) or are contradictory to the story. We can ask, "Do you observe that in the story? Where do you see that in the story? Is the story really indicating that?" In application questions we can ask: "Are there situations today in which people say, do and/or act the way the people in the story did? If so, what does that look like today?" And, "How does this story address that? What guidance, correction, or hope does this story offer for people in such situations today?" In the application, the Holy Spirit may apply an aspect of the story to hearts in ways the original hearers could not have anticipated.

It is said that *"story invites you into the room, but does not tell you where to sit."* You will choose to sit near to, and to look out from, the window on to the world from the direction or angle of your needs, concerns, interests or situation in life. In this way the story, and the teacher through the story, gently respects the free will and dignity of the hearers. This is the genius of the story or parable as a teaching approach.

---

[66] Bailey, *Through Middle Eastern Eyes*, 282.

Narrative 9: The Postmodern Moment and Its Prospects for Story

The philosophical and cultural trends that began in the Enlightenment (rejection of religious authority, utilitarianism, disengaged reason issuing into rationalism, scientism and secular liberalism) played out to a crisis in the 1960s disillusionments, revolutions, moral decline. The Baby Boom generation was the first to experience at the popular cultural level the consequences of what is called the "postmodern shift," or "late modernity" (because the postmodern is still also modern).[67]

The consequences of the postmodern shift are mostly morally and spiritually negative from a Biblical worldview perspective. But the cultural shift also proffers opportunities. Sociologists concerned with the postmodern shift describe our times as characterized by "incredulity to metanarratives." [68] The grand metanarratives that have driven modernity—Progress and the Perfectibility of Man through Science, Industrialism, Communism, Fascism, and other "isms"—have largely become "wasms" at the turn of the 21st century; they have lost their compelling power, no longer holding the same credibility.

Thus, the Western world is searching for a new metanarrative. In the Middle East, Islamism, especially in the ISIS, or the Islamic State (IS) movement, is advancing a powerfully renewed metanarrative of the seventh-century caliphate that shall rule the world by the sword. Western angry young men are susceptible to being recruited to this story because of the loss of a vital one envisioning and energizing them in the late modern West. There is a receptive climate in the twenty-first century in which to communicate God's master story.

Daniel Pink has argued that our postmodern moment in Western history is a time of "right brain rising." To put very simply the argument of his book: *"Left brain direction"* (rational, scientific, analytic, text-oriented, logical, linear, sequential, detail-oriented) was dominant during modernity. *"Right brain direction"* (artistic, aesthetic, emotional and relational expression, literary, synthesis, non-linear, context-oriented, big-picture, holistic, image, metaphor, and story-orientation) is rising in

---

[67] Bjoraker, "Faith," 9–74.
[68] Jean-Francois Lyotard, *The Postmodern Condition: A Report on Knowledge.* 1979, (Minneapolis: University of Minnesota Press, 1984), xxiv.

postmodernity out of human hunger for its lack during modernity. Right brain aptitudes are increasingly desired and needed. Left brain direction remains necessary, but it is no longer sufficient. We need a "whole new mind," a holistic mind.[69]

The larger metanarrative is the coming of Kingdom of God, His glory among the nations, inaugurated by Messiah's first coming, advancing now throughout This Age, the restoration of Israel, and to be consummated as his Second Coming and into the Age to Come. A spiritual renewal of the Zionist story and the American founding story infused by the Biblical master story can bring national revitalization to Israel and the United States. Thus, our moment in history is an auspicious one for a renewal and revival of storytelling in Messianic Jewish ministry and for reaching the world.

From Gutenberg to Zuckerberg

Another dimension of the momentous shift of our times is the communications revolution.

Our current digital revolution is certainly a cultural mega-shift. Communications theorists tell us the world has experienced only three major communications eras. There have been only three inventions that have served as hinges of history: (1) Writing and Reading, (2) Printing, (3) Electronic Media. The printing press changed the world and marked the end of the Middle Ages and opened a portal to the "Gutenberg Galaxy."[70] The personal computer, made accessible to the masses, opened the portal to the "Digitoral Galaxy."[71] Note also that the "Digitorality Era" has more similarities with the Orality Era than it does with the Textuality Era. This led Thomas Pettit to describe the Textuality Era as more of a "Gutenberg Parenthesis," a mere interruption in the broader arc of human communication. Our digital-media culture has brought us back again to a more original orality. The new kinds of literacy needed for the digitorality era are in some ways closer to the orality era. The three communication eras are compared in the following table:

---

[69] Daniel H. Pink, A Whole New Mind: Why Right-Brainers Will Rule the Future (New York: Riverhead Books, 2005).

[70] Marshall McLuhan, The Gutenberg Galaxy (Toronto: University of Toronto Press, 1962).

[71] Charles Madinger, "A Literate's Guide to the Oral Galaxy," Orality Journal 2, no. 2 (2013).

TABLE 2 – THREE COMMUNICATION ERAS

Orality Era	Textuality Era	Digitorality Era
Invention of the alphabet & writing (circa. 2000 BC)	Invention of movable type printing (Gutenberg, 1437)	Invention of personal computers and the Internet (1980s)
Pre-literate	Print literacy	Digital literacy
Ancient	Modern	Post- or Late Modern
Events, Stories	Words, Ideas	Images, Stories, Ideas
Oral communication by all, Storytellers, oral tradition	Books, newspapers, libraries, printed matter	Television, personal computers, plethora of electronic i-devices, etc.
Right Brain Dominant	Left Brain Dominant	Left & Right Brain Needed
Oral Galaxy	Gutenberg Galaxy	Digitoral Galaxy

When media changes, people are changed by those media. A question many observers are asking is, will our dependence on this new media rewire our brains? Younger generations today, though literate, have been conditioned by the digital revolution to prefer to get their information not from reading print, but from other electronic media. This mentality is termed "secondary orality" by orality and literacy theorist Walter Ong, a term he coined for the new electronically mediated culture of spoken, as contrasted with written, language.[72] The new media advances secondary orality, and secondary orality in turn is decreasing print literacy. This is not an entirely happy development.

One thing seems clear and constant however. Humans are *homo narrans*. All humans are hardwired for story, as part of the *Imago Dei* within us. Story and storytelling will always matter. And it matters more in the "Digitoral Galaxy" than it did in the "Gutenberg Galaxy." Late modern people do not, will not read their printed Bibles as much as they read their smartphones. But they will engage with oral, face-to-face Bible storytelling, and through Facebook, YouTube and Ning. Mark

---

[72] Ong, *Orality*, 11.

Zuckerberg invented Facebook, so Samuel Chiang of the "International Orality Network" deftly termed the transition we are experiencing as "From Gutenberg to Zuckerberg"[73] (Chiang 2014:4). It is of interest that Zuckerberg is Jewish. Jews, especially gifted in communication, have always been at the vortex of history-making movements and part of intellectual and culture-change movements. From the Hebrew prophets and apostles, to journalist Theodore Herzl's envisioning and writing *The Jewish State*, to the modern building of the Hollywood movie industry, Jewish people have been in the communications business and in the storytelling business. May the contemporary Messianic Jewish movement be at the vanguard, at the vortex, leading the way in creatively retelling God's master story to the masses! The "People of the Book" are the "People of the Story."

Narrative 10: Effective Use of Storytelling in Contemporary Jewish Ministry

Story and storytelling isn't everything in the ministry of the Word. It is something, however, and a big thing at that. If 70% of the Bible is in the story genre, a good rule of thumb may be to use storytelling in 70% of our teaching. The Hasidim were outstanding storytellers. Like Yeshua, they knew stories can be life-changing. Storytelling constitutes a life-giving act in itself. Here is one retold by Martin Buber:

A rabbi, whose grandfather had been a disciple of the Baal Shem Tov, was asked to tell a story. "A story," he said, "must be told in such a way that it constitutes help in itself." And he told this story: "My grandfather was lame. Once they asked him to tell a story about his teacher (the Baal Shem). And he told how the Holy Baal Shem used to hop and dance while he prayed. My grandfather, though he was lame, rose as he spoke, and was so swept away by his story that he began to hop and dance to show how the master (the Baal Shem) had done it. From that hour on he was cured of his lameness."[74]

---

[73] Samuel E. Chiang "Learning from My Own Mistakes," *Mission Frontiers*, May–June 2014, 1, accessed Dec. 14, 2014, www.missionfrontiers.org/issue/article/from-the-guest-editor.

[74] Buber, *I and Thou*, xvii.

The above Hasidic story about the Baal Shem illustrates a point: Stories can help us transcend our current condition or circumstance. It is important to distinguish between a story told with a moral, or to illustrate, like this story (or an *Aesop's Fable*). These stories have value and can even affect inner change. But if it is a *Bible story,* it is the Word of God. It can impart faith for healing and transformative change by the Holy Spirit. "So then faith comes by hearing, hearing the Word of God" (Rom. 10:17).

By "storying," or Bible storytelling, I mean the entire process of the oral and visual communication of *a Bible story* (not folk tales) followed by group discussion—learning, interpretation, application, accountability to the truth in the story, drama, and/or song and the retelling of the story such that the story is internalized by the group and can be retold to others. The approach can be called oral inductive Bible study.

It needs emphasizing that the story should be told, not read from a book. It should be told with the appropriate emotion, tone of voice, eye contact and eye movements, hand gestures and body movements; all that best communicate the story. The story should be brought to life. When a story is read from a text (especially if in expressionless monologue) and then dissected and analyzed verse-by-verse, something is lost.

Miller uses this illustration in *Simply the Story* training workshops. Suppose you see a beautiful butterfly. You admire its beauty, so you decide to take it home and dissect it on a corkboard. You pull out its wings and put them together. You pull off its legs and put them in a pile to analyze them. You pull out its antennae—but what has happened in the process? You may learn more about the class of insects in the order *Lepidoptera*, and there is a place for that, but in the dissection, the butterfly dies. You can no longer enjoy its living beauty. Let the story fly in its living beauty or something is lost.[75]

Storying is Jewish-friendly. No matter how religious or secular a Jewish person may be, virtually all, even if Biblically illiterate, know intuitively that these stories of the Hebrew Bible are their stories, the stories of their people, the stories of Israel. They are thus non-threatening and find a welcome response.

Storying is seeker-friendly. People of any faith or none can participate and not feel preached-to or lectured-at. Anyone can hear and discuss the story. Seekers feel on a more level playing field, because

---

[75] Miller, Simply the Story.

everyone in the group is discussing the story just told. All are looking for the treasures in the story together. And then the story does its work of speaking to hearts.

Conversational storytelling is a non-threatening, engaging means of Jewish evangelism. Simply described, conversational evangelistic storytelling is done on the go, in the streets and marketplaces. You are standing line at Starbucks, or waiting to collect your luggage at the airport baggage carousel, you make small talk, looking for an opening to say, "Hey that reminds me of a story, do you mind if I tell you one?" Virtually every one will agree to hear it. You tell a five-minute version of a Bible story and ask a question about it—and listen for the person's answer. Then you respond to that answer, and you will find yourself in a conversation about God. You let it go where it, or the Spirit, wills. Seeds are planted in that heart; a person is moved closer to Truth, to Yeshua.

The value of storying is it bypasses the pitfalls of apologetics and argumentation that go nowhere. Jewish people, and especially those schooled in Rabbinic thought, can argue and debate you to a standstill over who is the Messiah and theological issues. Head-to-head Messianic vs. Rabbinic apologetics is the "naked truth" approach. It becomes a fencing match, with each debater thrusting and parrying and unwilling to lose the match. However, reflecting upon a story, and keeping the group focused on drawing out its treasures, shifts the matter to a whole different dimension. We let the story do the work of speaking to hearts, rather than us trying to convince the defensive rational mind.

We live in a moment of history that calls for a recovery of the lost treasures of Story and storytelling in the ministry of the Word. We need to re-dig the wells of Story, of Hebraic narrative epistemology that have been plugged by modernity's forces and trends. In this "Digitorality Era," a major way the Messianic Jewish movement will advance the Kingdom of God and be a "light to the nations" is through creatively retelling the Biblical Story and stories of God, empowered by the Holy Spirit, to these late modern and the succeeding generations until Messiah returns.

Conclusion: "A Rope Long Enough?"

Recall Rabbi Hanina's counsel that what is necessary to reach the depths of the well of Torah, of the Word of God, was "a rope long enough." He said that rope was parable and story. This essay has made clear in **Narrative 1**, subheading *Hebraism and Hellenism*, that rigorous intellectual scholarship, including systematic theology has a proper place in loving God with all of our minds. But as we read and write and teach the "-ologies," let us recall that every systematic theology category is at least one step abstracted from its primal source in story. Let us keep Bialik's counsel from **Narrative 2**, applied thus:

> *Halacha* is the crystallization, the ultimate and inevitable quintessence of *Aggadah*; ... *Aggadah* is the plaintive voice of the heart's yearning as it wings its way to its haven; *Halacha* [read: systematic theology] is the resting place, where for a moment the yearning is satisfied and stilled. As a dream seeks it fulfillment in interpretation, as will in action, as thought in speech, as flower in fruit—so *Aggadah* in *Halacha* [read: systematic theology].

All systematic theology is the expression of a generation, or at most a century. They are a "crystallization" of a generation's or a century's, or a cultural context's or a region's work of abstracting, deducing, summarizing and systematizing their theological beliefs. But these will be expressed differently a century later, even if they are a Jewish expression. The Jewish experience changes over time and changes from one country to another; there are differences in American Messianic Jewish theology from Israeli Messianic Jewish theology.

A twenty-first-century Messianic Jewish systematic theology is itself an expression of, and part of the story of a twenty-first-century Jewish spiritual and social movement, from its historical context. In the same way that the "Book of the Covenant" (named in Exod. 24:7, but comprising Exod. 21–23), containing the social and religious laws of the first generation of Israel as nation, is a "theology" which is embedded in and a part of the story told in Exodus of that generation of Israel (albeit Exodus is inspired, authoritative Scripture and our theologies today are not).

But the canonical stories remain the "dream," the "will," the "thought" and the "flower," underlying a movement's systematic theologies' "interpretation," "action," "speech" and "fruit" as Bialik so beautifully put it. The stories will remain. As Brueggemann said, "Story in Israel is the bottom line." If we want to teach an "-ology," let us find a biblical story or stories in which the doctrine is embedded, with story as base line, and let our hearers, with our help as teacher-storytellers discover those truths in their life situation.

Recalling from **Narrative 3**, that God said, "Hear O Israel!" not "Read O Israel!" ... The Written Word must be continually accompanied by the Oralized Word, in order to complete its intended divine purpose to change and transform lives. Can we shake the still-dominant Enlightenment way of knowing described in **Narrative 4** enough to go back to the future to a Hebraic epistemology where, as is presented in **Narrative 5**, story truly is a way of knowing? **Narrative 6** sketches out what a contemporary expression of what the oralized *midrashic* tradition might look like. Adonai told Moses, "Teach them to sing it..." (Deut. 31:19). "Let me write the songs of a nation and I care not who writes their laws." Let us find speech-places, thousands of venues in the highways and byways, the Starbucks and YouTube, in churches and synagogues, to oralize these stories—conversationally, as performance art, with or without media technology, in sermon and *drash* times, formally and informally.

Recalling that 60–70% of Scripture is in story form, let us proportionately make 60–70% of our teaching and preaching ministry time and content be the stories of Scripture. Why do we usually invert that and make about 70% of our time and content from the New Covenant Epistles? As **Narrative 7** suggests, in Jewish apologetics and evangelism, let us use "the Nathan Principle," story to obliquely skirt and subvert Jewish resistance to the Gospel. From **Narrative 8** comes a challenge: Can we do better than Yeshua, who was primarily a metaphorical theologian, and used stories extensively? As **Narrative 9** intimates, we can we transition from the Gutenberg Galaxy to the Digitoral Galaxy, from "Gutenberg to Zuckerberg" in our postmodern moment by using media to oralize the ancient yet ever-new stories of God. **Narrative 10** evokes promises of the life-giving, healing, transformative power of the *Ruach*-inspired Bible stories. Is our rope long enough?

BIBLIOGRAPHY

Ausubel, *Nathan*, ed. A Treasury of Jewish Folklore: Stories, Traditions, Legends, Humor, Wisdom and Folk Songs of the Jewish People. New York: Crown Publishers, Inc., 1948.

Bailey, Kenneth E. Through Middle Eastern Eyes: Cultural Studies in the Gospels. Downers Grove, IL: IVP Academic, 2008.

Bauer, Walter, and Arndt Gingrich, eds. *A Greek-English Lexicon of the New Testament and Other Early Christian Literature*. 3rd ed. Chicago: University of Chicago Press, 2000.

Bialik, Chaim Nahman. Revealment and Concealment: Five Essays. 1917. Translated from the Hebrew by Zali Gurevitch. Jerusalem: Ibis Editions, 2000.

Bjoraker, William D. "Faith, Freedom and Radical Individualism in Late Modern America: A Missiological Evaluation." PhD diss., Fuller Theological Seminary, 2007.

Bradt, Kevin M. Story as a Way of Knowing. Kansas City: Sheed & Ward, 1997.

Buber, Martin. I and Thou. Translated by Walter Kaufmann. New York: Touchstone Books, 1970.

_____. Tales of the Hasidim: The Early Masters. New York: Schocken Books, 1978.

Calvin, John. A Commentary On the Psalms of David. Vol. 1. Oxford: Talboys, 1840.

Chiang, Samuel E. "Learning From My Own Mistakes." Mission Frontiers, May–June 2014. Accessed Dec. 14, 2014. www.missionfrontiers.org/issue/article/from-the-guest-editor.

Forest, Heather. Wisdom Tales From Around the World. Little Rock: August House, 1996.

Goldberg, Michael. Jews and Christians: Getting Our Stories Straight: The Exodus and the Passion-Resurrection. Eugene, OR: Wipf & Stock, 1991.

Guinness, Os. When No One Sees: The Importance of Character in an Age of Image. Trinity Forum Study Series. Colorado Springs: Nav Press, 2000.

Heidegger, Martin. "Letter on Humanism." In Martin Heidegger: Basic Writings, edited by David Farrell Krell, 213–66. London: Routledge, 1977.

Horowitz, Rosemary, ed. Elie Wiesel and the Art of Storytelling. Jefferson, NC: McFarland & Company, Inc., Publishers, 2006.

Jersak, Brad. "Noah: Who Are the Watchers and Why the Panic?" Clarion: Journal of Spirituality and Justice. Mar. 31, 2014. Accessed Dec. 14, 2014. www.clarion-journal.com/clarion_journal_of_spirit/2014/03/noah-who-are-the-watchers-and-why-the-panic-by-brad-jersak.html.

Lyotard, Jean-Francois. The Postmodern Condition: A Report on Knowledge. 1979. English translation, Minneapolis: University of Minnesota Press, 1984.

Lee, Morgan. "Noah Movie Sparks Massive Spike in Global Reading of the Bible's Book of Genesis." Christian Post Reporter. Apr. 4, 2014. www.christianpost.com/news/noah-movie-sparks-massive-spike-in-global-reading-of-bible-book-of-genesis-117334.

Lopez, Barry. Crow and Weasel. Illustrations by Tom Pohrt. San Francisco: North Point Press, 1990.

Maccoby, Hyam. Early Rabbinic Writings, Cambridge Commentaries on Writings of the Jewish and Christian World 200 BC to AD 200, Vol. 3. Cambridge: Cambridge University Press, 1988.

Madinger, Charles. "A Literate's Guide to the Oral Galaxy." Orality Journal 2, no. 2 (2013).

McLuhan, Marshall. The Gutenberg Galaxy. Toronto: University of Toronto Press, 1962.

Miller, Dorothy A. "Simply the Story" Handbook. Hemet, CA: The God's Story Project, 2012.

Moxom, Philip S. "The Insufficiency of Religious Toleration." In Addresses Before the New York Conference of Religion, edited by James M. Whiton, 85–99. New York: The New York State Conference of Religion, 1903.

Ong, Walter J. Orality and Literacy: The Technologizing of the Word. London and New York: Routledge, Taylor & Francis Group, 1982.

Parsons, John J. "Seventy Faces of Torah." Hebrew for Christians. Accessed Dec. 14, 2014. www.hebrew4christians.com/Articles/Seventy_Faces/seventy_faces.html.

Pascal, Blaise. Pascal's Pensées. New York: Dutton & Co., 1958.

Patai, Raphael. The Jewish Mind. New York: Charles Scribner's Sons. 1977.

Peterson, Eugene H. Working the Angles: The Shape of Pastoral Integrity. Grand Rapids: Eerdmans, 1987.

Pink, Daniel H. A Whole New Mind: Why Right-Brainers Will Rule the Future. New York: Riverhead Books, 2005.

Smith, George Adam. "The Hebrew Genius as Exhibited in the Old Testament." In The Legacy of Israel. Oxford. 1944.

Stein, Robert H. The Method and Message of Jesus' Teaching. Louisville: Westminster John Knox Press, 1994.

Steinbarg, Eliezer, ed. The Jewish Book of Fables. Dora Teitelbaum Center for
    Yiddish Culture, 2003.
Sternberg, Meir. The Poetics of Biblical Narrative: Ideological Literature and
    the Drama of Reading. Bloomington: Indiana University Press, 1985.
Walton, John H. and D. Brent Sandy. The Lost World of Scripture: Ancient
    Literary Culture and Biblical Authority. Downers Grove: IVP
    Academic, 2013.
Ward, Michael. "How Lewis Lit the Way to Better Apologetics." Christianity
    Today 57, no. 9 (Oct. 2013).
Weston, Paul. "The Making of Christendom." Zotero. Accessed Dec. 13, 2014.
    www.zotero.org/groups/westminstercam/items/itemKey/WGKTDRUI.
Wilson, Marvin R. Our Father Abraham: Jewish Roots of the Christian Faith.
    Grand Rapids: Eerdmans, 1989.
Woodhead, Leslie. "How the Beatles Rocked the Kremlin." Nov. 10, 2009.
    www.thirteen.org/beatles/video/video-watch-how-the-beatles-rocked-
    the-kremlin.
Wright, G. Ernest. God Who Acts: Biblical Theology as Recital. Studies in
    Biblical Theology. London: SCM Press, 1952.
Zion, Noam. "The Origins of Human Violence and the Crisis of the Biblical
    First Family: Cain and Abel in Torah, Commentary, Midrash, Art,
    Poetry, Movies and Thought." Notes from a class taught at the Shalom
    Hartman Institute. Jerusalem, 2014.

Approaching God: The Essence of Messianic Jewish Theology

Daniel C. Juster, Th.D.

Human Reasoning About God

As we have seen, Jews and Jewish Scripture make liberal use of stories and place a premium on storytelling. By contrast, many of the ancient Eastern and Western philosophers have discussed God through philosophical reasoning, sometimes called speculative philosophy. Many of them were looking for the nature of ultimate reality, namely that which remains stable through all the vicissitudes of our lived experience in this world. Some became very skeptical, like Buddha, who concluded that the ultimate was unknowable.[1] Some came to the idea of an ultimate personal god of some kind, such as the famous classical Indian philosopher Ramanuja.[2] Others, mostly among the Greeks, gave us ideas of gods that were abstract, removed from any personal characteristics and not involved in loving care for human beings. In Aristotle, there is an ultimate first cause, an unmoved mover that has to necessarily exist to explain the nexus of cause and effect in the observed world.[3] For Plato, there is an ultimate form of goodness and the pattern for all good. And in Plato, somehow, the soul pre-exists its incarnation into human bodies in the sensory world and will return after death to that timeless place. There is also a demiurge that stamps the forms of that timeless world into matter that produces the world as we know it.[4]

---

[1] Stuart Hackett, *Oriental Philosophy*. Madison, WI: University of Wisconsin Press, 1979, 80–81.

[2] Ibid., 158-160; John Hick, *An Interpretation of Religion*. New Haven, CT: Yale University Press, 253.

[3] Frederick Copleston, *A History of Philosophy*: Volume *I, Greece and Rome Part II*. New York: Image Books, 1962, 56–57.

[4] Copleston, *History and Philosophy*, 195–196.

Greek speculation has greatly influenced both Jewish and Christian theologians. Thomas Aquinas represents the height of this speculation among Christians, and Maimonides among Jews. [5] Both offered speculative reasons, coherent to Aristotle's philosophy, for the existence of God and the nature of creation. Louis Goldberg, one of the early pioneers of Messianic Jewish theology and a professor at Moody Bible Institute, argued in his master's thesis at Roosevelt University that the God of Maimonides (and sometimes of Thomas as well) was not really the God of the Bible. In their kind of abstract theology, with their understandings of God as timeless and unchanging, it became necessary to interpret all biblical language in such a way that most of its content about God was divested of biblical narrative, became abstracted and Aristotelian in worldview and was re-explained so as to make it incomprehensible and irrelevant to most. Yet, modern, 19th-century evangelical systematic theologies, in order to be deemed credible, often began with arguing for and concurring with these abstract theological ideas.[6] Ancient writers were less inclined.

The ancient world manufactured many myths of gods who war with one another, have sexual relationships with humans, produce semi-gods, and who are gods of nature and destruction. The meaning of their various gods is captured in the mythological stories handed down. There was also an idea of one ultimate God above the pantheon of gods.

Reasoning about the existence of God today prevails and is quite extensive. All philosophers and theologians generally concede the point that something must always exist as something cannot come from nothing.[7] The question then is what is this ultimate something? Is it pure energy, some combination of matter and energy, or something more akin to a mind, or a being with personal characteristics (e.g.,

---

[5] *Basic Writings of St. Thomas Aquinas*. New York: Random House, 1945, 25-90; Copleston, *History of Philosophy*, 55-81 (a compendium of his 13th-century writings); Richard A. Robinson, ed., *God, Torah, Messiah: The Messianic Jewish Theology of Dr. Louis Goldberg* San Francisco: Purple Pomegranate, 2009, 91–94.

[6] Augustus Hopkins Strong, *Systematic Theology*. Valley Forge, PA: Judson Press, 1907. Pages 52–89 summarize the 19th-century views from such famous writers as Charles Hodge (*Systematic Theology*), William Shedd (*Dogmatic Theology*) and James Boyce (*Abstract of Systematic Theology*).

[7] William Lane Craig and J. P. Moreland, *Philosophical Foundations for a Christian Worldview*. Downers Grove, IL: Intervarsity Press, 2003, 464–534; Richard Swinburne, *Is There a God?* Oxford: Oxford University Press, 1996, 45–48; Antony Flew, *There Is a God*. New York: HarperOne, 2007, 165; Daniel Juster, *The Biblical World View: An Apologetic*. San Francisco: International Scholars Publications, 1995, 155–172.

mind, will, intentionality)?[8] A mind seems the only explanation of there *being* minds. Or a conscious, personal being must be behind conscious, personal beings. Recent studies on intelligent design have produced very powerful arguments concluding the world around us is the product of an intelligent designer. Physicist Gerald Schroeder, an atheist-turned-Orthodox Jew, produced two books that represent these arguments brilliantly.[9] These arguments not only look at the fine-tuning of the universe to support human life, but also the complex design of the cell and microscopic life that can in no way be explained by naturalistic evolution. The arguments of the intelligent-design movement convinced the leading atheist in the English-speaking world, Professor Antony Flew, to argue that there is a God. His change to belief in God was monumental in the world of philosophy, since one of his areas of expertise was the philosophy of science. Dr. Flew's conversion was not to personal theism and a relationship with his Creator; it was a philosophical conclusion that did not include the idea that this Creator loves us. Due to the problem of evil, Flew claimed he had no idea why we were created.[10] For his part, though he did not conclude God exists, the famous American philosopher Thomas Nagel, in *Mind and Cosmos*, recently argued the theology of naturalistic evolution as a materialistic explanation of reality is totally impossible.[11] C. S. Lewis adds to these arguments the idea that our moral conscience, our sense of right and wrong, is a key indicator that we stand before our Creator as a moral being. If we are guilty, he believed, we are guilty before an ultimate judge.[12]

Recent Jewish and Christian theologians have taken a more biblical path. Some have tried to dismiss all philosophical speculation and natural theology as a waste of time. Karl Barth is the key 20th-century representative of this view.[13] Others grant some validity but choose an orientation to understanding God based on revelation, not the rational

---

[8] Ibid.

[9] Gerald Schroeder, *The Science of God*. New York: Free Press, 1997, 115–145. *The Hidden Face of God.* New York: Free Press. 2001, 47–128. (Much of both these books present this argument.) Michael Behe, *The Edge of Evolution.* New York: Free Press, 2007. Numerous other such titles also present these arguments well.

[10] Flew, There Is a God,156.

[11] Thomas Nagel, *Mind and Cosmos.* New York: Oxford University Press, 2012. This is the thesis of the whole book.

[12] C. S. Lewis, *Mere Christianity.* San Francisco: Harper, 1943, 2001,17–39.

[13] Emil Brunner and Karl Barth, Natural Theology: Comprising "Nature and Grace" by Professor Dr. Emil Brunner and the reply "No!" by Dr. Karl Barth. Eugene, OR: Wipf and Stock, 2002.

speculation of our minds. For Abraham Joshua Heschel, the knowledge of God is an immediate response to awakening to a world of grandeur that produces wonder:

> Awareness of the divine begins with wonder. It is the result of what man does with his higher incomprehension. ... Wonder or radical amazement, the state of maladjustment to words and notions is therefore a prerequisite for an authentic awareness of that which is. *Radical Amazement* has a wider scope than any other act of man. ... Grandeur or mystery is something with which we are confronted everywhere and at all times. ... The way to faith leads through acts of wonder and radical amazement.[14]

The amazing nature of human existence, the world around us of flora and fauna, and the cosmos above produce wonder. As German philosopher Immanuel Kant said at the end of the 18th century, the things that most filled him with admiration and awe were "the starry heavens above and the moral law within."[15] We see this in the eyes of a child, with the astonishment of discovery. Children awaken us from our doldrums to realize we live in a "wonderful world" (as Louis Armstrong sang). Dr. Clyde Kilby, the great friend of C. S. Lewis and my wife's literature professor, sought to awaken the students to wonder as a window into faith in God.

The books of Genesis, Psalms, Acts and Romans give some credit to the place of natural theology, but no place to technical abstract theologies that explain away the biblical metaphors that describe God. In the Bible, the knowledge of God is primarily based on God's history with his people—*it is the story of God and His people!*[16] This story centers on human encounters with God and confirms what Martin Buber presents in his classic *I and Thou*, that we are gripped in a relationship, immediately grasped or intuitively perceived, a personal relationship of *I and thou.*[17] Buber also uses stories to speak about God, the Hasidic

---

[14] Text taken from Fritz Rothschild, ed., Between God and Man: An Interpretation of Judaism From the Writings of Abraham Joshua Heschel. New York: Free Press, 1959, 41–42. Text taken from Abraham Joshua Heschel, God in Search of Man: A Philosophy of Judaism. New York: Farrar, Straus and Cudahy, Inc., 1955, 43–51.

[15] Immanuel Kant, *Critique of Practical Reason*. London: Abbot, 1889, 260.

[16] G. Ernest Wright, *God Who Acts: Biblical Theology as Recital*. London: SCM Press, 1952, 33–86. Wright anticipates the contemporary idea of theology as narrative, the story of God's actions in history.

[17] Martin Buber, *I and Thou*. New York: Charles Scribners and Sons, 1958, 77–104.

stories. What are the stories that represent what God is like in the *Haggadic* literature of Judaism and in the Chasidic tales that so inspired Buber?[18] They were often stories of extraordinary kindness, humility and self-sacrifice for others. These are stories of amazingly loving, faithful and obedient people, people of mercy and justice. They show us what God is like!

In summary, in the Bible, the way of understanding God is to say that *"God is the One who..."* We fill in the blank with all of God's actions as they are revealed in the biblical text. *God is known through the stories of His actions and by His self-declarations of His character.* In Scripture, God is a God of active involvement with His people, in His purposes and is working to accomplish His plans. We will now attend to the beginning of that Story. It will here be reintroduced to readers, with a deeper analysis to follow in the next chapter.

In The Beginning: Genesis 1–3

The first book of the Bible, Genesis, begins with an announcement: "In the beginning, God created the heavens and the earth" (Gen. 1:1).[19] God is introduced through the story of His actions in the world, which are then interpreted by His prophets in Sacred Literature. *The story of action and interpretation of action thus form the center of biblical revelation.* Prophetic words that stand independently of the acts of God are the other part of the revelation. Genesis 1 presents the acts of God in creating and then interpretation by the prophetic writer. In Genesis there is no argument for the existence of God, but rather a narrative story and a prophetic interpretation of how we are to understand the universe. God brought the universe into being in successive stages. We need not recount the entirety of Genesis chapter 1. God begins by creating light and separating it from darkness. He then brings into being the stars, the moon and the sun, the vegetables, and then the animals. At this point, we note that God is One—and One who delights in variety. It's a story of a great artist who brings into being a fabulous world of mutual interdependence for blessing: man depends on God; plants depend on the soil and the sun. Plants, animals and humankind are interconnected and depend on each other. All of creation is rooted in God. At the end of

[18] Martin Buber, *Tales of the Hasidim, Vols. I–II.* New York: Schocken Books, 1947–48.
[19] Scripture references are taken from the Tree of Life Version. Grand Rapids: Baker Publishing Group, 2015.

every day, God observes what He has done and declares it to be very good. His work was pleasing to Him; He had great pleasure in it. God's own appreciation is the basis of aesthetic judgment. Then finally, on the seventh day, God creates human beings in His image. This is the beginning of the story of God in relationship with humankind. Through this story we will learn what God is like, what pleases Him, what displeases Him, and how to live in fellowship with Him.

Genesis 1:26–27 says male and female were created in God's image. Karl Barth sees this as indicating there is a plurality in God.[20] Others have noted this as well. It is not based on the Christian argument that a Trinitarian God is revealed in the words "let *Us* make man in Our image" (though I do conclude the statement indicates some kind of plurality in God without indicating He is speaking to a heavenly court). Rather, it is that two people together are representing the image of God, so there is an everlasting fellowship in God Himself, or as Christians say, in the Godhead. Barth's understanding is debated, but many have found it a fruitful insight. I give it some credit. The meaning of "image of God" is debated. Some point to attributes that make humans like God: intelligence, will, freedom of action, the ability to love and much more. Mormons actually assert God was once a mortal and so it means physical likeness.[21] Yet it is certainly better to see this term as a functional one. Humans are like unto God because they can function as rulers over the earth. Humans, therefore, need all the capabilities that are like God's so that they can perform the function of ruling in fellowship with God.

Genesis 1:28 tells us God blessed the male and the female. In this text, blessing takes place by God speaking words over them that they might be enriched in life. Indeed, God said, "Be fruitful and multiply, fill the land and conquer it. Rule over the fish of the sea, the flying creatures of the sky, and over every animal that crawls on the land."

Genesis 2 gives additional information on the nature of man's ruling. It is ruling in deferential partnership with God. Adam is the steward of creation and is given a garden to till. He is responsible for taking good care of what God has made. Already there is a sense that humans cannot abuse creation and still have God's favor. God places the male and the

---

[20] Karl Barth, *Church Dogmatics: The Doctrine of Creation, Volume III, Part I.* Edited by G.W. Bromiley and T.F. Torrance. London: T&T Clark, 1986, 203.

[21] Walter Martin, *The Kingdom of the Cults.* Minneapolis: Bethany House, 1997, 220–23.

female in a paradise and gives them His commands: Be fruitful and till the garden. This becomes man's orientation. The male and female can eat of the tree of the knowledge of good and evil, die, and be their own masters, or they can submit to God's will and live in submitted partnership and fellowship with their Creator. God values the obedience of his human creatures.[22]

The creation of the female accentuates God's love and goodness in providing for intimate human fellowship. While Adam, the male, could appreciate the living creatures God placed around him, he could not find intimate fellowship through them. Rather, he was to find it in another human being—a female. If God had created another male, there would not be that wonderful aspect of similarity and distinction and full mutual interdependence. Eve was like Adam, yet so different. He was to love someone who was in many ways opposite of himself. God's intention for human beings is in the bonded partnership of marriage where the two become one.

Modern scholarship views Genesis 1–2 as eschatological, pointing to the ultimate purpose of God and the final destiny of creation with human beings as its steward. Paradise is to be restored, and Genesis gives us some idea of what it will be like. It will be a world of amazing and wonderful beauty, variety, fellowship and mutual blessing.[23]

The accounts of Genesis 1 and 2 show us a God who is creative, loving, providing and desiring of fellowship with us. All this is true, of course, but there's more. Genesis 3 introduces the idea that God actively judges sin and will not simply accommodate acts of rebellion. By eating of the forbidden tree, humans experienced divine judgment. They were cast out of the Garden and prevented from reentering. Yet man was not without hope. Gen. 3:15 looks forward to a reversal of the conditions ensuing from judgment. First the serpent who did the tempting is judged, with a curse that his head will be crushed by the offspring, but in turn, the offspring will be bruised on the heel. The head blow will be fatal. The bruise on the heel will be painful but not fatal. In his magisterial magnum opus *The Promise-Plan of God*, Walter Kaiser rightly sees this passage as the beginning of the great theme of the Bible, namely, God's

---

[22] Nahum Sarna, *Understanding Genesis*. New York: McGraw, 1966, 14–16. This is a highly recommended commentary from a Jewish point of view and covers well the early chapters of Genesis.

[23] R. Kendall Soulen, *The God of Israel and Christian Theology*. Minneapolis: Fortress Press, 1996, 117–134.

active involvement to reverse the effects of the Fall and to redeem the human race through the promised seed.[24]

So, what do we learn about God from the stories in the first chapters of Genesis? We learn that His Word communicates through stories—not lectures. We learn that God is awesome in power and wisdom, He is above the world He created, and He brought all things into being. God is transcendent—He is well beyond this finite world. He is everlasting. He loves variety. He is a great artist and declares that His creation is good. We also learn God is a delegator of authority. He entrusts human beings to manage the creation in submitted partnership with Him. God speaks blessing over them, and that blessing contains the destiny fulfillment of humans as God's partners in ruling the earth and multiplying children. There is also a not-so-subtle-hint that that there is a plurality in God. We also learn God is minded to enter into relationship with human beings. This fellowship is important to Him. Human obedience is critical to God.

God as the God of Judgment in Genesis 4–11

The early chapters of Genesis establish our understanding of God. After the expulsion of Adam and Eve from the Garden and the birth of their children, we read the difficult account of Cain and Abel. There is much speculation as to why Cain's offering did not please God. When I was young, I commonly heard preachers say it was due to him bringing vegetables and not a blood sacrifice. But the text does not say this, and vegetable offerings were part of later Temple worship. It was also commonly asserted in those sermons that it was a heart matter and Cain did not bring his best. Cain was also jealous. God's response to Cain was merciful. He did not ultimately reject him but encouraged him to master his wrong intentions and actions.

> Then Adonai said to Cain, "Why are you angry? And why has your countenance fallen? If you do well, it will lift. But if you do not do well, sin is crouching at the doorway. Its desire is for you, but you must master it." (Gen. 4:6,7)

---

[24] Walter Kaiser, The Promise-Plan of God: A Biblical Theology of the Old and New Testament. Grand Rapids: Zondervan, 2008, 848–856.

Even after Cain murders his brother, God acts in mercy and commands Cain not be killed or the person who does so will suffer severely. Yet Cain falls under severe judgment and is banished from the growing tribe of Adam's descendants. The idea comes to the fore that God is a God of justice; for Abel's "blood crying out to Me from the ground" (Gen. 4:10). So, Cain is under a curse and driven from the ground, which will no longer yield its crops for him. He is to be a restless wanderer on the earth. God will not simply overlook serious sins. There are both the consequences of sowing and reaping as well as the active judgment of God, an execution of a judicial penalty.

This idea of God's active judgment is very important for the story that follows of the Flood. Genesis 6 provides us with anthropomorphic language that has troubled classical theologians, from Thomas Aquinas and Maimonides, to classic statements from Hodge, Shedd and Strong (see footnote 6). Those scholars could not accept the idea that this language should just be embraced. Unable to come to terms with it, they had to reinterpret it to fit their understanding of a timeless, unchangeable God.

> Then ADONAI saw that the wickedness of humankind was great on the earth, and that every inclination of the thoughts of their heart was only evil all the time. So ADONAI regretted that he made humankind on the earth, and his heart was deeply pained. So, ADONAI said, "I will wipe humankind, whom I have created, from the face of the ground from humankind to livestock, crawling things and flying creatures of the sky because I regret that I made them. But Noah found favor in ADONAI'S eyes. (Gen. 6:5–8)

Human beings are shown to be responsible for their choices and hence free. Thus, they can embrace good or evil. If they embrace evil and wickedness, they can bring God's active judgment on themselves and others. That God responds to human behavior with emotions, emotions that are always in accord with His righteous nature (*i.e.*, never out of control) is the constant testimony of Scripture. C. S. Lewis notes that if man is created in the image of God, we should expect human language or anthropomorphic language to be the best possible language for describing God.[25]

---

[25] Lewis, *op. cit.*, 133–145.

In Genesis 8, we read that God remembered Noah. Thus, we should not think that God forgets or that His knowledge is limited, for numerous statements in the Bible imply His omniscience. Although the Bible does not use the word "omniscient," the biblical description of God's attributes indicates with certainty that He is "all knowing."[26] God remembering is normally interpreted as God visiting someone or a group of individuals. However, it is also a covenant concept whereby He does not forget to be faithful to those who maintain righteousness. So, God is actively involved in saving the righteous as well as punishing the wicked.

God ultimately desires to bless, not to curse. Hence in Genesis 8, after Noah's offering, a pleasing aroma to God (not only does God smell the roasting meat, but He perceives the intent of the heart), He commits Himself anew to the welfare of humanity in a covenant with Noah. So, God is a covenant making God who declares to Noah:

> Never again will I curse the ground because of man, even though every inclination of his heart is evil from childhood. And never again will I destroy all living creatures as I have done.
>
> > "While all the days of the land remain,
> > seedtime and harvest, cold and heat
> > summer and winter,
> > day and night will not cease." (Gen. 8:21–22)

Then God said to Noah and to his sons with him saying,

> "Now I behold, I am about to establish My covenant with you and with your seed after you, and with every living creature that is with you, including the flying creatures, the livestock, and very wild animal with you, of all that is coming out of the ark—every animal of the earth. I will confirm My covenant with you—never again will all flesh be cut off by the waters of the flood, and never again will there be a flood to ruin the land." (Gen. 9:8–11)

And God said,

> "This is the sign of the covenant that I am making between Me and you, and every living creature that is with you for all future generations. My rainbow do I place in the cloud, and it will be a sign of the covenant between Me and the land.

---

[26] 2 Chron. 6:30, Ps. 94:11, Isa. 46:10, Hos. 5:3, Jn. 16:30, Jn. 21:17, Col. 2:3.

Whenever I bring clouds over the land and the rainbow appears in the clouds, I will remember My covenant that is between Me and you and every living creature of all flesh. Never again will the waters become a flood to destroy all flesh. (Gen. 9:12–15)

God makes a solemn oath with covenantal language, confirming that He will limit His wrath against human wickedness. He adds,

And from every person man will I avenge it. From every person's brother will I avenge that person's life.

The one who sheds human blood,
    by a human his blood be shed,
for in God's image He made humanity. (Gen. 9:5b, 6)

This text is the basis of the idea of the so-called, Noachide Commandments. In ancient Judaism, it is the basis of universal laws of Torah that apply to all people.[27] God is the giver of law or legislation that orders the whole of the human community.

Genesis 10 and 11 bring us to another judgment, and an introduction to the backdrop of God's plan to bring the human community back together. The chapters first present an account of the origins of the nations that descend from the sons of Noah. These nations rebel against God and refuse His command to fill the earth. They instead seek to stay in the same place and build a tower as a marker of unity and to keep them together. The passage does not say they were building the tower to worship the heavenly hosts (a concept known from Ancient Near Eastern astrological texts) but to make a name for themselves—to bring them fame. Instead what God initiates is the scattering and dividing of nations through the division of languages. Walter Brueggemann connects this to God's desire for a plurality of ethnic people to enrich the earth. While language confusion could be seen as a curse, it could also be seen as a blessing in fulfilling God's desire for a plurality of peoples.[28] God is a God who loves variety. He calls forth Abraham with a mind to bring blessings to all peoples, not just Hebrew people!

---

[27] Markus Bockmuehl, *Jewish Law in Gentile Churches*. Grand Rapids: Baker Academic, 2000, 145–173.

[28] Walter Brueggemann, *Genesis: Interpretation: A Bible Commentary for Teaching and Preaching*. Louisville: John Knox, 1984. Commentary on Chapter 10.

Genesis 12–50: The God of Providence and World Redemption: The Stories of the Patriarchs

Genesis 12 expands the idea of the great reversal—the restoration of mankind to the blessings of God, and the reversing of the expulsion from Paradise. However, this reversal is to come through one family that will be the instrument of restoring the earth to blessing. We read,

> My heart's desire is to make you into a great nation, to bless you, to make your name great so that you may be a blessing.
> My desire is to bless those who bless you, but whoever curses you I will curse. and in you all the families of the earth will be blessed. (Gen.12:1–3)

Why was Abraham chosen? Much has been written about the choice as being arbitrary and inscrutable, as if nothing in him influenced this divine choice. But can we not say that as with Noah, Abraham found grace in the eyes of the LORD?[29] As well, Abraham was from the line of Shem, who had already gained God's favor at the time of his brother's sin (Gen. 9:24–27). *Galatians* 3:8 summarizes the call of Abraham and his descendants to bring blessing to the world, and says God spoke the Gospel to Abraham. The Gospel is the good news of the restoration of human life through God's blessing. The way of blessing for the nations is through alignment with Abraham and his seed.

In Genesis 15, God ratifies His covenant with an oath ceremony and passes between the cut pieces of sacrifices to show that His oath in the covenant is absolute. Herein we see a God who can so accommodate Himself to a human being so as to take a solemn oath before him.[30]

Jews speak through stories. Messianic Jewish theology must recover the usage of stories. The Bible speaks through stories. The stories of Genesis 12-50 show God to be the God of faithfulness to His covenant and the God of providential control over the events on earth, a control oriented to the fulfillment of His purposes for His covenant people. However, the story of the sacrifice of Isaac in Genesis 22 shows us that God is the God who also asks for total commitment to Him with everything we are and have. This strange account foreshadows the sacrifice of Yeshua. It also shows us, in a strange way, that God desires that Israel engage a literal human sacrifice or

---

[29] Gen. 26:4, 5.
[30] Kaiser, *op. cit.*, 1226–1234.

be engaged by one. It's a living sacrifice in Genesis, and one with interesting applications and implications.

One amazing account of judgment is found in Genesis 18–19. It raises questions about the nature of God. In the story, Abraham gives hospitality to three angelic figures. Two visit Sodom before the terrible judgments that befell it. The third remains with Abraham, who argues the town should not be destroyed if there is found in it a contingent of righteous men. The figure that looks like a man is called by the holy name of God, YHWH. Not just an angel, it could be said this is a theophany—a manifestation of God in human form. We find three significant details in this passage: (1) God's judgment is not merely individualistic (a modern Western idea) but also corporate. He takes into account a righteous remnant within the larger group and judges accordingly. (2) Abraham's intercession is significant in altering the situation. (3) God can take human form.

The third point raises the question: Does the Bible imply that YHWH/God has a physical body? The passage does not explicitly answer, but as God is the creator of all, any physicality one could attribute to God could resemble human physicality without being identical in all aspects. When one sees God appearing in human form, there is a special accommodation made so that what is seen is not the fullness of God, for He said, "no man can see me and live" (Ex. 33:20). There is a mitigating of the power of God so that any human who encounters God can handle the interaction without perishing. This type of manifestation is repeated in other passages.[31]

The Patriarchs were not perfect. They, like everyone else, fell short of fully trusting in God. Nevertheless, God intervened, as in the stories of Abraham and his family, in order to fulfill His purposes. *First*, Abraham sought to fulfill the promise by having a child through Sarah's handmaid, Hagar. Ishmael, her son, would be blessed by God, but he was not the child of promise. *Second*, when Abraham settled in Gerar, he thought his life was in danger. So he lied and said Sarah was his sister. Technically she was his sister—the daughter of his father but not his mother (see Gen. 20:12), but his statement was meant to deceive the king of Gerar, who took Sarah to live in his harem. God intervened in a

---

[31] C.F. Keil and F. Delitzsch, *Commentary on the Old Testament: The Pentateuch, Vol. 1.* Grand Rapids: Eerdmans, 1970, 228–231. Kaiser, *op. cit.,* 1108–1123; Asher Intrater, *Who Ate Lunch With Abraham?* Frederick, MD: Revive Israel Media, 2011, 13–14. All think this is a pre-incarnate manifestation of the Messiah.

dream to free her. *Third*, Isaac repeated the same lie to the king but again received divine protection. *Fourth*, Isaac resisted God's prophetic word, given at the birth of his twin sons, that the older would serve the younger. Isaac wanted the opposite, but God intervened so Jacob had greater prominence. Jacob schemed to steal his brother's birthright (double inheritance and prominence in the family), but it was God's will that Jacob receive these blessings. Providentially, Jacob escaped to his uncle Laban and served him for many years. Jacob fathered twelve sons. His name was changed to Israel, which has a double meaning: (1) one who strives with God and prevails; and (2) a prince with God.[32] As has been noted throughout, God communicates through stories, a Jewish trademark needing center-stage in Messianic Jewish theology.

From this point on, the story of God and the story of Jacob/Israel are really one. The story of Israel and God progressively reveals more and more about what God is like, our God who is *the One who...* Genesis provides stories of God's prophetic preservation of the promised seed (the nation in this case).[33] For example, Esau does not kill Jacob when he returns. While waiting for the confrontation with Esau, Jacob has a strange wrestling match in the night with the one who touches his hip and leaves him with a limp. Jacob calls the place *Peniel* ("face"), for "I've see God face to face and my life has been spared" (Gen. 32:31). This was more than a mere angel, and it is hard not to connect this account to the visit of the messenger who dialogued with Abraham in Genesis 18.[34] God shows up in the narrative, by intervening for His people and His purposes.

The children of Israel are saved from the famine by escaping to Egypt—a journey that includes an amazing set of circumstances. First is Jacob's sons' jealousy over Joseph, the first son of Jacob's favorite wife Rachel. Joseph was unwise to relate dreams that implied his future ascendancy over his parents and brothers. It was not well-received. But, he has a real prophetic gift, and the prophecies will prove true. Joseph's brothers are tempted to kill him, but instead sell him to Midianite traders who sell him to an Egyptian noble and military man, Potiphar. Joseph refuses Potiphar's wife's advances, so she accuses him of sexual

---

[32] Sarna, *op. cit.*, 206; Stuart Lasine, *"Israel,"* in *Eerdmans Dictionary of the Bible*, ed. David Noel Freedman, Grand Rapids: Eerdmans, 2000, 655.

[33] Walter Kaiser, *The Messiah in the Old Testament*. Grand Rapids: Zondervan, 1995, 46–50; *The Promise-Plan*, *op. cit.*, 1108–1123.

[34] Intrater, *op. cit.*, 3–8.

impropriety. landing him in prison with Pharaoh's cupbearer and baker. Joseph's interpretation of the servants' dreams opens a door for his deliverance from unjust incarceration. The baker's dream predicts his demise; the cupbearer's predicts his reinstatement to his position of service to Pharaoh. Two years later, Joseph is called upon to interpret Pharaoh's dreams. He reveals their meaning: Years of plenty and famine will soon come to the land of Egypt. For his revelation to Pharaoh, Joseph is made second in command over all of Egypt. The climax of the narrative occurs when Joseph reveals himself to his brothers and conveys the message of God's purposes:

> Don't be grieved and don't be angry in your own eyes that you sold me here—since it was for preserving life that God sent me here before you. For there has been two years of famine in the land, and there will be five more years yet with no plowing or harvesting. But God sent me ahead of you to ensure a remnant in the land and to keep you alive for a great escape. (Gen. 45:5–7)

The providence of God and His overarching rule over mankind's affairs is a great theme of Genesis, supported by other stories throughout the Bible. How our freedom as humans is real and ultimately subject to God's superintending providence, however, is a question never worked out philosophically in Scripture. Unlike the ancient Essenes of the Second Temple period and the classical Calvinists of the Reformation later, the Bible does not say everything that happens is only by God's causation. It *does* assert God's ultimate control over His creation. What was intended for evil against Joseph turns out for good, which was necessary in light of the covenant with Abraham and the promise to his seed. Indeed, Abraham was given a prophetic word by God Himself (Gen. 15) in the reaffirmation of the covenant (Gen. 12), and then told his descendants would live in Egypt and be enslaved, but brought out by the mighty hand of God (Gen. 15:13, 14). The nation of Israel was thus preserved from famine and strengthened in their identity by dwelling in Egypt. In the narrative, Jacob came to the end of his life and prophesied over the sons of Jacob and gave a distinct destiny to each one of them. For some, that destiny would be tempered by words of judgment, for the acts of the fathers do impact later generations; for others, there are words of unqualified blessing.

Reading the stories of Genesis, we know God is the Creator and Sustainer of the universe. He is a God who is awesomely beyond us (transcendent), and also intimately involved with His creation, especially with human beings (imminent). He cares about human beings. He is a God who seeks to save and chooses Abraham to bring the nations into a state of blessing. He is a God in control of history for the sake of fulfilling His covenant promises. He accommodates Himself to human beings and even reveals Himself in human form. He is a God of action and prophetic interpretation.

The Revelation of God in the Books of Moses

In speaking of the biblical doctrine of God, we normally identify God as *the One who*... By the time of the exodus, we know God is the One who identified with the enslaved Israelites and delivered them from bondage in Egypt. After delivering them from bondage, He gave them His Law (Torah) and brought them into the Promised Land. God's intervention in the life of Israel enables us to see God identifies with the poor and dispossessed, and desires to bring all people into a good inheritance prepared for them.[35]

In *The Torah Revolution*, Reuven Hammer discusses how the Torah contrasts the culture of the Israelites with that of the surrounding nations, both in their civil code and general way of life.[36] He argues the Torah's ideas were revolutionary.[37] The revolution is in monotheism itself. There is one God who rules over the whole world. He is the source of our moral or ethical laws. This one God is also Lord over Israel's civil law, including its legal and religious systems. Hammer's book is a sort of update of *The Old Testament Against Its Environment* by Harvard archaeology professor G. Ernest Wright[38]

That God identifies with the dispossessed, poor, widow, orphan and stranger (for the Israelites were strangers in Egypt) is a constant refrain

---

[35] The Reform Jewish Passover *Haggadot* (Passover family liturgy) emphasizes this truth. Example: Michael and Noam Zion, *A Night to Remember: A Haggadah of Contemporary Voices.* Cleveland: Zion Holiday Publications, 2012, 73. An Orthodox commentary also supports the universal meaning by the former Chief Rabbi of the United Kingdom, Rabbi Jonathan Sachs, *Pesah Haggadah.* Jerusalem: Maggid Books / Koren Pubs., 2013, 76–84.

[36] Reuven Hammer, *The Torah Revolution.* Woodstock, VT: Jewish Lights Publishing, 2011. This is the ongoing theme of Hammer's whole book. He is a leader in Conservative Judaism. On God's rule over the earth, 143, 233–336, 156–184 surmise 14 contrasting truths. For God as the source of moral and ethical laws that inform civil law, 623–715.

[37] Ibid.

[38] G. Ernest Wright, *The Old Testament Against Its Environment.* Chicago: Henry Regnery Company, 1950, 20–41.

of the Torah. Though some of the legislation looks stark, in contrast to the surrounding nations it was the most just legal system of the time. There was overlap with other law codes from that era, but so much of it is different as attested by its being so much more compassionate. We will return to this theme. The Torah was and is an essential revelation of God's character. *Torah* means "instruction." It includes law (legislation) but is much more than that.

The Torah testifies that the great deliverance of Israel from Egypt was not due to the merits of the nation (e.g., Deut. 8:5–6; 9:4). Rather, as Scripture reiterates, it was the gracious act of a loving God. The salvation of the nation was solely executed through divine grace. This establishes the biblical pattern that culminates in individual salvation, for salvation is always a matter of response to an offer of undeserved grace.[39]

Deuteronomy makes clear the relation of grace and law, as Samuel Schultz noted in his groundbreaking books. He penned two titles, *Deuteronomy: The Gospel of God's Love* and *The Gospel of Moses.*[40] They astonished a world of Evangelicals, many of whom did not understand the Torah. When we read it with God's grace and love in mind, we gain a new, deeper, better understanding. Scholars have pointed out the whole structure of *Deuteronomy* is in the form of an ancient Hittite vassal treaty; this itself was something of a covenant of grace, where the ruler offers a covenant that is totally undeserved.[41] Obedience is a proper response to the offer of grace. The texts of the Ten Commandments (the Ten Words) follow the same pattern. Kline calls it an abbreviated covenant. The words "I am ADONAI, your God who brought you out of Egypt, out of the house of bondage" are not to be listed as one of the commandments, but a preamble introducing the Ten Words (Ex 20: 2; Deut. 5:6); in the Ten Commandments, the mention of God's gracious act of deliverance precedes the call to obey His commandments. As Schultz notes, in the Torah and throughout the prophets, the offer of mercy always precedes judgment.[42] God desires to be merciful.

---

[39] Add Meredith Kline, *Treaty of the Great King*. Grand Rapids: Eerdmans, 1963, 17, 22, 23, 26; Samuel Schultz, *The Gospel of Moses*. New York: Harper & Row, 1974, 71–74, 110, 159–165.

[40] Samuel Schultz, *The Gospel of Moses*. New York: Harper and Row, 1974, 55–60; *Deuteronomy: The Gospel of God's Love*. Chicago: Moody Press, 1971.

[41] Ibid., and Meredith Kline, *op. cit.*, 38, 42–44. See especially footnotes 34 and 35.

[42] Schultz, *op. cit.*, 71–74.

The Torah presents the most magnificent picture of God's nature and character. This revelation was in response to Moses' request to see the glory of God. God says to Moses, "You cannot see my face, for no one may see me and live." Abraham and Jacob both saw God and lived, but the level of glory seen by them was mitigated. The full revelation of God's face can never be seen by a human being. Moses saw only His back.

> Then ADONAI passed before him, and proclaimed, "ADONAI, ADONAI, the compassionate and gracious God, slow to anger, and abundant in lovingkindness and truth, showing mercy to a thousand generations, forgiving iniquity and transgression and sin, yet by no means leaving the guilty unpunished, but brining the iniquity of the fathers upon the children and upon the children's children, to the third and fourth generation." (Ex. 34:6–7)

Jewish tradition notes that important passage attests to "thirteen attributes of God."[43] Partial lists of these attributes appear throughout the Hebrew Scriptures. [44] The text accentuates God's love and compassion so as to be more prominent in readers' minds than judgment. Yet when people remain unrepentant, the laws of sowing and reaping cause sin to be passed down intergenerationally, even if the specific sins are not repeated. *Ezekiel* 18 emphasizes that individuals are punished for their own sin, but the text states the individual must decide to be righteous and thus break from the chain of wickedness. We should not think that God is merely an indulgent grandfather, but that He will punish iniquity. The story of Israel's conquering the Promised Land is a case in point. In mercy God waited over 400 years until the Canaanites' iniquity had come to fullness (Gen. 15:16). At a certain point of wickedness, God's active wrath is engaged. In the Flood narrative, as in the Sodom and Gomorrah story, a line was crossed where God's active judgment had to be released (Gen. 18:20,21; 19:13). In *Deuteronomy*, we read that the Canaanites' wickedness demanded their destruction (Deut.9:4-6). Therefore God is also a God of wrath, though His mercy and love are the more dominant attributes.

---

[43] Hayim Halevy Donin, *To Be a Jew*. New York: Basic Books, 1972, 22. This is a very significant statement by a noted Orthodox rabbi.
[44] Other references: Num. 14:18; Ps. 78:38, 86:15, 103:8, 111:4, 130:3, 145:8; II Kings 13:28; II Chron. 30:9; Is. 30:18; Jer. 32:18, 33:8; Joel 2:13; Micah 7:18,19; Jon. 4:2; Neh. 9:17; Lam. 3:22, 23, 31, 32.

In studying the Bible, my conclusion is we should not think that every time a person sins, God's response is active wrath. Perhaps His level of protection diminishes, and we do experience the laws of sowing and reaping. However, there is a point of active wrath, and the Bible is consistent in pointing this out. God's active wrath can be severe.

This leads us to the Torah's teaching on God's holiness. God is perfect in His moral and ethical orientation toward His creation. He is glorious in His total majestic being. As such, God dwells in splendor and in an apartness, a holiness far beyond anything in the whole of creation. Holiness connotes a quality of awesome purity that involves separation. Hence when objects are consecrated for special holy use, they are separated from other usages. God calls His people to be holy, which is not only a matter of ritual purity with all of its symbolic meanings but is defined also by moral perfection. Holiness is a greatly neglected emphasis today. God's holiness draws us and repels us due to the right sense of awe or holy fear. Therefore, both morally and in ritual, God is to be treated with utmost reverence. Biblical rituals bring out these aspects of how to approach God. Moses is told to take off his shoes since he stands on holy ground before the burning bush where the Angel of God appears to him. So also, due to God's holy presence, the people are not to go beyond a boundary at the base of Mt. Sinai (Ex. 19:20–21). The priests who approach the mountain have to be specially consecrated or the LORD will break out against them. One sees the emphasis in the death of the Levites who brought unholy fire (Num. 16). God broke out against them. This emphasis on holiness continues in the story of Uzzah in the historical books. He was not qualified to touch the ark and therefore died in seeking to steady it on the cart (2 Sam. 6:6–7).

Holiness is connected to our moral/ethical position before God. Rituals convey the meaning of holiness, but the emphasis in the New Covenant is more on the moral aspects of holiness and the need to be protected by Yeshua's atoning blood. Thus, *I Corinthians* 11 warns people of sickness and death if they partake of the Messiah's supper in an unworthy manner—that is, with moral impurity, unconfessed sin, and a lack of intention to dedicate one's life fully to God and to live in His ways.

The study of the Torah is a spiritual gold-mine where one discovers the character of God. Much of it is universal law, as argued by Markus Bockmuehl in his reference to Hillel's distinction between universal law for all people and Jewish-specific law as part of our Jewish responsibility to live a distinct life.[45] Yes, some laws are hard to understand, but the Torah makes clear what kind of behavior God desires, wills, or likes, and what kind He abhors. When God gives a command and says the behavior is an abomination to Him, we understand there is an important universal requirement to the commandment. So, for example, mistreating the widow, the stranger and the alien have this kind of intense evaluation of God's abhorrence. Israel is therefore to leave the corners of the fields for the needy and is to pay tithes for the poor as well. Many times, God emphasizes the importance of a law by simply saying, "I am the LORD your God." It is His way of emphasizing that this is really important to Him.

Aberrant sexual relationships, adultery, homosexual relationships and promiscuity are heinous to God. He connects sexuality to covenant. Polygamy falls short of the ideal of Gen. 1–2 but is allowed in the Torah, but even polygamy requires a covenant commitment. Yet the Torah presents a view of sexuality with clear rules and limits.

Deuteronomy 1 and 16 are also very clear on honest courts that do not distinguish between the rich and powerful, the poor and powerless. There is to be no favoritism or bribe. The penalties for sin are reasonable. Capital punishment is for the most egregious violations, while restitution under communal supervision is the way for lesser offenses.

God shows He is against an oppressive system where one small class controls the wealth and oppresses the rest of the population. To mitigate such a possibility, there is a Jubilee system where lands are returned to the original families of ownership. The Sabbatical year as well is the time for the cancellation of debts and indentured slavery. God even cares for the land and provides rest and renewal of the land by allowing it to lie fallow every seven years.[46]

We should also note God's heart as revealed in the Temple-sacrificial system. The main point again is His mercy. Since people will sin and fall short, He provides a system where they can make an offering that has substitutionary symbolic meaning, and by sincerely bringing such an offering and repenting of evil, they are forgiven. There are many kinds of offerings, some to show gratitude and some for dedication. There is no explanation of the substitutionary character of the sin

---

[45] Bockmuehl, *op. cit.*,158–162.
[46] Hammer, *op. cit.*, 2399–2585.

offering and the guilt offering, either as voluntarily brought by an individual or as offered daily for Israel and especially on the day of atonement, Yom Kippur. The main point is that God is oriented not to bring destruction in judgment but to provide a way back for sinners that He might forgive them. The Torah is thus a textbook on the character of God. It is why the psalmist can say, "Oh how I love thy law, it is my meditation all the day long" (Ps. 119:97). The Torah of God is deeply inspirational and leads the psalmist to worship.

The Doctrine of God in the Historical Books and the Prophets

The historical books (*Joshua, Judges, I* and *II Kings, I* and *II Chronicles, Ezra, Nehemiah*), along with the major and minor prophets, affirm and re-emphasize what is taught in the Torah. Contrary to much of ethereal contemporary spirituality, in *Joshua* through *II Kings* and then at the end of the Jewish canon, *I* and *II Chronicles*, God empowers people for actual war. The anointing for battle enables the success of Joshua, and later, it empowers King David in his wars. Yet God is not a god who likes war. Because David was a man of war and bloodshed, he is not to build the Temple, but his son, who is to be a man of peace, will build the Temple in Jerusalem (I Chron. 28:2–3).

The control of the Holy Land is a necessary condition for Israel to fully be a light to the nations. She must avoid compromise with the gross sins of the nations of Canaan. Sadly, Israel often failed. *Joshua, Judges, Kings* and *Chronicles* show both sowing and reaping but ultimately God's active judgment in the destruction of the Northern Kingdom of Israel. Finally, the destruction of the city of Jerusalem, the Temple, and the captivity of the Southern Tribes who were taken to Babylon show God's active judgment and not just sowing and reaping. When Israel is faithful, she is protected from her enemies; when she falls into idolatry, immorality and social injustice, God withdraws His protection and the other nations have power over her. So, by means of the above, God's character is again revealed in the repeated patterns of judgment and deliverance in these books.

Two important passages stand out in developing a doctrine of God. First is God's covenant with King David. God enters into covenant with one whose heart pleases Him. David and his descendants are promised an everlasting throne, one that will eventually be established over the whole world (II Sam. 7: 8–17; Isa. 9:6, 7; Heb. 5, 6). This covenant has universal implications for the redemption of the whole world. The *Isaiah* passage especially states the extent of the rule of the descendant of David will be unlimited. We see this applied by *Isaiah* 11, where the shoot from the stump of David settles disputes between nations and brings about the universal peace and rule described in *Isaiah* 2.

Second is Solomon's prayer for the dedication of the Temple, and for it to be a place of prayer for all nations. The prayer's universalism is quite significant and reflects God's heart for all people. Solomon prays that all who turn toward the Temple in prayer will have their needs met. By Israel's being protected and preserved, and by having the prayers of many peoples answered, the hope is put forth so that "all the peoples of the earth may know that the ADONAI is God and there is no other" (I Kings 8:60). For this to happen, we read, "Let your heart, therefore, be wholly devoted to ADONAI Eloheinu, to walk in His statues and to keep all His commandments" (I Kings 8:61).

Two more aspects of the prophetic books are crucial for understanding God. The first is that God is described as torn within Himself, when He must inflict judgment upon His people when He allows for the destruction of the Northern Kingdom through an Assyrian invasion. Hosea reveals the pain God experienced as He contemplated judging His own people:

> How can I give you up Ephraim? How can I surrender you, Israel?
> How can I make you like Admah? How can I set you as Zeboim?
> My heart is turning over within Me. My compassions are kindled.
> I will not vent my fierce anger, I not again destroy Ephraim.
> For I am God—not a man—the Holy One in the midst of you.
> And I will not come in fury. (Hos. 11:8–9)

The meaning of God's heart turning over is that it is somehow conflicted within. One writer puts it this way: "God's heart was so moved within Him with compassion for Ephraim that he was torn between two decisions--to destroy or not destroy. Ephraim was so sinful there was nothing left to do but destroy, hence the pleadings of God for this nation to seek him and do that which was right so that He would not need to bring judgment." [47] This view differs drastically from those who

---

[47] Finis Dake, *Dake's Annotated Reference Bible*. Atlanta: Dake Bible Sales, 1963, 888.

advocate that God delights in punishing the wicked and blessing the righteous, who are in these states because God willed the wicked to be wicked and the righteous to be righteous.

God's desire for compassionate justice is pervasive in the prophets. Judgment for idolatry is always a prominent theme but not more prominent than judgment for injustice. *Isaiah* 58 and 59 shows in a magnificent way the character of God.

> Why have we fasted, yet You do not see?
> Why have we afflicted our souls, yet You take no notice?
> Behold, in the day of your fast you seek your own pleasure,
> And exploit all your laborers.
> Behold, you fast for strife and contention and to strike with a wicked fist.
> You should not fast as you do today to make your voice heard on high.
> Is this the fast I have chosen? A day for one to afflict his soul?
> Is it to bow down his head like a reed, and spreading out sackcloth and ashes?
> Yet on the day of your fasting you do as you please and exploit all your workers.
> Will you call this a fast and a day acceptable to ADONAI?
> Is this not the fast I choose: to release the bonds of wickedness, to untie the cords of the yoke, to let the oppressed go free, and to tear off every yoke.
> Is it not to share your bread with the hungry, to bring the homeless poor into your house?
> When you see the naked, to cover him, and not hide yourself form your own flesh and blood.
> Then your light will break forth like the dawn and your healing will spring up quickly.
> Your righteousness will go before you, the glory of ADONAI as your rear guard. Then you will call, and ADONAI will answer.
> You will cry and He will say, Here I am. …
> If you yourselves to the hungry and satisfy the desire of the afflicted, then your light will rise in the darkness, and your night will become like noonday. (Isa. 58:3–10)

The Bible teaches that every man is created in the image of God and worthy of being treated with compassionate justice. So, this is the heart of God. Note also the idea, also in the Torah, that evil speaking against others is one of those things most hated by God. Gossip and slander are an affront to God. *Isaiah* 59 carries this theme forward in what is perhaps the greatest justice passage in the Bible.

Behold, ADONAI's hand is not too short to save, nor his ear too dull to hear.

Rather, your iniquities have made a separation between you and your God.

Your sins have hidden his face from you, so that He does not hear.

For your hands are defiled with blood and your fingers with iniquity.

Your lips have spoken lies, your tongue mutters wickedness.

No one sues justly, and note pleads a case honestly.

They conceive mischief, and bring forth iniquity.

They hatch adder's eggs, and weave the spider's web— whoever eats their eggs dies; crack on open, a viper breaks out.

Their webs will not become clothing, nor will they cover themselves with what they have made.

Their deeds are works of iniquity, an act of violence is in their hands,

their feet run after evil. They rush to shed innocent blood.

Their thoughts are thoughts of iniquity. Violence and ruin are on their highways.

They do not know the path of peace, and there is no justice in their tracks.

They have made their paths crooked.

Whoever walks in theme will not experience *shalom*.

That is why justice is far from us and righteousness does not reach us.

We hope for light, but behold darkness, for brightness but we walk in gloom...

We hope for justice, but there is none, for salvation, but it is far from us.

For our transgressions are multiplied before You, and our sins testify against us...

Justice is turned back, and righteousness sands far off.

For truth has stumbled in the street and uprightness cannot enter.

So now truth is missing and whoever shuns evil becomes prey.

Now when ADONAI saw it, it was displeasing in his eyes that there was no justice.

He saw that there was no one—He was astonished that no one was interceding.

Therefore his own arm brought salvation for him, and righteousness upheld him.

He put on righteousness as a breastplate and a helmet of salvation on his head.

He clothed himself in robes of vengeance and wrapped Himself in zeal as a cloak.

According to their deeds, so He will repay: wrath to his adversaries, retribution to His enemies.

The LORD looked and was displeased that there was no justice.

He saw that there was no one, he was appalled that there was no one to intervene; so his own arm worked salvation for him and his own righteousness sustained him.

He put on righteousness as his breastplate, and the helmet of salvation on his head; he put on the garments of vengeance and wrapped himself in zeal as in a cloak.

According to what they have done, so will he repay,

To the Islands He will repay as due.

So from the west they will fear the Name of ADONAI, and his glory form the rising of the sun. (Isa. 59:1-19)

The passage concludes with the hope that a Redeemer will come to Zion, to those who repent of their sins. God again reaffirms His covenant with Israel, that He will give them His Spirit and that His words will not depart from them or their children forever. Though it is a day of judgment, in the midst of this, the promise of redemption is again affirmed.

When we read these magnificent passages, we gain a true understanding of the heart of God—One who is exacting in his standards of justice, who will bring judgment, but who longs to be merciful to those who will repent. In the midst of judgment, He is One who promises ultimate redemption. We would be remiss if we did not quote one more passage from *Micah*.

With what shall I come before ADONAI?

With what shall I bow myself before God on high?

Shall I present Him with burnt offerings, with year old calves?

Will ADONAI be pleased with thousands of rams, with hordes of rivers of oil?

Shall I offer my firstborn for my transgression, the fruit of my belly for the sin of my soul?

He has told you, humanity, what is good and what Adonai is seeking from you:

Only to practice justice, to love mercy and to walk humbly with your God.

This is our God, a God of compassionate love and justice. The meaning of that love and justice is defined by His law and His interventions in history as interpreted by His prophets.

Is God a Singular Being or a Uni-Plural Being?

Several passages in the Tanakh indicate God is more complex than the singular type of being, as Maimonides taught, where God is confessed as *Yachid* or absolutely singular. The mystery begins in Genesis 1 where God says, "Let Us make man in Our image." As noted, Barth saw the plurality of humans being created male and female indicated this plurality in God. This alone would not be a strong argument, but as we move forward we see many intriguing accounts. There is an angelic personage who is called by the holy name of God— YHWH—and who dialogues with Abraham over the judgment of Sodom and Gomorrah. The same kind of being—one who wrestles with Jacob—appears in Genesis 33. In Exodus, a burning bush appears to Moses. We are told it is an Angel of God who is later called by the name YHWH. Moses is told to say that YHWH sent him. God tells Moses He will send His Angel before Israel and that they are to heed Him or He will not forgive their sins. This Angel is in the pillar of fire by night and in the cloud by day, as Israel journeys in the wilderness. In *Judges*, it appears the Angel of the LORD is the God of Israel. We read:

> Now the angel of ADONAI came up from Gilgal to Bochim, and He said, "I brought you up out of Egypt and took you into the land which I swore to your fathers. I also said, 'I will never break My covenant with you. Now as for you, you must make no covenant with the inhabitant of the land. You must break their altars. But you have not listened to my voice. What is this you have done?' Therefore I also said, 'I will not drive them out from before you, but they will be thorns in your sides, and their gods will be a snare to you.'"
>
> Now when the Angel of the Lord spoke these words to all *Bnei-Yisrael*, the people lifted up their voice and wept. So they called the name of that place Bochim, and they sacrificed there to ADONAI. (Judg. 2:1–5)

The figure that appears to Manoah before the birth of Samuel in *Judges* 13 is also fascinating. Manoah seemingly realizes with whom he spoke. When he asks His name, he is asked in return, "Why do you ask My Name? It is wonderful" (Judg. 13:9). The angel ascended in the flame of the offering of Manoah. He and his wife fell to the ground. Then we read, "Then Manoah realized that he was the Angel of the ADONAI."

"We will surely die!" he said to his wife. "We have seen God" (Judg. 13:21,22). Passages such at these have prompted some to say that YHWH is the Angel of the Lord and that whenever YHWH is used it refers to the Angel. It is also claimed that the Angel is the pre-incarnate Messiah. I think it is saying too much to conclude that all uses of YHWH refer to the Angel and to the pre-incarnate Messiah. However, I think it is reasonable to think this is oftentimes the case.[48]

One more important passage on the nature of God is the mysterious passage in Daniel 7. The figure of the Messiah who comes before the Ancient of Days is given universal sovereignty over all peoples and an everlasting dominion. The New Covenant Scriptures make this figure part of the identity of God.

In *Borderlines* and *The Jewish Gospels*, Daniel Boyarin—an Orthodox Jewish professor at Berkeley—argues that the idea of a plurality in God, almost of distinct but unified persons, was well accepted in many circles of first-century Judaism. In his view, it was the majority view until it was intentionally cleansed from Judaism, as a polemic against Messianic Judaism and Christianity.[49]

The Revelation of God in the Psalms

The revelation of God in the book of *Psalms* is fully in accord with the revelation in the Torah and the prophets. *Psalms* argues that God is merciful, loving and just. His forgiveness is amazing, for He does not deal with us according to our sins (Ps. 103:8–14). He will rescue the poor and needy, deliver the oppressed, punish the wicked, and bring the nations to the knowledge of the truth (Ps. 82:3,4). The book of *Psalms* confirms our understanding of God is based on the history of His interventions in and for Israel, and on the prophets' interpretation of them. In addition, the prophetic declaration of God's will and character according to His Law and revealed will is key to our understanding.

Psalms reaffirms God's everlasting faithfulness to His covenant with Israel and connects His favor to her with the redemption of the nations (Ps. 102:13, 105:8,9). The psalms that affirm God's love for all nations and His commitment to bring them to the truth include 22:27, 28; 47:7–

---

[48] James Oliver Buswell, *A Systematic Theology of the Christian Religion.* Grand Rapids: Zondervan, 33; Intrater, *op. cit.,* 27–35.
[49] Daniel Boyarin, *Border Lines.* Philadelphia: University of Pennsylvania Press, 2004, 93–127; and *The Jewish Gospels,* New York: The New Press, 2012.

9; 47:6; 67; 72:17; 96:7–10; 102:15. Psalms that affirm the knowledge of God is revealed through Israel's history include 78, 105, 106, 136.

The book of *Psalms* show intimacy between the psalmist and God, sometimes through an honest complaint, but often ending with a note on God's ultimate faithfulness. The psalmists' expressions of emotion, pain and calls for vengeance do not always reflect God's higher standard of love and forgiveness. However, the *Psalms'* great proposition is that God is the kind of divine being who can be in an intimate relationship with His people both on the individual and corporate levels. Indeed, *Psalm* 139 shows God as involved in creating every human being with the most intimate of involvement and care.

God's tender care for creation is also noted in *Psalms* 67:9–13; 104; and 145:17. *Psalms* 19 and 119 powerfully affirm the greatness of the Torah. This is a great worship book that affirms most of what we have already concluded as the doctrine of God in the *Tanakh*. *Psalms* deepens our understanding of intimacy with God. The ideas of His faithfulness and promise to Israel and care for all nations is set in a context of worship.

Psalms presents God as completely wise, as One who always acts in the most judicious, righteous and practical ways to bring about His good ends. These good ends are based on His love, but also on His commitment to the free choices of the human beings He created in his image.

Expanding Our Knowledge of God Through the Gospels

The New Covenant Scriptures emphasize the faithfulness of God in bringing a redeemer for the sake of Israel and the nations. The same emphasis on God as a God of compassionate justice continues in the New Covenant. There is really no assertion contrary to what we have discovered in the *Tanakh*. However, our understanding of the depths of the love of God is expanded in the New Covenant Scriptures.

The coming of Yeshua is a fulfillment of God's promise, and God is a promise keeping God. The conception and birth stories in Luke completely vindicate the Hebrew Bible and are fully in line with these Scriptures. Miriam prays,

> "And his mercy is from generation to generation
> To the ones who fear him
> He has displayed his power with his arm.

He has scattered the proud in the thoughts of their hearts.
He has brought down rulers from thrones and exalted humble ones.
He as filled the hungry with god things and sent away the rich empty-
handed.
He has helped his servant Israel, remembering his mercy, just as he spoke
it to our fathers, to Abraham and his seed forever." (Lk.1:50–54)

Miriam's song emphasizes God's faithfulness to Israel. In addition, we see a great reversal of fortunes in this poem. The rich are sent away empty, but the poor and hungry are filled. This anticipates the teaching of Yeshua in the beginning verses of *Matthew* 5, the Beatitudes. In the same chapter, Zechariah emphasizes that the Messiah fulfills the oath to Abraham to rescue Israel.

Salvation from our enemies and from the hand of all who hate us!
So He shows mercy to our fathers and remembers his holy covenant, the
vow which He swore to Abraham our father, to grant us— rescued
fearlessly from the land of our enemies—to serve him, to serve him in
holiness and righteousness before Him all our days. (Lk. 1:71–75).

Furthermore, John the Immerser will prepare his way and give people knowledge of salvation and "through the forgiveness of sins, because of the tender mercy of our God, by which the rising sun will come to us from heaven" (Lk. 1:78). Simeon proclaims the Messiah will be "a light for revelation to the nations and for glory of Your people Israel" (Lk. 2:32).

Early in the gospels, we see God's heart for Israel and for all the nations. How is His love expressed? It is expressed first of all through the life, works and teachings of Yeshua. From the beginning of his ministry, Yeshua declared the Kingdom of God had come to earth (*Mark* 1:15: "The kingdom of God is near"). By responding to Yeshua, one can enter into the Kingdom of God and live in it. Although partially revealed to his followers, that Kingdom is indeed real and accessible. It is a Kingdom of love and righteousness. Its fullness on earth awaits the second coming of Yeshua.

Yeshua's actions demonstrate the presence of the Kingdom and a great reversal for those who respond. In *Matthew* the poor and grieving are blessed. Why?—because the Kingdom has broken into the world and delivers from poverty and grief. Those who hunger and thirst for righteousness will not continue in frustration but will be filled. His words to unjustly incarcerated doubting John the Immerser expand this change.

> Go report to John what you saw and heard; the blind see, the lame walk, those with *tzara'at* are cleansed, the deaf hear, the dead are raised, and the poor have the good news proclaimed to them. Blessed is he who is not lead to stumble because of Me." (Lk. 7:22)

The gospels present accounts that have no parallel in other non-biblical religions and literature. There are parallels to some of the teachings and miracle stories, but I speak of the astonishing level of miracle-working power that came through Yeshua and was shared with his disciples (Luke 9, 10). The dramatic reversals in the conditions of the sick and demonized through the ministry of Yeshua and his disciples are a manifestation of God's ultimate heart for people, for deliverance from the great and terrible pains of our existence after the Fall and in this present age. These miracles are motivated by divine compassion. From the paralytic who is lowered through a roof, has his sins forgiven and takes up his bed and walks (Mk. 2:1–12), to the deliverance of a demonized man who lives among the tombs and is constantly injuring himself (Mk. 5:1–20), the love of God is publicly demonstrated for the world to see. Never had the world experienced such an outpouring of compassion expressed by miraculous provision and power. The Gospels clearly show that the compassion of Yeshua is a reflection of the compassion of God Himself—for God so loved the world that He came to seek, heal and save the lost and broken (Lk. 19:10; Jn. 3:16). This shows the Kingdom of God broken into this earth. It is available to those who respond to God's invitation and enter in.

The teachings of Yeshua reaffirm the Torah (Mt. 5:15, 17) while simultaneously emphasizing the need for deeper heart transformation. Torah is not merely a matter of external acts; it is what springs from the heart that is the key to true ethical living. The Hebrew Bible speaks frequently of the intentions of the heart, but Yeshua's teachings bring new depth to this emphasis. Indeed, some have said there are rabbis who teach similar things, but no one has put such teachings together into one connected narrative. As we pursue the gospels, we find a deeper and deeper understanding of the love of God. The story of the prodigal son is the story of God's own love for a prodigal Israel and a prodigal human race. God rushes to forgive the returning sinner (Lk. 15:11–31). Indeed, there is great rejoicing in heaven over one sinner who repents (Lk. 15:7). Never had religious literature made love so much the central focus of God's will and of our relationship with God. Yeshua attracts sinners, the despised tax-collectors and prostitutes. Somehow, these individuals of ill-repute find their way to God through him. Yet this love is not just emotional indulgence without law. That would not really be love.

Yeshua's life and the totality of the Word shows love is passionate identification by a person for another person or people, that perceives their worth, and seeks their good guided by law. I use "passion" because there is an important emotional component to love. We love when we perceive the worth of another through God's revelation. This worth is based on the fact that humans are created in God's image and are called to rule in life as submitted partners to Him (Gen. 1:26–28). In addition, we seek others' good. In so doing, we come to share the same ultimate good we find in God, by having fellowship with Him (Deut. 6:4,5; John 15:9–12) and by enjoying loving fellowship with other persons who love God (Jn. 15:12, Acts 2:42–46, I Jn. 3:11). The good of others is God's will. For example, God usually wills marriage and family (some are called to be single, however) and speaks of provision for all our needs through the institution (Gen. 2:18). Love is guided by law (I Jn 3:4, Rom. 13:8). This prevents love from being degraded into mere human sentiment. This is why we tell a man he is not free to divorce his wife to marry his secretary, though he tells us that if we really loved him we would not deny him such fulfillment. True love is only found in God in accord with His law.

Understanding divine love helps us understand God's justice. My conclusion after years of reflecting on the Bible is that justice is the balancing of the scales, so that God can produce an order of righteousness that maximizes the destiny and fulfillment of every human being.

Love is highlighted further in *John* 13–17. In these chapters, Yeshua shows his servant leadership. He washes the feet of his disciples and teaches them to abide in his love and to love one another through concrete actions. *Matthew* 7 describes God's love by His tender provision for the birds of the air. Consequently, we, human beings, should not worry, for God will lovingly provide for us if we seek His Kingdom first (Mt. 6:33).

We have not even yet mentioned that God's Messiah, and Israel's ultimate corporate representative, Yeshua, is more than a mere man.

However, we would be remiss if we did not include the great warnings of divine judgment. Yeshua is no mere meek and mild lamb as in the poem by William Blake.[50] He overturns the tables of the money changers for compromising the holiness of the Temple (Mk. 11:15–17), which is a house of prayer for all nations, not a commercial bazaar (Mk. 11:17). In this account, religious hypocrites are condemned and warned of hellfire. For a person who would cause little ones to stumble, it would be better to be drowned in the sea with a millstone around his neck (Lk. 17:2, Mk. 9:42). Yeshua describes the fate of those who ultimately reject God and His ways as being consigned to hell (Gehenna) where the worm dies not and the fire is not quenched (Mk. 9:46). Indeed, in his parables, Yeshua warns of an ultimate judgment where the wheat will be gathered into the barn (those who respond to God and turn toward the ways of righteousness) while the wicked will be gathered as chaff to be burned (Mt. 13:30). Echoing Jewish thought, Yeshua affirms a final irreversible judgment.[51] All of this is the most profound teaching on the nature of the love of God and of His ultimate justice and judgment.

The gospels also present Yeshua as divine. It is more than Yeshua reflecting what God is like since he is in His image, for we also were made in His image. But Yeshua was sinless. A perfect human would reflect God's image more than any other creature. But the Bible also asserts his divinity (deity). When we look at Yeshua, we see what God is like. He is, as C. S. Lewis said, "God become focused"; the image is clear.[52] Three writers point out the gospels unmistakably present Yeshua as divinity/deity—the God-man. First is Daniel Boyarin, an Orthodox Jewish scholar, mentioned above. In his book *The Jewish Gospels*, he argues the gospels truly present Yeshua as divinity. He says the first-century controversy over Yeshua was not the theoretical claim of his divinity as a human, but whether or not he was that One, the Messiah to come into the world.[53] As noted, Boyarin says a plurality dimension in the unity of God was a common first-century Jewish idea derived from the Hebrew Bible, reflected in contemporary Jewish literature. That the Messiah could be a divine figure was deduced from the description of the figure in Daniel 7, through the one who comes before the Ancient of

[50] William Blake (1757–1827), *The Lamb* in *Songs of Innocence*, Stanzas 16-20.
[51] Talmud: Baba Metzia 58b, Sanhedrin 10a, 99b, 105a; Rosh Hashanah 16b–17a, Ecclesiastes Rabbah iii. 9.
[52] C. S. Lewis, *Mere Christianity*. 139–140.
[53] The material that follows is taken from Boyarin's *The Jewish Gospels* (New York: The New Press, 2012), 26–31, 38–43, 46–52.

Days is a god figure and is given universal sovereignty and everlasting rule. He is called the "son of man." Boyarin says this term has been misinterpreted to mean a human being and to merely describe Yeshua's humanity. For Boyarin, it is just the opposite. Though "Son of God" was taken to denote his deity, for Boyarin "son of man" is the clearer indicator. "Son of God" is a title for the Messiah, but also for the ancient Israelite kings and Israel; thus its deity implications are ambiguous. "Son of man" is used for a claim of deity when Yeshua applies Daniel 7 to himself at his trial (Mk. 14:62). In Mark's account, the high priest declares Yeshua guilty of blasphemy for quoting Daniel! He tore his clothes in the strongest revulsion against Yeshua's claim. But remember the high priest was a Sadducee who likely would not have accepted the book of Daniel as Scripture.[54] The majority of the Sanhedrin were Sadducees. The Pharisees who agreed to condemn Yeshua (at least two did not) may have done so for different reasons. The Bible notes envy and the extent of his popularity among the people. He also flouted some of the Pharisaic rules.

The second scholar is Larry Hurtado. In *How on Earth Did Jesus Become a God?*, he argues the level of worship Yeshua received during and after his earthly ministry provides solid proof for his divinity claim. Hurtado's lectures on Yeshua's divinity, at Bar-Ilan University in Israel, gave an important Jewish context to this claim of divinity.[55]

The third scholar, Richard Bauckham, one of today's premiere New Testament scholars and an expert in Jewish backgrounds of the gospels, argues that three things are markers for a claim to divinity. First is Yeshua's involvement in creating the universe, which we see clearly affirmed in *John* 1. Second is the assertion of universal authority, which Yeshua claims in *Matthew* 28:18, "All authority in heaven and earth has been given to Me." Thirdly is his status as One who receives worship from human beings. We see this in the post-Resurrection accounts and throughout the New Covenant (Mt. 28:17, Lk. 24:52, Jn. 20:28, Rev. 1:17,18, 5:9–14). The Son—the Word—pre-existed the creation, and that Word became flesh and dwelt among us (Jn. 1:14).[56] He who has

---

[54] Oskar Skarsaune, *In the Shadow of the Temple*. Downers Grove, IL: InterVarsity Press, 2002, 109–112. He sees the evidence for their acceptance of the prophets as ambiguous.

[55] Larry Hurtado, *One God, One Lord*. London: T&T Clark, 1998, 93–114; *How on Earth Did Jesus Become a God?* Grand Rapids: Eerdmans, 2005, 111–51.

[56] Richard Baukham, *God Crucified*. Grand Rapids: Eerdmans, 1998, 9–16. See also Oskar Skarsaune, *Incarnation: Myth or Fact?* (St. Louis: Concordia, 1991), 24–43.

seen Yeshua has seen the Father (Jn. 14:9, 10). In the beginning, He was the Word who was with God and was God, for through him all things were made (Jn. 1:3). Hurtado points out the amazing change that takes place in the ubiquitous language of worship in the New Testament. He calls it *"binitarian devotional language,"* especially where it relates to the gospels, while in the rest of the New Testament, Hurtado notes that the authors focus primarily on the close relationship between the Father and the Son.[57] We see this close relationships in the modified Sh'ma in I Corinthians:

> Yet for us there is but one God, the Father, from whom all things came and for whom we live; and there is but one Lord Jesus Christ through whom all things came and through whom we live. (I Cor. 8:6)

The question to be answered is, does the NT present a view of God as binitarian or trinitarian? Throughout the NT, emphasis regarding worship is placed on the Father and the Son—the Messiah—with constant references to the Holy Spirit. Is the Spirit just the Spirit of the Father? Or of the Son? Or is the Spirit a more distinct person? Is the Spirit a he, she or it? The New Covenant Scriptures speak of the Spirit in a way that seems more than just a personification. In *John* the followers of Yeshua are promised a Comforter or Counselor, but are told "the world cannot receive [him]" (Jn. 14:16, 17). Yeshua states the Counselor will teach the disciples, remind them of Yeshua's teachings and testify of him (Jn. 15:26). Also, in *John* 16:8–15, we read:

> When He [the Spirit] comes he will convict the world of about sin … He will guide you into all truth. He will not speak on His own, but whatever He hears, He will tell you. And He will declare to you the things that are to come. He will glorify Me because He will take from what is mine, and declare it to you. … For this reason I said that the *Ruach* will take from what is mine and declare it to you.

The development of the doctrine of the Spirit is anticipated in the *Tanakh*. We see this especially in *Ezekiel* 36:26–27, which says God will put His Spirit in each of His children. The Spirit is therefore the One who can dwell in the heart or center of a person (see John 3:3-8). In

---

[57] Hurtado, *op. cit.*, 93–124.

addition, *Acts* highlights the coming of the Spirit upon God's people, while the epistles focus on the Sprit dwelling in us and filling us (Acts 2:1*ff*, Eph. 5:18). The work of the Spirit effects an inner change in the heart of humans, what some call being "born again" or "born from above." The Messiah in us is the Spirit of God in us.

We should note that in speaking of these realities, we are using the functional language of the Bible. The Bible does not engage in abstract, metaphysical definitions. Yet by the time we finish reading the gospels, we are left with the mystery of a plurality in God Himself, a uni-plural God in fellowship at the deepest level in His own being. Hence the prayer of Yeshua referring to his pre-incarnation and even pre-creation existence: "Father, glorify me together with Yourself, with the glory which I had with You, before the world came to be" (Jn. 17:5).

Finally, the resurrection of Yeshua is the great vindication of his kingship and lordship over all the earth. It is the vindication of his sacrificial love for our sake. It proves the kind of God we serve is One who loves us even to the point of great suffering and pain, as expressed in the crucifixion of His Son. In this, the depth of God's love takes on an astonishing new dimension. God gives us His Son, who is part of Himself, as Bauckham says, is part of the identity of God,[58] to lay down his life for us. This shows the fullness of God's love for God, for God was in Messiah and also suffers for us. God's suffering love reaches its climax in the suffering of His Son. Indeed, when we accept that Yeshua suffered and died to show the greatness of his love and the Father's love, and if we believe this and turn to God, we are forgiven, freed from our sins and spared divine judgment, for Yeshua has died in our place as a supreme act of divine love.

The Apostle John shows God's essence is love (1 Jn. 4:16). Although all of God's attributes are important—omnipotence, omniscience, omnipresence, graciousness, truth, justice, faithfulness, etc.—but the greatest thing about God is He is a person and He is love. When we speak of God as a person, again, we are asserting God is an intelligent being with will and with personal attributes of love, motivations of justice, wisdom, and a divine emotional life. Through this, God becomes known as the God of our Lord Yeshua who raised him from the dead. Again, God is known by His acts and their prophetic

---

[58] Bauckham, *op. cit.*, 41–42.

interpretation. God is the God who loves us so much, He gave His Son to die for us all.

Expanding Our Knowledge of God From Acts to Revelation

In *Acts*, Yeshua's work continues through his disciples and through the broader community of believers who profess God is compassionate, loving and just. He is constantly seeking to save through the proclamation of the Gospel and to demonstrate His love through signs and wonders. But there is also a great warning against spurning His offer of salvation. Paul exhorts his listeners to turn from worthless idols to the living God, "who made the heaven and the earth and the sea and all that is in them. In past generations He allowed all the nations go their own way. Yet He did not leave Himself without a witness—He did good by giving you rain from heaven and fruitful seasons, filling your hearts with joy and gladness" (Acts 14:15b–17).

Parallel to this passage, Paul teaches the following to the Athenians:

> I even found an altar with this inscription; *"To an Unknown God."* Therefore what you worship without knowing, this I proclaim to you. The God who made the world and all things since He is the Lord of heaven and earth, does not live in temples made by hands as if he needed anything, since He himself gives everyone life and breath and all things. From one he made every nation of men to live on the face of the earth having set appointed times and he boundaries of their territory. They were to search for Him, and perhaps grope around for Him and find Him. Yet He is not far from each one of us, for "in Him we live and move and have our being."
>
> As some of your own poets have said, "For we also are His offspring." (Acts 17:23b–29) Since we are His offspring, we ought not to suppose the Deity is like gold or silver or stone, and engraved image of human art and imagination. Although God overlooked the periods of ignorance, now He commands everyone everywhere to repent. For He has set a day on which He will judge in righteousness through a man whom He has appointed. He has brought forth evidence of this to all men, by raising him from the dead. (Acts 17:29–31)

This passage, along with *Romans* 1–2, describes Paul's natural theology. He uses an argument from stoicism. If we are God's offspring, as the

Stoics taught, anything less than human cannot represent God. A Stoic would have been thinking in a panentheistic way (all is in God), but Paul uses the Stoic view to refute idolatry and argue that God is infinitely greater than the human who is His offspring and cannot be represented by idols. Human beings alone are the image-bearer. God cares for all creatures. He is the one who provides for all. He calls all men and women to acknowledge Him and turn from idols.[59]

The book of *Romans* contains the most important Pauline texts for understanding the doctrine of God. In *Romans* 1, Paul notes that any human being has no excuse for not embracing the basic truth about God. Paul argues:

> What can be known about God is plain to them—for God has shown it to them. His invisible attributes—His eternal power and His divine nature—have been clearly seen ever since the creation of the world, being understood through the things that have been made. So people are without excuse. (Rom. 1:19–20)

Paul continues to reveal the perversion of humans who fall easily into idolatry and turn to immorality. He concludes, "Though they know God's righteous decree—that those who practice such things deserve death—they not only do them but also approve of others who practice the same" (Rom. 1:32). This text has been the subject of great debates. Proponents of natural theology—who say humans can know important details about God through reason only—say Paul supports their position.[60] Others believe the minds of humans are corrupt to such an extent that, for them, natural theology is impossible. They interpret Paul to only be saying that at an earlier period in history the human race had an understanding of God but turned away.[61] I rather think Paul's argument fits the text from *Acts* 14 and 17. His natural theology is not a

---

[59] Ben Witherington III, *The Acts of the Apostles: A Socio-Rhetorical Commentary.* Grand Rapids: Eerdmans, 1998, 422–427, 511–535.
Hilary Le Cornu and Joseph Shulam, *A Commentary on the Jewish Roots of Acts.* Jerusalem: Netivyah, 2003, 780–784, 959–973.
[60] Many references to natural theology reference *Romans* 1: Norman Geisler, *Christian Apologetics*; J.P. Moreland and William Lane Craig, *Philosophical Foundations for a Christian Worldview*; Joseph Shulam, *Romans*; James Dunn, *Word Biblical Commentary: Volume 38A, Romans 1–8.* Dallas: Word Books, 1988.
[61] Campbell, D.A., *The Deliverance of God: An Apocalyptic Rereading of Justification in Paul.* Grand Rapids: Eerdmans, 2009, 317–18, 343, 344, 400–404. Campbell says Paul, quoting Jewish and Greek philosophers, used a rhetorical method to reject natural theology. C. Cranfield, *The Epistle to the Romans.* Edinburgh: T&T Clark, 1975, 116–7.

conclusion of an extended argument. It is the immediate intuitive grasp that we should know we are created by God, and the One who brought us into existence is far greater than any human being. We should be in awe toward the ultimate ground or source of our existence. The argument of *Romans* 1 may be more like that of Abraham Joshua Heschel, who describes the proper human response to realizing that one is living in a creation of extraordinary grandeur, and that human life itself is part of this grandeur. Reverence for the Creator is the only proper response.

Regarding unbridled hedonism, Paul had plenty of company among Stoic philosophers who condemned pagan behavior and hedonism and having an intuitive sense that such behavior is wrong and unfitting. In *Romans* 2, Paul does not say humans have common standards of right and wrong, rooted in their minds / consciences, thus proving they have a common origin from a Creator lawgiver whose law is written on their minds. Rather, Paul says we condemn others for things we do. Whatever standards we may profess, we do not live up to them. In condemning others we condemn ourselves. Edward John Carnell calls this the judicial sentiment. [62] Beyond these texts, no emphasis is placed on natural theology, but the knowledge of God is based on the revelation in the history of Israel and through Israel's representative King, the Messiah Yeshua.

Romans presents God as a God of love and justice. It presents the Gospel of the death and resurrection of Yeshua for us as the key to experiencing God's love and favor. It is good news since accepting the Gospel, or confessing Yeshua as Lord, gives us the confidence of everlasting life or a good final destiny. The way back to God is through Yeshua's sacrificial death and resurrection. When we believe in and embrace the work of Yeshua by faith, we are freed from the bondage of sin and death. *Romans* describes God's love on this basis, "But God demonstrates His own love toward us, in that while we were yet sinners Messiah died for us" (Rom. 5:8). In *Romans* 6, Paul speaks of the spiritual death and resurrection of the believers who identify with Yeshua's death and resurrection. In this regard, God the lawgiver does not do away with His law, but as in *Jeremiah* 31:31, where the law is written on the heart, Paul can say, "in order that the righteous

---

[62] Edward John Carnell, *Christian Commitment*. New York: MacMillan, 1957, 96–104.

requirements of the law might be fully met in us, who do not live according to the sinful nature but according to the Spirit" (Rom. 8:4).[63] Through identification in the death and resurrection in Yeshua, believers are forgiven and changed inwardly into a new man. God upholds His law and so we read, "Do we then nullify the *Torah* through faithfulness? May it never be! On the contrary, we uphold the *Torah*" (Rom 3:31).

A wrong understanding by some Evangelical Christian teachers in the calls into question what we have asserted as part of the doctrine of God.[64] They think justification does away with His law or the standards for humanity that express His character. God cannot change with regard to His basic ethical standards. Justification is a way for God to accept us while upholding His law; it leads to transformation so people will live according to His standards.

The message of God's love and escaping His judgment by embracing the salvation that is in Yeshua pervades Paul's epistles and the rest of the New Testament. (Rom. 6:18, 19, 8:1, 2, 10:9, 10) But those who do not turn back to God are in danger of a terrible judgment, for God does not treat wickedness lightly (Heb. 10:26, 31).[65]

A few more comments are in order about the rest of the epistles. *James* (*Jacob*) presents a strong case for upholding the law as a reflection of God's character. According to *James*, those who truly follow Yeshua and have a genuine faith in the Messiah live in accord with God's ways (Jas. 2:20–22). They do works of righteousness as proof of faith.

John makes a similar case in *I John*. His great epistle emphasizes God's love and our call to love one another. However, the way of love is not a life that indulges sin. John notes that sin is the transgression of the law, and those who have truly embraced the Gospel no longer walk in sin (1 Jn. 3:4). They may fall, but sin is unnecessary. John seems quite in accord with Paul, who taught that there is no temptation not common to all, but God provides a way of escape so we have no excuse for sin (I Cor. 10:13). The follower of Yeshua is characterized by a life of faithfulness or obedience. Love therefore fulfills the law, not by replacing it, but by naturally living in accord with it.

---

[63] James Dunn, *op. cit.*, 266–269, 306–333, 424, 425.

[64] This is especially well-represented by classical dispensational writers. Zane Hodges, *Absolutely Free: A Biblical Response to Lordship Salvation*. Corinth, TX: Grace Evangelical Society, 2014.

[65] Jn. 3:36; Mt. 13:42, 49, 50, 18:35, 25:41–46; Rev. 20:15, 21:8.

Finally, the book of *Revelation* is the greatest testimony on the consistency of the revelation of God in the *Tanakh* and in the *New Covenant Scriptures*. Any idea that God changed from the time of the revelation at Sinai to the time of Yeshua must be abandoned if one is to take the Bible seriously. The idea of God as a God of wrath in the Old Testament and a God of love in the New is completely false. God's great love is the same in both the *Hebrew Bible* and the *New Covenant Scriptures*. His great commitment to righteousness is the same, and His wrath for those who refuse Him is the same. One can argue whether or not the judgments in Revelation are just a matter of sowing and reaping, or show an active wrath of God, but it seems as with the Flood and Sodom and Gomorrah, the human race will come to a place where they will experience God's active wrath. Yet His offer of mercy before judgment and His offer of love and forgiveness for those who turn to Him remain throughout, as noted in the following passage:

> And then I saw another angel flying high in the sky, having a timeless message of good news to proclaim to those who dwell on the earth—to every nation, and tribe, and tongue and people. He said in a loud voice, "Fear God and give Him glory because the hour of his judgment has come. Worship the One who made heavens and earth and sea and springs of water." (Rev. 14:6)

Both the warning of God's judgment and proclamation of the Good News are announced together in *Revelation*. Chapter 7 describes a great number of the Jewish people (144,000 from the tribes of Israel) and a multitude that no one could count from every tribe, tongue and people. No doubt that description of *Revelation* 14 is parallel to *Revelation* 7 and gives great hope of an abundant harvest during these times of shaking. This is truly an expression of God's love and mercy.[66]

The themes of judgment and wrath come to an ultimate climax (Rev. 14:17–20). The grapes are gathered into the winepress of God's wrath. We read of Yeshua, "He treads the winepress of the furious of the wrath of Elohai-Tzva'ot" (Rev. 19:15). Revelation depicts a great final judgment and a separation forever of the wicked and the righteous (Rev.

---

[66] Daniel Juster, *Passover: The Key That Unlocks the Book of Revelation.* Clarksville, MD: Lederer Books, 2011, 30–32, 73–75. David Frankfurter, *The Jewish Annotated New Testament.* New York: Oxford University Press, 2011, 476–477. Steve Gregg, ed., *Revelation: Four Views: A Parallel Commentary.* Nashville: Thomas Nelson, 1997, 134.

20:11–15). Those who are excluded from salvation are listed near the end of the book. They are "the cowardly, and faithless and detestable and murderers and sexually immoral, and sorcerers and idolaters, and all liars—their lot is in the lake that burns with fire and brimstone, which is the second death (Rev. 21:8).

Again, the idea of God, His love, justice, mercy and wrath are basically the same in both the Hebrew Bible and the New Covenant Scriptures. Of course, the depth of the revelation of the love of God in the New Covenant Scriptures is much greater.

The doctrine of God as a uni-plural being is again established in *Revelation* with the most extensive assertions of the deity of Yeshua, who is part of the identity of God. He is called the Alpha and Omega, the beginning and the end (Rev. 1:8; 21:6, 12, 13). He is depicted in the center of the throne of God (5:6, 7:12). He is given worship with the Father, while the angel tells John to not worship him, since he is a creature (5:12–13; 22:8–9). He is given sovereignty over the whole earth (11:15).

God's love ultimately prevails for those who receive the Gospel and turn to Him. The glories of the New Jerusalem are described where God will wipe away tears from the eyes of the redeemed. There will be no more death or mourning, crying or pain. "Behold the dwelling of God is among men and, and He shall tabernacle among them. They shall be His people, and God Himself shall be among them and be their God" (Rev. 21:3). The New Jerusalem will include every many tribes and peoples bringing their glory into the city (Rev. 21:24). The New Jerusalem is especially connected to God's covenant faithfulness to His people, as the foundation stones will have the names of twelve Jewish apostles, and the entrances will be inscribed with the names of the twelve tribes of Israel.

I should note other texts from the Pauline epistles and Hebrews that also emphasize the deity of Yeshua, the hymn of *Philippians* 2 where Yeshua is described as one who, though in the form of God, did not hold on to this divine attribute, but emptied himself to become a servant even unto death. Now he is highly exalted and given the name that is above every name. So also in *Colossians* 1:17 we read that all things were created by him and through him. In *Hebrews* 1, we read that the Messiah is the very radiance of God's glory and the exact representation of His being, through whom He made the universe, sustaining all things by His powerful word and now sitting at the right hand of the Majesty in heaven. These claims for Yeshua are such that we can be certain of his deity and of the fact that we can understand God most fully by understanding him.

Conclusions About The Doctrine of God From Scripture

The Bible presents a very consistent doctrine of God. It affirms the following:

1. God is the Creator of the heavens and the earth. As such, He is beyond what we can grasp with our finite minds. The Bible asserts we cannot make sense of the universe without understanding God as Creator (Rom. 1; Acts 14). God is infinite—fully beyond creation, incalculable and beyond our full comprehension.

2. The Bible asserts God is ultimately in control of history and every human life (Ps. 139). He knows the end from the beginning. The Bible reveals that He knows the future since He has more knowledge of the directions of events than is humanly conceivable, and He is committed to fulfilling His plan until the end of times.

3. The Bible asserts that God is primarily known by His interventions in history as interpreted by His prophets. The history of God is bound up with the history of Israel, and that history is the definitive revelation of what God is like. God revealed Himself most fully in Yeshua, as Israel's King and Messiah. He is part of the history of Israel through which we know what God is like.

4. The Bible shows God desires to act in love, compassion, forgiveness and mercy toward every human being and His whole creation. But He is also a God of justice. While His is compassionate justice, it requires He allow the law of sowing and reaping to do its fearful work in bringing the good or painful results of our actions. Repentance can bring some mitigation of this (Ezek. 18). Beyond this, at a certain point of wickedness, God's active wrath is engaged, and He will act sometimes in severe judgment. The fullness of His love is seen in Yeshua. In his life, ministry, teaching, death and resurrection we see the greatness of God's offer of salvation. Yeshua also reaffirms God's justice, both in sowing and reaping and ultimately in active wrath against wickedness when there is no repentance. Yeshua teaches an ultimate separation of the righteous

and the wicked at the end of this age in a final judgment. *Revelation* fully reaffirms all these themes.[67]

5. God is beyond His creation, transcendent, but present in the midst of His creation. He dwells in the midst of His people and in the lives of individuals by the power of the Holy Spirit. He can have an intimate relationship with those who seek Him.

6. God is constantly described as holy. This is a quality of His awesome purity, righteousness and transcendent being in that it is greater than we can conceive. As such, God is love, yet we must not enter His presence lightly or presume upon His mercy. Rather, we must recognize that unrepented sin and failure to treat God as holy can lead to judgment. His holiness draws us but also elicits a reverent fear.

Finally, a word about the debates about God. For much of the 20th century, since the philosophy of Alfred North Whitehead, who presented a Theistic view where God was connected to time and developing, theologians have been breaking free of classical theistic ideas defining God as timeless, all-knowing, all-powerful, unchangeable, and having all future events as fixed in His present knowledge—that is, in His "ever-present nowness,"[68] He knows it all as if it has already happened. As Evangelicals, liberal Christian theologians and Jews have engaged these issues, some have asserted the views of God as connected to time and change are more in accord with a Hebraic understanding in the Bible than with the classical Christian and Jewish views derived from Greek philosophy. Some say God is growing and coming Himself to a higher plane of existence.[69] More moderate thinkers, who want to see a change in our understanding of God, have developed "open theism." The late Clark Pinnock would be a key asserter of this view.[70] Rabbi Harold Kushner also presents a similar view.[71] Some of the aspects of this essay are in agreement with open-theism scholars, both Jewish and Christian.

---

[67] Juster, *Passover*, 97.

[68] Alfred North Whitehead, *Process and Reality*. New York: MacMillan, 1929.

[69] John Cobb and Daniel Ray Griffin, *Process Theology: An Introductory Exposition*. Louisville: Westminster, 1996. Teilhard de Chardin, *The Phenomenon of Man*. New York: Harper Perennial, 1959.

[70] Clark Pinnock, *Most Moved Mover: A Theology of God's Openness*. Grand Rapids: Baker, 2001, 4–14.

[71] Rabbi Harold Kushner, *When Bad Things Happen to Good People*. New York: Anchor Books, 2004. Rabbi Kushner combines this with a view that God is finite and hence cannot prevent evil (asserted by the Boston personalist school of philosophy). Edgar Sheffield Brightman, *Philosophy of Religion*. New York:

It is true that it has been wrong to explain away and reinterpret the anthropomorphic language used to speak of God in the Bible. Sometimes such language is used in an exaggerated way, but in general God experiences emotions that are always within his righteous control. In addition, God loves, judges, and gets angry. God is unchangeable in His moral character. So we agree with the open theists on these aspects.[72] Open theists question the fixity of God as unchangeable and timeless as making language about God impossible. Relational language is time-conditioned, and the Bible is completely oriented toward relational language in speaking about God. He thus must know the past and the future as human beings interact with him. Open theists have a good point here. I grant that this view seems closer to the Bible.[73]

However, open theists hold different views concerning the certainties of the future. All hold that the actions of free human beings cannot be totally predicted and are not facts that can be known even to an omniscient being. So how free is the human race? Conservative open theists assert God has decreed future events and this age's ultimate conclusion. He will therefore bring it about. However, some think the direction of history is uncertain even to God. I cannot see how a radical open-history view squares with the many statements of the Bible that God knows the future, the end from the beginning, and has a commitment to bring about the eschatological end envisioned in the Bible.

I think a problem with open theism is in its assertions that we know things we cannot know. There is a creator-creature distinction, and, echoing Immanuel Kant, I do not think we can know God's in his ultimate experience and knowledge.[74] It is far beyond our understanding. We know what God has said. We are free to choose. Our choices can lead to salvation or to damnation. On the other hand, God has told us that He has fixed a day to judge the world. He has declared the end of all things and will bring it about. He will find willing people in sufficient numbers to move history to His goals.

Prentice Hall, 1940. Also the originator of this school, Borden Bowne, *Theism*. New York: Harper & Brothers, 1897.

[72] Pinnock, *Most Moved*, 56–60, 79–92.

[73] Oscar Cullman, *Christ and Time*. (Philadelphia: Westminster Press, 1964, 63–67. Cullman anticipates these open-theism views in his views of time. For example, God is everlasting, but not in an ever-present now where there is no change. Pinnock, 71.

[74] Immanuel Kant, *Critique of Pure Reason*, translated by Norman Kemp Smith. New York: St. Martin's Press, 1933, 266–73.

Addendum on the Trinity

No doubt perceptive readers of this chapter have noticed I did not respond to or assert the classic formulations of the Trinity, especially as presented in the Council of Nicaea. In very large measure, Messianic Jews believe in the deity of Yeshua and the personhood of the Holy Spirit. I am positive toward the creedal statements and, as my friend Dr. Mark Kinzer has stated in a Catholic Jewish dialogue we participate in, I think the formulations produced at the Nicaean Council were the best possible ones for a Greek- and Latin-speaking world. The creedal formulations safeguarded the biblical emphases against the Hellenistic trends of the day. In that day, to define God in singular terms would have been more compatible to Platonic and Aristotelian ideas. That said, for Messianic Jews I still think it best to stay closer to the Bible and its assertions concerning Yeshua and the Spirit. In a Jewish context, such texts give a very adequate formulation of the truth.

There are many Christian theologies that give a very good presentation and defense of Trinitarian theology. James Oliver Boswell's *A Systematic Theology of the Christian Religion* is one of the best older presentations.[75] Two more recent presentations that are quite clear and persuasive are Wayne Grudem's *Systematic Theology*, J. Rodman Williams' *Renewal Theology*.[76] I, however, prefer speaking in a manner that comports with Jewish sensibilities, and have endeavored to do so herein.

---

[75] James Oliver Buswell, *A Systematic Theology of the Christian Religion.* Grand Rapids: Zondervan, 1962, 102–29.

[76] Wayne Grudem, *Systematic Theology.* Grand Rapids: Zondervan, 1994, 226–61; J. Rodman Williams, *Renewal Theology, Vol. I.* Grand Rapids: Zondervan Academic, 1988, 83–94.

Messianism in the Hebrew Bible[1]

Seth Postell, Ph.D.

Introduction

In the Beginning was the Story

In the beginning... was THE STORY. The fact that the Torah begins with narrative rather than commandments, was, for the Medieval Rabbis, a problem in need of a solution. Rashi, the most famous of all Jewish Bible commentators, begins his commentary on the Torah by writing:

> Rabbi Isaac said, "The Torah should have begun with 'This month shall be for you' (Exod 12:2), since this is the first commandment with which Israel was commanded to keep." And what is the reason that it [the Torah] opens with 'In the beginning'?"[2]

Rashi goes on to explain that the Torah begins with a story, from creation to the exodus (Genesis 1–Exodus 12), in order to justify Israel's dispossession of the Canaanites from the Promised Land. Should the nations of the world accuse Israel of stealing the Land from the seven Canaanite nations, Israel's defense would be ... THE STORY: "The whole world belongs to the Holy One blessed be He. He created it, and He gives it to whomever He sees fit." The Story is Israel's "alibi;" both her title deed to, and justification for, the conquest of the Land. Though the Story provides the divine justification for Israel's claim to the Promised Land, truth is this is merely a subcategory of a far grander and universal purpose. It is my contention that the purpose of the Story, a

[1] I would like to thank Jo Blower (MA Haifa University) for the hours of time she spent reading and editing this chapter. I can literally see her fingerprints on every page of this chapter, and for this she is deserving of special thanks.
[2] *Miqraot Gedoloth* (Translation from Hebrew my own).

story that goes beyond Exodus to include the rest of the Torah as well as the Former Prophets (Joshua, Judges, 1-2 Samuel, 1-2 Kings),[3] does much more and provides the biblical "alibi" for both the Messianic hope and the eschatology in the Hebrew Bible.

A few thoughts about the shaping and the nature of this Story are necessary to set the stage for this rather bold assertion. First, the Hebrew Bible, or Tanakh (the Law, the Prophets, and the Writings), opens with a single continuous historical narrative that starts with the creation of the world and concludes with the exaltation of Jehoiachin son of David in the Babylonian Exile (2 Ki 25:27–30). This story accounts for nearly half of the entire Hebrew Bible in words.[4]

The Tanakh in Words

Torah	Prophets	Writings
Torah and Former Prophets (Gen–2 Kings) 211,012 words		Latter Prophets and Writings (Isa–2 Chron) 214,164 words

Particularly since the Hebrew Bible opens with a story whose scope is nearly half the Hebrew Bible in words, we can't even entertain the thought of understanding the Hebrew Bible's genealogies, laws, prophecies, psalms and prayers – especially in the second half of the

---

[3] For the purposes of clarity for those not familiar with the order of the Hebrew Bible, the order of Hebrew Bible differs from the ordering of the Protestant Christian canon. The Hebrew canon is divided into three major sections based on the acronym "Tanakh," the Torah, the Prophets, and the Writings. The Prophets, moreover, are divided into the Former Prophets (Joshua – Kings), and the Latter Prophets (Isaiah – Malachi). One significant justification for using this tri-partite arrangement in our study comes from Yeshua himself. Yeshua argued that the religious leaders would be held accountable for the blood of all the righteous martyrs from Abel (Gen 4:8ff.) to Zechariah (2 Chron 24:21; see Matt 23:35; Luke 11:51). Such a statement only makes sense when one thinks of the Hebrew Bible as beginning in the Torah and ending in Chronicles (i.e., Yeshua holds them accountable to the totality of revelation as expressed in the Hebrew Scriptures). Elsewhere, Yeshua provides the disciples an exposition of the Messianic hope of the Scriptures, namely, Moses, the Prophets, and the Psalms (Luke 24:44). At the very least, we can say that Yeshua's presentation suggests he understood the Scriptures in terms of three sections, though we might be further inclined to argue that Yeshua not only viewed the Hebrew Bible in terms of three sections, but that he conceived the third section in terms of Psalms – Chronicles. In that case, the term "Psalms" in Luke 24:44 may be used as a title for the entire third section of the Hebrew Scriptures.

[4] Stephen G. Dempster, *Dominion and Dynasty*, NSBT New Studies in Biblical Theology (Downers Grove, Il.: InterVarsity, 2003), 39.

Hebrew canon – without first attempting to grasp the meaning of this story, and thereby interpreting all that follows in this context.[5]

Second, the conclusion of this Story can be anticipated by the reader since its plot is already adumbrated in the introduction (Genesis 1–11).[6] In the world of literary theory, this phenomenon is known as *mise en abyme*[7] wherein the larger image contains a smaller copy of itself. In Rabbinic literature, this phenomenon falls under the category of *ma'asei avot siman l'banim*, meaning, "The deeds of the fathers are a sign to the sons."[8] In other words, the early chapters of this Story, particularly the *toledoth*[9] of Adam and Eve, are there not simply to tell us about what happened to Adam in the past but to tell what will happen to Israel in the future. Remarkably, and sadly, Adam's story in Genesis 1–3 becomes Israel's story in Joshua all the way through to 1–2 Kings (the gift of the Garden/Land, the receiving of the commandments, the failure to resist the temptations of the resident/s of the Garden/Land, disobedience, and exile to the east).

---

[5] Though a justification for interpreting the Primary History (Genesis – Kings) as a single story goes beyond the scope of this article, some words of explanation are in order. First, literary and canonical evidence strongly favors the integrity of the Torah as an individual composition, a narrative that begins at creation (Genesis 1) and concludes with death of Moses on Mt. Nebo (Deuteronomy 34). Second, the Former Prophets (Joshua – Kings) are loaded with allusions to and citations of the Torah, such that it's clear that its authors relied heavily on the Torah in the writing of their own compositions. There is a third, yet often overlooked point, however, when we consider the relationship of the Torah and the Former Prophets. Not only do we see evidence that the writers of the Former Prophets knew and made use of the Torah story, but also that the Torah knew and made use of the history as told in the Former Prophets. Two examples will suffice to make our point. First, Genesis 36:31 takes for granted that kings reigned over Israel. Second, Deut 2:12 takes for granted Israel's accomplished possession of the Promised Land. How can we account for these texts (and many others) without denying the Mosaic authorship of the Torah? One very plausible explanation is that once the Former Prophets were completed and joined together as the intentional continuation of the Torah Story, the Torah was then retrofitted into the Former Prophets to form a single comprehensive history from creation to Israel's exile. For more on the notion of the retrofitting of the Torah, see John H. Sailhamer's notion of Moses 2.0 in *The Meaning of the Pentateuch* (Downers Grove: IVP Academic, 2010), 200-201; on the importance of reading the Primary History as a whole, see Hans-Christoph Schmitt, "Das spätdeuteronomistische Geschichtswerk Genesis 1 - 2 Regnum 25 und seine theologische Intention," in *Congress Volume*, ed., J.A. Emerton, 261-79 (Leiden: Brill, 1997); T. Desmond Alexander, "Royal Expectations in Genesis to Kings: Their Importance for Biblical theology." *TynB* 49, no. 2 (January 1, 1998): 191-212.

[6] For an extended argument of this assertion, see Seth D. Postell, *Adam as Israel* (Eugene, Or.: Pickwick, 2011).

[7] Lucien Dällenbach, Le récit spéculaire. Essai sur la mise en abyme, Paris, Seuil, 1977.

[8] See *Gen Rabba* 48.7; Ramban's Commentary on Gen 12:6. For example, Abraham's sojourn in Egypt, which includes a famine in the Land, the taking of Sarah into Pharaoh's service, the plagues on Pharaoh's house, Abraham's departure with abundant gold, silver, and cattle, are clearly a "sign" to his sons, who likewise begin their sojourn in Egypt because of a famine, are taken into Pharaoh's service, set free through plagues, and depart with abundant gold, silver, and cattle. Abraham's exodus from Egypt serves to foreshadow Israel's exodus from Egypt.

[9] Namely, the story of what became of Adam and Eve.

Third, the prophetic nature of the Torah's introduction is reinforced by Moses' predictions at the end of the Torah:

> *ADONAI* said to Moses, "Behold, you are about to lie down with your fathers. Then this people will rise up and prostitute themselves with the foreign gods of the land they are entering. They will abandon Me and break My covenant that I cut with them. . . For when I bring them to the land flowing with milk and honey that I swore to their fathers, and they eat and are satisfied and grow fat—then they will turn to other gods and serve them, and they will spurn Me and break My covenant." (Deut 31:16–21[10])

Moses, the greatest of all the prophets of the Hebrew Bible, declares in no uncertain terms that Israel, like their father Adam, will enter a garden-like land, eat of its fruit, break God's commandments as expressed in the Sinai Covenant, and be driven away and into exile (see Deut 4:25–28; 30:1).

When we consider the introduction of the Story with its emphasis on Adam's disobedience and subsequent exile, Moses' explicit predictions of Israel's disobedience and subsequent exile, and the actual telling of Israel's disobedience and subsequent exile as narrated in Joshua 1 through to 2 Kings 25, a question forces itself upon us. Since Israel's disobedience and exile was completely anticipated (predicted) by Moses in the Torah, what's the point of the Story? For if Moses knew beforehand that Israel would break the Sinai Covenant and go into exile, and that is precisely what happens in the Former Prophets, then the Story could not have been written in an effort to encourage Israel's obedience. What's the point of the Hebrew Bible if Israel's disobedience and exile is assured? *We believe that the best answer to that question may be summed up in one word: "Messianism."* The Messiah, as we will see, is the point of the Story, and the Messiah of the Story becomes the "buzz" of Israel's later sacred writings (the Latter Prophets and the Writings). In the body of this chapter, we will have occasion to defend these two assertions.

---

[10] Tree of Life Version. All other quotations are from the Tree of Life Version unless stated otherwise. Personal changes to the TOL will be noted in italics.

Definition of Terms

Before we discuss the Messianism of the Hebrew Bible, it's necessary to define the terms "Messianism" and "Messiah" given the fact that these terms are not used in the Torah, and very infrequently in the Hebrew Bible for that matter, to describe the one about whom this chapter is written. The word messiah (*Mashiach*), "anointed one," is used 39 times in the Tanakh, and on some occasions, though rarely, it is used as a technical term to refer to the one whom the post-biblical writers called "the King-Messiah" (see for example Psalm 2:2; Dan 9:25–26).[11] In its non-technical sense, the term refers to the high priest (Lev 4:3), to kings (1 Sam 24:7), to prophets (Ps 105:15), and to Cyrus (Isa 45:1). In this chapter, I use "Messiah" as an all-inclusive term for the individual through whom God would ultimately reestablish His original purposes for His creation, a purpose that will be made clearer in the Last Days. At times, he is depicted as a king, other times as a prophet, and in some places as a priest. In some passages, he is described as a potentate, in others, a despised and rejected worm. In all cases, however, this multi-faceted figure is the lynchpin of God's plan to reestablish his blessed rule over a temporarily curse-ridden creation. "Messiah" in this article refers to the hero of this Story, and Messianism is a term used to highlight those features that are pertinent to His-Story.

Messianism in the Torah

The Creation Mandate as Plot

According to some Bible scholars, Messianism is a rather marginal topic in the Hebrew Bible.[12] In terms of counting heads, the seemingly limited number of overt Messianic prophecies[13] in the Hebrew Bible, particularly in the Torah, may cause intellectual dissonance with some rather clear statements in the New Testament about the centrality of the

---

[11] See Michael Rydelnik, *The Messianic Hope*, NAC Studies in Bible and Theology (Nashville: B&H, 2010), 2.

[12] See, for example, Gordon D. Fee and Douglas Stuart, *How to Read the Bible for All It's Worth* (Grand Rapids: Zondervan, 2003), 182; Grant R. Osborne, *The Hermeneutical Spiral*, revised (Downers Grove: IVPress, 2006), 264-65. In Osborne's words, "Fee and Stuart argue that less than 2 percent of the Old Testament prophecy is messianic, less than 5 percent relates to the new-covenant age and less than 1 percent concerns events still future to us.... Of course, this figure depends largely on exegetical decisions as to which so-called messianic prophecies were originally intended messianically. Nevertheless, the percentage either way would be relatively low."

[13] By overt, I mean those passages whose Messianism is grounded in the *peshat*, i.e., the grammatical-historical interpretation of the text (authorial intent).

Messiah in the Tanakh. For instance, Yeshua makes the following rather bold claim about the Torah: "Do not think that I will accuse you before the Father. The one who accuses you is Moses, in whom you have put your hope. For if you were believing Moses, you would believe Me—because he wrote about Me" (Jn 5:45–46). Other statements in the New Testament claim unreservedly that the Messiah is *a* central, if not *the* central theme of Moses and the Prophets.[14] As Messianic believers who accept the authority and veracity of the New Testament, we readily pay lip service to Yeshua's claims about the Torah, yet sadly many would likely be hard-pressed to defend those claims from the *Bema*[15] with just the *Chumash*[16] in hand. Does believing Moses really necessitate faith in Yeshua? In this section, we want to explore the claim that Messianism is a major theme in the Torah, and more, that it provides the foundation and the headwaters out of which Messianism flows to the rest of the Hebrew Bible.

If we seek to read the Torah according to its literary genre,[17] we would be wise to search for the key themes of the storyline – for the plot – in its opening chapters, given the fact that opening chapters in biblical literature, the Tanakh and New Testament alike, frequently introduce the key themes and ideas of the books as a whole.[18] As we shall see, Genesis 1:26-28 introduces the major themes that are developed in the remainder of the Torah:

> Then God said, "Let Us make man in Our image, after Our likeness! Let them rule over the fish of the sea, over the flying creatures of the sky, over the livestock, over the whole earth, and over every crawling creature that crawls on the land." God created humankind in His image, in the image of God He created him, male and female He created them. God blessed them and God said to them, "Be fruitful and multiply, fill the land, and conquer it. Rule over the fish of the sea, the flying creatures of the sky, and over every animal that crawls on the land." (Gen 1:26–28)

---

[14] See, for example, Luke 24:25–27, 44; John 1:45; Acts 3:18; 24:14; 26:22, 27; 28:23; Rev 19:10.

[15] Pulpit.

[16] Five books of Moses, or the Torah, which is in reality not five books, but one.

[17] Though the Torah contains many laws, genealogies, and poems, these have all been fitted into a chronologically continuous narrative framework.

[18] Patrick D. Miller, "The Beginning of the Psalter," in *The Shape and Shaping of the Psalter*, ed. J. Clinton McCann, JSOT Supp 159 (Sheffield: Sheffield Academic, 1993): 83, writes, "The beginning and end of a book are among the chief indicators of its subject matter."

There are two aspects of the creation account which break one or more of the features of the predictable literary patterns of the creation week (Gen 1:1–2:3). The typical pattern is as follows:

> "And God said" + "let there be" + "and there was morning, and there was evening, an X day."

The creation of humankind on the sixth day with divine deliberation, "Let Us make," and the seventh day lacking both divine speech and an end, clearly break the pattern. These disruptions of the pattern are intentional, drawing our attention to themes that will play an important role as the Torah's story continues to unfold. Given the fact that the Shabbat serves as the sign of the Sinai Covenant (Exod 31:12–17),[19] among other things, we should hardly be surprised to find it featured so prominently in creation. The broken pattern from "let it be" to "Let Us make" on the sixth day also draws the reader's attention to the theme of human rule over the land and everything in it, a very prominent feature of the creation mandate. A careful look at Gen 1:28 reveals three themes that are part and parcel of the promises contained in the Abrahamic Covenant. What is more, these three themes form the basis of God's dealings with, and purposes for, the people of Israel, namely; Blessing, Seed, and Dominion over the Land:

> God *blessed* them [BLESSING] and God said to them, "*Be fruitful and multiply* [SEED], *fill the land, and conquer it* [LAND[20]]. Rule over the fish of the sea, the flying creatures of the sky, and over every animal that crawls on the land." (Gen 1:28).

Two aspects of the creation mandate are directly tied to the Abrahamic Covenant, aspects which are generally masked by the English translations. First, the man and woman are called to exercise dominion[21] over the *eretz*, a word that may be translated as earth or land, depending on the context. When *eretz* is translated as "earth" one easily misses the

---

[19] The Hebrew Bible concludes by referencing the continual violation of the Land Sabbath as one of the primary reasons for Israel's exile to Babylon (2 Chron 36:21).

[20] The underlines and words in brackets added. True to the emphasis on the number seven in the creation account, "the land" is mentioned seven times in the creation mandate (Gen 1:26–30).

[21] The Hebrew word "rule" (*radah*) in Gen 1:26, 28, is not only used to describe Solomon's rule over the Promised Land (1 Kgs 5:4 [EVVs 4:24]), but also on several occasions to describe Messiah's rule over the entire earth (Num 24:10; Ps 72:8; 110:2).

fact that the creation mandate focuses on one of the three major components of God's threefold promise to Abraham, and to Israel, namely, the gift of the *eretz* (Land). Secondly, the creation mandate specifically includes a command to *kavash* the *eretz*. The typical translation, "subdue the earth" blurs the rather obvious connection to another key component of the Abrahamic Covenant, the conquest of the Promised Land (*kibbush ha'eretz*). Later on in the Torah and the Former Prophets, this phrase is used explicitly to refer to Israel's conquest of the Promised Land (Num 32:22, 29; Josh 18:1).

and the land [*eretz*] is subdued [*nikhbasha*] before ADONAI—then afterward, you may return and be free before ADONAI and Israel. Then this territory will be your possession before ADONAI. . . Moses said to them, "If the sons of Gad and Reuben cross over the Jordan with you, everyone armed for battle before ADONAI, when the land [*eretz*] is subdued [*nikhbasha*] before you, then give them the territory of Gilead as a possession. (Num 32:22, 29)	Then the whole congregation of *Bnei-Yisrael* assembled at Shiloh and set up the Tent of Meeting there, after the land [*eretz*] was now subdued [*nikhbasha*] before them. (Josh 18:1)[22]

What is more, this same verb is used of King David's conquest of the nations in 2 Sam 8:11, following on the heels of the making of the Davidic Covenant in 2 Sam 7.

In short, blessing, seed, and land,[23] all introduced in the very first chapter of the Torah, remain the central themes of the rest of the Hebrew Bible's Story from Genesis to 2 Kings. These themes also form the foundation for biblical eschatology. God's purpose in creation and in the election of Israel is to bless, to multiply, and to establish his rule over the Land through the seed of the woman (Gen 3:15).

When we look at the literary parallels between the creation mandate, the Abrahamic Promise-Covenant, and the calling of Israel, those who want to understand the Story as it relates to God's ultimate purpose for creation cannot ignore this trifold theme.

---

[22] Words in brackets added.
[23] Dietary restrictions in the creation mandate (Gen 1:29–30) also anticipate another theme in God's dealings with Israel (see Leviticus 11).

TORAH	
Creation	God blessed them [BLESSING] and God said to them, "Be fruitful and multiply, [SEED] fill the land, and conquer it. Rule [LAND DOMINION] over the fish of the sea, the flying creatures of the sky, and over every animal that crawls on the land." (Gen 1:28).
Noah	God blessed [BLESSING] Noah and his sons, and He said to them, "Be fruitful and multiply [SEED] and fill the land. The fear and terror of you will be on every wild animal, and on every flying creature of the sky, with everything that crawls on the ground and with all the fish of the sea—into your hand they are given. [LAND DOMINION].'" (Gen 9:1-2)
Patriarchs	Then ADONAI said to Abram, "Get going out from your land, and from your relatives, and from your father's house, to the land [LAND DOMINION] that I will show you. My heart's desire is to make you into a great nation, [SEED] to bless you, to make your name great so that you may be a blessing. I will bless those who bless you, [BLESSING] but whoever curses you I will curse, and in you all the families of the earth will be blessed." (Gen 12:1-3)
Israel	Yet Bnei-Yisrael were fruitful, increased abundantly, multiplied and grew extremely numerous—so the land was filled with them. [SEED] (Exod 1:7). God said to Balaam, "Do not go with them! Do not curse them, for they are blessed! [BLESSING]'" (Num 22:12). Moses said to them, "If the sons of Gad and Reuben cross over the Jordan with you, everyone armed for battle before ADONAI, when the land is subdued before you, [LAND DOMINION] then give them the territory of Gilead as a possession. (Num 32:29).
FORMER PROPHETS	
Joshua – 2 Kings	Then the whole congregation of Bnei-Yisrael assembled at Shiloh and set up the Tent of Meeting there, after the land was now subdued before them. [LAND DOMINION]" (Josh 18:1). When your days are done and you sleep with your fathers, I will raise up your seed, [SEED] who will come forth from you after you, and I will establish his kingdom. [LAND DOMINION]" (2 Sam 7:12).[24] Now Solomon ruled over all the kingdoms from the River to the land of the Philistines up to the border of Egypt [LAND DOMINION]. They brought tribute and served Solomon all the days of his life. . . For he had dominion over the entire region west of the River, from Tiphsah even to Gaza, over all the kings west of the River [LAND DOMINION]; and he had shalom on all sides around him. (1 Kings (5:1, 4; [EVVs 4:21, 24])[25] But King Solomon shall be blessed [BLESSING] and the throne of David established before ADONAI forever. [LAND DOMINION]" (1 Kings 2:45).[26]

[24] This clear allusion to Gen 15:4 here suggests that God's promise to David is directly related to the promises to Abraham with respect to the Seed.
[25] The wording of 1 Kings 5:1, 4 [4:21, 24 EVV] is remarkably similar to Gen 1:26–28. The author of Kings describes Solomon as fulfilling the creation mandate as a chosen seed who has dominion over the land.
[26] Words in brackets added.

Why did God create *adam* (humankind, male and female) in His image? He *blessed* them with the intent of establishing His *rule* over the *Land* and everything in it,[27] and it is only in light of this purpose that Messianism begins to make sense. And as we shall see, dominion over the Land is not only essential background knowledge for properly understanding Adam and Eve's encounter with the serpent in Genesis 3, but also the poetic pronouncement of its doom in Gen 3:15.

Adam as King-Priest, Adam as Israel

Having considered the creation mandate as the primary plot of the Story, we will now look more closely at Genesis 1– 3 in order to understand how these three themes converge in Adam and Eve; and how their story, in turn, anticipates Israel's story in terms of the reestablishment of God's creation purposes for humanity. We will also consider Israel as both a collective seed as well as an individual seed through whom the collective seed achieves its destiny.

Adam (male and female in the image of God) *is a king*. The terminology used to describe rule and dominion in the creation mandate is used elsewhere to describe the rule of kings, language that, "coincidentally," is also repeated in some well-known Messianic prophecies. The Hebrew word *radah* is the first of several dominion terms used in the creation mandate (Gen 1:26). "Then God said, 'Let Us make *adam* in Our image, after Our likeness! Let them rule [*radah*][28] over the fish of the sea, over the flying creatures of the sky, over the livestock, over the whole earth, and over every crawling creature that crawls on the land.'" This term is used to describe Solomon's rule over the Land in 1 Ki 5:4 [4:24 EVVs]. Remarkably, though not surprisingly, this verb also appears in three passages that are traditionally regarded as Messianic:

One from Jacob will rule [*radah*] and destroy the city's survivors. (Num 24:19)	May he have dominion [*radah*] from sea to sea, and from the River to the ends of the earth. (Psa 72:8[29])	ADONAI will extend your mighty rod from Zion: "Rule [*radah*] in the midst of your enemies". (Psa 110:2)

---

[27] This point is made quite evident in Psalm 8:5–9.

[28] The relationship of this waw+jussive to the previous cohorative ("Let Us make") suggests that its sense is telic, expressing the purpose for which God created *adam*: "in order to rule." See Joüon and Muraoka §116.116a; GKC §109f.

[29] See Zech 9:10b, another well-known Messianic prophecy whose words are nearly identical with Ps 72:8

God intends to establish his rule over creation through *adam* and his seed. *Adam is priest.* To appreciate Adam's priestly role, we must first recognize the extent to which Creation-Eden imagery permeates the Tabernacle. Scholars have long noted many thematic and verbal parallels[30] between the creation week and the Tabernacle Narrative (Exodus 25–31, 35–40),[31] some of which are worth noting here. First, as the creation week is divided into seven days (Gen 1:5, 8, 13, 19, 23, 31; 2:1), so the blueprints of the tabernacle are given in seven speeches (Exod 25:1; 30:11, 17, 22, 34; 31:1; 12), and in both cases, the seventh day and the seventh speech focus on the Sabbath. In the former, the Sabbath is the climax of creation, in the latter, the Sabbath is the sign of the covenant. Second, the creation and the construction of the tabernacle conclude with statements of completion (Gen 2:2; Exod 40:33b). Third, once creation/construction are completed, they are inspected (Gen 1:31a; Exod 39:43a). Fourth, the creation and tabernacle are blessed (Gen 1:22, 28; 2:3; Exod 39:43b). Fifth, "the Spirit" is vital to the creation/construction process in both (Gen 1:2; Exod 31:3; 35:31). Finally, the creation narrative and the tabernacle narrative both include accounts of a "fall" (Genesis 3; Exodus 32). In addition to these literary parallels, both accounts include a high degree of terminology unique to these narratives.[32]

---

[30] There is a great deal of shared language in the creation account and the Tabernacle Narrative, thus occasioning critical scholarships identification of both texts as being "priestly" (P).

[31] See, for example, Shimon Bakon, "Creation, Tabernacle and Sabbath." *Jewish Bible Quarterly* 25, no. 2 (April 1, 1997): 79-85; Eric E. Elnes, "Creation and Tabernacle: The Priestly Writer's "Environmentalism," *Horizons In Biblical Theology* 16, no. 2 (December 1, 1994): 144-155; Peter Enns, *Exodus*, NIV Application Commentary (Grand Rapids: Zondervan, 2000), 550-52; Michael A. Fishbane, *Biblical Text and Texture: A Literary Reading of Selected Texts* (Oxford: Oneworld, 1998), 12; Peter J. Kearney, "Creation and Liturgy: The P Redaction of Ex 25–40," *ZAW* 89 (1977): 375-87; Michael Morales, The Tabernacle Pre-Figured: Cosmic Mountain Ideology in Genesis and Exodus (Biblical Tools and Studies 15; Leuven/Paris/Walpole, MA: Peeters, 2012); Sailhamer, *The Pentateuch as Narrative* (Grand Rapids: Zondervan, 1992), 309; Daniel C. Timmer, *Creation, Tabernacle, and Sabbath: The Sabbath Frame of Exodus 31:12-17; 35:1-3 in Exegetical and Theological Perspective* (FRLANT, 227; Göttingen: Vandenhoeck & Ruprecht, 2009).

[32] The word for "lights" in Gen 1:14-16 are only used elsewhere in the Torah to describe the Menorah (Exod 25:6; 27:20; 35:8, 14, 28; 39:37; Lev 24:2; Num 4:9, 16). The process of "separation," so vital to creation (e.g., light from darkness, water from water, night and day) is also vital to the priestly legislation (Gen 1:4, 6–7, 14, 18; Exod 26:33; Lev 1:17; 5:8; 10:10; 11:47; 20:24–26; Num 8:14; 16:9, 21). The specific form of the verb for "yield seed" in Gen 1:11 is used elsewhere only in Lev 12:2. The distinction of the animals "according to their kind" in Genesis 1, 6–7, is elsewhere only used with respect to the classification of clean and unclean animals in the Torah (Gen 1:11–12, 21, 24–25; 6:20; 7:14; Lev 11:14–16, 19, 22, 29; Deut 14:13–15, 18). The Hebrew root for the word "expanse" is only used elsewhere in the Torah with respect to the tabernacle and its service (Gen 1:6–8, 14–15, 17, 20; Exod 39:3; Num 17:3–4). Finally, the focus on dietary provisions/restrictions in Gen 1:29-30 are essential to the Mosaic Law (see Leviticus 11; Deuteronomy 14).

Parallels between Creation and the Tabernacle[33]

	Creation	Tabernacle
Statement of Completion	God completed [*kalah*] — on the seventh day—His work [*malakha*] that He made. (Gen 2:2)	So Moses finished [*kalah*] the work [*malakha*]. (Exod 40:33b)
Inspection	So God saw [*v'yar*] everything [*et kol*] that He made, and behold [*hinneh*] it was very good. (Gen 1:31a)	When Moses saw [*v'yar*] the entire work [*et kol*], and that [*hinneh*] they had done it just as *ADONAI* had commanded (Exod 39:43a)
Benediction	And God blessed them [*v'yivarech otam*]. (Gen 1:22, 28; see 2:3)	And Moses blessed them [*v'yivarech otam*]." (Exod 39:43b)
Spirit of God	And the *Ruach Elohim* was hovering upon the surface of the water. (Gen 1:2)	and I have filled him with the Spirit of God [*Ruach Elohim*], with wisdom, understanding and knowledge in all kinds of craftsmanship (Exod 31:3)

In addition to the many parallels between creation and the tabernacle, there are also numerous links between the Garden of Eden and the Tabernacle.[34] First, we are told that God "walks" [*hithalekh*] in the midst of the Garden, the form of this verb with reference to God in the Torah is used to describe God's activity in the tabernacle (Gen 3:8; Lev 26:12; Deut 23:14). Second, God stations cherubim on the eastern entrance to the Garden, clearly parallel to the decorative cherubim whose presence on the veil guarded the eastern entrance into the Holy of Holies (Gen 2:24; Exod 26:31; Num 3:38). Third, the tree-like Menorah in the sanctuary is likely intended to be a replica of the Tree of Life in the midst of the Garden (Gen 2:9; Exod 25:32-36). Fourth, the precious metals that are mentioned in the Garden of Eden narrative are mentioned elsewhere in the Torah with reference to the precious metals used in the construction of the tabernacle (Gen 2:12; Exod 25:7; 28:9–14, 20; Num 11:7).[35]

---

[33] Postell, *Adam as Israel*, 111.

[34] For the classic treatment of the links between the Garden and the Tabernacle, see Gordon J. Wenham, "Sanctuary Symbolism in the Garden of Eden Story," in *I Studied Inscriptions before the Flood*, edited by Richard Hess and David Toshio Tsumura, 399–404, Sources for Biblical and Theological Study 4. Winona Lake, IN: Eisenbrauns, 1994. The following list of parallels draw heavily upon Wenham's work.

[35] It is clear enough that the prophets, by describing the future temple in terms of a renewed Eden, also regarded the Garden of Eden as the prototypical temple of creation from which all other sanctuaries were patterned (compare for instance, the river flowing out of Eden with the river flowing forth from the eschatological temple: Gen 2:10–14; Ezekiel 47).

Once we recognize that Eden is portrayed as the prototypical Creation-Sanctuary, Adam's role as the prototypical priest over all creation comes to light. First, we are told that Adam is placed in the Garden to work and to watch over it. This twofold commission over the Garden is, in fact, the same twofold commission given to the Levites, namely to work and watch over the tabernacle (Gen 2:15; Num 3:7–8).[36] Moreover, having sinned, God clothes [hilbish] Adam's nakedness with a tunic [kutonit], a phrase that is used most frequently in the Tanakh to describe the clothing of the priests in the tabernacle (Gen 3:21; Exod 29:7; 28:9-14, 20), which, significantly, was intended to cover their nakedness (Exod 28:40–43).

Adam was the prototypical high priest over all creation. All subsequent divinely ordained high priesthoods trace their origins back to Adam in the Garden. Aaron's annual task of passing beyond the images of the cherubim to the place where God walked with his people (Lev 16:2) served as a reminder of Adam's once privileged position in Eden before the Fall (see Gen 3:8, 24). The connection between Adam's original priesthood with the Aaronic high priesthood is most notably highlighted by the Prophet Ezekiel, who depicts the king of Tyre in the likeness of Adam in the Garden before his fall, adorned with all the stones upon the high priestly garments:

> You were in Eden, the garden of God. Every precious stone was your covering—ruby, topaz and diamond, beryl, onyx and jasper, sapphire, turquoise and emerald—your settings and your sockets a workmanship of gold— in the day you were created they were prepared. You were an anointed guardian *cheruv*. I placed you on the holy mountain of God. You walked among stones of fire. You were perfect in your ways from the day that you were created, until unrighteousness was found in you. (Ezek 28:13–15)[37]

---

[36] Schmutzer, Andrew J., "The Creation Mandate to 'be fruitful and multiply': A Crux of Thematic Repetition in Genesis 1–11," (PhD diss., Trinity Evangelical Divinity School, 2005), 348, writes, "Just as Eden is God's garden-sanctuary, the prototypical temple, so the terms 'keeping and guarding' . . . are used for priests who 'serve' God in the temple and 'guard' it from all unclean things."

[37] Though this passage has typically been understood as a reference to the fall of Satan, the depiction of this high priestly figure in Eden is more likely an allusion to Adam, given the fact that Genesis 2-3 portrays Adam, and not the serpent, as a priest. C. F. Keil and Delitzsch F., *Commentary on the Old Testament* (Accordance electronic ed. 10 vols.; Peabody: Hendrickson Publishers, 1996), n.p., write, "Ezekiel here compares the situation of the prince of Tyre with that of the first man in Paradise; and then, in vv. 15 and 16, draws a comparison between his fall and the fall of Adam." See Craigie, *Ezekiel*, 207; Taylor, *Ezekiel*, 196; Walther Zimmerli, Ezekiel 2: A Commentary on the Book of the Prophet Ezekiel, Chapters 25–48 (Hermeneia 26B; ed. Paul D. Hanson and Leonard Jay Greenspoon; trans. James D. Martin; Accordance electronic ed. Minneapolis: Fortress Press, 1983), 90-91.

Ezekiel's allusions to Eden are unmistakable. Significant, for our purposes, is the list of gemstones used to describe the covering. Note how these are the very stones that were used to adorn Israel's high priest (Exod 28:17–20; see also Rev 20:19–20).

What are we to make of the parallels between the creation narrative and the construction of the Tabernacle, and the Garden of Eden and the design of the Tabernacle itself? In a recent publication, Michael Morales looks at the lexical and thematic parallels between Genesis 1 – 3 and Israel's story in Exodus: from the parted seas (of creation/of the Exodus) to the Tabernacle of his presence (Eden/Tabernacle). [38] Morales highlights the parallels between the creation narrative with the construction of the Tabernacle (Gen 1:1–2:3; Exod 25–31, 35–40), and the priestly ministry of Adam in Eden with the priestly ministry of Aaron in the Tabernacle (Gen 2:4–3:34; Exod – Num). He argues, quite convincingly in my opinion, that the land in Gen 1:1–2:3 is depicted as the outer courtyard to a cosmic temple, with the Garden of Eden serving at its Holy of Holies (Gen 2:4ff.). [39] The effect of this depiction is rather straightforward: *God places Adam in the Garden Sanctuary as the high priest par-excellence; the High Priest in the Garden and King over all Creation. Adam's royal-priestly depiction clearly anticipates God's call on Israel collectively to be a royal priesthood (Exod 19:6), and God's call on Aaron individually to be the one who serves the God who walks with his people beyond the cherubim.* Mindful of this, we are now ready to consider the Royal-Priestly Adam as a prefiguration and sign of things to come (*ma'asei avot*), both in terms of *collective* Israel as well as a specially designated *individual* who will arise from Israel's midst.

---

[38] Michael Morales, The Tabernacle Pre-Figured: Cosmic Mountain Ideology in Genesis and Exodus (Biblical Tools and Studies 15; Leuven/Paris/Walpole, MA: Peeters, 2012), 51-120.
[39] Michael Morales, 73-90.

Adam's Story and Israel's Tale in Former Prophets

Israel's disobedience, according to the prophet Hosea, is in the likeness of Adam's disobedience. "But like Adam, they transgressed a covenant. There they dealt treacherously with Me." (Hos 6:7). Positively, *adam* (male and female) was blessed for the purpose of filling the *eretz* and conquering it (Gen 1:28). The author of the Torah, in describing Israel's phenomenal growth in the land of Egypt, draws a direct link to the creation mandate: "Yet Bnei-Yisrael [sons of Israel] *were fruitful, increased abundantly, multiplied and grew extremely numerous*—so *the land was filled with them*" (Exod 1:7).[40] It is clear enough that this growth can be none other than a result of God's promised *blessing* of Abraham's seed (cf. Exod 1:9; Gen 18:18; Num 22:6). It was in Egypt that God took a small family and turned them into a people. He created them to be a nation outside the Land, just has he created Adam outside the Garden, ultimately to then be brought into it. In fact, the term used for bringing or placing Adam in the Garden is specifically used in Deuteronomy and in Joshua to describe God's action of bringing Israel into the Promised Land.[41]

Then *ADONAI Elohim* took the man and GAVE HIM REST in the Garden of Eden in order to cultivate and watch over it. (Gen 2:15)	But when you cross over the Jordan and settle in the land that *ADONAI* your God enables you to inherit, and HE GIVES YOU REST from all your enemies around you, you will dwell in safety. (Deut 12:10; see 3:20; 25:19)	So now *ADONAI* your GOD HAS GIVEN REST to your kinsmen, as He said to them. So now, turn and go to your tents, to the land that is your possession, which Moses the servant of *ADONAI* gave you beyond the Jordan. (Josh 22:4; see 1:13, 15; 23:1)[42]

Adam was tasked with conquering the land which God specially prepared for him (Gen 1:28; 2:8-14). Though modern commentators

---

[40] Words in brackets and italicizes added.
[41] The geographical location of the Garden, like the Promised Land, is marked by the rivers surrounding it (Gen 2:10–14; 15:18).
[42] Emphasis added (all caps).

tend to downplay this militaristic term,[43] it is a term strategically chosen for the immediate context and as well as the larger one. In its immediate context, the word aptly describes what Adam is supposed to do with the rebellious serpent when God brings him into the Garden: he is to conquer it. Here we find vital clues for Israel's task in God's redemptive purposes. Although God promised to give the Land to Abraham and to his seed, it was Israel's task, like Adam's, to conquer this Land by subduing its rebellious inhabitants, the Canaanites.[44] Thus, the book of Joshua describes the initial fulfillment of Adam's unfulfilled task: the conquering of the Land and its rebellious inhabitants.

God blessed them and God said to them, "Be fruitful and multiply, FILL THE LAND, AND CONQUER IT. RULE OVER the fish of the sea, the flying creatures of the sky, and over every animal that crawls on the land." (Gen 1:28)	Then the whole congregation of *Bnei-Yisrael* assembled at Shiloh and set up the Tent of Meeting there, after the land was now SUBDUED before them. (Josh 18:1)[45]

It is likely not a coincidence that the term used for *conquering* in the creation mandate is later used to describe King David's subjugation of the nations; and the terms for *ruling* over creation and its animals are used to describe King Solomon's rule. Adam's mandate, and subsequently Israel's, is accomplished vicariously through Israel's reigning king (as can also be seen in Psalm 8).

God blessed them	These too King	Now Solomon	what is man, that

---

[43] See Kenneth A. Matthews, Genesis 1:1-11:26 (NAC 1A; ed. E. Ray Clendenen; Accordance electronic ed. Nashville: Broadman & Holman Publishers, 1996), 175; Gordon J. Wenham, Genesis 1-15 (WBC 1; Accordance/Thomas Nelson electronic ed. Waco: Word Books, 1987), 33. Ramban explains the word *kabash* as follows: "He gave them power and dominion on the earth to do according to their will with the cattle and with the creeping things and with all things that crawl on the dust, and to build, and to uproot what is planted, and to mine bronze from its mountains, etc." (translation from Hebrew my own). Similarly, the *NET Bible Notes* (W. Hall Harris, ed.: 1st, Accordance electronic ed. Richardson: Biblical Studies Press, 2005), n.p., write, "Elsewhere the Hebrew verb translated 'subdue' means 'to enslave' (2 Chr 28:10; Neh 5:5; Jer 34:11, 16), 'to conquer,' (Num 32:22, 29; Josh 18:1; 2 Sam 8:11; 1 Chr 22:18; Zech 9:13; and probably Mic 7:19), and 'to assault sexually' (Esth 7:8). None of these nuances adequately meets the demands of this context, for humankind is not viewed as having an adversarial relationship with the world. The general meaning of the verb appears to be 'to bring under one's control for one's advantage.' In Gen 1:28 one might paraphrase it as follows: 'harness its potential and use its resources for your benefit.' In an ancient Israelite context this would suggest cultivating its fields, mining its mineral riches, using its trees for construction, and domesticating its animals."

[44] Several parallels between the Noah's fall (planting a vineyard – taking of fruit of vineyard – nakedness and covering –curse upon Canaan) in Gen 9:21–27 with Adam's fall (planting of a Garden – taking of fruit of the garden - nakedness and covering – curse upon the serpent) in Gen 2:4– 3:34 strongly suggest an intentional link between the cursed serpent and the cursed Canaan. Canaan in the Promised Land is thus portrayed as an offspring of the serpent in the Garden who must ultimately be subjugated (cf. Gen 3:15; 9:25–26; 10:15–19).

[45] Emphasis added (all caps).

| and God said to them, "Be fruitful and multiply, fill the land, and CONQUER it. RULE over the FISH OF THE SEA, the FLYING CREATURES OF THE SKY, and over EVERY animal that CRAWLS on the LAND." (Gen 1:28) | David consecrated to *ADONAI*, along with the silver and gold that he had consecrated from all the nations that he had SUBDUED. (2 Sam 8:11) | ruled over all the kingdoms from the River to the land of the Philistines up to the border of Egypt. They brought tribute and served Solomon all the days of his life. . . FOR HE HAD DOMINION OVER THE ENTIRE REGION west of the River, from Tiphsah even to Gaza, over all the kings west of the River; and he had *shalom* on all sides around him. . . . He also spoke about TREES, from the cedar in Lebanon to the hyssop that grows out of the wall, and he spoke about BEASTS, BIRDS, CREEPING THINGS and FISH. (1 Kings 5:1, 4, 13 [EVVs 4:21, 24, 33]) | You are mindful of him? and the son of man, that You care for him? Yet You made him a little lower than the angels, and crowned him with glory and majesty! You gave him dominion over the works of Your hands. You put ALL THINGS under their feet: all SHEEP AND OXEN, and also BEASTS OF THE FIELD, BIRDS IN THE AIR, AND FISH IN THE OCEAN— all passing through the paths of the seas. (Ps 8:5-9 [EVVs 4–8])[46] |

Adam's continued habitation of the Garden was contingent upon obedience to God's commandments. Obedience meant life in the Garden, disobedience meant death in exile (Gen 2:16–17; 3:19, 23–24). Likewise, Israel's habitation of the Promised Land was contingent upon obedience to God's commandments. Obedience meant life in the Land,

---

[46] Emphases provided (all caps).

disobedience meant death in exile (Deut 30:15-20).[47] Once Adam is brought into the Land, however, the mandate to conquer the Land and rule over its inhabitants, and the commandment to choose life rather than death, are thwarted by an inhabitant of the Garden who is described as more *clever* (*arum*)[48] than the other creatures of creation (Gen 3:1). The serpent's rebellion results in his being cursed (Gen 3:14). Adam and Eve quickly succumb to the tempter's enticements. Likewise, Israel's initially successful military campaign to conquer the Land and its inhabitants is quickly undermined by very *clever*[49] yet subsequently cursed inhabitants.

But the serpent was more CLEVER [*'ārûm*] than any animal of the field that *ADONAI Elohim* made. (Gen 3:1) *ADONAI Elohim* said to the serpent, "Because you did this, CURSED ARE YOU above all the livestock and above every animal of the field. On your belly will you go, and dust will you eat all the days of your life". (Gen 3:14)	But when the inhabitants of Gibeon heard what Joshua had done to Jericho and Ai, they acted CRAFTILY [*b^e'ormāh*]. They went and traveled as ambassadors, took worn-out sacks for their donkeys and worn-out wine skins, cracked and patched up. (Josh 9:3–4) Now therefore, YOU ARE CURSED, and you will never cease to be servants, wood-choppers and water-carriers for the House of my God. (Josh 9:23)[50]

[47] The terminology used to describe Israel's choices and the consequences of disobedience in Deuteronomy 30:15–20 is an intentional allusion to Adam's choices and the consequences of disobedience in Genesis 2–3: Life and death, good and evil, blessing and curse.

[48] Though the word *'ārûm* is typically translated "crafty" (negatively), there are several reasons why I believe that "clever" (in a positive sense) is a far better translation. First, a homonym of the word used to describe the serpent in 3:1 is used positively to describe the nakedness of the man and the woman in 2:25: "the two of them were naked [*'^arûmmîm*]." By virtue of this juxtaposition, one would expect a positive meaning in 3:1. Second, the author uses a Hebrew word play to describe a reversal in the man and woman's condition before and after the fall. Before the fall, the man and the woman are described as *'^arûmmîm* [naked] and unashamed (2:25). After the fall, however, they are described *'ērummim* [a term used elsewhere in Deut 28:48 to describe Israel's pathetic condition under the curses of the law] and ashamed (3:7). Rashi perceptively notes a similar word play contrasting the serpent's condition before and after the fall. Whereas the serpent is described as " *'ārûm* more than all the beasts of the field" before the fall (3:1), it becomes " *'ārûr* [cursed] more than all the beasts of the field" after the fall (3:14). This word play strongly suggests that the description of the serpent should be understood positively in 3:1 (i.e., clever to cursed). Third, the word used to describe the serpent in 3:1 is used positively throughout the book of Proverbs (Prov 12:16, 23; 13:16; 14:8, 15, 18; 22:3; 27:12), notable for its other clear allusions to the Garden of Eden Narrative (see for example, Gen 2:9; 3:22, 24; Prov 3:18; 11:30; 13:12; 15:4). Fourth, early on in the history of interpretation, the description of the serpent in 3:1 was taken positively (see Gen 3:1 LXX; Matt 10:16). This cumulative evidence not only favors a positive interpretation of *'ārûm* in 3:1, but also suggests that Satan, like the man and the woman, also fell in Genesis 3.

[49] The fact that this word is used only rarely in the Primary History (Genesis–2 Kings) suggests that it has been purposefully employed in Joshua 9 to allude to the serpent (see Gen 3:1; Ex 21:14; Josh 9:4; 1 Sam 23:22).

[50] Emphases provided (all caps); transliterated Hebrew terms in brackets provided (it's important to note that these Hebrew words share the same Hebrew root).

The result of Joshua's covenant with these native inhabitants was the descent into apostasy as Israel turned to their gods. Subsequent exile from the Promised Land as punishment was their just deserve.[51] Thus Joshua, like Moses before him, could say with assurance that Israel would break the covenant by serving other gods, given the ongoing presence of the Canaanites in the Land (cf. Josh 23:15-16; Deut 31:16–21). Given these clear predictions in the Torah and in Joshua, we can expect to read in Judges about the terrible dangers awaiting Israel because of the continued presence of the Canaanites:

> Now the angel of *ADONAI* came up from Gilgal to Bochim, and He said, "I brought you up out of Egypt and took you into the land which I swore to your fathers. I also said, 'I will never break My covenant with you. Now as for you, you must make no covenant with the inhabitants of this land. You must break down their altars.' But you have not listened to My voice. What is this you have done? Therefore I also said, 'I will not drive them out from before you, but they will be thorns in your sides, and their gods will be a snare to you.' (Judg 2:1–3)

Returning to the story of Adam and Eve, we read that their disobedience resulted in their being cast out of the Garden, eastward, where they eventually died in exile (Gen 3:23–24; 5:5). Adam's children continued their easterly exilic direction, further and further away from the special Garden-Land, until they eventually find themselves in Babylon, the good guys with the bad guys (Gen 11:1–9). It is out of Babylon that God brings forth an individual seed – a descendent of Adam and Eve, of Seth, of Noah, and of Shem – back to the Garden-Land in order to conquer it, to rule over it and to reestablish the blessing which was so tragically lost through Adam's fall (Gen 11:10–12:9). In short, God chooses Abram and calls him from the east to restore His blessed rule over creation, through the seed of the woman. Are you noticing a story-line with all this?

Israel's story in the Former Prophets follows along these predictable lines. Though God chooses an individual dynasty of kings, through whom Israel will ultimately fulfill Adam's calling (the dynasty of

---

[51] The numerous references to the commands of Deut 7:1-4 (not to make a covenant with the Canaanites lest they tempt Israel to follow other gods) in Joshua 9 (see vv. 15, 24), strongly suggest that the author sees Joshua's covenant with the Gibeonites as the beginning of the end of Israel's successful campaign to conquer the Promised Land; and more importantly, to fulfill the creation mandate in Adam's stead (see Deut 11:16).

David), its fulfillment was not to be realized before Israel's foreseen covenant disobedience and subsequent exile to Babylon of all places (2 Kgs 25; see Deut 4:26–30). Here we see that the concluding verses of the Former Prophets serve as the sign to which the deeds of the fathers *(ma'asei avot)* in Genesis 1–11 pointed. Just as Adam's disobedience brought him and his descendants eastward to Babylon (Gen 11:1–9), so Israel's disobedience brought her and her descendants to eastward to Babylon (2 Ki 25). What is more, just as the tale of the "first Babylonian Exile" in Genesis 11 concludes on a hopeful focus on an individual seed (Abraham), through whom God would reestablish his creation purposes, likewise the telling of the "second Babylonian Exile" concludes with a hopeful focus on an individual seed (Jehoiachin) through whom God would ultimately reestablish His creation purposes:

Then *ADONAI* said to Abram, "Get going out from your land, and from your relatives, and from your father's house, to the land that I will show you. My heart's desire is to make you into a great nation, to bless you, to make your name great so that you may be a blessing. I will bless those who bless you, but whoever curses you I will curse, and in you all the families of the earth will be blessed." (Gen 12:1–3)	Now it came to pass in the 30-seventh year of the exile of King Jehoiachin of Judah, on the twenty-seventh day of the twelfth month, that King Evil-merodach of Babylon, in the year he became king, released King Jehoiachin of Judah from prison. He spoke kindly to him and set his throne above the throne of the other kings who were with him in Babylon. So he changed his prison garments, and regularly ate bread in the king's presence all the days of his life. As for his allowance, a regular allowance was granted to him by the king, an allotment for each day, all the days of his life. (2 Ki 25:27–30)

Adam's Story and the Messiah-King in the Torah's Poems

So, then, the Story is set in such a way that Israel's plight was entirely predictable. Adam sinned, was judged and cast out of Eden. Israel's collective failure later, under the Sinai Covenant, likewise resulted in punishment for disobedience and exile to the east. So much for the bad news. Similarly, it is prophetically anticipated that Israel's ultimate fulfillment of the creation mandate would be ultimately fulfilled through the coming of an individual king from the Tribe of Judah. In his groundbreaking work on the Deuteronomic History (Deuteronomy–2

Kings), Martin Noth pointed out one of the key literary devices by which the author interprets Israel's story, namely, through large speeches.[52] John Sailhamer, likewise, highlighted the significance of large speeches in the Torah's narrative, speeches that are poetic in genre[53] and appear in major junctions of the Torah Story.[54]

Poetic Speeches in the Torah Story[55]

Primeval History	Patriarchal History0	Story of the Exodus	Wilderness Journey to Sinai	Israel's Sojourn at Mount Sinai	Wilderness Journey to Promised Land	New Generation	Exposition of Torah on Border of Promised Land
Gen 1-11	Gen 12-5	Ex 1-14	Ex 15-18	Ex 19-Nm 10	Nm 10-25	Nm 26-36	Deuteronomy
Gn 3:14-		Gn 49	Ex 15				Nm 23 – 24

The common language and repeated themes shared by most if not all the poetic speeches in the Torah suggest that these poems do in fact provide both literary and theological cohesiveness to the story as a whole. Significantly, three of the four[56] largest poetic speeches found in the Torah are identified as events that will take place in the last days.

---

[52] "To assess the work as a whole, it is more important to notice certain aspects of the arrangement of the books Joshua - Kings which can be traced back to the work of Dtr. In particular, at all the important points in the course of the history, Dtr. brings forward the leading personages with a speech, long or short, which looks forward and backward in an attempt to interpret the course of events, and draws the relevant practical conclusions about what people should do." Martin Noth, *The Deuteronomistic History* (1981) p. 5

By saying that the speeches are a "literary device" we are by no means denying the historicity of these speeches. Rather, I am suggesting that the location of these speeches in key moments in Israel's history as told in the Former Prophets and the common-repeated themes contained therein strongly suggest that these speeches not only bring connectivity to Israel's history but also sense and meaning.

[53] Poetry in the Hebrew Bible is noted for its abundance of metaphors and similes, tersity, parallelism, and lack of the direct object marker.

[54] Sailhamer, *Pentateuch as Narrative*, 36, writes, "At three macrostructural junctures in the Pentateuch, the author has spliced a major poetic discourse onto the end of a large unit of narrative (Ge 49; Nu 24; Dt 31). A close look at the material lying between and connecting the narrative and poetic sections reveals the presence of a homogeneous compositional stratum. It is most noticeably marked by the recurrence of the same terminology and narrative motifs. In each of the three segments, the central figure (Jacob, Balaam, Moses) calls an audience together (imperative: Ge 49:1; Nu 24:14; Dt 31:28) and proclaims (cohortative: Ge 49:1; Nu 24:14; Dt 31:28) what will happen (Ge 49:1; Nu 24:14; Dt 31:29) in 'the end of days' (Ge 49:1; Nu 24:14; Dt 31:29)."

[55] Other poetic speeches not in this chart include Gen 2:23; 9:25-27; 12:1-3; 24:60; 27:28-29; Num 21:17–18, 27–30.

[56] The fourth poem is found in Exod 15:1-21, and is known as the Song at the Sea.

| Jacob called his sons and said to them: Gather together so that I can tell you what will happen to you in THE LAST DAYS. (Gen 49:1) | Now, behold, I am going back to my people. Come, let me counsel you what these people will do to your people in THE *LAST* DAYS. (Num 24:14) | For I know that after my death you will certainly act corruptly and turn aside from the way I have commanded you. So evil will fall upon you in THE *LAST* DAYS. . . (Deut 31:29)[57] |

For our purposes, we will discuss three significant poetic speeches in the Torah and their importance, not only for one's understanding of the theology of the Torah in general, but also in terms of the Messianism of the Hebrew Bible, in particular: Gen 3:14–19; 49:1–28; Num 24:1–24.

Genesis 3 and the Beginning of Days

In order to appreciate Genesis 3 in general and Gen 3:14–19 in particular, it is important to recall that Adam, who is portrayed as God's son,[58] is mandated by God to conquer the land and to rule over all its creatures. Given the fact that the Torah Story begins with "the beginning" of days, Adam's story in effect tells of humanity's first "king;" the king whose rule began in *the beginning of days*, who was tempted by the serpent, and who thereby failed to conquer the land and rule over it. He forfeited this divinely ordained rule over the land, was cast into exile, and by virtue of his banishment from the Garden-Sanctuary, lost his priesthood. It is only from the frame of reference of Adam's royal-priestly calling over creation that God's calling to Israel at Mount Sinai makes sense: "And you shall be to Me a *kingdom* of *priests* and a holy nation..." (Exod 19:6). In Gen 3:14–19, God not only pronounces judgment upon the serpent, the woman, and the man, but therein also He lays out (in intentionally ambiguous terms[59]) His plan to eventually restore the kingship and the priesthood to humanity. God intends to reestablish His dominion over creation through the Seed of the woman!

---

[57] Emphasis added (all caps); words in italicizes reflect changes I have made to the Bible (in both cases I have changed "later" to "last" in order to point out the fact that the Hebrew phrase in each of these poems is exactly the same).

[58] God, by virtue of his place at the head of the list of Adam's genealogies, implicitly portrays Adam as the son of God through whom God intends to rule over creation (see Gen 5:1-4). If Adam is Seth's father, and Seth is Enosh's father, who is Adam's father? The answer is clearly – God!

[59] Sailhamer, *Genesis* (EBC 2; ed. Frank E. Gaebelein and J. D. Douglas; Accordance electronic ed. Grand Rapids: Zondervan, 1990), n.p., commenting on Gen 3:15, writes, "Verse 15 still contains a puzzling yet important ambiguity: Who is the 'seed' of the woman? It seems obvious that the purpose of his verse has not been to answer that question but rather to raise it. The remainder of the book is the author's answer."

ADONAI Elohim said to the serpent, "Because you did this, Cursed are you above all the livestock and above every animal of the field. On your belly will you go, and dust will you eat all the days of your life. I will put animosity between you and the woman— between your seed and her seed. He will crush your head, and you will crush his heel." (Gen 3:14–15)

In our attempts to understand this text, particularly in terms of Messianism, it is necessary to answer three important questions:

1. Is the serpent just a garden-variety reptile?

2. Is the seed of the woman a reference to a collective entity (Israel) or an individual (the Messiah)?

3. Who receives the more deadly blow, the seed of the woman or the serpent?

Is the serpent just a garden-variety reptile? Although the Torah, or the whole Hebrew Bible for that matter, never identifies the serpent as the devil,[60] the text clearly portrays the serpent as unique among all His other created beings (with the exception of humans of course). The serpent is cleverer than all other beasts of the field, the evidence of which is demonstrated in its ability to talk, to reason, and even to oppose God's word. Moreover, though it's clear enough from the text that the serpent's rebellion results in ongoing battles between the serpent's seed and the woman's seed, the war will not come to an end until the serpent itself is dealt with. In other words, the text suggests that the serpent outlives its seed. We believe the NT writers were quite justified in identifying the serpent as humanity's archenemy, the devil.

Is the seed of the woman a reference to a collective entity (Israel) or an individual (Messiah)? In order to interpret this text, it is crucial to note the use of the word seed is intentionally ambiguous in this passage. In the Hebrew language, "seed" can be interpreted as a collective (descendants), but it can also be interpreted as an individual (descendant). In other words, *Gen 3:15 forces a strategically important question upon its readers, the answer to which must be found by carefully reading the rest of the Torah Story.* Is the seed who will crush the serpent's head a collective group of people (Israel), or is the seed of

---

[60] The New Testament, however, does in fact identify the serpent as the devil (Rev 12:9; 20:2; Rom 16:20 is very likely an allusion to Gen 3:15).

the woman an individual?[61] To answer this question, we must consider this passage syntactically and contextually. Jack Collins, in his careful study on the syntactical distinctions between the collective and individual use of the term "seed,"[62] concluded that pronouns are crucial in determining whether seed is collective or singular. Whenever seed refers to a collective entity, the pronouns referring to the seed are always plural. For instance, we read in Gen 15:13: "God said to Abram, 'Know for certain that your *seed* will be strangers in a land that is not *theirs* [plural pronoun], and they will enslave *them* [plural pronoun] and afflict *them* [plural pronoun] for four hundred years.'"[63] When seed, according to Collins, refers to an individual, its pronouns are always singular. One example will suffice. "And of the son of the maid I will make a nation also, because *he* [singular pronoun] is your *seed*" (Gen 21:13).[64] Here, seed clearly refers to Ishmael, and thus the singular pronoun "he" is used. Such is the case in Gen 3:15 as well: "And I will put enmity between you and the woman, and between your seed and her *seed*; he [singular pronoun] shall bruise you on the head, and you shall bruise *Him* [singular pronoun] on the heel."

Though Collins syntactical conclusions have been generally accepted,[65] they are not entirely conclusive. Particularly problematic to his theory is Gen 22:17–18: "Indeed I will greatly bless you, and I will greatly multiply your *seed* as the stars of the heavens and as the sand which is on the seashore; and your *seed* shall possess the gate of his [singular pronoun] enemies. In your *seed* all the nations of the earth shall be blessed, because you have obeyed my voice." Here we see the word seed is used three times, the first of which is unambiguously plural: "seed as the stars of the heavens." The second time seed appears, however, it is used with a singular pronoun: "And your *seed* shall possess the gates of *his* [singular] enemies." We are faced with an

---

[61] See, R. A. Martin, "The Earliest Messianic Interpretation of Genesis 3:15," JBL 84 (1965): 525-27, who argues that the LXX offers the earliest Messianic interpretation of Gen 3:15, by virtue of the translators use of the masculine pronoun "he" to modify the neuter noun "seed."

[62] Jack Collins, "A Syntactical Note (Genesis 3:15): Is the Woman's Seed Singular or Plural," *TynB* 48.1 (1997):139-49.

[63] Other examples of the word seed used with plural pronouns include Gen 17:7–10; 48:11–12.

[64] Other examples include 1 Sam 1:11; 2 Sam 7:12–15.

[65] See, for example, T. Desmond Alexander, "Further Observations on the Term 'Seed' in Genesis," TynB 48.2 (1997): 363-67; Rydelnik, *Messianic Hope*, 140. Chee-Chiew Lee, *The Blessing of Abraham, the Spirit, & Justification in Galatians* (Eugene, OR: Pickwick, 2013), 80; James M. Hamilton, Jr., *God's Glory in Salvation Through Judgment: A Biblical Theology* (Wheaton, Il.: Crossway, 2010) , 76; Jason C. Meyer, *The End of the Law: Mosaic Covenant in Pauline Theology*, NAC Studies in Bible & Theology, ed., E. Ray Clendenen (Nashville: B&H, 2009), 145.

exegetical-syntactical challenge. Does the first use of seed, which is clearly collective, determine the meaning of the second use of seed ("your *seed* shall possess that gate of *their* [singular pronoun with a collective meaning] enemies)? Or can we say that Collins' conclusions are valid, and thus interpret the second use of seed with reference to a single seed of Abraham: "your *seed* shall possess the gate of *his* [singular pronoun with singular meaning] enemies." And if that is the case, then the third use of seed in verse 18 ("in your seed all the nations of the earth shall be blessed") also refers to a single individual through whom the nations will find blessing.

As important as Collins' work may be we are forced to ask ourselves: Could Gen 22:17–18 be the exception that disproves the rule? Thankfully, there is evidence elsewhere in the Hebrew Bible that lends strong support to interpreting this verse in light of Collins' findings.

Psalm 72 is a structurally significant Psalm in the Psalter, serving as a conclusion to Books I and II of the Psalter. [66] Psalm 72 shares significant parallels with Psalm 2, a psalm which is formally recognized by many scholars, along with Psalm 1, as the introduction to Book I. [67] Psalm 2 and 72 focus on an exalted Davidic king whose rule extends to the ends of the earth (Ps 2:8; 72:8). What is more, Psalm 72 contains several allusions to some of the Torah's poetic speeches, [68] suggesting that its author looked to this King-Messiah, as one through whom the Torah's key prophecies would find fulfillment. Helpfully, Psalm 72:9 and 17 offer an inner-biblical interpretation of Gen 22:17-18 with respect to the identity of the seed:

Let desert dwellers bow before him, and his ENEMIES LICK THE DUST. . . May his name endure forever. May his name increase before the sun, and MAY ALL NATIONS BE BLESSED BY HIM and call him blessed. (Ps 72:9, 17)	I will richly bless you and bountifully multiply your seed like the stars of heaven, and like the sand that is on the seashore, and your seed will POSSESS THE GATE OF HIS ENEMIES. IN YOUR SEED ALL THE NATIONS OF THE EARTH WILL BE BLESSED. . . Gen 22:17-18)[69]

---

[66] Book I (Ps 1–41), Book II (42–72).

[67] See, for example, Robert L. Cole, *Psalms 1–2: Gateway to the Psalter* (Sheffiled, UK: Sheffield Phoenix Press, 2012); J. Clinton McCann, Jr., *A Theological Introduction to the Book of Psalms: The Psalms as Torah* (Nashville: Abingdon, 1993), 41.

[68] Compare Ps 72:8 with Num 24:19 and Zech 9:10–11, Ps 72:9 with Gen 3:14, and Ps 72:11 with Gen 27:29.

[69] Emphases provided (all caps).

Though some might argue against Ps 72:9 being an allusion to the possession of the enemy's gates in Gen 22:17 (but see Gen 3:14), it is quite clear that Ps 72:17 is a nearly verbatim allusion to Gen 22:18. It is clear enough that the author of this Psalm interprets the seed through whom all that nations will be blessed in Gen 22:18 as an *individual king.* It is difficult to understand how the author could have reached such an interpretive conclusion were he not to understand the previous verse, "your seed shall possess the gates of his enemies," as also referring to an individual seed of Abraham who would defeat his enemies. In brief, the inner-biblical interpretation of Gen 22:17-18 supports Collins' syntactical conclusions about the semantics of seed in Gen 3:15. We are forced to the conclusion that the seed of the woman is an individual, and that an individual "will crush your head," the serpent's head, that is.

Moving on to some contextual considerations regarding the identity of the meaning of seed in Gen 3:15, we are reminded of the popular saying: "The best commentary on Scripture is Scripture." Yet again, the meaning of seed in Gen 3:15 finds an interpretation in the immediate context. Before looking at this interpretation, however, we should consider the referent of the serpent's seed in the immediate context as well. Who or what is the serpent's seed? Several clues in the storyline of the Torah suggest that the serpent's seed does not refer to baby snakes, but rather to opponents to the chosen seed of the woman. For example, we read in the very next chapter of Cain, who, after opposing Abel, finds himself cursed (cf. Gen 4:11; 3:14). Likewise, Ham's perverted actions result in his son's sharing of the serpent's fate as well: "Cursed is Canaan" (Gen 9:25). Later on in Gen 12:3, we are told that all who curse Abraham (and his seed) will also share the serpent's fate: "And the one who curses you, I shall curse!" According to the Torah's storyline, therefore, the serpent's seed are those who curse the chosen seed, and thus share the serpent's fate.

So how is the seed of the woman understood in the text that follows? In the very next chapter, Adam's firstborn son kills Abel, and in response, God gives Eve another seed. Remarkably, Eve's commentary on God's provision uses terminology elsewhere in the entire Hebrew Bible only found in Gen 3:15.

Adam was intimate with his WIFE [woman] again, and she gave birth to a son and she named him Seth, "For God HAS APPOINTED me another SEED in place of Abel—since Cain killed him." (Gen 4:25)	I WILL PUT animosity between you and the WOMAN— between your seed and her SEED. He will crush your head, and you will crush his heel. (Gen 3:15)[70]

It is essential to note that the word wife in Gen 4:25 is the same word for woman in Gen 3:15. Moreover, Eve's statement "God has appointed" uses the same verb for "put" in Gen 3:15: "I will *put* enmity." Finally, Eve states that God has appointed her another "seed." Eve's allusions to Gen 3:15 in Gen 4:25 are quite clear in the Hebrew text. And it is quite clear that Eve has interpreted the reference to "her seed" in Gen 3:15, not in its collective sense, but with respect to an individual son who would defeat the serpent.

Who receives the more deadly blow, the seed of the woman or the serpent? For many people, the answer to this question is so clear that the question itself is not worth the asking. The truth be told, however, the question is a trap. The answer to the question is not either/or but both/and. Some might protest: "Wait a minute; a blow to the head is far more severe than a blow to the foot." That might be true enough if we are speaking of man versus man. But we are not. This is man versus serpent. When a man wants to kill a serpent, of course he goes for the head. But when a serpent wants to kill a man, he strikes at the foot, the truth of which is made abundantly clear in Gen 49:17: "Let Dan be a serpent beside a road, a viper beside a path, who strikes a horse's heels, so that its rider falls backward." Strangely enough, *God's judgment against the serpent includes a prediction that the seed of the woman shall also suffer a fatal blow.* Does this mean, however, that the Torah Story ends in tragedy: Nobody wins; everyone loses? Or does this mean that ultimate victory over the serpent will be achieved, but at great expense? As we look at the two other poetic speeches regarding the last days in the Torah, Genesis 49 and Numbers 24, we will see that the Torah Story is what the Greeks would call a comedy, that is, a story with

---

[70] Emphases provided; words in brackets provided.

a happy ending.[71] Returning to the Hebrew world, Gen 3:15 not only prepares the reader for predictions of the glories of the coming Messiah-King, but *the text also paves the way for appreciating the sufferings of the coming Messiah-King.* God's purposes in Gen 1:28 will come to fruition, but the reclamation of creation includes great suffering.

In summary, we see that in a very real sense, Gen 3:15 is the fountainhead of Messianism. Though, according to the textual narrative, Adam abdicated both his kingship and his priesthood over creation, and though collective Israel will be like Adam, *Gen 3:15 anticipates the coming of an individual seed of woman, a priest-king, another Adam, who will ultimately defeat the serpent and his descendants, though not without a terrible struggle.* In order to more fully appreciate the meaning of Gen 3:15, we must briefly consider the story of Noah, another Adam-like person, a king-priest, a man who is called to reestablish God's creation purposes.

That the Torah's author sees the seed of the woman as a future Adam-like figure is evident in his presentation of Noah. This is most evident in the occasion by which Noah ("rest" in Hebrew) is given his name. "And he named him Noah [rest] saying, 'This one will comfort[72] us from our work and from the pain of our hands because of the ground which ADONAI cursed.'"[73] The clear allusions to the poetic speech Gen 3:14-19, particularly to Gen 3:17-19, suggests that Noah is portrayed as a seed of the woman who will, at least in a limited sense, restore the creation to its pre-fall conditions. How will Noah, Mr. *Rest*, bring *rest* to creation? We will have occasion to answer this question in a moment.

---

[71] For an interesting analyses on reading the Bible in terms of tragedy/comedy, see Norman K. Gottwald, "Tragedy and Comedy in the Latter Prophets," *Semeia* no. 32 (January 1, 1984): 83-96; Martin J. Buss, "Tragedy and Comedy in Hosea," Semeia no. 32 (January 1, 1984): 71-82; David M. Gunn, "The Anatomy of Divine Comedy: On Reading the Bible as Comedy and Tragedy," *Semeia* no. 32 (January 1, 1984): 115-129. I must make clear that I am applying these terms in their broadest and most general sense, and in no way am suggesting that these categories are intentionally appropriated by the author of Torah. Here, I agree with Yair Zakovitch's, response to the aforementioned articles when he writes, "[Tragedy] and [Comedy] in the Bible," *Semeia* no. 32 (January 1, 1984):109, "The terms comedy and tragedy are, of course, alien to the Bible and its sphere of origin and growth.... But while these authors employ the expression 'at first glance' and 'seemingly' in order to moderate their claims, and at least acknowledge the fact of dealing with something alien, I nevertheless cannot overcome my impression that the terms 'comedy' and 'tragedy,' borrowed from the world of Greek drama, are entirely alien to biblical literature."

[72] The Hebrew word for "comfort" shares two of the same Hebrew consonants with the word "rest," and is clearly used as an intentional word play on Noah's name.

[73] Words in brackets provided.

But for now we must stop and ponder the importance of the figure of Noah for our understanding of the meaning of, and the author's expectations for, the fulfillment of Gen 3:15.

The anticipated seed of the woman will be another Adam who will reverse Adam's failures. In terms of *ma'asei avot siman l'banim*, we should expect to see, and therefore find, many clear parallels between Noah and Adam, both in terms of their victories, and sadly enough, in terms of their defeats and downfalls. First, we see that like Adam before him, God also brings the animals to Noah as a demonstration of his dominion over creation (Gen 2:19; 7:9; cf. 1:28). Secondly, once God brings Noah and his children safely through his judgment, Noah receives a slightly revised form of the creation blessing and mandate.

God blessed Noah and his sons, and He said to them, "Be fruitful and multiply and fill the land. The fear and terror of you will be on every wild animal, and on every flying creature of the sky, with everything that crawls on the ground and with all the fish of the sea—into your hand they are given. Every crawling thing that is alive will be food for you, as are the green plants—I have now given you everything. Only flesh with its life—that is, its blood—you must not eat!" (Gen 9:1–4)	God blessed them and God said to them, "Be fruitful and multiply, fill the land, and conquer it. Rule over the fish of the sea, the flying creatures of the sky, and over every animal that crawls on the land. Then God said, "I have just given you every green plant yielding seed that is on the surface of the whole land, and every tree, which has the fruit of a tree yielding seed. They are to be food for you. Also for every wild animal, every flying creature of the sky and every creature that crawls on the land which has life, every green plant is to be food." And it happened so. (Gen 1:28–30)

Noah, like his father Adam, is blessed (BLESSING), is commanded to fill the land (SEED), and is given authority over the creatures of creation (LAND). And in both cases, the mandates are followed by dietary provisions as well as dietary restrictions. Not only is Noah like Adam in his dominion over the animals, and in his creation mandate, but third, he is like him in his downfall. Earlier we noted the similarities between the Adam Fall Narrative and the Noah Fall Narrative: the planting of a garden/vineyard (Gen 2:8; 9:20), the taking of its fruit (Gen 3:6; 9:21), shameful nakedness (Gen 3:7; 9:21), the knowing of something shameful (Gen 3:7; 9:24) the covering up of nakedness (Gen 3:7, 21; 9:23), and the pronouncing of a curse involving subjugation (Gen 3:14;

9:25). Sadly, Noah's fall shows that he, in fact, is *a* seed of the woman, but not actually *the* seed of the promised woman-to-come. His victory is partial, but not final, and thus the war between the seed of the woman and the seed of the serpent, in this case the Canaanites (Gen 9:25), will continue on through the generations.

But now we must ask ourselves: in what sense did Noah bring rest from the curse of Genesis 3? By building an ark? By surviving the flood? No! Noah's greatest achievement, in terms of the story, was not the building of the ark and the surviving of the Flood, but by fulfilling a priestly role, by building an altar and offering of a sacrifice! This is most clearly marked by the poetic use of Noah's name, or forms of it, throughout the story. Note the poetic nuances, ones lost through English translations. Noah (*noach*), we're told, will bring comfort (*nacham*) to the land (Gen 5:29). God regrets (*nacham*) that he made man, but Noah (*noach*) finds favor (*chen* = *noach* spelled backwards) in God's eyes (Gen 6:6-8). The ark rests (*nuach*) upon the mountain in the seventh month (Gen 8:4), but the dove does not find a resting place (*manoach*) for its foot (Gen 8:9). The climax of the narrative is reached when Noah builds an altar, and sacrifices offerings to the Lord (Gen 8:20). The aroma, we're told, is *pleasing* (*nichoah* = from the same root as Noah's name) to the Lord (Gen 8:21). It is only at this point in the story when Noah's actions do justice to the meaning of his name, "to give rest (comfort) from the curse." And so we read in Gen 8:21: "When *ADONAI* smelled the soothing [restful] aroma, *ADONAI* said in His heart, 'I will never again curse the ground on account of man, even though the inclination of the heart of humankind is evil from youth. Nor will I ever again smite all living creatures, as I have done.'" In short, noteworthy for our purposes is that the seed of woman, the new Adam of Gen 3:15, will reestablish God's purposes for creation, not merely by reigning as a king, but also by functioning as a priest. The priest offers sacrifices to restore peace and rest. The New Adam (the singular seed) will enjoy the glories of victory (crushing the head) as well as having to pay the sacrifice of suffering and death (being struck in the heel), to reclaim that which was lost in Genesis 3. Here we must pause to make a crucial point for the Messianism of the Hebrew Bible. Though separated by tribal distinctions under the Sinai Covenant, *all kingship and priesthood in the Tanakh ultimately finds its origins in one figurehead: Adam!* And *all Messianism in the Hebrew Bible, be it royal or priestly, all of it finds its source in Adam as well.*

Genesis 49 and the Last Days

The importance of the coming seed of the woman, a New Adam, is most apparent in the genealogies of Genesis. Very quickly the lines are divided, and the author of the Torah blazes a genealogical trail from Adam, through Shem (Gen 9:26–27), to Abraham (Gen 12:1–3), to Isaac (Gen 22:17–18), to Jacob (Gen 27:28–29), all the while separating the men (the chosen seed of the woman) from the boys (the un-chosen seed) in order to find Adam's truest descendent. Oddly though not surprisingly, the story of Judah and Tamar is rather abruptly inserted into an otherwise seamless narrative about Jacob's beloved son Joseph (Genesis 38),[74] the point of which, both in terms of the genealogical concerns in Genesis, and in terms of the Davidic line in the Primary History,[75] is to move from Adam, through Judah, to Perez (Gen 38:29; see Ruth 4:18[76]). Subtle clues in Perez's birth narrative, in fact, depict Perez as another Jacob, thereby making him the physical heir through whom the fullness of God's promises to Jacob in Gen 25:23 and 29:28–29[77] would come:

Now when it was time for her to give birth, behold THERE WERE TWINS IN HER WOMB. While she was giving birth, one stuck out his hand, and the midwife took a SCARLET THREAD and tied it to his hand saying, "This one came out first. But as he was pulling his hand back in, behold, his brother came out. So she said, "How you have broken through! The breach is because of you." And he named him Perez. AFTERWARD HIS BROTHER, ON WHOSE HAND WAS THE SCARLET THREAD, CAME OUT. And he named him Zerah. (Gen 38:27–30)	Isaac prayed to *ADONAI* on behalf of his wife because she was barren. *ADONAI* answered his plea and his wife Rebekah became pregnant. But the children struggled with one another inside her, and she said, "If it's like this, why is this happening to me?" So she went to inquire of *ADONAI*. *ADONAI* said to her: "Two nations are in your womb, and two peoples from your body will be separated. One people will be stronger than the other people, but the older will serve the younger. When her time came to give birth, indeed THERE WERE TWINS IN HER WOMB. Now the first came out REDDISH, all of him was like a fur coat, and they named him Esau. AFTERWARD HIS BROTHER CAME OUT WITH HIS HAND HOLDING ONTO ESAU'S HEEL—so he was named Jacob. Isaac was 60 years old when he fathered them. (Gen 25:21–26)[78]

---

[74] Wenham, *Genesis*, 363, writes, "At first blush, chap. 38 seems to have nothing to do with the Joseph story. If it were omitted, the narrative would progress from 37:36 to 39:1 very smoothly. It does not appear to be necessary for understanding chaps. 39–50."

[75] The single narrative history from the creation of the world to the Babylonian Exile (Genesis–2 Kings).

[76] Ruth, though not included in the Former Prophets, is of vital importance for filling an important gap between the Messianism of the Torah specifically to the House of David. David is not only of the Tribe of Judah, he is also a descendant of Perez.

[77] We will have occasion to discuss this passage momentarily.

[78] Emphases provided (all caps).

The birth narratives of Perez and Jacob are remarkably similar. Both tell of twins who struggle in their mother's womb. In both cases, the younger supplants the older brother, the former by grabbing his brother's heel, the later by pushing his brother aside. And in both narratives, the displaced brother is identified by the color red: the former by his hair, the later by the scarlet thread attached to his hand.

Having highlighted this important, yet frequently overlooked parallel between Jacob and Perez, we are now ready to consider the significance of Genesis 49 for the Messianism of the Hebrew Bible, and of the Torah in particular.

To recall, Jacob's poetic blessing is explicitly identified as a prophecy about the Last Days in Gen 49:1: "Jacob called his sons and said to them: 'Gather together so that I can tell you what will happen to you in the *last days.*'" Though identified as a blessing in Gen 49:28, Jacob's words about Reuben, Simeon, and Levi in Gen 49:2–7, are anything but a blessing. Reuben is called out for sleeping with Bilhah (Gen 35:22). Simeon and Levi are destined to be scattered in Israel because of their cruel deception and violent actions to the men of Shechem (Gen 34:25–30). Jacob's harsh words of *"anti*-blessing" to Reuben and Levi just prior to his death and burial contrast so starkly with Moses's words of blessing to Reuben (see Deut 33:6) and Levi (see Deut 33:8–11) [79] just prior to his death and burial that it begs the question: Why is Jacob so harsh to the first three of his twelve sons? The answer to this question has to do with the purpose of Jacob's blessing in the larger context of Genesis. Genesis' consistent focus on tracing the chosen line has led us from Adam, through the seed of woman, to Abraham (Gen 6:9; 11:10, 27), to Isaac (Gen 25:19), and to Jacob (Gen 37:2). And though all of Jacob's twelve sons are the chosen people (Gen 49:28; Exod 1:1-5; Deut 33:1, 29), *the storyline drives us on to a single seed,* the New Adam, who will rule over the nations and defeat the serpent and his seed. Thus, Jacob's "casting aside" of his first three sons in the blessing is clearly not their being cast aside from the people of Israel, but rather their stepping aside to make way for the King!

> Judah, so you are—your brothers will praise you: Your hand
> will be on your enemies' neck. Your father's sons will bow
> down to you. A lion's cub is Judah— from the prey, my son,

---

[79] Simeon does not appear in the Blessing of Moses.

you have gone up. He crouches, lies down like a lion, or like a lioness—who would rouse him? The scepter will not pass from Judah, nor the ruler's staff from between his feet, until he to whom it belongs will come. To him will be the obedience of the peoples. Binding his foal to the vine, his donkey's colt to the choice vine, he washes his garments in wine, and in the blood of grapes his robe. His eyes are darker than wine, and teeth that are whiter than milk. (Gen 49:8–12)

Jacob's blessing of Judah has been traditionally, and correctly, interpreted as a Messianic prophecy that the Messiah-King would come from the Tribe of Judah.[80] But for our purposes, we must not overlook the ways in which Jacob's prediction of the King of the Last Days fits within the larger storyline. First, it is crucial to notice that Judah's role as a Tribe in the promise-plan of God is to receive his brothers' allegiance – "your brothers will praise you... your father's sons shall bow down to you" (v. 8). Jacob's words concerning Judah – *"your father's sons shall bow down to you"* – are practically identical to Isaac's words to Jacob. "May peoples serve you and may nations bow down to you. Be master over your brothers. *May your mother's sons bow down to you.* May those who curse you be cursed and may those who bless you be blessed" (Gen 27:29).[81] What is striking about Isaac's oracle concerning Jacob, "be master of your brothers... may your mother's sons bow down to you," is the extent to which the Jacob-Esau story contradicts the promise! First of all, Jacob only had a single brother, thus "your brothers" and "your mother's sons" simply do not fit. Secondly, though Jacob is called to be the master of his brothers, in the story of Jacob and Esau's reunion, Jacob consistently refers to himself as "your servant" (Gen 32:4–5, 10, 18, 20; 33:5, 14) and Esau as "my lord" (Gen 32:4–5, 18; 33:8, 13–15). Third, though Isaac prophecies concerning Jacob that "your mother's sons bow down to you," we are explicitly told that Jacob and his family are the ones that bow down to Esau (Gen 33:3, 6–7). Why does the author go to such great lengths to show that Jacob's relationship with Esau doesn't line up with Isaac's prediction? The answer, it would appear, is that Isaac's words, though spoken to Jacob, would ultimately be fulfilled through Jacob's seed,

---

[80] See, for example, Targum Onkelos; M. Sanhedrin 98.72; Genesis Rabba 98.8; Midrash Bereishit 97.13; Rashi; Ramban.

[81] Emphases provided.

whom Jacob later identifies as the king from the tribe of Judah (Gen 49:8). It is through this king that the blessings and/or the curses of the Abrahamic Covenant would come: "May those who curse you be cursed and may those who bless you be blessed" (Gen 27:29b; see Num 24:9b).

Significantly, a later biblical author notices and comments on the promises to Jacob in Gen 27:29 and its connection with the Tribe of Judah in Gen 49:8. In 1 Chron 5:1-2, we read:

> The sons of Reuben the firstborn of Israel—he was the firstborn, but when he defiled his father's bed, his birthright was given to the sons of Joseph son of Israel—so he is not reckoned as the firstborn in the genealogical record. Though Judah was the strongest among his brothers, and a ruler came from him, the birthright belonged to Joseph.

The Chronicler's phraseology betrays his biblical sources. His comments concerning Reuben are taken from Gen 49:3-4. The reference to the birthright blessings being given to Joseph are clearly taken from Gen 48:1-22; 49:22-26. What of the comment, "Though Judah was the strongest among his brothers, and a ruler came from him"? Remarkably, the Hebrew form of this phrase is found in only one other place in the Hebrew Bible: Gen 27:29 ("be master of your brothers"). By alluding to Gen 27:29, the writer of Chronicles also makes Isaac's blessing of Jacob and Jacob's prediction concerning Judah explicit. Peoples will serve Jacob, the nations will bow down to Jacob, Jacob will be master over his brothers, and blessings will come to Israel and the nations (see Gen 27:29) through Jacob's greatest descendent.

Returning to the reference to the father's sons bowing down to Judah (Gen 49:8), one is also immediately struck by the similarity of this prediction concerning Judah to the story of Joseph. In fact, the whole point of the Joseph Narrative is to tell the story of how Joseph's eleven brothers would bow down to him as the divinely chosen ruler (Gen 37:7-10; 42:6; 43:26, 28; 48:12), much to their chagrin and in spite of their opposition. What is the point, therefore, of telling the Joseph Story if God's purposes for world redemption will ultimately come through Judah? *Ma'asei avot, siman l'banim*: the deeds of the fathers are a sign for the sons. It would seem that Joseph's story is intended to be illustrative, a prophecy in story, of future events. The story of Joseph's rise to power by rejection, suffering, and ultimate triumph is the dramatized version of Jacob's poetic oracle in Gen 49:8-12.

There are important details in Gen 49:8-12 that serve to bind Jacob's prediction into the larger storyline. For instance, this king of the Last Days will grab his enemies by the back of the neck (v. 8), or in other words, by the head! Moreover, the obedience of the nations will be his (v. 10; see Gen 27:29). Triumph over enemies and dominion over the nations is a consistent and oft repeated theme in the promises to Abraham, Isaac, and Jacob (see Gen 22:17; 24:60; Num 24:18), and can only be fully appreciated in light of Adam's original mandate and the predictions of Gen 3:15. The seed of the woman, from the Tribe of Judah, a King in the Last Days, will be the one to take the serpent and his seed by the neck! He will be the one who will reestablish Adam's mandate.

Numbers 24 and the Last Days

Just as Jacob's poetic speech predicted the coming of the King-Messiah in the Last Days, likewise Balaam's oracles speak of the same King and the Last Days, and as we shall see, both poems share important similarities. Before we look specifically at the Messiah in Numbers 24, it is essential to consider the Balaam Narrative in its larger context, particularly in light of the importance of understanding the Messianism of the Torah as integrally related to the Torah's broader storyline, and not merely as random fragments of disconnected prophecies.

Is Balaam a good guy or a bad guy? What are we to make of Balaam in Numbers 22 – 24? Whose side is he on? On the one hand, he is presented as a Spirit-filled prophet who refuses to compromise the word of God (Num 22:18; 24:2). On the other hand, he is depicted as a pagan diviner (Num 24:1; Josh 13:22) with less spiritual insight than a donkey (Num 22:34).[82] What is more, he is eventually put to death by the sword because of his involvement with Israel's prostitution at Peor (Num 31:8, 16). Before we look at what Balaam says about the Messiah, we must first figure out whether we should listen to him at all. After all, how can we trust the words of a pagan diviner who speaks from both sides of his mouth?

Some rather obvious parallels between the stories of Balaam and his donkey (Num 22:22-35) and Balak and Balaam (Num 22:36 – 24:25) show us that we not only can, but must believe the message in spite of

---

[82] His brutishness is even reflected in his name, Balaam son of Beor, his father's name apparently a pun on the Hebrew word for "fool" (see Prov 30:2).

the messenger. In the account of Balaam and his donkey, the spiritually blind Balaam unwittingly tries to force his spiritually insightful donkey to circumvent the Messenger of the Lord three times (Num 22:28, 32, and 33). Likewise, in the account of Balak and Balaam, the spiritually blind Balak tries to force the spiritually insightful Balaam to curse Israel three times (Num 23:7; 23:18; 24:3, 10). In both accounts, Balaam's third attempt (to force his donkey/to curse Israel) culminates in a divinely enabled "opening of the eyes" (Num 22:31; 24:4, 15) to behold things he had not seen before (22:31; 24:17).[83]

Then *ADONAI* OPENED BALAAM'S EYES, AND HE SAW THE ANGEL OF *ADONAI* standing in the road with his drawn sword in his hand. So he fell on his face. (Num 22:31)	the oracle of one hearing God's speech, one seeing *Shaddai*'s vision, one fallen down, YET WITH OPEN EYES. . . I SEE HIM, yet not at this moment. I BEHOLD HIM, yet not in this location. For a star will come from Jacob, a scepter will arise from Israel. He will crush the foreheads of Moab and the skulls of all the sons of Seth. (Num 24:4[84],17)[85]

These parallels provide the reader with a frame of reference for evaluating Balaam's message in chaps. 23–24 with respect to his personal character. The blind and perilous Balaam unwittingly fighting against the Messenger of the Lord in chap. 22 anticipates the blind and perilous Balak unwittingly fighting against God in chaps. 23–24. Likewise, the perceptive donkey refusing to circumvent the Angel of the Lord in chap. 22 anticipates the perceptive Balaam refusing to curse Israel in chaps. 23–24. These parallels encourage us to accept the message regardless of the messenger. How can such a dubious person speak forth such spiritually significant oracles? In the same way that a typically brutish beast is supernaturally enabled to see the Messenger of the Lord and to speak forth the truth. If God can speak through a donkey he can do the same through a pagan prophet. And if, like Balaam in chap. 22, and Balak in chaps. 23– 24, we fail to heed the words of the donkey and the words of the prophet, we do so only at our own peril.

---

[83] These parallels are particularly important for drawing the reader's attention to the significance of the oracles flowing out of Balaam's third attempt to curse Israel.

[84] see Num 24:15

[85] Emphases provided (call caps).

Context, context, context. In order to fully appreciate Balaam's poetic speeches, it is essential to read it in the context of the larger story, namely the restoration of God's creation purposes through the Seed of the woman, through Abraham and his descendant. Several allusions to, and citations of, other key texts in the Torah make it clear that the focus of Numbers 22– 24 is the outworking of the promised blessings and curses of the Abrahamic covenant, the culmination of which is the reign of King-Messiah in the last days (Num 24:14, 17ff.). Balak's statement to Balaam that, "He whom you bless is blessed, and he whom you curse is cursed" (Num 22:6; see v. 12; 24:9), draws directly from God's promises to bless those who bless Abraham and his seed and to curse those who curse Abraham and his seed (see Gen 12:3; 27; 29).[86] Noteworthy are the numerous references to the verbs "bless"[87] and "curse"[88] throughout this section, the highlight of which Balaam learns the unchangeable truth that it is "pleasing in the eyes of *ADONAI* to bless Israel" (24:1). Moreover, the implicitly royal connotations of the Abrahamic Covenant as expressed in Gen 27:29 (see below) and later amplified in Gen 49:8-12 are, as in Jacob's prophecy, explicitly tied to Israel's king in Numbers 24.

May peoples serve you and may nations bow down to you. Be master over your brothers. MAY YOUR MOTHER'S SONS BOW DOWN TO YOU. MAY THOSE WHO CURSE YOU BE CURSED AND MAY THOSE WHO BLESS YOU BE BLESSED. (Gen 27:29)	Judah, so you are—your brothers will praise you: Your hand will be on your enemies' neck. YOUR FATHER'S SONS WILL BOW DOWN TO YOU. (Gen 49:8)	He crouches like a lion or a lioness— who would rouse him? HE WHO BLESSES YOU WILL BE BLESSED, AND HE WHO CURSES YOU WILL BE CURSED. (Num 24:9)[89]

---

[86] Clearly related to the blessings and curses of the Abrahamic Covenant is the promise of numerous descendants, the fact of which causes Balak to fear and to call for reinforcements (Num 24:3-6; cf. Exod 1:12). The theme of abundant descendants is central to the Torah's theology (compare Exod 1:7, 9, 10, 12 with Gen 1:28; 9:7; 17:2; 18:18; 22:17; 26:4, 24; 28:3; 35:11; 47:27; 48:4).

[87] Num 22:6, 12; 23:11, 20, 25; 24:1, 9, 10.

[88] Num 22:11, 12, 17; 23:7, 8, 11, 13, 25, 27; 24:9, 10.

[89] Emphases provided (all caps).

These textual threads binding *Parashat Balak*[90] into the fabric of the Torah's story are unmistakable. How does *Parashat Balak* tie the blessings (and curses) of the Abrahamic Covenant specifically to the Messiah? *I see him, but not now!* Numerical patterns are quite common in Scripture. In the case of Balaam Narrative three's a charm. Earlier we looked at the parallels between Balaam and his donkey and Balak and Balaam. In both stories, the third attempt to fight against God's will results in the opening of Balaam's eyes to behold individuals of supernatural significance. Several textual clues in the narrative suggest that the author goes to great lengths to signal the reader's attention to the importance of the "third attempt" (to curse Israel) oracles in Numbers 24. First, we are told that Balaam does not use enchantments as he had with the previous oracles (24:1). Second, the narrator states that Balaam is empowered by the Spirit of God, a phenomenon attributed to only two other individuals in the Torah (compare Num 24:2 with Gen 41:38 and Exod 31:3; 35:31). Third, we are told that, unlike the other oracles where Balaam sees only a portion of the people of Israel, he sees all of Israel encamped tribe by tribe (24:2; see 22:41; 23:13). Fourth, we are told that Balaam utters these oracles with "open eyes" (24:3–4, 15). Finally, the "third attempt" oracles are identified as prophetic utterances (*neum*) six times: vv. 3 (twice), 4, 15 (twice), 16; this term is used elsewhere in the Torah only two times (Gen 22:16; Num 14:28).

Why does the author go to such great lengths to draw attention to Balaam's third oracle? It seems the purpose is to emphasize the content of the vision Balaam receives when his eyes are supernaturally opened. In chap. 22, Balaam is supernaturally enabled to see the Messenger of the Lord. In chap. 24, Balaam's eyes are opened to see things that would take place in the "Last Days;" namely, the coming of the Messiah, the one through whom Adam's dominion over creation would once again be established; the one who would defeat the enemy by crushing his head (see Gen 3:15); the one who would dispossess his enemies (see Gen 22:17; 24:60).

> Now, behold, I am going back to my people. Come, let me counsel you what these people will do to your people in the latter days. . . I see him, yet not at this moment. I behold him,

---

[90] Numbers 22:2 - 25:9.

yet not in this location. For a star will come from Jacob, a scepter will arise from Israel. He will crush the foreheads of Moab and the skulls of all the sons of Seth. Edom will be conquered[91]— his enemies will conquer Seir, but Israel will triumph. One from Jacob will rule and destroy the city's survivors. (Num 24:14, 17–19)

Though Rashi limits the Messianism of Balaam's prophecy to Num 24:19, evidence suggests that all of Balaam's "third-attempt" oracles (24:7-9, 17–24) are Messianic. First, it is essential to note that Balaam's "third-attempt" oracles (including Num 24:7–9) are remarkably similar to Judah's blessing in Genesis 49. Both places describe a royal figure (a lion, a scepter) who will come in the "last days."

Lion's cub is Judah— from the prey, my son, you have gone up. HE CROUCHES, LIES DOWN LIKE A LION, OR LIKE A LIONESS—WHO WOULD ROUSE HIM? The SCEPTER will not pass from Judah, nor the ruler's staff from between his feet, until he to whom it belongs will come. To him will be the obedience of the peoples (Gen 49:9–10)	His king shall be greater than Agag,[92] his kingdom will be exalted. God is bringing him out of Egypt. Like the strong horns of a wild ox. He devours nations hostile to him. He will crush their bones. His arrows will pierce them. HE CROUCHES LIKE A LION OR A LIONESS— WHO WOULD ROUSE HIM? He who blesses you will be blessed, and he who curses you will be cursed. . . I see him, yet not at this moment. I behold him, yet not in this location. I see him, but not now; I behold him, but not near; a star shall come forth from Jacob, a *SCEPTER* shall rise from Israel (Num 24:7b–9, 17a)[93]

---

[91] Though less apparent in the English versions, Balaam's prophetic words concerning the triumph of the Messiah over Seir in Num 24:18 ("his enemies will conquer Seir, but Israel will triumph") are nearly identical to God's words to Abraham about the triumph of his seed over the gates of his enemies in Gen 22:17 ("your seed will possess the gate of his enemies."). "Seir" in Num 24:18 is clearly a play on the word "gate" in Gen 22:17. Balaam's Messianic interpretation of the second use of "seed" in Gen 22:17, as in the case of Ps 72:17, further supports Collin's findings, discussed earlier with reference to Gen 3:15, on the syntactical distinctions between seed as a collective noun and seed as an individual!

[92] Text critically, there is strong support against the Masoretic Text's "Agag" in favor of "Gog," the enemy of Israel who will arise against them in the Last Days (see Ezek 38:14-16). The Septuagint, Qumran, the Samaritan Pentateuch, Aquila, Symmachus, and Theodotian all read "Gog."

[93] Emphases provided (all caps).

These similarities strongly suggest that these passages refer to the same individual, namely the Messiah.

Second, though some may argue against the Messianic interpretation of Num 24:8–9 since the wording of the text is so similar to Num 23:22, 24, (a passage clearly referring to Israel as a whole), the grammatical, syntactical, and contextual differences between these two passages suggest that Num 24:8–9 is not merely a repetition of Num 23:22, 24. Similar does not mean the same, however.

God is bringing THEM from Egypt with the strong horns of the wild ox! (Num 23:22)	God is bringing HIM out of Egypt. Like the strong horns of a wild ox. (Num 24:8a)[94]

It essential to notice the differences in the pronouns used in Num 23:22, "them," and in 24:8, "him." Are these merely stylistic differences or do they serve a strategic purpose? To answer the question we need to take a look at the immediate context in which these verses are found.

No misfortune is to be seen in Jacob, and no misery in Israel! ADONAI their God is with them—the KING'S shout is among THEM! God is bringing them from Egypt with the strong horns of the wild ox![95] (Num 23:21-22)	Water will flow from his buckets, his seed by abundant water. His KING will be greater than Agag, his kingdom will be exalted. God is bringing HIM out of Egypt. Like the strong horns of a wild ox. (Num 24:7-8)

---

[94] Emphases provided (call caps).

[95] The second half of this verse ("with the strong horns of the wild ox;" so also 24:8), however, has been variously translated since the singular pronoun in Num 23:22b is also ambiguous ("for him"). Robert Alter's, The Five Books of Moses: A Translation with Commentary (W. W. Norton & Company, New York; London, 2004), 808, more literal translation brings out the ambiguity of the second half of the verse: "El who brings them out from Egypt, like the wild ox's antlers for him." Who is "him" in the second half of the verse? Does it refer to Israel (so JPS, NASB, NET, NIV, NRSV, RSV) or to God (ASV, KJV, NKJV)? Alter obviously prefers the latter interpretation. In his own words:
To whom does this simile refer? The more cautious reading is that it is a representation of the fiercely triumphant Israel, now a militant people after its liberation from Egyptian slavery. It may, however, be more in keeping with the archaic character of the poem to see the animal imagery as a representation, in accordance with the conventions of Canaanite epic, of the fierce God who has freed Israel from Egypt. (emphasis my own).
There are at least two reasons why Alter's interpretation is more likely. First, God's power and work (not Israel's) are in focus within the immediate context (vv. 21, 23). It makes more sense, therefore, to interpret the second half of v. 22 as a reference to God's powerful and ferocious act of redemption. Verse 22b is likely a poetic elaboration of the manner in which God rescued his people from Egypt. Second, if the author intended to shift the focus away from God to Israel in v. 22b, it would have been more natural to use a plural pronoun ("them") instead of the singular "him" in keeping with the parallelism of the first half of the verse.

When we take a closer look at Num 24:21-22 we'll notice that v. 21 refers to a king who is with the people of Israel, most likely the Lord in this context. [96] It is important to notice that "Jacob" and "Israel" in the verse, like "king," are all singular nouns, yet "Jacob" and "Israel" refer collectively to the whole people (they/them), whereas "king" (he/him) does not. In order to make it clear to the reader that Balaam is referring to Israel-Jacob and not to the king in the following verse, the author must use a plural pronoun ("them"), even though the plural pronoun does not agree in number with the singular "Israel/Jacob": "God is bringing THEM [Israel] from Egypt with strong horns of the wild ox!" This is obviously a reference to Israel's exodus from Egypt.

Turning our attention to Num 24:7-8, we see that 24:7, like 23:21, also refers to Israel's king. "His [Israel's] king will be greater than Agag, his [the king's] kingdom will be exalted." In this case, the king no longer refers to the Lord, but to a future king who will arise out of the people of Israel. [97] When we look at the continuation of Balaam's oracle in 24:8, we can now appreciate the significance in the shift of pronouns: "God is bringing HIM out of Egypt. Like the strong horns of a wild ox." Why the shift? In Num 23:22, the author used the plural pronoun "them" in order to make it abundantly clear that God brought Israel-Jacob (singular noun with a plural sense) out of Egypt. By using the singular pronoun in 24:8, the author wants to make it just as clear that he is NOT referring to Israel; rather, he is referring to Israel's king, a king who will prevail over Israel's enemies, a king whose kingdom will be exalted (24:7). In Num 23:22, God BRINGS Israel ("them") out of Egypt. In Num 24:8, however, God WILL BRING Israel's king ("him") out of Egypt!

Why does this interpretation of Num 24:8 make more sense? There are three reasons. First, this interpretation is supported by the grammar and syntax of the verse itself. Second, the intent of the "third-attempt" oracles (Numbers 24) is to point to spiritual realities that Balaam could not see in the earlier oracles. He now sees reality through spiritually

---

[96] See Philip J. Budd, *Numbers* (WBC 5; Accordance/Thomas Nelson electronic ed. Waco: Word Books, 1984), 268; R. Dennis Cole, *Numbers* (NAC 3B; ed. E. Ray Clendenen; Accordance electronic ed. Nashville: Broadman & Holman Publishers, 2000), 413.

[97] Numbers 24:17, "For a star will come from Jacob, a scepter will arise from Israel" is in all likelihood intended to clarify and explain the rather enigmatic poetry in Num 24:7: "Water will flow from his buckets, his seed by abundant water." What does "water will flow from his [Israel's] buckets" mean? Numbers 24:17 explains it: a king will come forth from the people of Israel (compare Num 24:7, 17 in the LXX).

opened eyes (see Num 24:3-4, 16-17). A repetition of the description of Israel's exodus in 24:8 is foreign to the overall flow of the text. Although Balaam uses words quite similar to 23:22 to describe what he sees in 24:8, the changes in wording point to a previously unseen spiritual reality. In 23:22 he could only see Israel's exodus from Egypt as a past event. In 24:8, he discovers harbingers of the future by consider Israel's exodus (*ma'asei avot, siman l'banim*).[98] Just as God brought Israel out of Egypt, so God will bring Israel's Messiah out of Egypt. Third, the identification of the "him" in 24:8 with the coming Messiah (not Israel) is confirmed in 24:9 ("He crouches like a lion or a lioness— who would rouse him? He who blesses you will be blessed, and he who curses you will be cursed") a nearly verbatim quotation of another Messianic prophecy (Gen 49:9): "Lion's cub is Judah— from the prey, my son, you have gone up. He crouches, lies down like a lion, or like a lioness—who would rouse him." It is this King through whom the promises of blessing to the patriarchs and in the mandate to Adam will be fully realized: "He who blesses you will be blessed, and he who curses you will be cursed." (Num 24:9b; see Gen 27:29b; Ps 72:17).

Summarizing the Messianism of the Torah

Before we move on to the Messianism of the Former Prophets (Joshua – Kings), it's crucial to stop for a moment in order to connect the various dots. The Torah's Messianism is grounded in the creation mandate and occasioned by Adam's fall. Adam, the royal-priest (the one to watch over, work in and rule the Garden-Sanctuary) of the Beginning of Days fails to conquer the land, forfeits his dominion over creation, and is cast out of the Garden eastward into exile. But God plans to redeem creation by choosing another man, Abraham, and a people Israel. And in spite of Israel's anticipated disobedience and exile, God's purpose cannot be thwarted, and so *Israel's success, and God's, is tied to an individual seed of Abraham through whom God would bless the world, provide numerous seed, and reestablish dominion over creation.* Genealogy and poetry are the means by which Moses leads the reader to this King, of the Tribe of Judah, a descendant of Perez, who will ultimately accomplish Israel's recreation mandate... And it is here, where the story of the Former Prophets seamlessly picks up the Torah

---

[98] Remarkably, Micah 5 is the *Haftorah* reading for *Parashat Balak*, where we are told that the Messiah will be born in Bethlehem (having already been told by Balaam that the Messiah would be brought out of Egypt).

Story. Joshua's initial conquest of the Land prepares us for the story of David's family, of the Tribe of Judah, from the line of Perez...

Messianism in the Former Prophets

In one sense, the Former Prophets, from Joshua to 2 Kings consists of four books: Joshua, Judges, Samuel (I–II), and Kings (I– II). And in another sense, the storyline is such that the four are really just one continuous telling of Israel's history from the initial conquest of the Promised Land until the Babylonian Exile. Truth be told, we can say that the books of Genesis–Kings are one continuous telling of Israel's story (and humanity's), from her pre-history (Genesis 1–11) until her exile (2 Kings 25). The prophetic authors of this history tell this history from God's perspective, and do so in a cohesive and coherent manner. The creation of the world and the election of Abraham as told in the Torah are specifically linked to the house of David in the Former Prophets. We can only truly understand the telling of Israel's history in the Former Prophets, particularly in terms of covenant disobedience and exile, when we see it as a fulfillment of Mosaic prophecy. "*ADONAI* said to Moses, 'Behold, you are about to lie down with your fathers. Then this people will rise up and prostitute themselves with the foreign gods of the land they are entering. They will abandon Me and break My covenant that I cut with them.'" (Deut 31:16). Likewise, we can only truly understand the election of David's house and the final verses of the Former Prophets about the reversal of Jehoiachin's fortunes in Babylon (2 Kgs 25:25-30) with reference to the Abrahamic Covenant and the Torah's poetic speeches about the Last Days and the redeeming King-Messiah who would come from the Tribe of Judah. "The scepter will not pass from Judah, nor the ruler's staff from between his feet, until he to whom it belongs will come. To him will be the obedience of the peoples" (Gen 49:10). And because David's story is a necessary outworking of the Torah Story, we can say that Gen 3:15 is the headwaters of David's story whose final destination is ultimately the Messiah-King through whom creation's Edenic conditions will one day be restored as foretold by the Latter Prophets (see Isa 11:1-9; 65:25). This Story, from creation to the reversal of Jehoiachin's fortunes in exile, not only provides the alibi for Israel's Messianic hope, but also provides the context for making sense of the Messianism in the Latter Prophets and the Writings.

Crucial to the Torah's storyline is the election of Abraham, through whom would come an individual seed from the Tribe of Judah. By way of comparison, David's election and rise are similarly crucial to the storyline of the Former Prophets. As we shall see, *the prophetic authors of the Former Prophets understood God's covenant with David as the continued outworking of the Abrahamic Covenant as well as the poetic promises of the coming king* in Gen 49:8-12 and Num 24:7-9, 17-24. And for this reason we see that God's promises to David have several allusions to God's promises to Abraham:[99]

... My heart's desire is to make you into a great nation, to bless you, TO MAKE YOUR NAME GREAT so that you may be a blessing. (Gen 12:2)	... I will MAKE YOUR NAME AS GREAT as the greatest on earth. (2 Sam 7:9)
Then Abram said, "Look! You have given me no seed, so a house-born servant is my heir. Then behold, the word of *ADONAI* came to him saying, "This one will not be your heir, but in fact, ONE WHO WILL COME FROM YOUR OWN BODY will be your heir." (Gen 15:3–4)	When your days are done and you sleep with your fathers, I will raise up your SEED, who WILL COME FORTH FROM YOU after you, and I will establish his kingdom. (2 Sam 7:12)[100]

The capitalized phrases in 2 Samuel 7 are used elsewhere only in the Abraham Narrative. Ronald F. Youngblood makes this connection explicit when he writes:

> Verses 9b–11a contain three elements: The Lord will (1) make David's "name great" (v.9b), (2) "provide a place" for Israel (v.10), and (3) give David "rest" from all his enemies (v.11a; ...). The divine promise to make the name of David great is a

---

[99] That other biblical writers also saw the connection between the Abrahamic Covenant and the House of David is clear enough from the Book of Ruth, a book that tells the story of David's origins through Ruth with numerous allusions to the Abraham Narrative (cf. Gen 12:1 with Ruth 2:11; cf. Ruth 4:18–22 with the genealogical patterns of ten generations linking Adam to Abraham in Genesis; cf. Ruth 4:11–12 with the stories of the Matriarchs in Genesis. The link between the Abrahamic Covenant and the House of David is also explicit in Ps 72:17 (cf. Gen 22:17-18; also Gen 18:18; 28:14).

[100] Emphases provided (all caps).

clear echo of the Abrahamic covenant (cf. Gen 12:2), which in turn stands in sharp contrast to the self-aggrandizing boasts of the builders of the tower of Babel: "so that we may make a name for ourselves" (Gen 11:4). An example of David's name becoming great is 8:13, where the narrator reports that David "became famous" (lit. "made a name"; cf. 1 Kings 1:47) after defeating the Edomites (cf. similarly 1 Sam 18:30). But again David testifies to his reliance on God's power as he affirms that redemption takes place in the context of God's determination to "make a name for himself" (vv.23, 26; cf. Jer 13:11; 32:20; see 1 Sam 12:22 and comment).[101]

God's plan for David and a Seed from David's house is rooted in his purposes for electing Abraham and a single seed from his line. And God's purposes for electing Abraham are rooted in God's purposes for creating Adam to rule over creation and to conquer the Land (see 2 Sam 8:11). It is part of this established pattern, therefore, that Solomon – David's second greatest descendent, and quintessential paradigm of the son of David and son of God ruling over God's kingdom (2 Sam 7:12-16) – is described as a new Adam, both in terms of his rule over the Land and its creatures (1 Kgs 5:1, 4, 13 [EVVs 4:21, 24, 33), and in terms of his fall (cf. 1 Kgs 11:1-4; Gen 3:1-6)![102] And Solomon's fall, like Adam's before his, occasions the coming of yet another descendent who will never fall (compare 1 Chron 17:13 with 2 Sam 7:14). Moreover, it is only through the lens of a new Adam that we make sense of Solomon's dual role as king over creation and builder of God's house.[103] Solomon is portrayed in a priestly light due to the numerous parallels between the temple that he built and the tabernacle of Moses, both of which hark back to Adam's Eden.[104] God's promise to build a house for David, and David's descendant building a house for God is therefore, in effect, New Adam theology: God will build a house for

---

[101] Ronald F. Youngblood, 1 and 2 Samuel (EBC 3; ed. Frank E. Gaebelein and J. D. Douglas; Accordance electronic ed. Grand Rapids: Zondervan, 1992), n.p.

[102] There are numerous links between Genesis 1-3 and the Solomon Narrative (1 Kings 1–11). For an extended analysis, see Postell, *Adam as Israel*, 131-34; John A. Davies, "'Discerning Between Good and Evil': Solomon as a New Adam in 1 Kings," *Westminster Theological Journal* 73, no. 1 (March 1, 2011): 39-57.

[103] Solomon's prayer to know the difference between good and evil (1 Kgs 3:5) is clear allusion to Adam in the Garden (Gen 2:17; 3:5, 22).

[104] Seed Postell, *Adam as Israel*, 132.

David, thus David's heir will rule as an eternal king of an eternal kingdom (2 Sam 7:12, 16). David's heir will also build a house (2 Sam 7:13), a temple for God, thus David's heir will function as a high priest par excellence (a New Adam), at least in the sense of providing a place of worship for Israel and all nations.

It is this concern with the coming of the new Adam that informs our understanding of Joshua, both the conqueror (Josh 18:1) who stands upon the heads of his enemies (Josh 10:24; Gen 3:15), and the one who failed to conquer the Land completely because of the deception of the Gibeonites (Josh 9:4, 23; Gen 3:1, 14). And it is the Torah's poetic promises to bring a New Adam from the tribe of Judah that informs our understanding of the Book of Judges' preoccupation with and idealization of the Tribe of Judah.[105] It is entirely fitting, therefore, that Hannah's song (poetic speech) at the beginning of 1 Samuel calls for the coming of this king (1 Sam 2:10),[106] and that the Samuel Narrative ends with David's similar longing for God to raise up one of his descendants who will rule forever (2 Sam 22:1–23:7).[107] And it is in keeping with God's faithfulness to His creation purposes, through the seed of Abraham, through the Tribe of Judah, through the House of David, that God continues to show His favor to David's House in the Book of Kings during the darkest days of his dynasty, even after the collapse of the Davidic throne in the Babylonian Exile!

---

[105] Marc Brettler, "The Book of Judges: Literature as Politics," JBL 108/3 (1989): 395–418, has done a stellar job in demonstrating that Book of Judges in all its parts is focused on the importance of the Tribe of Judah as the rightful tribe of Israel's future kings. In the Prologue (1:–2:10), the Tribe of Judah is portrayed as the hero of the story (see 1:2–10, 13, 19, 21 [cf. Josh 15:63]). In the body of the book (2:11–16:31), only the judge from the Tribe of Judah who appears first in a list of morally declining anti-heroes, is presented with no flaws (3:7–11). And in the conclusion, it is Judah and Bethlehem that is exonerated (where, coincidentally, King David of the Tribe of Judah is from: 1 Sam 17:12), and it is Gibeah of Benjamin (where, coincidentally, Saul of the Tribe of Benjamin is from: 1 Sam 10:26) where a terrible sin is committed. It is clear enough that the chaos at the end of the book of Judges (Judg 17:6; 18:1; 19:1; 21:25) can only be corrected by a king who will come from the Tribe of Judah, thus a major purpose of the Book of Judges is prologue of sorts for the Book of Samuel and the election of David.

[106] "Those who oppose *ADONAI* will be shattered. He thunders against them in heaven. He judges the ends of the earth. He gives strength to His king, exalting the horn of His anointed one." Given the juxtaposition of Hannah's prayer with the Book of Judges, it is clear that this king for whom Hannah longs, must be from the tribe of Judah.

[107] "He is a tower of salvation to His king, He shows loyal love to His anointed—to David and to his seed, forever" (2 Sam 22:51).

To his son I will give one tribe so that My servant David may have a lamp every day before Me in Jerusalem, the city that I chose for Myself to put My Name there. (1 Ki 11:36)	Nevertheless, for David's sake, *ADONAI* his God gave him a lamp in Jerusalem, raising up his son after him and establishing Jerusalem. (1 Ki 15:4)	Nevertheless, *ADONAI* was not willing to destroy Judah, for the sake of David His servant, since He had promised to him a lamp for his children for all days. (2 Ki 8:19)	Now it came to pass in the 30-seventh year of the exile of King Jehoiachin of Judah, on the twenty-seventh day of the twelfth month, that King Evil-merodach of Babylon, in the year he became king, released King Jehoiachin of Judah from prison. He spoke kindly to him and set his throne above the throne of the other kings who were with him in Babylon. So he changed his prison garments, and regularly ate bread in the king's presence all the days of his life. As for his allowance, a regular allowance was granted to him by the king, an allotment for each day, all the days of his life. (2 Ki 25:27–30)

For those who have carefully followed the storyline of the whole Story (Genesis – 2 Kings), its conclusion really comes as no surprise. Of course, Israel would go into exile just as God predicted in the Torah (Genesis 1–3; Deut 31:16-21). And of course, God would remain faithful to the seed of the woman, from the Tribe of Judah, a descendant of David, through whom God's purposes for creation, for Abraham, for Israel, for the nations, would ultimately come to fruition (Gen 49:8-12; Num 24:7-9, 17-24). And it is only when we read this Story that we can rightly and truly understand the message of the Latter Prophets and the Writings, *it is only then that we can understand and appreciate how Messianism is patterned in the Hebrew Bible.*

Messianism in the Latter Prophets

Given the shaping of the Hebrew Bible (Torah, Prophets, Writings) and given the fact that Genesis – Kings (Torah and the Former Prophets) reads as one continuous story, our interpretation of the Latter Prophets (Isaiah – Malachi) and the Writings (Psalms – Chronicles) is necessarily influenced, and must be guided, by this Story. The Messianism of the Latter Prophets is, in essence, an elucidation of the meaning and implications of the Story, particularly as it is expressed in the poetic speeches of the Torah (Gen 3:14–19; Gen 49:1, 8–12; Num 24:7–9, 17–24; Deut 32:1–43; 33:7) and the Former Prophets (1 Sam 2:1–10; 2 Sam 7:12–16; 2 Sam 22:1–51; 23:1–7).[108] The Apostle Peter's comments in his first epistle suggest that this was in fact the apostolic understanding of the Hebrew Bible as well. Peter writes, "As to this salvation, the prophets who prophesied of the grace that would come to you *made careful searches and inquiries*, seeking to know what person or time the Spirit of Messiah within them was indicating as He predicted the sufferings of Messiah and the glories to follow."[109] How did Peter know that the prophets searched? What did the prophets search? There is ample evidence within the Hebrew Bible suggesting that the prophets searched in the words of their earlier sacred writings, particularly the Torah, and that Peter could know this to be true simply by reading his Bible! The most explicit example of a prophet searching a prophet can be found in the ninth chapter of Daniel where we find the prophet studying the words of the prophet Jeremiah in order to understand more precisely the timing of the coming Messiah (see Dan 9:1-2, 24-27). Based on the content and wording of Daniel's prayer moreover, it is quite clear that the prophet had been searching the prophecies of Moses as well in order to more fully appreciate what God was doing in his days and about to do in the days to come.[110] Daniel, however, is one example among many of the prophets searching the prophets.

The Prophets carefully searched the Torah and the writings of the prophets that preceded them, and found a wealth of knowledge and hope about the coming Messiah, both in terms of his sufferings as well as his glory. Given the scope of the Messianism in the Latter Prophets

---

[108] A word of explanation about the Prophets' awareness of the whole story is in order. It is evident that the pre-exilic prophets were not reading the finalized version of the Story, a story whose final recorded event is the reversal of Jehoichin's fortunes during the Babylonian exile. Given the frequent reference to written sources in Kings (1 Kings 14:19, 29; 15:7, 23, 31; 16:5, 14, 20, 27; 22:39, 45; 2 Kings 1:18; 8:23; 10:34; 12:19; 13:8, 12; etc.), however, it would not be a stretch to argue that the pre-exilic prophets did have access to and were reading pre-canonical versions of the Story. Furthermore, the prophets' understanding of the Torah Story facilitated and guided their understanding of their own histories. They were living out the Torah's prophecies of the election of a king from the Tribe of Judah, of covenant disobedience, of covenant curses, etc., and in a very real sense, their historical ministries and the inclusion of their messages in books were deeply influenced by the Story.

[109] 1 Pet 1:10-11.

[110] Compare Dan 9:4 with Lev 26:40; Dan 9:5 with 1 Ki 8:47; Dan 9:7 with Deut 30:1, 4 and Lev 26:40; Dan 9:19 with 1 Ki 8:30, 34, 36, 39, 50. Daniel 9:12-13, in fact, makes explicitly clear that Daniel saw Israel's exile as the fulfillment of Moses' predictions.

and the Writings, we simply want to provide illustrative passages that demonstrate that Israel's Prophets knew the Torah Story quite well, and frequently alluded to it in order to describe the King-Messiah, and that their Messianism is well integrated into the Story as a whole (Genesis – Kings).

The Book of Isaiah is particularly rich in allusions to the Messianism of the Story, and is quoted often in the New Testament. A few examples from Isaiah will suffice. First, we find that Isaiah's prophecy of the coming of a son who will rule forever on David's throne is taken nearly word for word from God's promises to David in 2 Samuel 7:

For to us a child is born, a SON will be given to us, and the government will be upon His shoulder. His Name will be called Wonderful Counselor, Mighty God My Father of Eternity, Prince of Peace. Of the increase of His government and *shalom* there will be no end—ON THE THRONE OF DAVID AND OVER HIS KINGDOM—TO ESTABLISH IT AND UPHOLD IT THROUGH JUSTICE AND RIGHTEOUSNESS FROM NOW UNTIL FOREVERMORE. The zeal of *ADONAI-Tzva'ot* will accomplish this. (Isa 9:5-6 [EVVs 6–7])	When your days are done and you sleep with your fathers, I will raise up your seed, who will come forth from you after you, AND I WILL ESTABLISH HIS KINGDOM. He will build a house for My name, and I will establish his royal throne forever I will be a father to him, and HE WILL BE A SON TO ME. If he commits iniquity, I will correct him with the rod of men and with the strokes from sons of men. Yet My loving kindness will not be withdrawn from him as I withdrew it from Saul, whom I removed from before you. SO YOUR HOUSE AND YOUR KINGSHIP WILL BE SECURE FOREVER BEFORE YOU; YOUR THRONE WILL BE ESTABLISHED FOREVER. (2 Sam 7:12–16)[111]

Another example is found in Isaiah's depiction of the Messiah in 11:1–9, and in the parallel passage in 65:25. The description of the Messiah as one upon whom rests the Spirit of God, wisdom, insight, knowledge, etc. in 11:2 is practically the same description of Bezalel from the Tribe of Judah who was called to build God's house in Exodus (see Exod 31:3, "I have filled him with the Spirit of God, with wisdom, understanding and knowledge in all kinds of craftsmanship"), thereby merging the two roles of King Messiah: the royal (from Judah), and the priestly (God's

---

[111] Emphases provided (all caps).

house). The description of the cessation of violence among the animals of creation in Isa 11:6–8 practically screams "New Adam," as we are reminded of Adam and Noah's authority over the animals (see Gen 1:28; 2:19; 7:9; 9:2). And we are reminded of Solomon whose wisdom and dominion over the animals (1 Ki 5:11–14 [4:31–34]) is but a shadow of Messiah's wisdom (Isa 11:2) and dominion over the animals (Isa 11:6–8). Remarkably, in a parallel passage in Isaiah 65:25 describing the days of Messiah's reign, it is clear that Isaiah has been studying the poetic speech in Genesis 3 and has correctly understood it with respect to the defeat of the serpent in the Days of the Messiah:[112]

The wolf and the lamb will feed together. The lion will eat straw like the ox, but dust will be the serpent's food. They will not hurt or destroy in all My holy mountain," says *ADONAI*. (Isa 65:25)	*ADONAI Elohim* said to the serpent, "Because you did this, Cursed are you above all the livestock and above every animal of the field. On your belly will you go, and dust will you eat all the days of your life. (Gen 3:14)

Isaiah 52:13-53:12, the fourth of Isaiah's Servant Songs,[113] a passage that is almost always included in the testimonies of Jewish people who believe in Yeshua, is also typically "under-read" in terms of its relationship to the Story. In his article on Isaiah's Servant Songs, Hugenberger has convincingly demonstrated, not only that the New Exodus[114] is a key theme in Isaiah 40– 55, but that we cannot rightfully appreciate the Servant's role in this New Exodus without reference to a New Moses (see Deut 18:15).[115] In other words, Isaiah's reading of the story of Moses and the Exodus was guided by the principle *ma'asei avot, siman l'banim*: the royal and priestly roles of the Servant are rightfully interpreted in the light of Moses, who himself served in both priestly and royal roles. And *the death of the Servant in Isaiah 53 is no shock to those who have already anticipated that Messiah's deadly blow to the serpent's head would necessarily involve the serpent's deadly blow to the Messiah's foot* (see Gen 3:15).

---

[112] The fact of which was also recognized by traditional Jewish interpreters (see Toledoth Yizhak Beraishit Parashat Beraishit 3; Daf al HaDaf Zara 30.71; Radak on Genesis 3; Malbim on Genesis 3.)

[113] Isa 42:1-4; 49:1-6; 50:4-9; 52:13-53:12.

[114] By "New Exodus," I am referring to an eschatological act of deliverance that is intentionally patterned after Israel's exodus out of Egypt.

[115] G. P. Hugenberger, "The Servant of the Lord in the 'Servant Songs' of Isaiah: A Second Moses Figure, in The Lord's Anointed: Interpretation of Old Testament Messianic Texts, eds., P. E. Satterthwaite, R. S. Hess, G. J. Wenham, 105-40 (Grand Rapids: Baker, 1995).

Later in Isaiah, the prophet describes the coming of a mighty conqueror whose garments are reddened like the one who treads in the wine presses (Isa 63:1-3). This description is almost certainly taken from Jacob's prophecy about the King-Messiah in Gen 49:11: "He ties his foal to the vine, and his donkey's colt to the choice vine; he *washes his garments in wine, and his robes in the blood of grapes*."[116]

Zechariah, like Isaiah before him, was also inspired by this specific prophecy in describing the Messiah's coming, for only in Gen 49:11 and Zech 9:9 do we find a reference to a future king coming on a foal and a colt: [117]

The SCEPTER will not pass from Judah, nor the RULER'S staff from between his feetcf. Rev. 19:15. , until he to whom it belongs will come [until SHILOH COMES]. To him will be the obedience of the peoples. Or tribute comes or Shiloh comes . . . Binding his FOAL to the vine, his DONKEY'S COLT to the choice vinecf. Zech. 9:9-10; Matt. 21:5; John 12:15. , he washes his garments in wine, and in the blood of grapes his robe. (Gen 49:10-11)	Rejoice greatly, daughter of Zion! Shout, daughter of Jerusalem! Behold, YOUR KING IS COMING to you, a righteous one bringing salvation. He is lowly, riding on a donkey—ON A COLT, THE FOAL OF A DONKEY. (Zech 9:9)[118]

Zechariah goes on to describe this king as one whose "dominion[119] will be from sea to sea, and from the river to the ends of the earth" (see Ps 72:8). Zechariah's words suggest he has understood the point of the Story, and recognized the centrality of the Messiah to retake what Adam forfeited in his disobedience, namely dominion over the Land. Finally, Zechariah's description of Messiah who is both king and priest in Zech 6:9-13 can only rightfully be understood when considered against the background of the Torah's expectation for the New Adam, a Royal-Priest, the One through whom Israel's calling to be a royal priesthood (Exod 19:6) will be fully and completely realized.

Messianism in the Latter Prophets is a promising field of study. From but a brief treatment of it, we can safely say that these prophets had meditated long and hard on the Story. And given the numerous allusions to this Story, particularly in those places that have long been

---

[116] This connection was also noted by the Jewish interpreters (see *Bereishit Rabati, Parashat V'yichi*).

[117] See Michael Fishbane, *Biblical Interpretation in Ancient Israel* (Oxford: Clarendon; New York: Oxford, 1985), 501-502.

[118] Emphases provided (all caps).

[119] Cf. Num 24:19.

regarded as Messianic, we see that their vision was neither spontaneous nor random. Rather, *it was forged in the furnace of prolonged meditation on Moses and their steadfast hope against all hope that his predictions about the Last Days would indeed come to pass.*

Messianism in the Writings

We come now to the final section of the Hebrew Bible, the Writings (Psalms – Chronicles). Given the fact that scholars are agreed that the section called the Writings was the last of the tripartite section of the Hebrew Bible to be completed,[120] it is quite remarkable that King David and God's covenantal promises to him continue to make the headlines!

How does David make the headlines in the Writings? First of all, in terms of a pure headcount, David has Moses beat 365 to 40![121] Secondly, David serves as the bookend figure of the Writings,[122] appearing 88 times in the opening book of the Writings (Psalms), and 261 times in the closing book of the Writings (Chronicles). Lastly, the Davidic Covenant stands in structurally significant places in both books.

Moreover, recent studies in the Psalter have demonstrated that Davidic-Royal Psalms do not appear in random places, but are strategically located in the introductions and/or conclusions of the major books of the Psalter.[123] Psalm 2 and 72 are both Psalms dealing with God's promises to the house of David. They serve as the bookends to Books I and II, and are all the more striking given the compositional gloss in Ps 72:20 linking these books together. Book III also concludes with a prolonged focus on the Davidic Covenant, as the author agonizes over the possibility that Israel's exile means the promises are no longer valid (see Ps 89:38–51). David is conspicuously and intentionally absent from Book IV,[124] only to reemerge again in the introduction (Psa 108:1;

---

[120] For an in depth treatment of the issues, see Rodger Beckwith, *The Old Testament Canon of the New Testament Church* (Grand Rapids: Eerdmans, 1985).

[121] David mentioned 710 times in the Prophets (including Former and Latter Prophets), 672 times in the Former Prophets, 38 times in Latter Prophets.

[122] Regardless of whether one considers Ruth or Psalms as the opening of the Writings, David's importance in the book still puts David as the dominant figure in the introduction and conclusion to the Writings (see "CANON," *AYBD*, 1:840.).

[123] See Gerald H. Wilson, "The Use of Royal Psalms at the 'Seams' of the Hebrew Psalter," *Journal For The Study Of The Old Testament* no. 35 (June 1, 1986): 85-94; David C. Mitchell, "Lord, Remember David: G H Wilson and the Message of the Psalter," *Vetus Testamentum* 56, no. 4 (January 1, 2006): 526-548. The Psalter is divided into five books: Book I (Psalms 1-41), Book II (Psalms 42-72), Book III (Psalms 73-89), Book IV (Psalms 90-106), and Book V (Psalms 107-150).

[124] Moses, not David, is the key figure in Book IV, appearing both its opening and closing Psalms as bookends (Psa 90:1; 99:6; 103:7; 105:26; 106:16, 23, 32). David, on the other hand, is only mentioned twice

109:1; 110:1) and conclusion to Book V (Ps 144:1, 10; 145:1),[125] with the David Covenant taking center stage yet again (Ps 110; 132).

Finally, Chronicles, like the Psalter, gives significant attention, not only to King David, but it also repeats the Davidic Covenant in 1 Chron 17:11–14 with one significant difference. Unlike its counterpart, 1 Chronicles 17 does not even suggest the possibility of failure on the part of David's house (cf. 2 Sam 7:14; 1 Chron 17:13). Noted therein is that God will set a descendant of David on an eternal throne. Period.

A truly remarkable aspect of the significance of David and the Davidic Covenant in the third section of the Hebrew Canon is why this should be the case at all! After all, both the Psalter[126] and Chronicles[127] were composed at a time when David's line was no longer on the throne. In other words, *why should the David and the Davidic Covenant be such a hot topic at a time when Judea was being ruled by a foreign power?* The only explicable reason for the centrality of David and the Davidic Covenant long after the exile must be the hope for the coming David-related, Messiah-King, in fulfillment of God's unconditional promises to David, and to Abraham before him!

The place of David and the Davidic Covenant in the Writings, in spite of the reality of Israel's covenant disobedience and exile, can only mean that its authors also understood the point of the Story, particularly those places in the Story where God promised to restore creation through the coming Messiah (Gen 3:15; 49:1, 8–12; Num 24:7–9, 17–24; 1 Sam 2:10; 2 Sam 7:12–16; 22:1–51; 23:1–7). Thus the writer of Chronicles, at the end of the canon, can write with inspired confidence: "Yet the LORD was not willing to destroy the house of David because

---

(Psa 101:1; 103:1). Recent studies suggest that the purpose of Book IV is to highlight the kingship of God during the time of Israel's exile (see Wilson, "Use of Royal Psalms"). Though a son of David is not on the throne in Jerusalem, God is still on the throne in heaven! Moses, rather than David, serves as a source of hope, for he too died in exile without losing his faith in the promises of God!

[125] Psalms 146-150 function as the final doxology of the Psalter as a whole. For an excellent defense of regarding Ps 146-150 as the conclusion to the Psalter, see Michael Snearly, "Coda: Psalms 146-150 as the Conclusion of the Psalter," unpublished paper, https://www.ibrbbr.org/files/pdf/2014b/Snearly%20OT%20Essay.pdf, accessed December 27, 2014 (Michael Snearly received his Ph.D. under the well-known Psalms scholar, David Howard, Jr.); see also Gerald H. Wilson, *The Editing of the Hebrew Psalter*, SBLDS 76 (Chico, CA: Scholar's Press, 1985), 193–94; *idem*, "The shape of the book of Psalms," *Interpretation* 46, no. 2 (April 1, 1992): 132-33; Tremper Longman III, "From Weeping to Rejoicing: Psalm 150 as the Conclusion to the Psalter," in The Psalms: Language for All Seasons of the Soul, ed. Andrew J. Schmutzer and David M. Howard, Jr. (Chicago: Moody, 2013): 226.

[126] The Psalter in its canonical form had to have been completed after the composition of Psalm 137, a Psalm that was written during the Babylonian Exile. If Psalm 126 was composed when the Israelites returned from exile, that would mean the Psalter was completed in the postexilic period.

[127] For the issues involved in the dating of Chronicles, see "CHRONICLES, BOOK OF 1–2," AYBD, 1:994-995.

of the covenant which He had made with David, and since He had promised to give a lamp to him and his sons forever" (2 Chron 21:7).

Before we bring this section to a close, it's worth considering the ways in which the Messianism in the Writings is rooted in the Story, and how it features the Messiah as the one through whom God would reestablish His creation purposes. In short, how, and in what sense will the Messiah be the New Adam? In an earlier section of this chapter, we looked at Psalm 8, a Psalm which, in its literary context as a Psalm of David, the psalm depicts the rule of the Davidic king as a fulfillment of the creation mandate. Given the depiction of King Solomon's rule in 1 Kings, it's clear enough, moreover, that this belief was well established in Israelite thinking.

God blessed them and God said to them, "Be fruitful and multiply, fill the land, and conquer it. Rule over the fish of the sea, the flying creatures of the sky, and over every animal that crawls on the land." (Gen 1:28)	Now SOLOMON RULED OVER ALL THE KINGDOMS FROM THE RIVER TO THE LAND OF THE PHILISTINES UP TO THE BORDER OF EGYPT. They brought tribute and served Solomon all the days of his life. . . FOR HE HAD DOMINION OVER THE ENTIRE REGION west of the River, from Tiphsah even to Gaza, over all the kings west of the River; and he had *shalom* on all sides around him. . . He also spoke about trees, from the cedar in Lebanon to the hyssop that grows out of the wall, and HE SPOKE ABOUT BEASTS, BIRDS, CREEPING THINGS AND FISH. (1 Kings 5:1, 4, 13 [EVVS 4:21, 24, 33])	What is man, that You are mindful of him? And the son of man, that You care for him? Yet You made him a little lower than the angels, and crowned him with glory and majesty! YOU GAVE HIM DOMINION OVER THE WORKS OF YOUR HANDS. YOU PUT ALL THINGS UNDER THEIR FEET: ALL SHEEP AND OXEN, AND ALSO BEASTS OF THE FIELD, BIRDS IN THE AIR, AND FISH IN THE OCEAN— ALL PASSING THROUGH THE PATHS OF THE SEAS. (Psalms 8:4-8)[128]

---

[128] Emphases provided (all caps).

Thus it is natural that the Psalter's Messiah would be given rule over everything in creation, even till the ends of the earth (Psa 2:8; 72:8; see 22:28). Of particular interest is Ps 72's depiction of the Messiah in terms borrowed from the poetic speeches of the Torah.

May he have dominion from sea to sea, and from the River to the ends of the earth. (Ps 72:8)	God blessed them and God said to them, "Be fruitful and multiply, fill the land, and conquer it. Rule over the fish of the sea, the flying creatures of the sky, and over every animal that crawls on the land." (Gen 1:28)
Let desert dwellers bow before him, AND HIS ENEMIES LICK THE DUST. (Ps 72:9)	*ADONAI Elohim* said to the serpent, "Because you did this, Cursed are you above all the livestock and above every animal of the field. On your belly will you go, and dust will you eat all the days of your life. I will put animosity between you and the woman— between your seed and her seed. He will crush your head, and you will crush his heel". (Gen 3:14–15)
So let all kings bow down before him, and all nations serve him. (Ps 72:11)	May peoples serve you and may nations bow down to you. (Gen 27:29) To him will be the obedience of the peoples. (Gen 49:10)
Long may he live! May gold from Sheba be given to him. May he pray for him continually, AND BLESS HIM ALL DAY. (Ps 72:15)	He crouches like a lion or a lioness— who would rouse him? HE WHO BLESSES YOU WILL BE BLESSED, and he who curses you will be cursed.. (Num 24:9)
May his name endure forever. May his name increase before the sun, AND MAY ALL NATIONS BE BLESSED BY HIM and call him blessed. (Ps 72:17)	… and your seed will possess the gate of his enemies. IN YOUR SEED ALL THE NATIONS OF THE EARTH WILL BE BLESSED. (Gen 22:17–18)[129]

It is difficult if not impossible to understand the depiction of the Messiah-King in Ps 72 without reference to the Messianism of the

---

[129] Emphases provided (all caps).

Torah, particularly as it is rooted in the creation mandate. This is particularly evident in the choice of words describing Messiah's rule in Ps 72:8 and 110:2: *radah*. This verb is not only used in the creation mandate (Gen 1:26, 28), but also to describe the reign of the star from Jacob who will crush the enemies' head in the Last Days (Num 24:19; see vv. 14, 17). Also not surprising is the reference to the priesthood of the Messiah-King in Ps 110:4, particularly in light of the paradigmatic significance of Adam's (and Israel's) royal priesthood. Of course Messiah-King, the New Adam, will also be a priest! Brief mention must also be made to the "suffering king" of the Psalter. Recent studies in the Psalter have focused on the compositional unity of the whole of the Psalter with Psalms 1-2 functioning as the introduction to the work as a whole.[130] Psalm 2, though describing Messiah's rule as universal, begins with recognition that the establishment of this rule will face fierce opposition: "The kings of earth set themselves up and rulers conspire together against *ADONAI* and against His Anointed One" (Ps 2:2). This verse is crucial for understanding the place of David's bitter laments in the Psalter. Yes, God has called David and one of his descendants to rule forever. But we can expect opposition, even unto death! David is elsewhere described as a prophet filled with the Spirit of God (2 Sam 23:1-2), thus it is neither foreign to the context nor exegetical contortionism to read David's lament Psalms as, in a very real sense, simultaneously prophetic descriptions of the bitter opposition and laments of the Messiah as well as expressions of his own suffering (see, for example, Ps 22:1-22 [MT]). And *for those who are familiar with the Story, it comes as no surprise that the Messiah's victory over the serpent necessarily includes suffering and death* (Ps 16:10; cf. Gen 3:15).

The book of Daniel is rich with Messianism, and is a study in itself. It is important to note here that when Daniel tells the king that God has made known to him how God will establish His eternal kingdom in the Last Days (Dan 2:28, 44; see 7:13–14), we are reminded of a similar situation wherein Balaam also declared to another non-Israelite king how God would establish His kingdom in the Last Days. This illustrates that Daniel's Messianism does not fall from heaven in a vacuum, but is thoroughly rooted in the Torah's Messianism:

---

[130] Brevard S. Childs, Introduction to the Old Testament as Scripture (Augsburg: Fortress, 1979), 504-525; Gerald Wilson, Editing of the Hebrew Psalter; David C. Mitchell, Message of the Psalter: An Eschatological Programme in the Book of Psalms, JSOTSup 252 (Sheffield: Sheffield Academic, 1997). Cole, Psalm 1-2: Gateway to the Psalter.

But, there is a God in heaven who reveals mysteries. He has made known to King Nebuchadnezzar the things that will happen in THE LATTER DAYS. . . . Now in the days of those kings, THE GOD OF HEAVEN WILL SET UP A KINGDOM THAT WILL NEVER BE DESTROYED, nor will this kingdom be left to another people. IT WILL CRUSH AND BRING TO AN END ALL OF THESE KINGDOMS. BUT IT WILL ENDURE FOREVER. (Dan 2:28, 44)	Water will flow from his buckets, his seed by abundant water. HIS KING WILL BE GREATER THAN AGAG, HIS KINGDOM WILL BE EXALTED. . . Now, behold, I am going back to my people. Come, let me counsel you what these people will do to your people in THE LATTER DAYS. . . I see him, yet not at this moment. I behold him, yet not in this location. For a star will come from Jacob, a SCEPTER will arise from Israel. He will CRUSH.... (Num 24:7, 14, 17)[131]

And, likewise, it is not entirely unexpected when we see Daniel's exalted Son of Man (Dan 7:13-14) that He is elsewhere described as a Messiah who is cut off as part of God's purposes, "To put an end to transgression to bring sin to an end, to atone for iniquity, to bring in everlasting righteousness" (Dan 9:24, 26). This deep into the chapter, we should be well aware that the Messiah's suffering, sacrifice, and death are part of God's plan for reestablishing the Second Adam's rule over creation. It all evolves out of Genesis.

And now we come to the capstone of the Hebrew Bible, a book at the other end of the Hebrew canon: the Book of Chronicles. Chronicles, unique among the other books of the Hebrew canon, appears to be designed as a conclusion to the Hebrew canon.[132] The book begins with a reference to the first book in the Hebrew Bible (1 Chron 1:1; see Gen 5:1) and concludes with a reference to the penultimate book in the Hebrew Bible (2 Chron 36:2-223; see Ezra 1:1-3[133]). It is clear enough from the introduction to the Book that the Chronicler is not particularly concerned with all the tribes of Israel, but almost exclusively concerned with one tribe, Judah, and one family line through Perez, David's (1 Chron 2:3-4). Moreover, the Chronicler begins his genealogy with Adam. It would be difficult to understand the Chronicler's genealogy from Adam to Perez were in not for the Story, whose genealogy also begins with Adam and leads us to a child of Judah, Perez (Gen 5:1; 38:29; 49:8). When the Chronicler repeats Nathan's words to David in 1

---

[131] Emphases provided (all caps).

[132] Hendrik J. Koorevaar, "Die Chronik als intendierter Abscluß des alttestamentlichen Kanons," Jahrbuch für Evangelische Theologie 11 (1997): 42-76.

[133] In the Hebrew canon, Ezra does not stand alone, but is part of a larger work known as Ezra-Nehemiah.

Chron 17:11-14, therefore, we rightfully understand this particular king as the truest heir of Adam:

> It will be that when your days are fulfilled to go with your fathers, I will raise up your offspring after you, one of your own sons, and I will establish his kingdom. He will build a house for Me and I will establish his throne forever. I will be a father to him and he will be a son to Me, I will not withdraw My loving kindness from him, as I withdrew it from the one who ruled before you.

It is this seed of Adam (and Eve), who is both David's son, as well as God's, *a king who rules and a priestly figure who establishes a place of worship.* As Adam's greatest heir, He is a priest-king! It is this Seed of Adam (and Eve), who is both the son of David and the son of God, this Seed is a king who rules and, as noted, is also a priestly figure who establishes a place of worship. This Seed is Adam's greatest heir; He is a priest-king!

As the Hebrew canon comes to a close, we are surprised (or perhaps not so surprised) to find an abbreviated version of Cyrus' speech taken from Ezra 1:

Now in the first year of King Cyrus of Persia—fulfilling the word of *ADONAI* by the mouth of Jeremiah—*ADONAI* stirred up the spirit of King Cyrus of Persia so that he sent a proclamation throughout all his kingdom and also put it in writing, saying: Thus says King Cyrus of Persia '*ADONAI*, the God of heaven, has given me all the kingdoms of the earth. He has appointed me to build Him a House in Jerusalem, which is in Judah. Whoever among you of all His people may go up and may *ADONAI* his God be with him.' (2 Chron 36:22–23)	Now in the first year of King Cyrus of Persia, in order to accomplish the word of *ADONAI* from the mouth of Jeremiah, *ADONAI* stirred up the spirit of King Cyrus of Persia to make a proclamation throughout his entire kingdom, announcing in a written edict, saying: Thus says King Cyrus of Persia: *ADONAI*, the God of heaven, has given me all the kingdoms of the earth. He has appointed me to build a House for Him in Jerusalem, which is in Judah. Whoever is among you from all His people—may his God be with him—may go UP TO JERUSALEM, WHICH IS IN JUDAH, AND BUILD THE HOUSE OF *ADONAI*, THE GOD OF ISRAEL—HE IS THE GOD WHO IS IN JERUSALEM. AS FOR ANYONE WHO REMAINS, WHEREVER THEY MAY BE LIVING, LET THE PEOPLE OF THOSE PLACES SUPPLY HIM WITH SILVER AND GOLD, WITH GOODS AND LIVESTOCK, AND WITH FREEWILL OFFERINGS FOR THE HOUSE OF GOD IN JERUSALEM. (Ezra 1:1–4)[134]

---

[134] Emphasis provided (all caps).

The author of Chronicles simply pulls the plug on Cyrus's speech. Why? Sailhamer has noted that the abbreviated speech fits well with the Chronicler's compositional purposes.[135] Whereas the author of Ezra-Nehemiah regards the return of the exiles and the building of the second temple as in some fashion fulfilling Jeremiah's 70 years, for the Chronicler, only the Son of God and Messiah - not the exiles - would build the house of God and establish God's eternal kingdom (compare 2 Chron 36:24 with 1 Chron 17:12). Jeremiah's 70 years in Ezra-Nehemiah becomes Daniel's 70 weeks of years in Chronicles (see Dan 9:1–2, 24ff.).

The final words of the Hebrew canon, therefore, should be understood as nothing less than a call for the New Adam, the Son of God, the Messiah, to "go up and build" an eternal house for God. And what more fitting introduction to the New Testament writings than a genealogy (Matt 1:1ff). One could say a seamless transition from the genealogies of Chronicles to the genealogies of Matthew, both of which are keen on demonstrating that God's creation purposes will be accomplished through a scion of David.

Conclusion

When we attempt to understand the Messianism in the Hebrew Bible, by looking first at various verses and oracles in the writings of the prophets, there is a sense in which the Messianic prophecies are scattered, random, and disconnected. The texts present to us without contexts. Moreover, when we try to understand the Messianism in the Torah (or the Hebrew Bible for that matter) through the lens of isolated verses, the Messiah hardly seems to merit any attention at all. Messianism from this perspective, it would appear, is not as significant to the writers of the Hebrew Bible as it obviously was to the writers of the New Testament, who utilize verses to proof text their narratives! The New Testament assertion that the Messiah was a central theme of the Hebrew Bible seems more a case of "extra-Jesus"[136] than of careful exegesis of the Hebrew text itself, if only a few prophetic passages are studied in isolation. So it may seem; but the look can be deceiving.

---

[135] I have been unable to locate Sailhamer's publication on the purposes of Cyrus' abbreviate speech in Chronicles, but recall classroom discussions with John Sailhamer on the topic; see also Nahum Sarna, "The Bible: The Canon, Texts, and Editions," in *Encyclopedia Judaica* (Jerusalem: Keter, 1971), 4:831.

[136] I first heard this pun used by my doctoral mentor, John Sailhamer.

This typical approach to Messianism, however, really doesn't do full justice to the shaping of the Hebrew Canon, the first half of which is a single seamless story; nor does it take seriously the interconnected web of citations and allusions to this thread within the prophetic writings.[137] Truth be known, Messianism and Messianic prophecies in the Hebrew Bible are neither scattered nor random when placed within their own natural context: the Story (Genesis – Kings). In this chapter, we have argued that the Story presents the reader with two parallel expectations, expectations that provide a grid through which to read and understand the Latter Prophets and the Writings. First, that Israel would break the Sinai Covenant, and they would go into exile. Second, that God would bring a king from and to His people Israel in the Last Days: "The scepter will not pass from Judah, nor the ruler's staff from between his feet, until he to whom it belongs will come. To him will be the obedience of the peoples" (Gen 49:10). Because this king is Israel's king, and because we know that Israel's king will triumph over His enemies (Gen 3:15; Deut 33:7), we can also know that Israel will ultimately triumph over her enemies in spite of her failures (Deut 33:29). Israel, by God's grace, is destined to win! And because Israel is destined to win, all nations are destined for blessing. The Torah's remarkable vision of Gentiles and Jews praising God together (Deut 32:43) will become a reality, because God will remain faithful to His promises to Abraham and because He is committed to the triumph of His creation purposes, purposes which may be summed up in three words, BLESSING, SEED, and LAND (Gen 1:28)

What exactly does "triumph" mean in the context of this Story? Triumph means doing what Adam failed to do in Genesis 1–3. Triumph

---

[137] Nor does this approach satisfactorily explain the manner in which the New Testament writers interpreted the Tanakh. Richard B. Hays, *Reading Backwards: Figural Christology and the Fourfold Gospel Witness* (Waco: Baylor University Press, 2014), expresses well the importance of the Story in Luke's presentation of Yeshua when he writes, 15-16, "If we learn from the Gospel of Luke how to read the OT, we will see that the whole story of Israel builds to a narrative climax in the story of Jesus. In other words, we do not simply scour the OT for isolated proof texts and predictions; rather, we must perceive how the whole story of God's covenant promise unfolds and leads toward the events of Jesus' death and resurrection." On that same note, he summarizes the interpretive approach taken by the Gospel writers, 105-106: "For the Evangelists, Israel's Scripture told the true *story* of the world. Scripture was not merely a repository of ancient writings containing important laws or ideas or images; rather, it traced out a coherent story line that stretched from creation, through the election of Israel, to the *telos* of God's redemption of the world.... One significant implication of this is that a Gospel-shaped hermeneutic will pay primary attention to large narrative arcs and patterns in the OT rather than treating Scripture chiefly as a source of oracles, proof texts, or halakhic regulations. The Evangelists, who are themselves storytellers, are much more interested in the OT as story than as prediction or as law" (words in italics original).

means doing what Israel failed to do in Joshua through to 2 Kings. Triumph means the reclamation of the Land and ruling over it. Triumph means blessing, lots and lots of blessing, through Eve's seed, through Abraham's seed, to Israel and to all nations (Gen 12:1–3; 22:17–18; 27:29; 49:10; Num 24:9; Ps 72:17). God is determined to bless, and so blessings, not curses, have the first and the last word in the Torah Story. Curses are penultimate (Gen 3:14, 17; Deut 27:15–26; 28:16–20), blessings are ultimate (Gen 1:22, 28; 2:3; Deut 33:1, 11, 13, 20, 24). And it is only because of the Messianism in the Hebrew Bible that blessings are ultimate, for only He can succeed where all others have failed.

The world will never be what it was intended to be until the Seed of Woman, the King of Israel, is reigning and ruling over the Land. With full anticipation of this biblical hope for the True King to take up His rule from Zion, we conclude this chapter with the final words of the Hebrew Bible, "Let him go up!" (2 Chron 36:23).

BIBLIOGRAPHY

Alexander, T. Desmond. "Royal Expectations in Genesis to Kings: Their
    Importance for Biblical theology." *TynB* 49, no. 2 (January 1, 1998):
    191-212
_____. "Further Observations on the Term 'Seed' in Genesis," TynB 48.2
    (1997): 363-67
Alter, Robert. *The Five Books of Moses: A Translation with Commentary* (W.
    W. Norton & Company, New York; London, 2004),
Bakon, Shimon, "Creation, Tabernacle and Sabbath." *Jewish Bible Quarterly*
    25, no. 2 (April 1, 1997): 79-85;
Beckwith, Rodger. *The Old Testament Canon of the New Testament Church*
    (Grand Rapids: Eerdmans, 1985)
Brettler, Marc. "The Book of Judges: Literature as Politics," JBL 108/3 (1989):
    395–418
Budd, Philip J. *Numbers*, WBC, vol. 5 (Waco: Word Books, 1984)
Buss, Martin J. "Tragedy and Comedy in Hosea," Semeia no. 32 (January 1,
    1984): 71-82
Childs, Brevard S. *Introduction to the Old Testament as Scripture* (Augsburg:
    Fortress, 1979)
Cole, R. Dennis. *Numbers*, NAC, vol. 3B (Nashville: Broadman & Holman
    Publishers, 2000)
Cole, Robert L. *Psalms 1–2: Gateway to the Psalter* (Sheffiled, UK: Sheffield
    Phoenix Press, 2012)
Collins, Jack, "A Syntactical Note (Genesis 3:15): Is the Woman's Seed
    Singular or Plural," *TynB* 48.1 (1997):139-49
Craigie, Peter C. *Ezekiel*. Daily Study Bible. (Philadelphia: Westminster Press,
    1983)
Dällenbach, Lucien, *Le récit spéculaire. Essai sur la mise en abyme* (Paris,
    Seuil, 1977).
Davies, John A. "'Discerning Between Good and Evil': Solomon as a New
    Adam in 1 Kings," *Westminster Theological Journal* 73, no. 1 (March 1,
    2011): 39-57
Dempster, Stephen G. *Dominion and Dynasty*, NSBT New Studies in Biblical
    Theology (Downers Grove, Il.: InterVarsity, 2003)
Elnes, Eric E. "Creation and Tabernacle: The Priestly Writer's
    "Environmentalism," *Horizons In Biblical Theology* 16, no. 2 (December
    1, 1994): 144-155
Enns, Peter . *Exodus*, NIV Application Commentary (Grand Rapids:
    Zondervan, 2000), 550-52
Fee, Gordon D. and Douglas Stuart, *How to Read the Bible for All It's Worth*
    (Grand Rapids: Zondervan, 2003)

Fishbane, Michael A. *Biblical Text and Texture: A Literary Reading of Selected Texts* (Oxford: Oneworld, 1998)

_____. *Biblical Interpretation in Ancient Israel* (Oxford: Clarendon; New York: Oxford, 1985)

Gesenius, Wilhelm, E. Kautzsch, and A. E. Cowley. *Gesenius' Hebrew Grammar*. Oxford: Clarendon Press, 1910.

Gottwald, Norman K. "Tragedy and Comedy in the Latter Prophets," *Semeia* no. 32 (January 1, 1984): 83-96

Gunn, David M. "The Anatomy of Divine Comedy: On Reading the Bible as Comedy and Tragedy," *Semeia* no. 32 (January 1, 1984): 115-129

Hamilton, James M. Jr., *God's Glory in Salvation Through Judgment: A Biblical Theology* (Wheaton, Il.: Crossway, 2010)

Harris, W. Hall, ed. *NET Bible Notes* (W. Hall Harris, ed.: 1st, Accordance electronic ed. Richardson: Biblical Studies Press, 2005).

Hays, Richard B. *Reading Backwards: Figural Christology and the Fourfold Gospel Witness* (Waco: Baylor University Press, 2014)

Hugenberger, G. P. "The Servant of the Lord in the 'Servant Songs' of Isaiah: A Second Moses Figure, in The Lord's Anointed: Interpretation of Old Testament Messianic Texts, eds., P. E. Satterthwaite, R. S. Hess, G. J. Wenham, 105-40 (Grand Rapids: Baker, 1995)

Joüon, Paul, and T. Muraoka. A Grammar of Biblical Hebrew. Roma: Pontificio istituto biblico, Gregorian & Biblical Press, 2006.

Kearney, Peter J. "Creation and Liturgy: The P Redaction of Ex 25–40," *ZAW* 89 (1977): 375-87

Keil, Carl Friedrich, and Franz Delitzsch. *Ezekiel*, Vol. 9, Commentary on the Old Testament. Peabody, Mass: Hendrickson, 1996.

Klein, Ralph W. "Chronicles, Book of 1-2," 992-1002 in vol 1 of *The Anchor Bible Dictionary*, ed. D. N. Freedman (New York: Doubleday, 1992).

Koorevaar, Hendrik J. "Die Chronik als intendierter Abschluß des alttestamentlichen Kanons," Jahrbuch für Evangelische Theologie 11 (1997): 42-76

Lee, Chee-Chiew. *The Blessing of Abraham, the Spirit, & Justification in Galatians* (Eugene, OR: Pickwick, 2013)

Longman, Tremper III, "From Weeping to Rejoicing: Psalm 150 as the Conclusion to the Psalter," in The Psalms: Language for All Seasons of the Soul, pp. 219-230, ed. Andrew J. Schmutzer and David M. Howard, Jr. (Chicago: Moody, 2013).

Martin, R. A. "The Earliest Messianic Interpretation of Genesis 3:15," JBL 84 (1965): 425–27

Matthews, Kenneth A., Genesis 1:1-11:26 (NAC 1A; ed. E. Ray Clendenen; Nashville: Broadman & Holman Publishers, 1996)

McCann, J. Clinton Jr., *A Theological Introduction to the Book of Psalms: The Psalms as Torah* (Nashville: Abingdon, 1993),

Meyer, Jason C. *The End of the Law: Mosaic Covenant in Pauline Theology*, NAC Studies in Bible & Theology, ed., E. Ray Clendenen (Nashville: B&H, 2009)

Miller, Patrick D. "The Beginning of the Psalter," in The Shape and Shaping of the Psalter, ed. J. Clinton McCann, JSOT Supp 159 (Sheffield: Sheffield Academic, 1993)

Mitchell, David C. "Lord, Remember David: G H Wilson and the Message of the Psalter," *Vetus Testamentum* 56, no. 4 (January 1, 2006): 526-548

_____. *Message of the Psalter: An Eschatological Programme in the Book of Psalms*, JSOTSup 252 (Sheffield: Sheffield Academic, 1997).

Morales, Michael .The Tabernacle Pre-Figured: Cosmic Mountain Ideology in Genesis and Exodus (Biblical Tools and Studies 15; Leuven/Paris/Walpole, MA: Peeters, 2012)

Noth, Martin. *The Deuteronomistic History* (Sheffield: JSOT Press, 1981).

Osborne, Grant R. *The Hermeneutical Spiral*, revised (Downers Grove: IVPress, 2006)

Postell, *Adam as Israel* (Eugene, Or.: Pickwick, 2011)

Rydelnik, Michael . *The Messianic Hope*, NAC Studies in Bible and Theology (Nashville: B&H, 2010)

Sailhamer, John H. *The Meaning of the Pentateuch* (Downers Grove: IVP Academic, 2010)

_____. *The Pentateuch as Narrative* (Grand Rapids: Zondervan, 1992)

_____. *Genesis*, EBC vol. 2, ed. Frank E. Gaebelein and J. D. Douglas (Grand Rapids: Zondervan, 1990)

Sanders, James A. "Canon," 837-852, in vol 1 of *The Anchor Bible Dictionary*, ed. D. N. Freedman (New York: Doubleday, 1992).

Sarna, Nahum. "The Bible: The Canon, Texts, and Editions," 816-41, in *Encyclopedia Judaica* 4 (Jerusalem: Keter, 1971).

Schmitt, Hans-Christoph, "Das spätdeuteronomistische Geschichtswerk Genesis 1 - 2 Regnum 25 und seine theologische Intention," in *Congress Volume*, ed., J.A. Emerton, 261-79 (Leiden: Brill, 1997)

Schmutzer, Andrew J., "The Creation Mandate to 'be fruitful and multiply': A Crux of Thematic Repetition in Genesis 1–11," (PhD diss., Trinity Evangelical Divinity School, 2005)

Snearly, Snearly. "Coda: Psalms 146-150 as the Conclusion of the Psalter," unpublished paper, https://www.ibrbbr.org/files/pdf/2014b/Snearly%20OT%20Essay.pdf, accessed December 27, 2014

Taylor, John B. *Ezekiel: An Introduction and Commentary* (London : Tyndale, 1969).

Timmer, Daniel C. *Creation, Tabernacle, and Sabbath: The Sabbath Frame of Exodus 31:12-17; 35:1-3 in Exegetical and Theological Perspective* (FRLANT, 227; Göttingen: Vandenhoeck & Ruprecht, 2009)

Wenham, Gordon J. "Sanctuary Symbolism in the Garden of Eden Story," in *I Studied Inscriptions before the Flood*, edited by Richard Hess and David Toshio Tsumura, 399–404, Sources for Biblical and Theological Study 4. 1994 ,Eisenbrauns :IN ,Winona Lake

_____. *Genesis 1-15*, Word Biblical Commentary, vol. 1 (Waco: Word Books, 1987)

Wilson, Gerald H. "The Use of Royal Psalms at the 'Seams' of the Hebrew Psalter," *Journal For The Study Of The Old Testament* no. 35 (June 1, 1986): 85-94.

_____. *The Editing of the Hebrew Psalter*, SBLDS 76 (Chico, CA: Scholar's Press, 1985)

_____. "The Shape of the Book of Psalms," *Interpretation* 46, no. 2 (April 1, 1992): 129-42

Youngblood, Ronald F. *1 and 2 Samuel*, EBC, vol. 3, ed. Frank E. Gaebelein and J. D. Douglas (Grand Rapids: Zondervan, 1992)

Zakovitch, Yair, Comedy and Tragedy in the Bible," *Semeia* no. 32 (January 1, 1984):107-14.

Zimmerli, Walther, Frank Moore Cross, and Klaus Baltzer. Ezekiel: A Commentary on the Book of the Prophet Ezekiel. Fortress :Philadelphia .1979 ,Press

Messianism in Jewish Literature Beyond the Bible

Vered Hillel, Ph.D.

Provost, Messianic Jewish Theological Institute

"Any discussion of the problems relating to Messianism is a delicate matter, for it is here that the essential conflict between Judaism and Christianity has developed and continues to exist." Gershom Scholem[1]

"Let God arise!" Messianic Judaism stands at the crossroads of the "essential conflict" mentioned by Gershom Scholem in his influential essay on the messianic idea in Judaism, because Messianic Judaism shares a communal context with both Judaism and Christianity. Scholem touches on one of the core challenges when he explains, "A totally different view of redemption determines the attitude toward messianism in Judaism and Christianity."[2] To be sure, his contrasts are overdrawn, but they do point out Christianity and Judaism have different understandings and views of messianism, which have developed over time in different communal contexts. How will God make His entrance onto the stage of the human drama? Messianic Judaism has the challenge of drawing from both communal contexts in tendering an answer. In the past, it has largely drawn from a Christian communal setting context in developing a Messianic Jewish theology. More familiarity with extra-biblical texts that give a window into how ancient Jews saw the Bible will enable us to draw more deeply from the wells of

---

[1] Gershom Scholem, "Toward an Understand of the Messianic Idea in Judaism," *The Messianic Idea in Judaism and Other Essays on Jewish Spirituality*, NY: Schocken, 1971, 1–36, quote 1.

[2] Ibid. W. S. Green challenges Scholem's postulations and the influence they have had on subsequent scholarship; see his article "Messiah in Judaism: Rethinking the Question," *Judaisms and Their Messiahs at the Turn of the Christian Era*. J. Neusner, W.S. Green and E.S. Frerichs, eds. Cambridge: Cambridge University Press, 1987, 1–13.

Jewish communal context in the development of a decidedly Messianic Jewish theology.

In this chapter we will survey Jewish texts beyond the Bible, for their witness to messianism and the Bible. We will limit our survey to texts from the 2nd Temple and early rabbinic literature—2nd century BCE to 7th century CE. These Jewish documents witness to the Jewish people's faith and traditions and provide developments in Jewish theology and ideology that are essential for understanding the Jewish communal context from which Messianic Jewish theology germinates. One of this chapter's goals is to move past seeing these texts as "off-limits" because they are not canonical, "valueless" or even "blasphemous," to seeing them for the contribution they make toward a Messianic Jewish understanding of "messianism" and ultimately for all Messianic Jewish theology.

Before we begin, a few methodological comments, including about terminology. "Messiah" and "messianism" are often used interchangeably and defined in different ways. [3] Sometimes "messianism" is used very broadly to describe any eschatological event that involves the salvation of Israel, whether it includes a "messiah" or not; other times it is restricted to the expectation of "the messiah."[4] John Lust offers a useful definition: "Messianism is the expectation of an individual human and yet transcendent savior. He is to come in a final eschatological period and will establish God's Kingdom on earth. In a more strict sense, messianism is the expectation of a royal Davidic savior at the end of time."[5] Two caveats here: First, this broad definition tends to make "messianism" an umbrella term for a divinely commissioned messianic figure who plays an eschatological role, yet the ancient body of Jewish literature does not attest to one uniform

---

[3] The term messianism is derived from משיח (*mashiach*), the Hebrew word for messiah, which in the Tanakh denotes something "anointed," as in the anointed high priest (Leviticus 4:3, 5, 16) or an anointed king (e.g., 1 Samuel 2:10; cf. Cyrus in Isaiah 45:1). For the biblical meaning of משיח see the article "Messianism in the Tanakh" by Seth Postell in this volume; Joseph Fitzmyer, "The Term Messiah," *The One Who Is to Come*, Grand Rapids/Cambridge: Eerdmans Publishing Company, 2007, 1–7 and *idem.*, "The Use of משיח in the Old Testament," *The One Who is to Come*, 8–25.

[4] The term "messiah" has limited and inconsistent use in early Jewish texts. For more information, see for example, M. de Jonge, "The Use of the Word 'Anointed' in the Time of Jesus," *Novum Testamentum* 8 (1966):132-148. Idem and A.S. van der Woude, "Chrio, etc.," TDNT 9 (1974):509–527; J.H. Charlesworth, "The Concept of the Messiah in the Pseudepigrapha," *Aufstieg und Niedergang der Romischen Welt* II/19.1 (1979): 189–218.

[5] J. Lust, "Messianism and Septuagint," *Congress Volume: Salamanca 1983*, SupplVT 36, J.A. Emerton, ed., Leiden: Brill, 1985, 174–191, quote 175.

"messiah" but several eschatological protagonists whose messianic role scholars still debate.[6] Second, messianism does not always include the hope the Davidic line will be restored but presents a variety of agents of salvation, including a priestly messiah.[7] Additionally, we cannot simply assemble the various texts chronologically and say this constitutes messianism's historical development. The truth is, it did not develop in one straight chronological line, but in different ways among different Jewish groups. So neither chronology nor specific terminology can be the only determiners for our study. Therefore, we will examine specific texts for their conceptual framework and influential historical events, as well as for their vocabulary and chronological relationships to one another. Tracing the texts in this manner will enable us to distinguish certain patterns or trends of messianic thought and provide us a more detailed and accurate picture.[8]

Second Temple Period Literature

Any idea of messianism in the 2nd Temple period literature, and in rabbinic literature for that matter, begins with biblical exegetical tradition: the scepter of Judah (Genesis 49:10); the Star out of Jacob (Numbers 24:17); and the seed of David that was to be established forever (2 Samuel 7:12–16). This three-pronged theology is echoed again and again throughout the prophets,[9] as well as in Apocrypha, Pseudepigrapha and Qumran. Two further dominating characteristics are the historical setting and the religious orientation of the community.

Gershom Scholem points out two typologies of messianism in the Tanakh: Davidic Rule and the Day of the Lord. The Davidic messiah is

---

[6] In ancient Jewish literature a messiah is not essential to the apocalyptic genre nor is it a prominent feature in ancient apocalyptic writings (J.H. Charlesworth, "From Jewish Messianology to Christian Christology," *Judaisms and Their Messiahs*, 225–264; J.J. Collins, *The Apocalyptic Imagination*, New York: Crossroad, 1984).

[7] The Dead Sea Scrolls report at least two messiahs, one Davidic and one priestly, neither of which is specifically an eschatological figure. The DSS also apply the term משיח to prophets who are not necessarily eschatological figures. See A. Hogeterp, *Expectations of the End, A Comparative Traditio-Historical Study of Eschatological, Apocalyptic and Messianic Ideas in the Dead Sea Scrolls and the New Testament*, STDJ 83, Leiden/Boston: Brill, 2009, 428–434.

[8] For more information on this methodology, see Schiffman, "Messianism and Apocalypticism," *The Cambridge History of Judaism IV: The Late Roman-Rabbinic Period*, S.T. Katz, ed., Cambridge: Cambridge University Press, 2008, 1053–1076, esp. 1054.

[9] See for example, Isaiah 4:2; 9:7; 16:3–16; Jeremiah 33:15–30; Ezekiel 34:23, 24; 37:24, 25; Amos 9:11; Daniel 2:44; Joel 2:32; Micah 5:2–3; Zechariah 6:12–13; 14:1–9.

the anointed one mentioned in 2 Samuel 22:50–51 (Psalm 18:50–51) and whose rule is explained in Isaiah 11:1–9. The Day of the Lord is found in the prophets who speak of the punishment of the wicked, the establishment of justice and a change in the destiny of the world. At that time God will act suddenly and decisively to destroy evil and to establish righteousness and justice. The Day of the Lord has a motif of wailing and darkness, and an underlying sense of doom. Scholem classifies these two typologies as restorative and utopian.[10] Restorative messianism reconstitutes the ancient glories of the Davidic dynasty,[11] while utopian construes an even better future—a day when the wicked will be destroyed. Zechariah 6:9–16 combines the two views in two messianic figures—a high priest and a king.

These two typologies represent opposite ends of a pole that vie with one another in 2nd Temple period literature. However, not all messianic references fit neatly into one of these categories; both approaches share elements with the other. Some documents emphasize the kingly, Davidic messiah, and others a priestly messiah; some include both messianic figures without any attempt to reconcile inconsistencies, and others do not clearly distinguish between the two. Apocalyptic ideas, such as those in the Qumran Scrolls, further muddy the waters. Nevertheless, restorative and utopian messianism are useful determiners that will be used throughout the rest of this chapter.

Apocrypha and Pseudepigrapha

A brief survey of Apocrypha and Pseudepigrapha shows that *ben Sira* and *Psalms of Solomon* are essentially restorative, while the older strata of the *Ethiopic Book of Enoch* (*1 Enoch* 90:16–38) and the *Assumption of Moses* are almost exclusively utopian. No Davidic messiah is mentioned in either of these books, nor in *Jubilees*, *2 Enoch* or the *Sibylline Oracles*. However, they all "contain prophetic passages in which some messiah might reasonably have been expected to make an appearance."[12] Two pre-destruction books, *Psalms of Solomon* and the *Similitudes of Enoch* (*1 Enoch* 37–71), specifically speak of a royal, Davidic messiah, similar to that in *4 Ezra* and *2 Baruch*, two-post

---

[10] Scholem, "Messianic Idea."

[11] For David in Second Temple literature, see K.E. Pomykala, *The Davidic Dynasty Tradition in Early Judaism: Its History and Significance for Messianism*, SBLEJL 7, Atlanta: Scholars Press, 1995, 127–229.

[12] Morton Smith, "What is Implied by the Variety of Messianic Figures?" *JBL* 78 (1959): 66–72, quote 68.

destruction books.[13] The books of the Maccabees do not look forward to a Davidic restoration or a utopian messianism, but some eschatological motifs do appear.[14]

Wisdom of ben Sira

The *Wisdom of ben Sira* (*Sirach*), also called *Ecclesiasticus*, conveys the views of a pious scribe at the beginning of the 2nd century BCE. The document is a work of ethical teachings originally written in Hebrew in Jerusalem and translated into Greek in Egypt by the author's grandson, thus accounting for the two names *ben Sira* (Hebrew) and *Sirach* (Greek). *Ben Sira* originated at a time of international political struggle before the Maccabean revolt, but was translated after the rebellion and its aftermath.

The book has little interest in eschatology, except to express hope for a better future (36:11–22) in which God will rescue and reassemble His people (51:12),[15] and sees no need for any divine agent. The term "messiah" as an "anointed one" (Hebrew משיח or Greek χριστός) does appear in 46:19 where it refers to an unnamed king, probably Saul. The cognate verb "to anoint" appears three times in the book, where it is applied to Aaron the priest (45:15; cf. Lev. 8:12), to kings Saul and David (46:13; cf. 1 Sam. 10:1; 16:13) and to "prophet(s)" presumably Elisha (48:8; cf. 1 Kings 19:16).[16] No messianic king is mentioned. *Ben Sira* does, however, foresee Elijah returning before the eschaton to fulfill some type of eschatological function (48:10–11).[17]

Ben Sira has an ambivalent attitude toward the Davidic monarchy, although the author does praise David at some length in 47:1–11. We must be careful, however, not to construe *ben Sira's* statement that God has exalted his (David's) horn forever (47:11) as theological support of a

---

[13] Pre-destruction refers to books written before the destruction of the Temple and Jerusalem in 70 CE and post-destruction after that date.

[14] See É. Shürer, *History of the Jewish People in the age of Jesus Christ (175 B.C. –A.D. 135)*, rev. ed. G. Vermes, F. Millar and M. Black, eds., Edinburgh: T&T Clark, 1979, 2:500.

[15] B.G. Wright discusses the eschatology in ben Sira in "Eschatology Without a Messiah in Ben Sira," *The Septuagint and Messianism, Bibliotheca Ephemeridum Theologicarum Lovaniensium* 195, M.A. Knibb, ed., Leuven/Leuven: Leuven University Press/Peeters, 2006, 313–323.

[16] For more information on messianism in Hebrew *ben Sira* and Greek *Sirach* see J. Corley, "Messianism in Hebrew *Ben Sira* and Greek *Sirach*," *The Septuagint and Messianism*, 301–312.

[17] Both the Hebrew and Greek texts are problematic and difficult to understand. Plus, key sections of the Hebrew are missing. See Wright, *Eschatology*, 319–322 and É. Puech, "Ben Sira 48.11 et la Résurrection," *Of Scribes and Scrolls: Studies on the Hebrew Bible, Intertestamental Judaism and Christian Origins*, H.W. Attridge, JJ. Collins and Th.H. Tobin, eds., Lanham, MD: University Press of America, 1990: 81–90.

revived Davidic dynasty.[18] Indeed, 49:4–6 notes that except for David, Hezekiah and Josiah, God gave the "horn"/"power" of all the Davidic kings to foreigners who burned Jerusalem. For *ben Sira*, the glory of David belongs to the past. The composition is more interested in the legitimacy of priestly rule over Israel. This is seen in 45:6–25, which contrasts the Aaronic and Davidic covenants, stating that Aaron's was an "eternal covenant," a phrase not used in the biblical text. When *ben Sira* mentions God's covenant with David, he minimizes its importance and suggests it is inferior in some respects. There is no doubt *ben Sira* viewed the High Priest Simon as a hero, the ideal cultic and political leader (50:1–21).

Psalms of Solomon

The *Psalms of Solomon* is a collection of 18 poems that incorporate an unknown Jewish group's response to persecution and the capture of Jerusalem by the Romans in 63 BCE. Most of the *Psalms of Solomon* grapples with the same topics as those in the canonical psalter and in the *Hodayot* scroll from Qumran. The last two psalms in the document have an eschatological and messianic motif: 17 and 18 emphasize the kingship of God, the reign of a messianic king, and the permanent nature of the Davidic dynasty. The concept of an "anointed one" becomes concretized in 17 and 18 through the use of two messianic titles, "son of David" and "Lord Messiah." This is the first instance of the usage of "son of David" in Jewish literature, and the only usage of "Lord messiah."

Pss. Sol. 17 incorporates a wonderful mixture of language drawn from Psalm 2, Isaiah 11 and Ezekiel 34 to describe the future son of David who will oppose the unrighteous Roman rulers who have overrun the land. The Psalm appeals to God to defeat the unrighteous rule and Gentile domination of Jerusalem. This can only be done through a legitimate king who will lead Israel against the occupying forces and re-establish the Davidic kingdom. The anticipated Davidic king will crush Israel's enemies and cleanse Jerusalem of the Gentiles (17:23–27). He will gather Israel and redistribute the land among the tribes (26, 28). Gentiles will serve the king and come up to Jerusalem to see the glory of the Lord (17:30–31). The king, the "anointed of the Lord" (17:32), will

---

[18] See Wright, *Eschatology*, 317–319.

rule in righteousness and all the people will be holy, because their king will be "Lord Messiah" (17:32 and 18:5, 7). *Pss. Sol.* 17 and 18 clearly present the messiah as a Davidic king, a real king of Israel, who rules over the entire world,[19] and thoroughly reflect Scholem's restorative messianism. The Roman domination of Jerusalem in the author's time may have fostered his longing for a Davidic king and the reconstitution of his dynasty.

Assumption of Moses

The *Assumption of Moses*, most likely written around the turn of the era, is known from a single Latin manuscript, published by A. Ceriani in 1861 and now identified with the work known in antiquity as the *Testament of Moses.*[20] The *Assumption* is largely a rewriting of Deuteronomy 31–34 and purports to contain Moses's farewell discourse to his successor, Joshua; it does not, however, mention the assumption of Moses. The messianic section of the text can be classified as utopian because chapter 10 portrays God as the define warrior who destroys the wicked and wreaks vengeance on the nations, and establishes a heavenly afterlife. The text mentions a messianic figure (10:2), which it identifies as a messenger of God and His agent of vengeance. However, no human agent of redemption or restoration is mentioned. The idiom "filled the hands of" in 10:2, however, seems to indicate the messenger is also a priest.[21]

1 Enoch

1 Enoch 90:16-38

This section of *1 Enoch* is located at the end of the *Animal Apocalypse* (*1 Enoch* 85–90), which "recounts in allegorical form the history of the world from Adam to the end-time. Human beings are depicted as animals, the rebel watchers are fallen stars, and the seven archangels are human beings."[22] The *Animal Apocalypse* was written

---

[19] Shürer, *History of the Jewish People*, 2:503–505.

[20] J. Tromp defends the title "Assumption of Moses" warning that the ancient title cannot be inferred from the modern text (*The Assumption of Moses: A Critical Edition with Commentary*, SVTP 10; Leiden: Brill, 1992, 115). The *Stichometry* of Nicephorus mentions both a *Testament* and an *Assumption* of Moses.

[21] See for example, Exodus 28:41; 29:29, 33, 35; Leviticus 8:33; Judges 17:5; 1 Kings 13:33; Ezekiel 43:26 and *TLevi* 8:10.

[22] G.W.E. Nickelsburg, "Salvation Without and With a Messiah: Developing Beliefs in Writings Ascribed to Enoch," *Judaisms op. cit.*, 49–68, quote 55.

during the Maccabean revolt, between 165–160 BCE. The document supports the Maccabees; so much so that the only identifiable eschatological human figure is the Ram, which is understood to be Judas Maccabeus. Some have identified the great white eschatological bull (90:37–38) as the Davidic Messiah.[23] However, George Nickelsburg holds that the bull's importance lies in whom he is and not in what he does, *i.e.*, in his patriarchal status and not in messianic functions.[24]

1 Enoch 90:16–38 paints a picture of utopian messianism. The Gentiles, in their final attack against the Jews, are defeated by God's miraculous intervention. Then God sits in judgment on His newly erected throne. He replaces old Jerusalem with a new one, where the pious Israelites will dwell and the Gentiles will pay homage. After these events the messiah will appear, and all the Gentiles will adopt the ways of the Lord. Notice that God heralds the eschaton and the messiah only enters in at the end of the process, which is contrary to the usual depiction of a Davidic messiah.[25]

The Similitudes

The Enochic *'Book of Parables'* (or *Similitudes, 1 Enoch* 37–71), written in Hebrew toward the end of the first century BCE or early first century CE[26], comprises 3 parables (*1 Enoch* 38–44, 45–57, 58–69). The term "messiah" appears twice in the second parable in reference to a messiah of the 'Lord of Spirits' (48:10, 52:4). No specific reference is made to the Davidic king, messiah or dynasty. The *Similitudes* instead designate the messianic figure by four names: the chosen one; the righteous one; the anointed one; and the son of man. These four epithets are conflated to embody the three parallel figures of Davidic king, Isaianic servant of the Lord and Danielic one like a son of man and significantly transform them from their original positions in Israelite religious tradition into an expected messianic figure.[27] Thus the author

[23] See for example, R.H. Charles, *The Book of Enoch or 1 Enoch*, Oxford: Clarendon, 1912, 215–216, and more recently Jonathan Goldstein, "How the Authors of 1 and 2 Maccabees Treated the Messianic Prophecies," *Judaisms op. cit.,* 69–96, esp. 72–73.

[24] Nickelsburg, "Salvation Without and With a Messiah," 56.

[25] G.W.E. Nickelsburg, "Salvation Without and With a Messiah"; cf. Schiffman, "Messianism and Apocalypticism," 1058.

[26] For a discussion on the dating of Enoch see G.W.E. Nickelsburg, Jewish Literature Between the Bible and the Mishnah: A Historical and Literary Introduction, Minneapolis: Fortress Press, 2005, 254–256.

[27] For an in-depth explanation of the conflation of these traditions, see G.W.E. Nickelsburg and J.C. VanderKam, 1 Enoch 2: A Commentary on the Book of 1 Enoch Chapters 37–82, Minneapolis: Fortress Press, 2012, 43–44; VanderKam, "Righteous One, Messiah Chosen One and Son of Man in 1 Enoch 37–71,

presents the messiah as a pre-existent, transcendent figure from heaven and not simply a human son of David.[28] The conflated savior character in the *Similitudes* appears in other Jewish literature written after the fall of Jerusalem in 70 CE, particularly *4 Ezra* and *2 Baruch*, and provides a missing link in the chain of tradition that led from Daniel's "one like a son of man" to the Gospels' widespread use of the epithet.[29]

4 Ezra and 2 Baruch

4 Ezra and *2 Baruch* were composed within a few decades after the destruction of the Temple in 70 CE.[30] These two apocalypses represent the reactions of Jews to the shock of the destruction and the impact it had on the Jewish faith. There are many parallels between the books, some of which are concepts—such as messianism and the authors' struggle to understand their religious world in the aftermath of the destruction—various arguments and phrases, literary form, vision experiences, and dialogues between the seer and God.[31] The authors of both books are deeply distressed by the destruction of Israel and eagerly await divine vindication. The messiah plays an important role in the process of vindication and in the development of the eschatological events. Both texts seem to imply the preexistence of the messiah (*2 Baruch* 30:1, 40:1; *4 Ezra* 11:37–46).

The preexistence of Messiah seems to imply Davidic descent—*4 Ezra* 12:31–34 specifically states that messiah "will arise from the posterity of David"—yet *4 Ezra* 13 depicts him as a man who ascends

The Messiah: Developments in Earliest Judaism and Christianity, J.H. Charlesworth, et. al., Minneapolis: Fortress Press, 1992, 169–91. Not all scholars agree the "son of man" represents a messianic figure. For example, Sigmund Mowinckel understands the "son of man" to be a representation of the people of the Most High (*He That Cometh: The Messiah Concept in the Old Testament and Later Judaism*, G.W. Anderson, trans., Grand Rapids/Cambridge, UK: Eerdmans, 2005, 348–53).

[28] Cf. M. Black, "The Messianism of the Parables of Enoch: Their Date and Contributions to Christological Origins," *The Messiah*, 145–168; A. Laato, *A Star Is Rising: The Historical Development of the Old Testament Royal Ideology and the Rise of the Jewish Messianic Expectations*, Atlanta: Scholars Press, 1997, 285–316; J.J. Collins, *The Scepter and the Star: The Messiahs of the Dead Sea Scrolls and Other Ancient Literature*, 2nd ed., Grand Rapids: Eerdmans, 2010, 52–148.

[29] See Leslie W. Walck, "The Son of Man in the Parables of Enoch and the Gospels," Enoch and the Messiah Son of Man: Revisiting the Book of Parables, G. Boccaccini, ed., Grand Rapids: Eerdmans, 2007, 299–337.

[30] For more information on *4 Ezra*, see M.E. Stone, *Fourth Ezra*, Hermeneia, Minneapolis: Fortress Press, 1990 and on *2 Baruch*, see A.F.J. Klijn, "2 (Syriac Apocalypse of) Baruch," *Old Testament Pseudepigrapha*, J.H. Charlesworth, ed. Garden City, NY: 1983-1985, 1:615–652.

[31] On the material shared by both texts, see Nickelsburg, *Jewish Literature*, 270-285; cf. M.E. Stone and M. Henze, *4 Ezra and 2 Baruch: Translations, Introductions and Notes*. Minneapolis: Fortress Press, 2013.

out of the sea[32] and *2 Baruch* 29:1–33:3 as an earthly king who embodies all the dreams attributed to the kings of ancient Israel. Ancillary is the description in both texts of the messiah's activities in legal terms—his victory is gained through judgment rather than by military exploits—thereby downplaying the messiah's role as warrior (*2 Baruch* 72, *4 Ezra* 12:32); final judgment is in God's realm. Furthermore, in the book of *4 Ezra* the messiah will die preceding the eschaton (7:29). Consequently, it seems clear the restoration of the ideal Davidic monarchy did not play a major role in these authors' messianic expectations.

The messianic kingdom is presented as finite in *2 Baruch* 36–40, though it is also presented as eschatological and eternal in chapters 73 and 74. According to *2 Baruch* 30, only the righteous will arise with the advent of the messiah. However, according to *4 Ezra* 7:28–29, both the righteous and the unrighteous will be resurrected, but only after the messiah dies, and the interlude of primeval silence begins and ends. Despite these contradictory traditions, both texts record that the messiah is not the one who raises the dead; resurrection is in God's realm.

Qumran Documents

The Qumran corpus exhibits the same three-pronged biblical theology based on Genesis 49:10 (the scepter of Judah), Numbers 24:17 (the Star out of Jacob) and 2 Samuel 7:12–16 (the seed of David) and the same variety of messianic motifs found in the Apocrypha and Pseudepigrapha (e.g., restorative and utopian messianism, Davidic messiah, human and transcendent figures). However, the community's apocalyptic worldview and religious orientation profoundly impacted their messianic beliefs and views. The community's existence for about three centuries contributed to the complex theology and messianic motifs in Qumran literature; Qumran theology is not monolithic. The study of messianism in the Qumran corpus is complicated by the lack of firm dating of individual documents and the variety of messianic and apocalyptic ideas nestled in documents of diverse genre, as well as the vast amount of literature generated from studies of the literature.

---

[32] This imagery is an allusion to "a son of man" in Daniel 7:2. See, for example, Stone, *4 Ezra*, 383 and Collins, *The Scepter and the Star*, 207.

Volumes have been written on messianism and messiah(s) at Qumran.[33] Consequently, we will extract from these documents only those minutiae that help us understand the messianic expectations among the Jews who wrote these texts or at least used them in developing their ideological and theological conceptions.

Messianism in the Qumran corpus is novel and valuable, as it combines a priestly messiah alongside a royal Davidic one. The Messiah of Aaron—the priestly messiah—was expected to govern religious matters, while the messiah of Israel—the royal, Davidic Messiah—was to rule over temporal and political matters. The kingly messiah was subordinate to the priestly messiah. Nevertheless, both would preside over the eschatological messianic banquet that would usher in the new age (1Q28a 2.11–15). The Messiah of Israel corresponds to Scholem's restorative approach and the messiah of Aaron to the utopian.

Additional messianic protagonists can be discerned from these texts: a messianic prophet[34] and other eschatological figures such as a teacher of righteousness, who will interpret Torah in the end days,[35] and the Prince of the Congregation (נשיא העדה), who is a military leader. He, along with messiah (משיח) and branch of David (צמח דוד), usually designates the messianic figure from the royal house of David.[36]

Messianism is well-represented among the Qumran documents, both in sectarian and non-sectarian documents, but not elucidated. [37] Conflicting ideas about these messianic figures are presented without trying to reconcile them. Some texts refer to messiah (singular) of Aaron and Israel (CD 12:23–13:1, 14:18–19, 19:10–11, 19:35–20:1)[38], and others to messiahs of Aaron and Israel (1QS, 4Q174; see below). For years, scholars debated whether this meant there was one messiah with

---

[33] Many studies have been devoted to Qumran messianism, see M.G. Abegg, C.A. Evans, G.S. Oegema, "Bibliography of Messianism and the Dead Sea Scrolls," *Qumran Messianism*, Tübingen: Mohr Siebeck, 1998, 204–214 and the Orion Center's comprehensive bibliography on the Dead Sea Scrolls and related literature, http://orion.mscc.huji.ac.il/resources/bib/bibliosearch.shtml.

[34] On king, priest, and prophet as basic paradigms of earthly messianic figures at Qumran, see Collins, *The Scepter and the Star*, 12.

[35] The statement "until he comes who shall teach righteousness at the end of days" in CD 6:11 is quite controversial. Collins discusses this at length in *The Scepter and the Star*, 110–148.

[36] VanderKam, "Messianism in the Scrolls," *The Community of the New Covenant*, E. Ulrich and J.C. VanderKam, eds., Notre Dame: University of Notre Dame, 1994, 211–234, esp. 212–219 on these terms as titles of 'the Davidic Messiah.'

[37] e.g., 1QS 9.2, 9.10–11; 1QM 5.1; CD 12.23–13.1, 14.18–19, 19:10–11, 19.33–20.1; 4Q161[Pesher Isaiah A] 8–10, 11–25, 4Q174 3.11–13, 4Q252 1 5.1–5, 11QMelch, 4Q246, 4Q521, 4Q541.

[38] See L. Schiffman, "Messianic Figures and Ideas in the Qumran Scrolls," *The Messiah*, 116–129, esp. 117–119.

different functions, or two messiahs each with a different function. Scholarly consensus now favors a plural understanding of the expression.

4Q174 (4QFloriligium), a collection of passages with eschatological significance, points to two eschatological figures in its interpretation of 2 Samuel 7:11–14 that are elsewhere called messiahs: the Branch of David and the Interpreter of the Law. Lines 11–13 say, "This passage refers to the Shoot of David, who is to arise with the Interpreter of the Law, and who will [arise] in Zi[on in the La]st Days, as it is written, 'And I shall raise up the booth of David that is fallen.' This passage describes the fallen Branch of David, [w]hom He shall raise up to deliver Israel."[39] The idea of two messiahs also appears in *Rule of the Community* 9.10–11. The *Rule of the Community* (1QS, *Serekh HaYahad*) is one of the first scrolls removed from Cave 1 in 1947. It is a lengthy scroll containing the strict rules of conduct that ordered the life of the *Yahad*, a celibate group of Jewish males who had withdrawn to Qumran in the Judean Desert. 1QS 9.10–11 states, "They shall govern themselves using the original precepts by which the men of the *Yahad* began to be instructed, doing so until there come the Prophet and the Messiahs of Aaron and Israel." [40] From this text we learn three eschatological figures were expected to appear sometime in the future; it does not tell us anything about them or their functions. Not much is written about the anticipated eschatological prophet (cf. Deuteronomy 18:15); he could be Elijah or a divine guide sent to Israel in the final days. Nevertheless, 1QS expected the prophet together with the messiahs of Aaron and of Israel (1QS 9.2).

One further eschatological protagonist that must be mentioned is Melchizedek (11QMelk). The Qumran sectarians viewed him as a high-priestly, angelic deliverer. He was chief of the sons of heaven and was to preside over the last judgment of Melchiresha or possibly Belial or Satan. This final judgment was the great liberation, which was to take place on Yom Kippur at the end of the 10th Jubilee cycle.

The pattern of priestly and non-priestly messiah continues throughout the messianic texts at Qumran. 4Q252 (a *pesher* on Genesis) frag. 1 5.1–5—commenting on the scepter of Judah (Genesis 49:10)—

---

[39] Translation taken from J.C. VanderKam and P. Flint, The Meaning of the Dead Sea Scrolls: Their Significance for Understanding the Bible, Judaism, Jesus and Christianity, NY: HarperSanFrancisco, 2004, 265.

[40] Translation from VanderKam and Flint, *Meaning*, 265.

calls the Messiah of Israel "the Branch of David" (צמח דוד). 4Q285, The War of the Messiah, 5.3–6 also mentions the Branch of David and supplies the additional title "Prince of the Congregation" (נשיא העדה). Although this fragment is full of lacunae and quite controversial, its military context is important as it implies a warrior messiah. These two texts, 4Q252 and 4Q285, associate the Messiah of Israel with the Branch of David and Prince of the Community, the kingly messiah.

The *Damascus Document* (CD) is a sectarian document clearly related to the *Community Rule* (1QS), yet decidedly different in that it consists of admonitions and explicit legal provisions for those who live in the camps "marrying and begetting children" (7.6–7) and "live by these rules in the era of wickedness, until the appearance of the Messiah of Aaron and Israel" (12.23–13.1). Here "messiah" is singular, as in the other three instances of the expression in CD. However, CD 7.18–21, a section dealing with Balaam's oracle concerning the Star of Jacob (Numbers 24:15–19), [41] mentions two individual messianic figures. "…The 'star' is the interpreter of the Torah who came to Damascus, as it is written: 'A star stepped forth out of Jacob, a staff arose out of Israel.' 'The staff' is the prince of all the congregation, and when he arises, 'he will destroy all the sons of Seth'…" (7.18–21). [42]

The passage clearly understands the star of Jacob (Numbers 24:17) to be a priestly messiah who is also the Interpreter of the Torah, and the staff (Genesis 49:10) as the Prince of the Congregation, a kingly Davidic messiah. [43] This interpretation agrees with 4QFloriligium (4Q174), which distinguishes the Messiah of Israel and the Interpreter of the Torah as two separate individuals, demonstrating that the star of Jacob cannot refer to the Davidic, royal messiah, but only to a priestly messiah. Thus, the evidence attests to both a messianic "Prince of the Congregation" (royal, Davidic messiah) and a messianic priest (Interpreter of the Torah) in the Damascus Document.

The Messiah of Israel is the King Messiah, the classic concept of a Davidic Messiah. He is a royal, military figure who destroys the enemies

[41] This oracle is also understood in a messianic sense in 4QTestimonia (4Q175) and in other ancient Jewish literature, e.g. *y. Ta'an.* 68d–69a and various Targumim, cf. *T. Levi* 18:3; *T. Jud.* 24:1; as well as in Revelation 22:16.

[42] Quote from Joseph L. Angel, "Damascus Document," *Outside the Bible: Ancient Jewish Writings Related to Scripture*, L.H. Feldman, J.L. Kugel, L.H. Schiffman, eds., Philadelphia: JPS, 2013, 3:2975–3935, esp. 2996.

[43] Some scholars see a priestly messiah with royal characteristics in this passage. For a good explanation of the textual difficulties underlying this passage see Collins, *The Scepter and the Star*, 87–91.

and reestablishes the glory of days old, of the Davidic kingdom. The Messiah of Aaron, on the other hand, represents utopian messianism. This priestly messiah would not restore the temporal Davidic kingdom but would usher in an even better time. He would bring about the utter destruction of evil and wickedness, and establish everlasting joy for the elect. The priestly messiah had pride of place; he was first in order of precedence. The Messiah of Israel—that is, the King Messiah—was to defer to the Messiah of Aaron, the priestly messiah for general authority.

The scrolls indicate a great diversity of messianic expectations in the years around the turn of the century. The Qumran literature, like the Apocrypha and Pseudepigrapha, describes restorative and utopian tendencies based on the biblical prophetic visions. Yet the Qumranians went much further. They combined messianic, apocalyptic and eschatological motifs apparent in other 2nd Temple period texts with their own religious orientation creating a unique messianism—one that expected both a royal and kingly messiah and the imminent advent of the messianic age.

Early Rabbinic Literature

Early rabbinic literature, meaning Tannaitic and Amoraic literature, is not monolithic, and neither are its attitudes toward messianism and messianic motifs. This corpus reflects differing views of the sages in Israel and in Babylon ranging over 700 years, as well as different types of literature: halakha, aggadah, midrashim, targumim, etc.[44] Historical events and political circumstances also greatly influenced the material; for example, the Tannaitic period, 10 BCE–220 CE, experienced two revolts, both of which had messianic overtones, and political governance during the Amoraic period (200–500 CE) was split between Christian rule in Israel and Sasanian in Babylon. Furthermore, both Judaism and Christianity were developing and defining their self-identity, as well as their relationship to one another. Christianity was dealing with the influx of non-Jewish adherents and its self-definition apart from Judaism, and Judaism was busy determining how to live pure and holy lives on a daily basis in an unclean world without the Temple, the priesthood and the sacrifices. The various time periods, influences and events must be

---

[44] For a detailed discussion of the messianic material in rabbinic traditions, see J. Neusner, *Messiah in Context: Israel's History and Destiny in Formative Judaism*, Philadelphia: Fortress Press, 1984.

considered when studying messianism in rabbinic literature. Consequently, we will examine this literature by time periods and by classification. Despite these variables, rabbinic literature reflects the same characteristics of messianism apparent in Apocrypha and Pseudepigrapha and in the Qumran corpus: the ideas of restorative and utopian messianism, as well as that of Davidic and priestly messiahs. However, these elements are not clearly delineated, and their significance waxes and wanes throughout the corpus. One trend is that apocalyptic elements are non-existent in Tannaitic literature but prominent in Amoraic literature.

Tannaitic Literature

Mishnah

The Mishnah, codified around 220 CE, is a law code for the Jewish people in Israel. Its principle point is sanctification, not salvation.[45] Written in the aftermath of the destruction of the Temple and the bar Kokhba debacle, when the rabbis were trying to define life without the Temple and blood atonement, the Mishnah looks forward to a time when God's anointed, an heir of the Davidic dynasty, would restore the Temple and rule of Israel. The messiah (משיח) in the Mishnah indicates an anointed priest (*m. Mak.* 2:2, 3, 7; 3:4, 5), an unidentified person who does not figure prominently into the situation or resolve any major religious issues of the day. The Mishnah does, however, differentiate between the messiah (anointed one) of this age and the one of the future, of "the days of the Messiah" (*m. Ber.* 1:5). Though the figure of the messiah comes at the end of time, his role is inconsequential. This is clearly seen in *m. Sotah* 9.9–15, the most significant messianic passage in the Mishnah. *M. Sotah* 9:15 mentions "the footsteps of Messiah"—the time of desolation, corruption and religious decline that immediately precedes the coming of the messiah—and Elijah as the harbinger of the end times (cf. *m. Sheqal.* 2:5, *m. B. Met.* 1:8, 2:8, 3:4–5). They are both mentioned rather matter-of-factly as part of the inherited background material, neither to be emphasized nor ignored. Conspicuously absent are references about false messiahs or how to recognize false messiah.

---

[45] J. Neusner, *Messiah in Context*, 17–25; *idem*, "Mishnah and Messiah" *Judaisms and Their Messiahs*, 265–282; cf. B.M. Bokser, "Messianism, The Exodus Pattern in Early Rabbinic Judaism," *The Messiah*, 239–258.

Tosefta

The Tosefta is a companion volume to the Mishnah. It is a collection of halakhic and aggadic traditions stemming from the mishnaic period. It is organized according to the order of the Mishnah, shares its rhetorical patterns, and basically operates within the parameters established by the Mishnah. The Tosefta repeats the picture of the messiah depicted in the Mishnah; he is mentioned only incidentally and generally in the same contexts, and avoids any mention of false messiahs. Nonetheless, further clarifications about the time of the Messiah are found in the Tosefta: *t. Ta'an.* 3:1 alludes to what will happen to the nations in the time of the messiah and *t. Arak.* 2:7 suggests the "days of messiah ... form a differentiated interim period, between this age and the age to come".[46] But, as in the Mishnah, the Tosefta simply states these points as a matter of fact and does not elaborate on them.

The messiah plays no role as a redeemer or savior in the eschatological passages associated with the world to come. In fact, passages that explicitly refer to the rebuilding of the Temple and Jerusalem are void of any allusion to the messiah.[47] It could be inferred that the redactors of the Tosefta did not know the traditions surrounding the messiah, the days of the messiah or the rule of the messiah. However, we read in *t. San.* 4:9 that the rule of the house of David will be forever. The redactors simply choose not to associate messiah with the eschatological hope of a Davidic messiah.

Tannaitic Midrashim—

Mekhilta de R. Ishmael, Sifra, Sifre Numbers, Sifre Deuteronomy

The Tannaitic Midrashim do little more than rehearse the messianic material already presented. The few statements on messiah in *Mekhilta de R. Ishmael*—a halakhic midrash on the book of Exodus that stays very close to the biblical narrative—are discrete and routine (2:161; 2:120, Lauterbach ed.).[48] In *Sifra*—a systematic exegesis of Leviticus that also remains close to the Scripture—"the messiah" only refers to an anointed high priest as in Leviticus itself. *Sifre to Numbers*, like *Sifra*,

---

[46] Neusner, Messiah in Context, 54.
[47] See *t. San.* 13.5; *t. B. Bat.* 2.17; *t. Men.* 13.22–23; *t. Ber.* 6.3–6; *t. Zev.* 13.6. These references and others are discussed by Neusner, *Messiah in Context*, 53–63.
[48] Jacob Lauterbach, tr., *Mekhilta de Rabbi Ishmael*, 2nd ed., Philadelphia: Jewish Publication Society, 2004.

refers only to the messiah as the anointed high priest. However, *Sifre Num.* 40 does mention the messianic age that will be preceded by a time of trouble, but does not allude to the messiah. *Sifre to Deuteronomy* contains a number of references to the "age of the messiah" in contrast to "this age" (16, 104, 188, 351, 362, 363, 372, 398, 401), and has one passage on the anointing of David (17; cf. 1 Samuel 16:6), which has no messianic orientation.[49]

Targumim

The Targumim, Aramaic translations of Scripture, are a varied set of writings with no firm evidence as to their dates or translators. Thus all we can say about messianism in them is the translators drew on ideas and motifs that circulated before their time.[50] The Targumim follow a similar policy to that of *Sifra* and the *Sifres* and do not introduce the theme of the messiah unless the text specifically demands or invites it. One example will suffice. *Onqelos* interprets the phrase "until Shiloh comes" (Genesis 49:10) as "until the messiah comes, to whom the Kingdom belongs, and whom nations obey" and Numbers 24:17 ("a star shall step forth out of Jacob, and a scepter shall arise out of Israel") as "when a king shall arise out of Jacob and be anointed the Messiah out of Israel."

Amoraic Literature

Jerusalem Talmud (Yerushalmi)

The Jerusalem Talmud is a systematic exegesis of the Mishnah redacted around 400 CE, but is not symmetrical with that of the Mishnah. It makes no attempt to introduce messianic concepts into its interpretation of tannaitic material where they are not already present (e.g., *y. Sheqal.* 3:3; cf. *m. Sot.* 9:15–16). New concepts are only introduced in the independent discourse of the Amoraim, which evidence a widespread knowledge of messianism and exhibit many of the same restorative and utopian ideas seen in 2nd Temple Literature. The Yerushalmi expects the return of the Davidic dynasty (*y. Naz.* 7:1) with a Davidic messiah (*y. Kidd.* 4:1) and the resurrection of the dead in the messianic era (*y. Ket.* 12:3).

---

[49] Neusner, *Messiah in Context*, 133–137.

[50] For more detailed information of messiah in the Targumim, see Neusner, *Messiah in Context*, 239–247.

The Yerushalmi moves from allusions to suggestive stories. *Y. Ber.* 2:4 relates that the Messiah-king, Menahem son of Hezekiah, was born in Bethlehem on the day the Temple was destroyed, and hidden away by the spirit, presumably until his expected later revelation. This story is important because it expects a "Davidic messiah" who is not specifically a descendant of David. Furthermore, its identification with a known historical figure rejects Akiva's view that Bar Kokhba was the messiah as found in *y. Ta'an.* 4:5. This may be an indirect statement against false prophets. The Yerushalmi basically picks up ideas latent in tannaitic texts and brings them to the forefront. It is void of the utopian concept of messianism so prominent during the Second Temple and focuses on restorative messianism with its central Davidic messiah.[51]

Babylonian Talmud

The Babylonian Talmud (Bavli) is the second and most important systematic exegesis of the Mishnah. It reached closure in the 6th century. Like the Yerushalmi, the Bavli consists of Mishnah and Gemara, which is commentary on the Mishnah. The Bavli presents the most developed form of messianism in rabbinic literature. From *b. San.* 96b–99a, the fullest statement on messianism in the Bavli, we learn the coming of the messiah will be inaugurated by a time of trouble,[52] it is ill-advised to calculate messiah's coming but not forbidden,[53] the messianic era constitutes the third part of the history of the world,[54] the messiah will be sent by God to a generation that repents of its sins, and the messiah will come from the House of David.[55] In the midst of this discussion on messianism, the rabbis inquire as to the name of the messiah. Each school put forth a name that honored its teacher by using

---

[51] For more detailed information on messiah in the Jerusalem Talmud see Neusner, *Messiah in Context*, 79–130 and Schiffman, "Messianism and Apocalypticism," 1064–1065.

[52] The concept that the time of the messiah will be preceded by terrible tribulations (e.g., b. Shabbat 118a and *b. Ket.* 111a–112b) goes back to the concept of the Day of the Lord found in the Prophets and to Scholem's utopian approach. Cf. *b. Hull.* 63a; *b. Ber.* 57a.

[53] Three times are proposed: Nisan, the season of Israel's first redemption (*b. Rosh Has.* 11a), in a sabbatical year (*b. Meg.* 17a), or on a weekday, but not a Sabbath or mo'ed (*b. Erub.* 43a–b). Despite the fact the actual time is to remain hidden (*b. Pes.* 54b; *b. Meg.* 3a) one sage calculated the date as 4231 from creation, the year 468 CE (*b. Av. Zar.* 9b).

[54] *B. Zev.* 118b.

[55] Cf. *b. Pes.* 118a; *b. Shabb.* 118a, 118b; *b. Ket.* 111a, 112b; *b. Hull.* 63a; *b. Av. Zar.* 9b; *b. Meg. 17*b; *b. Suk.* 52a–b; *b. San.* 93a–b, 94a; *b. Yev.* 76b; *B. Bat.* 14b; *b. Ber.* 4a; 7b; *b. Moed Qat.* 16b. Neusner, *Messiah in Context*, 169–91 provides an analysis of these sources; cf. Schiffman, "Messianism and Apocalypticism," 1065–69.

a play on words: The school of R. Shila said Shiloh (Gen. 49:10), of R. Yannai, Yinnon (Psalms 72:17), of R. Hananiah, Hananiah (Jeremiah 16:13), and others said Menachem son of Hezekiah (Lamentations 1:16). In the end they say, "His name is חיוורא (Soncino: "leper scholar") as it is written, *"Surely he hath borne our griefs, and carried our sorrows: yet we did esteem him a leper, smitten of God, and afflicted"* (Isaiah 53:4; quote from *b. San.* 98b). This title stems from an encounter recorded in *b. San.* 98a, between Rabbi Joshua ben Levi and the prophet Elijah in response to a question about the timing of the messiah's coming. Elijah sends R. Joshua to inquire of the messiah himself. R. Joshua finds the messiah in the city gate sitting among the poor and diseased, re-bandaging their leprous sores. The rabbis connected the first passage with one of the names of messiah associating him with suffering. From these two passages we learn Isaiah 53 was interpreted as applying to a messiah. The interpretation of Isaiah 53 and related passages (*i.e.*, Isaiah 49:10, 11; Micah 5:2: Psalm 18) shifted in the Middle Ages after Rashi (1040–1105) wrote his biblical commentary, where he interprets Isaiah 53 to refer collectively to Israel. As can be seen from this example, different names and functions were associated with the messiah in the Bavli. The Bavli assumes that the name messiah is pre-existent (*b Ned.* 39b; *b. Pes.* 5a; 54b), that he would free the Jewish people from foreign rulers (*b. San.* 97a), who, in turn, would submit to him (*b. Ta'an.* 14b) and that he would usher in an era of peace (*b. San.* 91b; *b. Shabb.* 63a; 151b; *b. Pes.* 68a).

The idea of multiple messiahs surfaces in the Bavli but does not play a systematic role in the Talmud's larger framework. Messiah ben Joseph is introduced in *b. Suk.* 52a alongside Messiah ben David. These two messiahs represent the two aspects of restorative and utopian (apocalyptic) messianism. Messiah ben Joseph is the messiah who dies during an eschatological battle. Though he fights and loses, he does not suffer; Isaiah's suffering servant is not applied to him. "He [Messiah ben Joseph] is a redeemer, who redeems nothing..."[56] After the death of Messiah ben Joseph, Messiah ben David comes to the forefront and all of the utopian bliss becomes concentrated in him. This very apocalyptic passage includes additional eschatological/messianic figures such as Elijah and Melchizedek.

---

[56] Scholem, "Messianic Idea," 18.

Despite the strong apocalyptic perspective of many of the Amoraic teachers, there were also those who rejected the idea. Samuel, a Babylonian sage from the early 3rd century, exemplifies stringent anti-apocalypticism. In opposition to R. Hiyya b. Abba, Samuel states, "The only difference between this age and the Days of the Messiah is the subjection [of Israel] to the nations" (*b. Ber.* 34b). Another strong rejection of apocalypticism in Amoraic texts appears in *Song of Songs Rabbah* 2(7).1, where God adjures Israel not to seek to hasten the end of days and warns them not to repeat the messianic failures of the past. While many of these concepts occur elsewhere in rabbinic literature, in the Bavli they have been infused with apocalyptic and utopian understandings: *e.g.*, the appearance of two messiahs, the messiah's ability to judge, the notion of four kingdoms based on Daniel. Still the Bavli is devoid of certain apocalyptic motifs characteristic of 2nd Temple texts, such as a complete description of an eschatological war or the destruction of the wicked. The utopian has come back, but it has been "rabbinized" into a different form.[57]

Amoraic Midrashim—Midrash Rabbah and Pesikta de-Rav Kahana

The Amoraic Midrashim, primarily compilations of traditions of the Palestinian Sages, continue the same tendencies seen in the Babylonian Talmud. For example, *Leviticus Rabbah* 13.5 (cf. *Lamentations Rabbah* 1.42 and *Esther Rabbah* 1) reworks and expands the sequence of Daniel's four kingdoms and *Song of Songs Rabbah* 2(13).4 expects the messiah to come during a time deserving of punishment and misfortune. The most explicit passage with apocalyptic elements is *Pesikta de-Rav Kahana* section 5.9. The section exhibits a strong utopian trend: well-known eschatological figures such Elijah, the messiah, Melchizedek, and the War Priest; the expectation of a great pestilence that will destroy the wicked; the coming of messiah only to a sinful generation that will be destroyed; and a description of the full restoration of Zion that surpasses even the glory of the giving of Torah at Sinai.[58]

The above survey of messianism in rabbinic literature does not include every reference to messiah or to his functions. It does however, capture the concepts of messiah, his functions and messianic expectations found in Classic Rabbinic Literature.

---

[57] Schiffman, "Messianism and Apocalypticism," 1069.

[58] Much of this section is drawn from Schiffman, "Messianism and Apocalypticism," 1069-1070.

Conclusion

Our survey of Jewish literature beyond the Bible has revealed basic messianic motifs and trends that run throughout the literature from the return from Babylonian captivity through the rabbinic eras. One prominent feature is the two typologies drawn from biblical traditions, of restorative and utopian messianism. Restorative messianism speaks of the reconstitution of the ancient glories of the Davidic dynasty and the utopian of a future perfect society. These two aspects circulated separately until they came together in Qumran literature in the messiahs of Aaron, the priestly messiah, and of Israel, the royal, Davidic messiah. The Qumran community's religious orientation and apocalyptic worldview also profoundly affected their adaptation of various messianic motifs common in the Apocrypha and Pseudepigrapha. Tannaitic literature continues these same trends and motifs, but moves away from apocalyptic influences and utopianism, whereas these 2nd Temple traditions re-emerge in Amoraic literature.

Although our survey stops just before the Medieval period, these messianic traditions do not. They continue to play a role in the ongoing development of Jewish messianic and apocalyptic speculation through the Middle Ages into modernity. The esoteric element and strong apocalyptic characteristic of Qumran literature spills into the Middle Ages, manifesting in mysticism and false messiahs. The tension between halakah and messianism in early rabbinic literature resurfaces in the conflict in the messianic movements of the 12th century CE with the advent of antinomianism. Anti-apocalypticism was crystallized in Maimonides' formulations of messianism. His views still dominate Judaism today.

Epilogue

The ideas stemming from the above survey profoundly impact Messianic Jewish concepts of Messiah and messianism because they supply part of the essential Jewish communal context. The motifs, trends and concepts expounded in this article, along with the bibliographical references, provide a foundation for the continued development of Messianic Jewish theology. Their consideration and infusion will bring about insights and clarity.

There are many ways the study of these documents impact Messianic Judaism today. Seth Klayman in his article "Messianic Expectations 'Messy-Antic' Realizations: Evaluating the Influence of Messianisms on Jewish Identity in the Second Temple Period" *Kesher* 12 (Winter 2000) 3–79 list five reasons the study of messiah in Jewish extra-biblical texts are important for Messianic Jews today. [59] His reasons relate to messianic prophecies, expectations, realizations and outreach. The above study expands these five to include theology, especially in developing a mature Messianic Jewish Christology. First, studying 2nd Temple texts outside the Bible for Messianic Jewish theology provides a sound methodology. Messianism, messianic expectations, traditions, etc. have changed radically since the coming of Yeshua until today. The destruction of the Temple, the marriage of the Church and the Roman empire under Constantine, the Middle Ages, the Enlightenment and Jewish Haskalah, and the Holocaust are historical events that have greatly impacted Christian and Jewish views of messiah and messianism. The documents presented in this study provide a glimpse into the ideas and concepts before or contemporary with these historical events, allowing us to trace the development of theological ideas of messiah/messianism and understand how they were influenced by the various historical events. This in turn affords the ability to understand various theological points and to discern which to build upon and which to discard. Secondly, the study of these texts provide a Jewish communal context that is more or less contemporary with the time and events recorded in the Apostolic writings and the development of early Christianity. As such, they provide insights into the concepts, thoughts, worldview and questions people were asking at the that time. These in turn afford a wider background so the doctrine and theology of the Apostolic Writings we can be understood more deeply and clearly. Lastly, the texts presented in this chapter demonstrate how the Jewish community in the 2nd Temple period and shortly thereafter exegeted the Tanakh in regard to messiah and messianism. They interpreted the biblical prophecies messianically, just as Messianic Jews do today. Our study revealed diverse understandings of these prophecies.

---

[59] Klayman's five reasons are expounded on pages 72-73 in "Messy-Antic."

Understanding the ancients' exegesis of these prophecies provides us with more hermeneutical tools to rightly divide the Word of Truth today (2 Timothy 2:15), much as learning how ancients understood and applied the Bible for purposes of faith and practice, yesterday, will enable us to see and walk more sure-footedly today.

BIBLIOGRAPHY

Abegg, M.G., Evans, C.A. and G.S. Oegema. "Bibliography of Messianism
        and the Dead Sea Scrolls." *Qumran Messianism.* Tübingen: Mohr
        Siebeck, 1998, 204–214.
Angel, Joseph L. "Damascus Document." *Outside the Bible: Ancient Jewish
        Writings Related to Scripture.* L.H. Feldman, J.L. Kugel, and L.H.
        Schiffman, eds. Philadelphia: JPS, 2013, 3:2975–3935.
Black, M. "The Messianism of the Parables of Enoch: Their Date and
        Contributions to Christological Origins." *The Messiah: Developments
        in Earliest Judaism and Christianity.* J.H. Charlesworth, et. al.
        Minneapolis: Fortress Press, 1992, 145–68.
Bokser, B.M. "Messianism, The Exodus Pattern in Early Rabbinic Judaism."
        The Messiah: Developments in Earliest Judaism and Christianity. J.H.
        Charlesworth, et. al. Minneapolis: Fortress Press, 1992, 239–258.
Charles, R.H. *The Book of Enoch or 1 Enoch.* Oxford: Clarendon, 1912.
Charlesworth, J.H. "The Concept of the Messiah in the Pseudepigrapha."
        Aufstieg und Niedergang der Romischen Welt II/19.1 (1979): 189–218.
_____. "From Jewish Messianology to Christian Christology." *Judaisms and
        Their Messiahs at the Turn of the Christian Era.* J. Neusner, W.S.
        Green and E. Frerichs, eds. Cambridge: Cambridge University Press,
        1987, 225–264.
Collins, J.J. *The Apocalyptic Imagination.* New York: Crossroad, 1984.
_____. *The Scepter and the Star: The Messiahs of the Dead Sea Scrolls and
        Other Ancient Literature.* 2nd ed. Grand Rapids: Eerdmans, 2010.
Corley, J. "Messianism in Hebrew *Ben Sira* and Greek *Sirach.*" *The Septuagint
        and Messianism. Bibliotheca Ephemeridum Theologicarum
        Lovaniensium* 195. M.A. Knibb, ed. Leuven/Leuven: Leuven
        University Press/Peeters, 2006, 301–312.
de Jonge, M. "The Use of the Word 'Anointed' in the Time of Jesus." *Novum
        Testamentum* 8 (1966): 132–148.
de Jonge, M., and A.S. van der Woude. "*Chrio,* etc." TDNT 9 (1974):509–527.
Fitzmyer, J. *The One Who Is to Come.* Grand Rapids/Cambridge: Eerdmans
        Publishing Company, 2007.
Goldstein, J. "How the Authors of 1 and 2 Maccabees Treated the Messianic
        Prophecies." *Judaisms and Their Messiahs at the Turn of the Christian
        Era.* J. Neusner, W.S. Green and E.S. Frerichs, eds. Cambridge:
        Cambridge University Press, 1987, 69–96.
Green, W.S. "Messiah in Judaism: Rethinking the Question." *Judaisms and
        Their Messiahs at the Turn of the Christian Era.* J. Neusner, W.S.
        Green and E.S. Frerichs, eds. Cambridge: Cambridge University Press,
        1987, 1–13.

Hogeterp, A. *Expectations of the End, A Comparative Traditio-Historical Study of Eschatological, Apocalyptic and Messianic Ideas in the Dead Sea Scrolls and the New Testament*. STDJ 83. Leiden/Boston: Brill, 2009.

Klayman, Seth. "Messianic Expectations 'Messy-Antic' Realizations: Evaluating the Influence of Messianisms on Jewish identity in the Second Temple Period." *Kesher* 12 (Winter 2000): 3–79.

Klijn, A.F.J. "2 (Syriac Apocalypse of) Baruch." *Old Testament Pseudepigrapha*. J.H. Charlesworth, ed. Garden City, NY: 1983–1985, 1:615–652.

Laato, A. *A Star Is Rising: The Historical Development of the Old Testament Royal Ideology and the Rise of the Jewish Messianic Expectations*. Atlanta: Scholars Press, 1997.

Lauterbach, Jacob. tr., *Mekhilta de Rabbi Ishmael*. 2nd ed. Philadelphia: Jewish Publication Society, 2004.

Lust, J. "Messianism and Septuagint." *Congress Volume: Salamanca 1983*. SupplVT 36. J.A. Emerton, ed. Leiden: Brill, 1985, 174–191.

Mowinckel, S. *He That Cometh: The Messiah Concept in the Old Testament and Later Judaism*. G.W. Anderson, trans. Grand Rapids/Cambridge, UK: Eerdmans, 2005.

Neusner, J. *Messiah in Context: Israel's History and Destiny in Formative Judaism*. Philadelphia: Fortress Press, 1984.

Neusner, J., et. al. *Judaisms and Their Messiahs at the Turn of the Christian Era*. Cambridge: Cambridge University Press, 1987.

Nickelsburg, G.W.E. "Salvation Without and With a Messiah: Developing Beliefs in Writings Ascribed to Enoch." *Judaisms and Their Messiahs at the Turn of the Christian Era*. J. Neusner, W.S. Green and E.S. Frerichs, eds. Cambridge: Cambridge University Press, 1987, 49–68.

_____. Jewish Literature Between the Bible and the Mishnah: A Historical and Literary Introduction. Minneapolis: Fortress Press, 2005.

Nickelsburg, G.W.E. and J.C. VanderKam. 1 Enoch 2: A Commentary on the Book of 1 Enoch Chapters 37–82. Minneapolis: Fortress Press, 2012.

Pomykala, K.E. *The Davidic Dynasty Tradition in Early Judaism: Its History and Significance for Messianism*. SBLEJL 7. Atlanta: Scholars Press, 1995, 127–229.

Puech, É. "Ben Sira 48.11 et la Résurrection." *Of Scribes and Scrolls: Studies on the Hebrew Bible, Intertestamental Judaism and Christian Origins*. H.W. Attridge, JJ. Collins and Th.H. Tobin, eds. Lanham, MD: University Press of America, 1990: 81–90.

Schiffman, L. "Messianic Figures and Ideas in the Qumran Scrolls." *The Messiah: Developments in Earliest Judaism and Christianity*. J.H. Charlesworth, et. al. Minneapolis: Fortress Press, 1992, 116–129.

_____. "Messianism and Apocalypticism." *The Cambridge History of Judaism: IV The Late Roman-Rabbinic Period.* S.T. Katz, ed. Cambridge: Cambridge University Press, 2008, 1053–1076.

Scholem, G. *The Messianic Idea in Judaism and Other Essays on Jewish Spirituality.* NY: Schocken, 1971.

Shürer, É. *History of the Jewish People in the Age of Jesus Christ (175 B.C. – A.D. 135).* rev. ed. G. Vermes, F. Millar and M. Black, eds. Edinburgh: T&T Clark, 1979.

Smith, M. "What Is Implied by the Variety of Messianic Figures?" *JBL* 78 (1959): 66–72, quote 68.

Stone, M.E. *Fourth Ezra.* Hermeneia. Minneapolis: Fortress Press, 1990.

Stone, M.E. and M. Henze. *4th Ezra and 2 Baruch: Translations, Introductions and Notes.* Minneapolis: Fortress Press, 2013.

Tromp, J. *The Assumption of Moses: A Critical Edition with Commentary.* SVTP 10. Leiden: Brill, 1992.

VanderKam, J.C. "Righteous One, Messiah Chosen One and Son of Man in 1 Enoch 37–71." *The Messiah: Developments in Earliest Judaism and Christianity.* J.H. Charlesworth, et. al., Minneapolis: Fortress Press, 1992, 169–91.

_____. "Messianism in the Scrolls." *The Community of the New Covenant.* E. Ulrich and J.C. VanderKam, eds. Notre Dame, IN: University of Notre Dame, 1994, 211–34.

VanderKam, J.C. and P. Flint. *The Meaning of the Dead Sea Scrolls: Their Significance for Understanding the Bible, Judaism, Jesus and Christianity.* NY: HarperSanFrancisco, 2004.

Walck, L.W. "The Son of Man in the Parables of Enoch and the Gospels." *Enoch and the Messiah Son of Man: Revisiting the Book of Parables.* G. Boccaccini, ed. Grand Rapids: Eerdmans, 2007, 299–337.

Wright, B.G. "Eschatology Without a Messiah in Ben Sira." *The Septuagint and Messianism. Bibliotheca Ephemeridum Theologicarum Lovaniensium* 195. M.A. Knibb, ed. Leuven/Leuven: Leuven University Press/Peeters, 2006, 313–323.

The Rise of Messianic Jewish Experience in Antiquity

Jeffrey L. Seif, D.Min.

Introduction

Christianity, so called, began as a renewal movement *within* Judaism. Jews hoped for a Messiah in the 2nd Temple Period, and the earliest Jewish followers of Yeshua/Jesus understood Him to be that awaited Messiah. Not everyone agreed. Problems with the intra-Jewish struggle over who Jesus was within the Jewish world, noteworthy is the fact that the fledgling movement of Jesus believers came into its own in a precarious world, one wracked by political intrigue and social unrest. Two political revolts failed in Judea, debacles that had devastating consequences for Jews in the troubled eastern Roman province. A North African Jewish insurgency failed as well, with dire consequences for the Hebrew people in the region. There, tragically, hundreds of thousands perished, with equal numbers of survivors eventually uprooted and displaced.

Surviving Jews, be they Jewish Jesus believers or nonbelievers, were left dispirited on a number of levels. Ancient Jews were numerically depleted, emotionally devastated and spiritually disoriented, as a result of their being socially and geographically uprooted. The story of Jesus' first followers is a story of a refugees in recovery, of displaced persons seeking new spaces in new places, of post-traumatic stress survivors looking for some needed sunshine in very gloomy worlds.

In the interest of telling the story of the first Jews who embraced Jesus-Messianism, we will begin with an accounting of the First Jewish Revolt in Judea, consider the Jewish Revolt in North Africa, and then the Second Jewish Revolt in Judea. We will consider how Jews uprooted from their ancestral lands reconstituted their lives in other people's worlds, and the impact messianic understandings and experience had upon them in the process of their so doing. From there we will look at *insider* Messianic Jewish writings, to ascertain what we can about their experiences; from there, we will consider what *outsiders* said about them, in order to learn more about them. If successful, we will walk away with a better understanding of Messianic Jewish experience just after the movement's inception.

Jewish Wars Leading up to the 130s AD

The First Jewish Revolt in Judea

In the mid-first century CE, tensions flared in Judea in response to news that the Caligula intended to set up a statue of his own in the Jerusalem Temple. Disconcerted Jews and anti-Semitic Greeks came to blows in Caesarea; riots subsequently spread inland and to Jerusalem proper. News reached King Agrippa II, who attempted to put a lid on the cascading unrest, but his hollow appeals for calm proved unfruitful.[1] Seeing an opportunity to seize the moment by exploiting the unrest for his own purposes, the nefarious and provocative procurator Gessius Florus (64–66CE) was all too happy to fan the flames of discontent. Perturbed by Florus' incessant abuses, chagrined Judeans appealed to the Roman governor in Antioch, Syria, a legate named Cestius Gallus. Their appeals fell on deaf ears, however. Unmitigated Jewish discontent ran its course, and pent-up furies found expression with the rapid mobilization of ad-hoc Jewish militia. Upon learning of this, and in response, Gallus disembarked from his headquarters in Antioch, Syria with the Legion XII *Fulminata* (meaning the "Thundering One") along with two thousand regulars from other Syrian-based legions—e.g., the Legion III *Gallica*, the VI *Ferrata* and the X *Fretensis*. The Syrian-tied

---

Portions of this chapter are available under his book title *To The Ends of the Earth*, published by Messianic Jewish Publications.

[1] His father, Agrippa I, was the Herodian monarch who persecuted Jewish believers in Judea and who killed Ya'akov/James (Acts 12:1–2), and whose son gave Gallus his willing hand. Luke records Agrippa I's death by stomach "worms" in Acts 12:19–23, which correlates with Josephus' account of his being "gripped in his stomach by an ache" in *Ant.* 19:346. This Messianic martyr-maker was survived by a few daughters and a young son, Agrippa II, under whose subsequent administration the entire Jewish kingdom was handed over to the ultimate supervision of the governor of Syria—Gallus, as previously noted.

Agrippa II[2] supplied foot soldiers and cavalry to assist Gallus in getting the better of his own Jewish people in Israel.[3]

Gallus' XII *Fulminata* proved to be more thunder than striking lightning, at the outset. The Legion not only lost its striking power, it even lost its symbol: the "eagle." Bested by circumstances and shamed by its losses, the floundering XIIth was forced to retreat from Jerusalem. The initial triumph over the Romans encouraged Jewish masses; many construed the turn of events in their favor as a sign that Providence was finally shining upon them. Intoxicated with encouragement, they geared up for an all-out eschatological contest with the Romans, assured of their ultimate victory in the otherwise-suicidal war.

Vespasian was apprised of the situation at his eastern front. To Gallus' aforementioned initial response-forces, Vespasian added the Legion XV *Apollinaris*, called up by his son Titus, who was dispatched to Alexandria, Egypt to mobilize more forces for the Judean campaign. Vespasian traveled over land and proceeded to Syria, where he marshaled other troops. Forces reconstituted and galvanized under Vespasian were invigorated by new energies. They re-launched an assault and began getting the better of the Jewish revolutionaries as they moved southward through the Galilee and Judea.

Vibrations from the Roman armies' approaching drumbeats created no little stir amongst the Jewish people—*prompting mass evacuations*, even before the great eschatological war was officially contested and decided in Jerusalem. Josephus mentioned that Vespasian gave "his right hand for their preservation," a reference to those who came over to him during the war (*Wars*, 4.130, 444). This conciliatory move was similarly followed by Titus, according to Josephus (*Wars*, 4.115), and then Placidus (*Wars*, 4. 438).[4] In *Wars* 4.377 Josephus said "on numerous occasions large numbers of people fled from the city to seek refuge with the Romans."[5] Josephus himself encouraged Jews to do just that, as he himself did, to the chagrin of many afterwards—and for centuries to

---

[2] *Ant.* 19:363–365; *War* 2:220; culled from Anson F. Rainey and R. Steven Notley, *The Sacred Bridge*, 384, my principal source for my reconstruction of events culminating in the destruction of Judea in the first and second wars.

[3] According to Tacitus, he had previously sent troops to assist the Romans in their campaign against the Parthians. (See *Ann.* 13.)

[4] Dan Jaffee (ed.), *Studies in Rabbinic Judaism and Early Christianity: Text and Context* (Leiden/Boston: Brill, 2010), 119. Dr. Bourgel is the principal source for my reconstruction of the argument, along with Professors Rainey and Notley. (See below.)

[5] *Ibid.*, and 129; see also *Wars* 4.397, 410.

follow. *"Many there were of the Jews that deserted every day, and fled away from the Zealots,"* said Josephus (*Wars*, 4.377, italics mine). Josephus later records that the Temple was destroyed on the 10th of Av, in *War* 6:250—*not* on the ninth. Eusebius and Epiphanius noted that after the first revolt, Jewish believers eventually "returned" to Judea,[6] where they reconstituted (*Ecc. Hist.* 4, 5:2). He is explicit in noting their presence until the invasion of Hadrian, to quell the Bar Kochba Revolt, approximately sixty years later, from 132–135CE. Before we get to the second Jewish revolt in Judea, a word about how kindred Jews in North Africa fared between the Judean wars is worthy of some consideration.

The North African Revolt

In "The Jews of Alexandria," Professor Erich Gruen reports: "Jews [in Alexandria] enjoyed productive and rewarding lives in the greatest of the Hellenistic cities. Integration in the social, economic and cultural life of Alexandria was open to them, and they took advantage of that opening. Jews served in the armies, obtained administrative posts, took part in commerce, shipping, finance, farming and every form of occupation, reaching posts of prestige and importance, and played a role in the world of the Hellenic intelligentsia."[7]According to Dr. Gruen, Jews fared reasonably well in North African Egypt. Tragically, however, things changed and the Jewish community was eventually annihilated in North Africa—a process that began shortly after the closing of its now long-forgotten temple, one that rivaled the Jerusalem Temple. We will consider sacred Jewish space in North Africa, and then Trajan's war and its effect on the Jews.

This once-famous (now forgotten) Jewish temple in Leontopolis, Egypt was *the only place, outside of Jerusalem, in antiquity where sacrifices were offered by Jews.* A word about this site is in order, in part because just introducing the idea of an independent Jewish temple outside Jerusalem may be new to so many. The Egyptian-based, Jewish sanctuary's origination was spirited along by Onias III's son, who once

---

[6] That aside, and in the wake of the Temple's demise, in the aftermath of the war, "Titus," we're told, "left the Legion X *Fretensis* in Jerusalem, while stationing the Legion XII *Fulminata*, "besides the Euphrates near the confines of Armenia and Cappadocia" and retained the Legions V *Macedonia* and XV *Apollinaris* with himself (*War* 7.17–19). See Anson F. Rainey and R. Steven Notley, *The Sacred Bridge*, 394.

[7] Erich S. Gruen, *Diaspora: Jews Amidst Greeks and Romans* (Cambridge: Harvard University Press, 2002), 69.

fled Syrian persecutions and took refuge in Alexandria, Egypt. Josephus says Philometor, King of Egypt, gave him quarter. After petitioning him and his sister/wife Cleopatra (not the famous one) to allow him to build a sanctuary in Egypt like the one in Jerusalem, a temple comparable to the one in Jerusalem (though smaller) was subsequently built. It was constructed atop the ruins of the temple of Bubastis, in Heliopolis, 180 stadia from Memphis, Egypt.[8] Professors Gottheil and Krauss explain how "Jewish support was crucial in rescuing Julius Caesar at Alexandria, leading him to grant privileges to Jews throughout the Roman empire."[9] The political ingratiation facilitated the aforementioned temple construction. Dr. Livia Capponi published a work on the Jewish temple in Egypt[10] in 2007; her work was reviewed by Professor David Noy, of the University of Wales Lampeter, for the *Bryn Mawr Classical Review* (2008.09.37).

The basic story is, shortly after the Jerusalem Temple was destroyed in the aforementioned 70 CE debacle, the Egyptian Temple in Leontopolis was closed by the Roman authorities. It was closed either by Lupus, the governor of Egypt, or by his successor, Paulinus, about three years after the destruction of the Temple at Jerusalem... fearing that through this temple, Egypt might become a new center for [another] Jewish rebellion.[11] In his *Historia Romana* (LXVIII), the Roman historian Dio Cassius noted how Roman fears were not unwarranted and how an uprising destabilized North Africa, resulting in utter destruction and displacement of North African Jewry.

In 115CE, Trajan bested the Parthians in the east, extending western-based Roman hegemony to Armenia, Mesopotamia and Assyria in the east. Roman troops, previously employed to keep the *Pax Romana* ("Roman Peace") in North Africa, were dispatched to the eastern front for the new Parthian campaign. As a consequence, Roman holdings in North Africa were left less protected. Seething under oppressive Roman racial policies, and unable to get redress for their grievances, North African Jews in Cyrene and Cyprus took to arms and caused no little stir. As their pent-up furies and enthusiasms were running their course, many non-Jewish people were plundered and the pagan temples of

---

[8] From www.jewishencyclopedia.com/articles/9772-leontopolis.

[9] http://bmcr.brynmawr.edu/2008/2008-09-37.html

[10] In Il temio di Leontopoli in Egitto: Identita politica e religiosa dei Giudei di Onia. Pubblicazioni della Facolta di Lettere e Filosofia dell'Universita di Pavia.

[11] From www.jewishencyclopedia.com/articles/9772-leontopolis.

Apollo, Artemis, Hecate, Demeter, Isis and Pluto were leveled. The
death toll was enormous. Gentile refugees fled to Alexandria en masse
and subsequently exacted their revenge upon Jews living there. Two of
Alexandria's five districts were Jewish, with many Jews living in non-
Jewish quarters. The Jewish population in the city alone is said to have
been about 150,000. Many Jews were slaughtered. Not to be either
outdone or undone Alexandria's Jews regrouped, after which they spent
their furies on even more North African peoples and places. The temples
of Nemesis, Hectate and Apollo were laid waste by their response.
Cyrenaican Jews similarly laid waste the Romanized-Egyptian
countryside. Fomenting discontent spread.[12] The uprising was quelled by
Marcius Turbo, but not before about 200,000 Romans and Greeks had
been killed, according to Dio Cassius (lxviii. 32). The Roman governor
Marcus Rutilius Lupus dispatched the III *Cyrenaica* and XXII
Deiotariana legions to protect the non-Jewish inhabitants of Memphis.
To these Trajan then added the Legion VII *Claudia*, along with forces
under Quintus Marcius Turbo, a trusted military man well-known to him
through his service as prefect of the Praetorian Guard and as the
commander of the *Classis Misenensis*, the Roman navy's senior fleet.
Trajan threw his best at his foes, besting Jewish forts and forces. Myriad
Jews in Alexandria and Cyrene were slaughtered, and the campaign was
swiftly brought to a close in favor of the Romans. Wanting finally to
both resolve the cascading uprising and take pains to ensure it would not
happen again, *the Romans depopulated North Africa of Jews*—and this,
of course, included Jewish followers of Yeshua/Jesus. Wanting
furthermore to keep the North African revolt contained—after a revolt in

---

[12] Discontent had been brewing for some time. Located to the west in modern Libya, Cyrene was an
important Greek colonial city midway between the major port cities of Carthage and Alexandria. Located on
the slopes of the Green Mountains, Cyrene was a short distance from the sea, close to the Greek
Peloponnesus and the Greek island Thera. It was the fourth-largest city in the Roman world at its prime. Its
success was spirited along by its proximity to the port city Apollonia, which gave it access to international
markets. Flavius Josephus wrote that during the Ptolemies' reign in Egypt, many Jews took up residency in
Cyrene (*Ant*. 14.7, 2). There, says Strabo, people "were divided into four classes: citizens, farmers, resident
aliens, *and Jews*." Relegated to a low, distressed class, Lucullus was once dispatched to Cyrene by Sulla to
quell disturbances perpetrated by the disenfranchised Hebrews. The Romans recommended concessions to
the Jews, to keep the precarious peace (*I Macc*. 15. 15-24), and Cyrenians were notified accordingly.
Tensions were long-abiding, however, and Jews felt them. According to Josephus, Jewish Cyrenians were
oppressed by the autonomous Greek population (*Ant*. 16. 6.1). As a consequence, Romans met with
opposition in Cyrene, where a Jewish "Zealot" named Jonathan incited Jews to riot. Josephus said the
disturbance was quickly suppressed by the governor Catullus (*Wars*. vii. 7.11.1; *Vita*, 76). More serious than
that disturbance was the insurrection of the Jews of Cyrene under Trajan (117 C.E.).
www.newworldencyclopedia.org/entry/Cyrene,_Libya; www.jewishencyclopedia.com/articles/4826-cyrene

both Judea and now North Africa, now—and fearing it may well spread from North Africa to the newly acquired, disquieted eastern, Syrian-Mesopotamian provinces, Trajan called upon the commander of some North African auxiliaries, a cavalry officer named Lusius Quietus. Quietus subsequently imposed himself upon the Jews in Cyprus, Mesopotamia and Syria, and effectively *annihilated the Jews*, as had Turbo.[13] Quietus thus kept the quiet. Jews in North Africa were quieted, through a little-told holocaust. Judea erupted shortly afterward, for a spirited revolt in the 130s.

The Second Jewish Revolt in Judea

The dogs of war were again unleashed in Judea. Dio Cassius says the Bar Kochba Revolt resulted in hundreds of thousands of Jews killed—with estimates as high as 500,000. It was a holocaust, to be sure. According to him, the revolt sparked because "the Jews deemed it intolerable that foreign races should be settled in their city and foreign religious rites planted there," after the 70 CE revolt (Dio Cass. 69.12.1-2). This is a possibility. The holocaust of Hebrews in North Africa must surely have been a factor, as well, as with all else happening to Jews in the region. Some consider Emperor Hadrian's vacillation the primary cause, however. Though initially game to assist with the building of a new Jewish Temple in Jerusalem in 130 CE, Hadrian was said to have changed his mind. Disinclined, he opted to make Jerusalem a decidedly non-Jewish city. Chagrined, some Jews started stockpiling weapons and plotting revenge, under the leadership of Simon Bar Kochba. War erupted, and it went horribly for the Jews, leaving hundreds of thousands dead in its wake. In the wake of the failed revolt, the province known as Iudaea was renamed *Syria Palaestinia*, with perennial Jewish banishment as punishment for the insurrection—save for "visiting rights" on the ninth of Av.

The reasons for the second revolt are varied and debated, but not the consequences: *Jews were subsequently forbidden access to Jerusalem—including Messianic Jews.* Eusebius sums up the Messianic believers' banishment in *Hist. Eccl.* 4, 6:4: "...when the city came to be bereft of

---

[13] As a reward for his efficiently effecting the demise of the Jews, Quietus was appointed governor of Judea. Death claimed him in the summer of 118 CE—as it does us all. Though forgotten by many today, as he lay silently in his grave, Judaism's sages could not keep quiet. They remembered Quietus in the Talmud. There, because of his endeavors to destroy Jewish people and culture, Jewish fathers were beckoned to not teach their sons Greek (*Mishnah Sota*, 9.14).

the nation of the Jews, and its ancient inhabitants had completely perished, foreigners of the Church colonized it... it was composed of Gentiles."

With this I bring to close a brief treatment of Jewish wars and rumors of wars, happening all the while a Messianic movement was getting a foothold in and around Judea. *Those who followed Jesus at the time were making their passages through time amidst the turbulence of those perilous and trying times.* All Jews—Messianic or otherwise— then made their journeys from their wombs to their tombs as displaced persons. (1) They lived without a homeland and (2) suffered the loss of their religious center of gravity; (3) uncertainty would have prevailed in their thinking and emoting; and (4) their thoughts were no doubt clouded by memories of their present-world gone bad. While this is surely descriptive of the thinking and feeling of Jews in general, one group of Jews in particular found hope still—a hope amply attested in *the Gospel According to the Hebrews.*

The Gospel "According to the Hebrews"

For his part, Jerome *mistakenly* tied Matthew's Gospel to the land of Judea—but, in so many ways, it was no longer the habitat of the Hebrews. The assumption is not without merit, given how Matthew's document (1) includes Aramaic words without translation (5:22; 6:24; 27:6) and (2) assumes knowledge of Jewish customs and evidences "forms of speech that are more typically Semitic than Greek."[14] Still, if Fuller Theological Seminary's professors Dr. Carson, Dr. Moo and Dr. Morris are to be believed—and most all other New Testament scholars, for that matter, concur—*Antioch, Syria is to be preferred for Matthew's place of origination*, based, in part, on the fact that, like in the Antiochan faith community, constituted as it was by waves of immigrant Jews from the wars, the document: "breathes a [very] Jewish atmosphere and yet looks upon the Gentile mission in a favorable light."[15]

The Gentile-friendliness of the Jewish document, as Duke University's Professor Stanley Hauerwas notes, is evidenced alongside Matthean themes like "the relation between the church and Israel, the

---

[14] D.A. Carson, Douglas Moo and Leon Morris, *An Introduction to the New Testament* (Grand Rapids: Zondervan Publishing, 1992), 75. 79, as well, refers to there being "so many Jewish features."
[15] Ibid., 75.

continuing status of the law, [and] the significance of the Temple."[16] To these, Professor Warren Carter, of the Brite Divinity School in Ft. Worth, adds that Matthew's people—or the people of "the Gospel according to the Hebrews"—know Torah practices like (1) Sabbath-keeping, (2) purity laws, (3) tithing, (4) oaths, all of which are interpreted by Yeshua/Jesus, as per 5:17; 22:37–39, with premiums going to justice, mercy and faithfulness in 23:23.[17] With *knowing* being experiential, not just intellectual, we are well served to consider that Matthew's recipients lived like Jews, as opposed to just thinking like them or being sympathetic toward them. *The same is true with the ethos of the new Tree of Life version of the Bible, produced by Rabbi Mark and Daniah Greenberg, and the Messianic Jewish Family Bible Society.*

The ancients actually noted Matthew's decidedly Jewish nature for quite some time. Among them were the likes of Papias,[18] Ireneus (*Adv. Haer.* 3.1.1, quoted in Eusebius in *H. E.,* 5.8.2), Tertullian (*Against Marcion.* 4.2) and Origen (quoted by Eusebius in *H. E.* 6.25.3–6), to name but a few.[19] The strident, anti-Messianic churchman Epiphanius—arguably and sadly of Jewish extract himself!—claimed the "Ebionites" (*i.e.,* ancient Messianic Jews) had a Matthean text they mutilated to manufacture their defective book called *According to the Hebrews.* Lacking that sort of vitriol, Irenaeus says the early Jewish believers used a Matthew text, much as the celebrated philologist St. Jerome claims he "translated the 'Gospel According to the Hebrews' into both Greek and Latin."[20] Jerome claims that Nazarenes (*i.e.,* ancient Messianic Jews) assisted with the translation,[21] and is known to have been grateful and polite by way of response.

With its provenance in or around Antioch, Syria and an understood post-war date in the 80s with circulation and appreciation to follow for years as givens, we do well to ask: *What can we learn about Messianic Jewish experience* (or ancient "Christianity") in Antioch) *from the Gospel that originated there*—their lives and circumstances?

In his *The Formation of Christianity in Antioch: A Social-Scientific Approach to the Separation Between Judaism and Christianity,*

---

[16] Stanley Hauerwas, *Matthew* (Grand Rapids: Brazos Press, 2006), 20.
[17] Richard A. Horsley (ed), *Christian Origins,* 156.
[18] Ibid., 68.
[19] Ibid., 70.
[20] Ibid., 71.
[21] Ibid.

Professor Magnus Zetterholm postulates a population of 300,000–
400,000 people in Antioch, at the time when Messianic Judaism was
getting a hold there.[22] Others claim a higher number. Going with his
conservative appraisal, however, the city's density amounts to about 195
people per acre.[23] Considering Calcutta has about 122 people per acre,
and Mumbai 185, Dr. Zetterholm surmises that non-elite residents in
Antioch—the likes of which would have been represented by the better
part of the transplanted Jewish refugees who fled the war—would have
indeed been *hard-pressed*.

Leaning upon Seneca (4/5BCE–65CE), who complains about
conditions in Antioch, Dr. Warren Carter adds: "Most inhabitants of
Antioch lived in atrocious and cramped conditions, marked by noise,
filth, squalor, garbage, [exposure to] human excrement, animals, disease,
fire risk, crime, social and ethnic conflicts, malnutrition, natural disaster
(especially flooding) and unstable dwellings."[24] Non-elite slaves and
plebians, as distinguished from higher-ranking senatorial and equestrian
classes of people, had low life expectancies in this environment: 25–40
was the average life expectancy for males; it was much less for females.
Infant mortality was particularly high, as well, at 1:5, not to mention
increased deaths for the mothers laboring to bring the children into their
miserable world. Most did not have running water, requiring folk to
bring in water in jugs. Urine and feces were deposited in the streets and
left there. For those living at the time, life came replete with many
challenges.

Josephus spoke of a dense Jewish population in Antioch (*Ant.* 7.43).
Professor Zetterholm estimates there were approaching 22,000 Jews in
the city, and approximately thirty synagogues, but knows of no distinct
Jewish quarter, per se, as was the case in Sardis, Alexandria and Rome.[25]

Jews had secured some benefits in Antioch. Jews, for example, had
already earned the cherished right to assemble as a legal *collegia*, to
observe the Sabbath and other festivals, to collect and send the Temple
tax to Jerusalem, to observe dietary laws, to be exempted both from
obligations to the imperial cult and from mandatory military service.

---

[22] Others have argued for 500,000.
[23] Magnus Zetterholm, The Formation of Christianity in Antioch: A Social-Scientific Approach to the
Separation Between Judaism and Christianity (London and New York: Routledge, 2003), p. 29.
[24] In his chapter "Matthew's People," found in Richard A. Horsley (ed), *Christian Origins* (Minneapolis:
Fortress Press, 2010), 146.
[25] Zetterholm, *The Formation, op. cit.*, 37.

Though Jews enjoyed a legal status, many were nevertheless accused of impiety, misanthropy and xenophobia, and seen by some outsiders as "evil incarnate."[26] Josephus said Jews helped found the city of Antioch, initially, and had a long history in the city since inception (*Against Apion* 2.39; *Ant.* 12.119). Difficulties every now and again aside, overall, political life was reasonably tranquil for Jews in Antioch.

Waves of newcomer immigrants from the aforementioned wars were forever being absorbed by Jews there; and this, of course, taxed Jewish benevolence systems that would easily be stretched too thin. The recently resettled Messianic Jews were in a particularly precarious place, socially. They, of course, would have been assisted by Messianic Jews already resident there before the wars (see below), much as they would have been helped along through the larger Jewish community's largesse. Tacitus noted "Jews were "extremely loyal toward one another, and always ready to show compassion" (*Hist.* 5.5).[27] Still, challenging as the times were, issues associated with food production, distribution and consumption would have weighed heavy on the hearts and minds of the myriad non-elite Jewish peasants who lived almost one hundred years after Jesus.

Endemic undernourishment would have prompted sickness and its evil cousin contagion, with concomitant malnutrition making people especially prone to malaria, diarrhea, dysentery, cholera, typhus and *Bacillus meningitis*. Inadequate sewage and water would similarly have contributed to swollen eyes, skin rashes, measles, mumps, scarlet fever and smallpox. Mindful of the above, Professor Carter wonders: "Is it any wonder then that food production, distribution and trade and consumption and diet [stories] figure predominantly in the Gospel [of Matthew]?"[28] What else can we find there that contributes to understanding early Messianic Jewish experience?

The Torah-observant, Messianic Jewish community knew Yeshua/Jesus did not come to "abolish the Torah" for Jews (Matt. 5:17). Nobody ever heard Him or any immediate disciple of his say He did. Those who recall the famous 2 Macc. 6–7 story, of a woman who gave up her sons in defiance of the regnant powers' insistence they assimilate (cf. Heb. 11:35), might do well to consider that the story originates in

---

[26] Ibid., p. 113.
[27] Ibid.,. p. 127.
[28] Ibid., p. 157

Syria, Antioch. As for advocating a restrictive diet, would not stricter Torah-compliance assist Jews in an environment where plague was rife—as was the case in Europe? One would think so. In any case, the premium on charity in the abysmal world is particularly noteworthy here.

Matthew's Messianic believers heard stories of "the poor" who had "the Good. News preached to them" (Matt. 11:5). They learned that people mattered more than livestock (12:11–12) and that miracle provisions were to be had by the faithful (6:25–34). Whatever Matthew says about Yeshua/Jesus and Torah observance aside, stories of planting and harvesting (13:3–9, 18–24; 12:1), of vineyards (20:1–16; 21:28–32, 33–35), of day laborers (20:1–16), of fieldwork (24:40–41), of fishing (4:18–22; 13:47–50), of trading (13:45–46), of marketplaces (11:16), as with noting food staples like fish (7:9–10), bread (15:9–10) and wine (26:26–29) most surely would have spoken the loudest, and been heard by people burdened by deep-felt yearnings associated with life's menacing problems. *Nobody felt burdened by Torah observance; they all felt burdened by life.* People who "labor and are burdened" were invited to come to Yeshua/Jesus for their daily necessities (11:28–30), to pray for "daily bread" (6:11) and were beckoned to not worry too much about "what we will eat and drink" (6:25–34), as seems so much the case with humans who find themselves pressed amidst the turbulence of trying times.[29]

Deficiency and contagion would have been ubiquitous for hearers who dwelt in impoverished ghettos. Numerous summary passages to that effect are noted (4:23–25; 9:35; 11:4–5); and those, coupled with various miracle scenes (8–9; 12:9–14, 22; 15:21–28; 17:14–20; 20:29–34), of the healing of lepers (8:1–4; 11:5), of removing blindness (9:27–31; 11:5; 12:22; 15:30–31; 20:30; 21:14), of relieving pains (4:24), along with besting various types of deformities and paralysis (4:24; 8:6; 9:2; 11:5; 12:9–14; 15:30; 21:14). Yeshua/Jesus is seen helping and healing, and forcefully confronting and condemning the regnant spiritual/political powers in that world—on behalf of Jewish people (and all people)—time and time again, in 4:24; 8:16, 28, 33; 9:32; 15:22. One

---

[29] Stories told of crops threatened by aggressive and poisonous weeds (13:24–30), threatening famines (24:7) and beggars (9:27–31; 20:29–34) would have spoken to, for and about the needs of many, as with their associates.

illustration is particularly striking—and telling in that regard, especially in a first-century, Jewish context.

As noted at the outset, the Roman Legion X *Fretensis* was stationed in Syria with a variety of other legions. The Tenth transferred and fought against Jerusalem in 66–70 CE, however, and was stationed on the Temple Mount for many, many years afterward. Its mascot was a pig—an affront to Jews, to be sure. In Mark's accounting of a miracle scene, a demoniac was bested by a demon named "Legion" (see Mk. 5:9). In both Matthew and Mark's reckonings of his deliverance, after being excised from the unfortunate man, "Legion" entered pigs who, in turn, ran down an embankment to be finally destroyed in the Sea of Galilee/Tiberias (Matt. 8:28–34). Whatever else could be garnered from the story, the social implications would not have gone unnoticed by the story's Jewish hearers who would have rejoiced to see a symbol of the Xth being destroyed by Israel's Messiah.

Beyond whatever they garnered from vindication stories, they had interests that were uniquely related to the Gospel's own needs: *to expand the Messianic Kingdom into worlds and cultures beyond Judea.* Their Messianic Judaism was both *cosmopolitan* and *global-oriented* is evidenced by how the baby King's arrival was said to have been celebrated by "wise men" from the nations (2:1–12), by the Kingdom's being likened to a "dragnet cast into the sea that gathered *all kinds of fish*" (13:47) and by the Kingdom's messengers being under a mandate to then "Go into *all the world*... and make disciples of *all nations*" (28:19–20), to name but a few samplings in support of the point.

To be sure, they were poor people, living out precarious lives in a foreign land. They lived as Jewish people in that foreign land, however. No longer the dominant group in Syria as they were in Judea—even a Hellenized Judea—they developed socially as a sub-culture within the larger Levantine cultural milieu. It might be for that reason that, more so than what was typically afforded in a narrower traditional, Pharisaic approach to Judaism, Matthew's cosmopolitan, Messianic people were more open to, and indeed very much oriented toward, individuals of non-Jewish extract. This is only to be expected; after all, *this was their world and it was their way*—and their ways invoked the ire of others, both Gentiles and Jews alike!

Gentiles, Jews and Early Messianic Jews

How did Jews fare amongst the Greeks, generally? How did Messianic Jews fare among them, particularly, in and around 130 AD? In *Diaspora: Jews Amidst Greeks and Romans*, Dr. Erich S. Gruen, professor emeritus in the Department of History, University of California, says the population of Rome virtually "exploded" and shifted in the first and second centuries B.C.E., resulting in many "Jewish communities... in the late Republic and early Principate."[30] Gentile views of newly arriving, displaced Jews *vacillated*—in Rome itself, as elsewhere. Valerius Maximus reported in 139 B.C.E. that marginalized Jews invoked the ire of some resident Romans and that Cornelius Hispanus had them expelled from Rome, for "peddling their ancient wisdom" and "attempting to transfer their sacred rites to the Romans" (*Val. Max.* 1.3.3).[31] Seneca is on record describing Jews as a most pernicious people. Because he nowhere else speaks directly of Jews in his vast writings—save for this extract culled from St. Augustine's *City of God*—one cannot say Seneca was particularly obsessed with Jews and given to their slander. Others were, however. The satirist Juvenal disparaged Jews for adherence to *dietary laws, Sabbath, circumcision* and the like, but construed the practices "more laughable than dangerous."[32] Tacitus was tolerant of Jews, but "angrier at the [Gentile] converts [to Judaism] than at the Jews... who have deserted their native gods, ancestral traditions, homeland and families"[33] to affiliate with these odd foreigners.

That quite a few Gentiles were actually inclined toward Jewish vision, however, and the Jewish practices that nurtured it, was evidenced by Josephus, who observed how many Gentiles "adopted Jewish customs and manners" (*War* 2.463), and that Jews in the Greco-Roman world were "constantly attracting to their religious ceremonies multitudes of Greeks" (*Wars* 7.45). Elsewhere he said—and perhaps not hyperbolically: "[t]here is not one [single] city, Greek or barbarian, to which our [Jewish] customs... have not spread" (*Against Apion* 2.282).

---

[30] Erich S. Gruen, *Diaspora: Jews Amidst Greeks and Romans* (Cambridge: Harvard University Press, 2002), 15. In "Immigration and Cosmopolitanization," *Cambridge Companion to Ancient Rome*, 77–92, esp. 79 and fn 6, Claudia Moatti lists the Jewish population from 20,000–40,000 in the first century CE.

[31] Ibid., 16, and 260, n. 7.

[32] Ibid., 45.

[33] Ibid., 46–47.

Particularly, says he, beyond the Imperial City—Rome "... *[in] the whole of Syria... each city has its Judaizers*" (*War* 2.262–63, italics mine). Jewish influence was not inconsequential. Flavius further stated: "in Damascus [Syria] men noted how 'wives had all become subject to the Jewish religion'" (*War* 2.559–60). There most surely is some overstatement with the implication that *all* wives were coming over to Judaism. Still, the point is clear—as is the chagrin: *Judaism was popular enough to draw such hyperbolic scorn.* To continue, Dio Cassius said Jews were "converting many of the natives to their [Jewish] ways" (*Roman History* 57.18.5a). Tacitus similarly spoke of "those who come over to [the Jewish] religion" (*Histories* 5.5). Lending even more credence to *the attractiveness of Jewish vision* and speaking perhaps in a disparaging manner about it, Horace said: "we, like Jews, will compel you to join our throng" (*Satires* 1.4.142–143). Epigraphic evidence in Asia and Rome, for example, corroborates there being "proselytes"[34] in higher echelons who appreciated the Jewish world and ways. "Veturia Paula," for example, was remembered as "a proselyte [to Judaism] for 16 years under the name of Sarah, mother [or patroness] of the synagogues of Campus and Voluminus." Julia Severa, another example, was a patroness of the Jewish community, and was known to have financed a synagogue in Phrygia. Her son, L. Servenius Cornutus, served in the Senate under Nero in 73 CE and was legate to the proconsul in Asia. Another relative, L. Iulius Severus, served as a consul. *Jewish faith and culture seems to have had a certain amount of street appeal on the main boulevards* and *not just on society's lower-class alleyways.* According to Josephus, other Jewish-friendly friends in very high Roman places include Emperor Nero's mistress Poppaea Sabina, who "pleaded on behalf of the Jews." Titus, the elder son of Vespasian—both of whom participated in the "sack" of Jerusalem in the late 60s—took a Jewish woman named Bernice as his mistress with him back to Rome after the war, which would give him a Jewish-friendly voice in the bedroom, at the very least. Lastly, to finish the point, Professor Magnus Zetterholm, in *The Formation of Christianity in Antioch*, alights upon Judaism's presence and influence in Roman culture, by referencing St. Augustine in *Civ.* 6.11, citing Seneca who exclaimed: "the *customs of the accursed [Jewish] race have gained such influence* that they are now received. The vanquished have given laws to

---

[34] Ibid., 13.

the victors." [35] Surely much of this is overstated. Still, *what was Judaism's appeal*?

The reasons Jewish faith and practice had street appeal in Roman antiquity—*particularly for non-Jewish women*—vary. One telling example may suffice for our purposes—by giving a window in why Jewish faith and culture were attractive. Writing around 200 C.E., in his *The Roman History: The Reign of Augustus*, the Roman historian Dio Cassius noted an "extreme shortage of females" in Roman culture.[36] Dr. J. C. Russell posited there were 131 males for every 100 females in the city of Rome itself, and 140 males for every 100 in Italy.[37] In *The Ancient World: Manners and Morals*, Dr. Jack Lindsay noted how even in large, reasonably wealthy families, "more than one daughter was practically never reared."[38] This diminished number of Roman women, according to Professor Rodney Stark, can only be attributed to some artificial engineering of human life, or of "tampering" with it.

With no offense to Roman culture and morals, *many, many non-Jewish baby girls were left to die at birth in Greco-Roman culture*—as were males with deformities. Undesired Gentile girls were simply left to die at dumps at the edge of Roman cities; some, however, were picked up and raised as prostitutes. Seneca regarded the disregarding of unwanted children "reasonable" and "commonplace." [39] Plato and Aristotle recommended infanticide as a legitimate state policy and lent their credence to the pathetic practice. In no uncertain terms, Jews did not. In *The Histories* 5.5, Tacitus construed the Jewish notion that it is "a deadly sin to kill an unwanted child" as one of the Jews' "sinister and revolting" ways of thinking.[40] Torah-minded Jews were on record

---

[35] Zetterholm, *The Formation, op. cit.*, 127, italics mine.

[36] This claim has not gone uncontested. See J.-U. Kraus, *Witwen und Waisen im römischen Reich: Rechtliche und soziale Stellung von Waisen*. Stuttgart: Steiner, 1994–1995.

[37] Since his 1958 work *Late Ancient and Medieval Population*, much more work has been done, especially with the number of archaeological finds and with work in funerary inscriptions in ancient Rome. Studies on Roman families have been greatly revised since the 1980s. See, for example, Saller and Shaw, "Tombs and Roman Family Relations in the Principate: Civilians, Soldiers and Slaves," *Journal of Roman Studies* 74, (1984), 124–156. His dating of the data is contested, as is the reference by Jack Lindsey (see footnote 38).

[38] Jack Lindsay, *The Ancient World: Manners and Morals* (New York: J.P. Putnam's Sons, 1968), 168. Of 600 families with inscriptions left in Delphi, only six reported raising more than one daughter—thus only 1%. Astounding! Troubling, is it not?

[39] Rodney Stark, The Rise of Christianity: A Sociologist Reconsiders History, 118.

[40] Ibid., 118. My friend and respondent Dr. Vered Hillel refers to my excessive reliance on Professor Stark's work here as "intellectual suicide." She's correct, of course. While I grant there are gaps in my thinking that need filling, and the need for re-visioning, further refinement and the development of it through the

disdaining the murderous practice outright, and they were game to boldly criticize it. Josephus noted: "The [Jewish] law, moreover, enjoins us to bring up our offspring, and forbids women to cause abortion or to destroy it afterward; and if a woman appears to have done so, she will be a murderer of her child." In his *Sentences of Pseudo-Phocylides,* an ancient Alexandrian Jew reflects the same Jewish sentiment, saying: "a woman should not... throw it [i.e. her newborn baby] before dogs and vultures of prey."

Given Judaism's stalwart disparagement of divorce, marital infidelity, fornication and polygamy,[41] *it is not hard to understand why non-Jewish women would be attracted to Jewish vision*—and virtuous men. Kindness and nurture were accentuated in Jewish-based faith communities, in Israel-proper and throughout the ancient Roman world. Jewish culture was virtue-rich, whereas pagan culture operated with an extreme virtue deficit. Greco-Roman utilitarianism humbled and dehumanized human beings—even the citizens of the empire. Reducing non-citizens of lesser race, class and gender to less-than-hoped-for lives, the doomed unfortunates were socialized into accepting their unfortunate lot. Most knew they were little more than utilities to be used and abused in the gladiatorial games, to be harvested as slave-stock for the mines, and used as human chattel to serve the various needs and interests of oppressive overlords: as agricultural slaves, sex-slaves of both sexes, whatever... Though this ubiquitous dehumanization tended to prevail in the larger culture, and on quite a grand scale, *an attractive Torah-influenced Messianic Jewish subculture within the regnant culture cast a loftier moral vision and an intoxicating future vision, where all people— irrespective of race, class or gender—had inalienable, God-given dignity and rights, and where the powerful, wicked wealthy would eventually be judged.* That these "rights" extended to women in the decidedly patriarchal-oriented culture may well account for why women from all classes were attracted to Jewish vision originally, and then why many women preferred Judaism's daughter religion as it got a foothold in antiquity: Messianic Judaism.

That Jews and non-Jews alike were being drawn into Messianic Jewish experience *upset Jewish elites bent on exerting their influence*

---

assimilation of more and more-current data, I nonetheless am confident enough in Stark's appraisals to go with them here, construing him as I do, to be an extremely importance resource.
[41] As per restrictions in the Old and New Testaments.

amongst disenfranchised Jews in the wake of the Temple's demise. Not only were Jewish women and men embracing an understanding that did not comport with the sages' sensibilities, but growing inventories of Jewish-friendly, Gentile women and men—who may well have otherwise come under the sages' growing sway—were increasingly attracted to the new movement. *Jewish authorities believed the bleeding had to be stopped.*

Rabbinic Antipathy Toward Messianic Jews in Antiquity

The Latins referred to Jewish believers as *hebraeus Christianus*. In the early rabbinic sources, Judaism's ancient sages chose not to call them by that name, or any other name to speak of. They in fact ostensibly ignored the *hebraeus Christianus*, opting instead to cryptically refer to Jewish believers in and around 130 AD by other, disparaging terms. *Min* or *minim* was one such designation, derived from the common noun for "kind," "genus" or "species." *Minim* refers to another type of people—to non-people, to lesser mortals, to "heretics." *Meshummad* was another disparaging designation, traditionally translated as "apostate," or "someone who destroyed himself"—as with others, by association. Yet another was *mumar*, denoting "exchange," or "someone who has converted," a person who has set aside former values and associations. Akin to *Parushim*—meaning the Pharisees—*perushim*, from the word "separate," was employed to note separatist Jewish believers, seen by the rabbis as "seceders" and "renegades." *Masor* was yet another name, meaning to "hand over," as in a Jew who betrays another Jew and hands them over to Roman authorities. This is the equivalent of being a "turn-coat" in the American Revolution. *Hisonim* was yet another name for Jewish believers, from the adjective *hison*, "outsider"—hence those beyond our pale. Jewish believers were also referred to as *Epiqorsim* (*i.e.*, an Epicurean), denoting once again "separateness," but adding connotations of being "disrupters of families," those given to "sexual immorality" and to "moral depravity" generally. For the rabbis, *hebraeus Christianus* represented a disease. Beyond the aforementioned proscriptive designations, the words *Noseri* or *Noserim* were employed by the rabbis, unambiguously in these cases, referring to the followers of the One from Nazareth. Judaism's sages cast aspersions on Jewish believers in Jesus. What was it about this sub-group of Jews that invoked the ire of the ancient rabbis? Let's dig deeper, consider that question and then what we can learn about Messianic Jewish experience one hundred years after Calvary, through the survey.

M. Sanh. 10:1 says: "All Israelites have a share in the world to come... [But t]hese are they who have no share in the world to come... an *epiqoros* (an immoral, depraved one). Rabbi Akiva says: "Also he who reads the outside books, or who utters a charm over a wound and says: 'I will put none of the diseases upon you which I have put on the Egyptians; for I am the Lord that heals you' (Ex. 15:26)." "Outside books" harks to the canon of Messianic literature—what many call the New Testament; "utters a charm over a wound" harks to healing—in Jesus' Name. *T. Sanh.* 13:4–5 further reads: "... the *minim* (*i.e.,* heretics), and the *meshummadim* (*i.e.,* apostates) and the *epiqoris* (*i.e.,* immoral) and the *poreshim* (*i.e.,* those who separate or depart)... [For them] *Gehinnom* (hell) is shut in their faces, and they are judged there for generations of generations... Why has this befallen them? Because they stretched forth their hand against *Zevul* (i.e., the Temple)."

Professor Eyal Regev, of the Department of Land of Israel and Archeology at Bar-Ilan University, concurs. He observes how Christians have "tended to presume (without demonstration) [that the New Testament has] a completely negative approach toward the Temple," seeing Yeshua/Jesus as having completely "*substituted*" it, as per Dr. D. Juel, "*condemned*" its "corruption," according to Dr. W.H. Kelber, and bringing "to an end its commercial and cultic activities," says Dr. F.J. Moloney. [42] Leaning lastly on Professor E.P. Sanders, he reminds, "nothing Jesus said or did which bore on the Law led his disciples after his death to disregard it [Temple participation.]" [43] *Fidelity to the ancestral religion is attested everywhere.* Blaming Jewish believers in Jesus for the Temple's destruction goes beyond any and all known facts. The facts be damned! The sages had a problem. Not content to cast aspersions on unreasonably vilified Jewish believers, steps were taken to outright exclude them from Jewish communal experience, with the addition of a social death-sentence in the form of a nineteenth benediction to the *Amidah.*

---

[42] The Temple in Mark: A Case Study About the Early Christian Attitude Toward the Temple, 139–140, italics mine.
[43] Ibid., 155; from Sanders *Jesus and Judaism,* 268. Worth noting is that Jewish scholars seem to prefer parroting the misunderstanding. See Professor Cook, above, from Hebrew Union College.

B. Ber 28b-29a tells the story: "Rabban Gamliel said to the Sages: 'Is there no-one who knows how to compose a benediction against the *minim*?'" Someone rises to the occasion. Here's what Jews recited: "For apostates (*meshummadim*) may there be no hope... May the Christians (*noserim*) and the heretics (*minim*) perish in an instant. May they be blotted out of the book of the living. And may they not be written with the righteous." Speaking of books, in *t. Sabb.* 13(14):5, "The *gilyonim* (the Gospels) and books of heretics (*sifrei minim*) are not saved but are left where they are to burn... Rabbi Ishmael said: '...books of heretics, which cause enmity, jealousy and strife between Israel and their Father in heaven, [should] be erased.'" Not content to simply exclude Jewish believers' spiritual resources, Jewish believers' material resourcing was to be effected by the religious ban. Jewish believers were ostracized from every day, workaday life, with a premium placed on *freezing trade with them in its entirety*. *T. Hul.* 2:20–23 notes: "If meat [for sale]... is found in the hand of a *min*, it is forbidden [to acquire it]... For they said: The slaughtering of a *min* is idolatry..." The rabbis suggested we not take their work-product or their byproduct—their children: "their children are *mamzerim* (*i.e.*, bastards)" and, as a result, unfit to marry. They go on: "We do not sell to them, nor do we buy from them... We are not healed by them, neither healing of property or healing of life." In *y. Sabb.* XIV.14d, "The grandson [of Rabbi Joshua ben Levi] had a choking fit. There came a man and whispered [something] to him in the name of *Yeshua ben Pandira* [*i.e.*, Jesus] and he recovered... [Rabbi Joshua] said: 'It had been better for him to have died than that this should have happened.'" Better to die than be healed in Jesus' Name...

The aforementioned invectives were articulated because *the rabbis perceived Jewish believers as a threat*. *Qoh. Rab.* 1.8 is telling in this regard. "They said, Rabbi Jonathan, go tell your mother that you have not turned and looked upon us [the *minim*]; for *if you had turned and looked upon us... you would have pursued us*." Jewish believers were desirable, quite seductive, according to the rabbis. As a result, the people of Israel were told to keep away and not so much as give them a glance. Unlike pagans, who were very clear about their paganism, followers of Yeshua/Jesus understood themselves to be Jews, still, though not of a sort that comported with the rabbis' sensibilities. Their popularity amongst Israel's rank-and-file, as with those of non-Jewish extract who were kindly disposed towards Jews and developing Judaism, was no doubt spirited along by signs, wonders and attested healings among them and through them, to others. This was the problem! To quote from *b. Sanh.* 107a-107b (par. *b. Sotah* 47a): "... *Yeshua ha-Nosri* practiced magic and led Israel astray."

Jewish believers and their Gentile associates were a marginalized people, kicked to the curb by Judaism's religious elites. How did they fare amongst their non-Jewish counterparts in and around the time?

Bishops' Antipathy Toward Messianic Jews in Antiquity

The *Epistle of Barnabas*, so called, was written between 100–150 CE at a place and time when Jewish vision was apparently exerting considerable street-level influence in the empire, and upon Christians of non-Jewish extract—likely in either Alexandria or Syria, or both. Written with a mind to help Christians "not be shipwrecked by conversion to their law," [44] in the *Epistle of Barnabas* an obvious premium was placed on insisting that newly minted non-Jewish Christians avoid fasting, circumcision, food laws and the Sabbath observance,[45] hoping to ensure they *not* "rush forward as rash acceptors of their [Jewish] laws" [46] (*Barn.* 3.8), and thus take refuge in a religious Jewish world that had long since been "abandoned," according to the anti-Messianic churchman (*Barn.* 4.7).

Folk can lament later. Sometimes it is good to listen hard to critics (even nasty ones) for what they tell about those they are criticizing. In this case, the press to avoid fasting, circumcision, dietary restrictions and the Sabbath attests to the fact that many *early Christians/Messianics lived within the parameters of a Jewish faith, worldview and culture.* Professor Adolf Hilgenfeld surmised that the *Epistle of Barnabas* was written "at the close of the first century" and "with the view of *winning [folk] back, or guarding [some] from, a Judaic form of Christianity.*"[47]

First and arguably foremost among those minded to guard against so-called "Judaizing tendencies" was the famous bishop Ignatius of

---

[44] Murray, *Playing, op. cit.*, 47–48. Dr. Murray's text is the source for many of the passages noted herein to underscore the point.

[45] Ibid., 50.

[46] Speaking with regard to the Sabbath, for example, in *Barnabas* 15 the author postulates: "...concerning the Sabbath in the Decalogue... Attend my children to the meaning of this expression: "He finished in six days"... and then "six days, that is six thousand years, all things will be finished..." This can only be construed as meaning: "when his Son comes [again]" then the rest will be fulfilled. For now, however, applicable are the texts against its literal keeping, which read: "Your new moons and Sabbaths I cannot endure" and "your present Sabbaths are not acceptable to me."

[47] Ibid., 135, italics mine.

Antioch. The third bishop of Antioch, and a disciple of the Apostle John, according to Eusebius, Ignatius was martyred in the eleventh year of Trajan, or 108 CE. Condemned to die for reasons unknown to us, Ignatius was transported from Antioch to Rome to meet his fate. Undaunted, the intrepid bishop used his final trip to pass on final words—in the form of half a dozen letters to various congregations in Asia Minor. Of these, statements written to the Magnesians and the Philadelphians are particularly noteworthy for our purposes here.

In *Magn.* 10:3, Ignatius said: "It is monstrous to talk of Jesus Christ and to practice Judaism." In *Phld.* 6:1, he further opines: "If anyone interpret Judaism to you do not listen to him; for it is better to hear Christianity from the circumcised than Judaism from the uncircumcised." Seeing an amalgamation of "Jesus Christ" and the "practice of Judaism" as a "monstrous[ity]" is both interesting and troubling. Pressing individuals to not give those who "interpret Judaism" a hearing, similarly underscores a *troubling devaluation of Jewish influence and experience. Phld.* 6:1–2 further demonizes Jewish influence as being "tombstones and sepulchers of the dead," as with comments of its being associated with "the wicked arts and snares of the prince of this world." In *Magn.* 8:1–2 Ignatius states his position succinctly: "...if we are living until now according to Judaism, we confess that we have not received grace." Ignatius employs the term "Christian" 17 times, mostly in *contrast* to "Judaism." [48] The differentiation is obvious; so is the distaste. The reasons for both are *not*. What is going on here? Why is it happening? What might this reveal about early Messianic Jewish experience?

Professor Thomas Robinson surmises that Ignatius' "Judaizers... [are still] members of his [Christian] community" in Antioch,[49] and "were meeting on the Sabbath for their separate eucharists, whereas Ignatius' church appears to have conducted its corporate religious life primarily on Sundays.[50] Ah! A divide over the retention of Jewish communal practices. These were not *outsider* Jews much as they were *insider* Jesus-believing Jews who were still informed by Jewish sensibilities and cultural practices. Can't have that, now, can we? If he is correct, and there is good reason to think he is, then we do well to *not*

---

[48] Thomas A. Robinson, Ignatius of Antioch and the Parting of the Ways: Early Jewish-Christian Relations, 88.

[49] Ibid., 99.

[50] Ibid., 104.

rush too soon to distinguish between "Christianity" in Antioch, Syria and "Messianic Judaism," as it would seem they were still *intertwined,* well after the passing of the Apostles. "Many [Gentiles]," says Robinson, "would have had their first substantial exposure to elements of Judaism from within their new [Christian] environment,"[51] which would have made them "curious"[52] at the least. In sum, Dr. Robinson believes that *Ignatius' "Judaizing" opponents were "Gentiles who converted to Christianity but were attracted to elements of Judaism,* beyond that which was sanctioned by Bishop Ignatius."[53] This was the problem.

In support of what was adjudged to be a problematic connectivity, Suetonius spoke of "those who *without* publicly acknowledging that faith yet lived as Jews."[54] What does he mean by folk "living as Jews" *without* really being Jews? He could well be talking of Messianic Gentiles in early Christian communities. In 67.14.1–2, Dio Cassius noted that "Domitian… slew along with many others, Flavious Clemens, the consul… and [his wife] Flavia Domitilla," both relatives of the emperor, because they "drifted into Jewish ways."[55] What did "drifting into Jewish ways" mean? Too Jewish-friendly?! Did they become Messianic Jewish Gentiles? Possibly. After Domitian's assassination in 96 CE his successor Nerva adopted a more Jewish-friendly disposition. Dio Cassius reported: "Nerva said… no persons were permitted to accuse anybody of adopting the Jewish mode of life" (68.1.2). As stated at the outset, policies vacillated. That aside, there is an argument that Jewish visions and ways had a compelling draw upon Gentile Christians—and for quite some time.

Classical Jewish scholar Dr. Shaye J. D. Cohen—Littauer Professor of Hebrew Literature and Philosophy in Harvard's Department of Near Eastern Languages and Civilizations—spoke to the issue of Gentile Christian infatuation with Jewish vision and practice when commenting on Ignatius: "In both *Philadelphians* and *Magnesians* the 'Judaism' that arouses Ignatius' attention and anger is within the church. *The Judaism is the 'Judaism' of Christians within the Christian community,* not the

---

[51] Ibid., 111.
[52] Ibid., 110.
[53] Ibid., 117, italics mine.
[54] Zetterholm, *The Formation, op. cit.,* 186-187.
[55] Ibid., 187.

'Judaism' of Jews 'out there' beyond it."[56] According to Cohen, the anger was directed toward a formidable proclivity in ancient Christianity: *Gentile believers' affection for Jewish vision and for Messianic Jewish experience.* When was the last time you heard that point made? In *Playing a Jewish Game: Gentile Christian Judaizing in the First and Second Centuries CE,* Professor Michele Murray, professor of early Christian studies at Bishop's University, weighs in on Cohen's side and opines: "the need to ridicule Jewish observance perhaps derives from its being *too closely intertwined with Christian behavior and identity.*"[57] As evidence of Judaism's abiding influence in Antioch, Syria (and elsewhere)—well over 200 years later—she elsewhere noted that, as late as 386/387 CE—and *this is over 200 years removed from Ignatius*—some of Bishop John Chrysostom's congregants in Antioch "attended synagogues [on the Sabbath] and observed certain Jewish rituals including circumcision, dietary laws and rites of purification."[58] With Dr. Murray, I am inclined to believe *the tension reflects Jewish connections that were judged too-close-for-comfort.* A century after Jesus, Jewish believers were still living as Jews—but there was something noticeably different about them.

Assessing Messianic Jewish Faith and Practice Through the *Odes of Solomon*

Disparaged individuals look beyond their marginalization in the hopes of recovering their equilibrium. To help us get a window into how Messianic Jews attended to this business in and around 130 AD, we'll hear from Princeton University's Professor James Charlesworth, who gathered a group of scholars to work on an impressive collection of ancient documents, some of which are reportedly from the Messianic Jewish world, around 130AD. The collection is called *Old Testament Pseudepigrapha.* One particularly telling collection, said to be from in or around Antioch, Syria in the late first or early second century, is our focus here—the *Odes of Solomon.* Dr. Charlesworth attributes the *Odes to* "the earliest group of Jewish Christians" (to use his language) and is disposed to grant their origination in "Edessa or one of the many Jewish

---

[56] Ibid., 224, italics mine.
[57] Ibid., 54, italics mine.
[58] Murray, *Playing, op. cit.,* 43.

Christian communities that dotted the region between Edessa and Antioch."[59] Professor Charlesworth said that "with a strong Jewish tone," these Syriac/Aramaic songs' importance cannot be overestimated, and that they "preserve precious reminders of the first [Jewish] attempts to articulate the unparalleled experience of the advent of the Messiah."[60] They, according to him, are "so Jewish in tone and perspective that scholars from the beginning until the present have been persuaded, incorrectly, that they are *essentially Jewish*"[61]—*i.e.*, Hebraic, but not in a Messianic Jewish sense. What we have here are the first worship voices from the people and period in view. Let us consider the *Odes,* in brief.

Walking by faith and in the power of the Spirit energized early Messianics. Noteworthy in the *Odes of Solomon* are *Messianic Jewish attestations of supernatural wonderment and miraculous healings.* In *Ode* 6:1, for example, the songwriter says: "The Spirit of the Lord speaks through my members," and then in vv. 15–16 with "[e]ven lives who were about to expire they have seized from death, and members which had fallen, they have restored and set up." The Messianic Jewish *Odes* are more explicit yet in 18: "Infirmities fled from my body, and it stood firm for the Lord by his will; because his Kingdom is firm." That there "was no sickness or affliction or suffering" in a healed body is noted in 21:4, prompting the Messianic Jewish Syrian psalmist to say: "I raised my arms on high, on account of the grace of the Lord" in v. 1. Speaking of raising, in 25:9 the Messianic Jewish psalmist says: "because your right hand raised me" it has "caused sickness to pass from me." Attested in the literature are powerful, faith-filled experiences, ones that enabled believers to stand firm.

Transcending less-than-hoped-for circumstances is further spirited along by inspirational worship. Antiochan Messianics got an "arm up" on prevailing circumstance by so doing, which gave rise to their extending their arms upward in praise to God. In 35:7, for example, the ancient Messianic songwriter demonstrates this when saying: "I extend my hands in the ascent of myself, and I directed myself near the Most High, and I was saved near him." Abundant are the examples of what's articulated here, through depictions of orants in ancient worship spaces.

---

[59] James Charlesworth, *Old Testament Pseudepigrapha*, Vol. II (Garden City: Doubleday & Company, 1985), 727.

[60] Ibid.

[61] Ibid., 725, italics mine.

This up-reaching form of praise and prayer is further attested in 27:1–3, "I extend my hands and hallowed my Lord; for the expansion of my hands is his sign; and my extension is the upright cross"[62]—a striking remembrance of the Cross. The question of who would be included in the "I," as in "I extend my hands" above, is a question of no little significance—especially among the early Messianic Jews.

Were the Messianic Jewish worshipers in the *Odes* open to non-Jewish membership in their communities? In and around Antioch, Syria, around 130 AD, it seems Gentiles were fully admitted and associated with believers of Jewish extract at the time. The *Odes* in particular were *inclusive*. As proof thereof, let's look at 10:5, where the statement and implications are unmistakable: "[T]he Gentiles who had been scattered were gathered together, but I was not defiled by my love (for them), because they had praised me in high places." Is this not telling—and striking? Not being "defiled" by my love for Gentiles harks to understandings and prejudices that resonated the more so in some circles in the first centuries BCE and CE. The words are here put in the Messiah's mouth: saying, in effect, because "they praised me," I praise and accept them. The "they," of course, are Jewish-friendly Gentiles, who, according to the one who wrote the psalm and those who sung it, were *construed as included within the commonwealth of Israel by virtue of their association with Yeshua/Jesus and the people who felt obligated to Him.*

Conclusion

Though life was difficult for Messianic Jews and their Gentile associates in late-first and early-second-century Syria (and thereafter), it seems Jewish believers were able to walk in victory individually walk collectively with others (*i.e.,* *to inclusively walk as Jews and with Gentiles*), and maintain an overall positive disposition, difficulties notwithstanding. This was Messianic Jewish experience in the early second century—and *it tells a positive story in an otherwise-negative world.* Sadly, game to construe a disparaged "Judaizing Church" (so called) as hopelessly and theologically out of step with the "new [post-

---

[62] Praying in a manner designed to remember the Cross distinguishes these early Messianics from modern ones, who, because of the bad connotations associated with the Cross for Jews, with the passage of time, get little utility by remembering it.

Jewish] Christian era," by virtue of its assorted Judaistic proclivities, *leaders in both the traditional synagogue and church have been all too happy to ignore, marginalize, minimize and anathematize ancient Messianic Jewish people and experience*, on the whole—as with modern Messianic Jewish experience. Believing the jaded telling to be both overly simplistic and problematic, this presentation invoked a variety of stories to offer a decidedly *Jewish-friendly account of early Christian history*—what really is an extension of early Jewish history, and not a simple and distinct "Christian" history at all.

Sadly, through time and circumstance, the story of early Christianity's Jewish heritage was ignored and forgotten. Churchmen bent on offering a telling of Christian experience that comported with their own experience and sensibilities had little to-no interest in recovering ancient Jewish experience and retelling its relationship to early Christianity. Happily, more and more women and men are looking back with open eyes. Some are looking forward, too, and asking questions. Having rediscovered the Jewish origin of the Christian faith in antiquity, some wonder if and how they might appropriate the new insights and apply them in modernity to their faith insights and worship practices. Having considered the way we once were, in this chapter, we'll move on to consider the way we are now.

BIBLIOGRAPHY

Cook, Michael, *Modern Jews Engage the New Testament: Enhancing Jewish Well-Being in a Christian Environment.* Woodstock: Jewish Lights Publishing, 1996.

Gruen, Erich, Diaspora: *Jews Amidst Greeks and Romans.* Cambridge: Harvard University Press, 2002.

Ferguson, Everett, *Backgrounds of Early Christianity.* Grand Rapids: Eerdmans, 1993.

Flusser, David, *The Sage From Galilee: Rediscovering Jesus' Genius.* Grand Rapids: Eerdmans, 2007.

Hagner, Donald, *The Jewish Reclamation of Jesus: An Analysis and Critique of the Modern Jewish Study of Jesus.* Eugene: Wipf and Stock, 1997.

Horsley, Richard (ed.), *Christian Origins.* Minneapolis: Fortress Press, 2010.

Lindsay, Jack, *The Ancient World: Manners and Morals.* New York: G. P. Putnam's Sons, 1968.

Meeks, Wayne, *Jews and Christians in Antioch in the First Four Centuries of the Common Era.* Missoula: Scholars Press, 1975.

Milavec, Aaron, *The Didache: Faith, Hope and Life of the Earliest Christian Communities 50-70CE.* Mahwah: Paulist Press, 2003.

Murray, Michele, *Playing a Jewish Game: Gentile Christian Judaizing in the First and Second Centuries C.E.* Waterloo: Wilfrid Laurier University Press, 2004.

Neusner, Jacob, *Christianity, Judaism and Other Greco-Roman Cults.* Leiden: E. J. Brill, 1975.

Robinson, Thomas, *Ignatius of Antioch and the Parting of the Ways: Early Jewish-Christian Relations.* Peabody: Hendrickson, 2009.

Rudolph, David, *A Jew to the Jews: Jewish Contours of Pauline Flexibility in 1 Corinthians 9:19-23.* Tubingen: Mohr Siebeck, 2011.

Rutgers, Leonard Victor, *The Jews in Late Ancient Rome: Evidence of Cultural Interaction in the Roman Diaspora.* New York: E. J. Brill, 1995.

Seif, Jeffrey, *Evolution of a Revolution: Reflections on Ancient Christianity in its Judaistic, Hellenistic and Romanistic Expressions.* Landham, MD: University Press of America, 1994.

Stark, Rodney, *The Rise of Christianity: A Sociologist Reconsiders History.* Princeton: Princeton University Press, 1996.

Testa, Emmanuel, *The Faith of the Mother Church: An Essay on the Theology of the Judeo-Christians.* Jerusalem: Franciscan Printing Press, 1992.

Zetterholm, Magnus, The Formation of Christianity in Antioch: A Social-Scientific Approach to the Separation of Judaism and Christianity. London: Routledge, 2003.

History and Practices in the Messianic Jewish Movement

Jacob Rosenberg, Ph.D.

Though it was the original form of Jesus-believing faith experience, Messianic Jewish congregational experience itself has largely been dumped by most, relegated to the periphery of Christian experience. Herein the task is tell what newly emerging Messianic Jewish experience is, what it does, and why. In days past, someone who visited a Messianic Jewish congregation or interacted with a Messianic para-ministry may well have felt confused about Messianic theology and religious practice. A non-Jew can find it foreign to their culturally and religiously loaded worldview and practices; though familiar with Jewish expression and experience, a Jew may well perceive Jewish expressions in a Jesus context as anachronistic, not in sync with their understanding. Problems with first impressions and misrepresentations aside, with the crystallization of modern Messianic Jewish experience and expression, clarity has improved, and there has been a positive move toward common core practices and a more sophisticated theology that gives the reasons for them.

While there are definite variations and unique expressions of faith, practice and polity throughout the modern movement as a whole, one may argue there has been a common core that unites adherents. This core is somewhat overlooked because of past internal political struggles and allegiances. Yet there is more that has historically united the movement than divided it, and it's worth considering what those common cores are. There is a commitment to a belief in God, the divine nature (deity) of Yeshua the Messiah, the work of the Holy Spirit, the Hebrew language, a high view of the Old and New Covenant Scriptures, a premium on Synagogue-style worship, celebrating Jewish life-cycle events, replete with the biblically based holidays, festivals and calendar.

There is a common recovered understanding that our historic heritage stems from both the Old Covenant and New Covenant world, and that we are a product of both worlds theologically. Richard Harvey writes, "The Majority of Messianic Jews argue it is possible to have a theology of Yeshua which is completely Jewish and also compatible with Orthodox Christian theology."[1] Building upon Seif's previous chapter, the purpose of this one is to explore and understand the core practices of the modern Messianic movement in light of our shared Jewish identity and belief in Yeshua the Messiah.

Yeshua

There is nothing and no one more central to modern Messianic Judaism than the belief in Yeshua, that He is the promised divine Messiah of Israel. The divinity of the Messiah is a theme present in Torah, the expectation of the prophets of Israel, and at times even mainstream Jewish tradition and ancient literature. In fact, unlike many forms of mainstream Judaism, the existence of God is an overall assumption and presupposition of Messianic Judaism. Richard Harvey writes,

> [Messianic Jewish Theology] does not attempt to prove the existence of God, regarding it as a 'first truth' that is axiomatic for all further discussion. This truth is asserted in scripture and confirmed by philosophical arguments for the existence of God.[2]

In turn, all messianic congregational and para-congregational/mission organizations function under the belief there is one God, who reveals Himself as a triune being, and part of God's triune nature is the Messiah Yeshua. Messianic believers, while they may approach the doctrine of God with different methodologies, all agree in His Unity, Transcendence, Immanence, Omnipresence, Eternality, Omniscience and Perfection.[3] The belief in God has been a core value of mainstream

---

[1] Harvey, Richard. *Mapping Messianic Jewish Theology: A Constructive Approach*. Milton Keynes, U.K.; Colorado Springs, Colo.: Paternoster, 2009, 96.

Ibid., 60.

[3] See "Yeshua the Messiah: The Shaping of Messianic Jewish Christology," in *Mapping, op. cit.*,, 96–139; Mark S. Kinzer, "Finding Our Way Through Nicaea: The Deity of Yeshua, Bilateral Ecclesiology, and Redemptive Encounter With the Living God," *Kesher: A Journal of Messianic Judaism* 24 (2010): 29–52. Cited 1 March 2012. www.kesherjournal.com/index.php?option=com_content&view=article&id=135;

Judaism until recently. Skepticism impacts many segments of society, secular and religious. Scholars give different reasons for the shift in some liberal-bent Jewish theologies. Conservative for the most part, Messianic believers hold to the traditional concept that a belief in God is a requirement of Judaism. The belief in Yeshua's unity with God has been a core value of Jewish believers for well over two thousand years.

Because Messianic believers assert and believe Yeshua is the image of the invisible God (Col. 1:15) and the promised Messiah, He is our king, prophet, and the high priest who continues to mediate between us and Himself, as God. This is how we can recite the oneness of God through the *Shema* and assert Yeshua's divinity at the same time. All Messianic organizations understand Scripture's prophetic expectation for a physical, earthly and historic incarnation. Each group agrees on the Messiah's divine nature, that He has existed eternally and is worshipped as God.[4] Historically, all Messianic practice centers on this core value, that we follow Yeshua's teachings and practice. They all agree following Yeshua and His commands are the basis for all our faith and practice. Thus, all messianic organizations agree salvation depends on faith in Yeshua as our Lord God and promised Messiah.

Scripture

The central concept in Messianic Judaism is the Messiahship of Yeshua. Practices and theologies within the mainstream are dependent on the high view of Scripture most of us hold. All messianic organizations agree the entire Bible (Old and New Covenants) is the authoritative Word of God; meaning that life and practice of a Messianic believer comes primarily from an interaction and interpretation of the Bible. While different interpretive traditions inform different organizations' customs, the core essential is that the Bible is the supreme authority on life and practice. This said, there are no Messianic

---

Akiva Cohen, "The Christology of Matthew's Gospel and the Trinitarian Baptismal Formula," *Mishkan: A Forum on the Gospel and the Jewish People* 39 (2003): 59–64; Michael Schiffman, "Messianic Jews and the Tri-Unity of God," in *Return of the Remnant: The Rebirth of Messianic Judaism* (Baltimore: Lederer, 1996), 93–104. cf. Richard Bauckham, *Jesus and the God of Israel: God Crucified and Other Studies on the New Testament's Christology of Divine Identity* (Grand Rapids: Eerdmans, 2008).

[4] "Who Is Yeshua?" *UMJC*. UMJC, n.d. 9 Dec. 2014. www.umjc.org/who-is-yeshua. *MJAA*. Messianic Jewish Alliance of America, n.d. https://mjaa.org/statement-of-faith; "Statement of Faith." *Doctrinal Statement*. Chosen People Ministries, n.d. Web. 9 Dec. 2014. https://chosenpeople.com/site/our-mission-statement/doctrinal-statement. "Statement of Faith." *Statement of Faith*. Jews For Jesus, n.d. Web. 9 Dec. 2014. https://jewsforjesus.org/about/statement-of-faith.

communities of (or) organizations that regard Scripture as merely historic literature or reduce it to cultural myth. While the trend within mainstream Judaism is moving toward an a-religious secular Jewish perspective, based on social and ethnic expression rather than a biblical reality, Messianic Judaism strives to preserve the notion that the Scriptures are the inspired Word of God.

Messianic Judaism tends to focus on the continuity between the Old and New Covenants, rather than the discontinuity, something common in many Gentile organizations and churches. However, how one understands the interrelationship between the Covenants is an ongoing debate for both Jews and Gentiles. In addition, Messianic Jewish theologians differ on the role of Jewish and non-Jewish interpretive communities. While all agree the primary source of authority is found in the text itself, the disagreement surrounds the possibility of separating the text itself from contextual interpretations.[5] David Rudolph argues this debate takes on two main points of view: "The positions of Juster and Kinzer on the place of tradition in the interpretation of Scripture represent the views of two branches of Messianic Judaism and are emblematic of broader disagreements in the movement over the place of traditional practices in Messianic Jewish life."[6] However, differences aside, these discussions are still functioning as interpretive expressions based on the authority of the Bible, and not on purely ethnic or social expressions of Jewish experience.

The majority of Messianic Judaism believes in a real and living God, a life and practice based on the Scripture as the Word of God, and believers interpret Scripture within a prophetic reality and expectation that plays out in real historic events. Messianic Judaism believes in a real and personal Messiah who entered and had a profound effect on history and God's people. Therefore, the distinguishing practice and core values of Messianic Judaism are a dependence on the Bible as authoritative and the expectation and realization of the divine nature of Yeshua the Messiah.

---

[5] Daniel Juster, "Biblical Authority," in *Voices of Messianic Judaism: Confronting Critical Issues Facing a Maturing Movement* (ed. Dan Cohn-Sherbok; Baltimore: Lederer, 2001), 23. 4. Kinzer, "Scripture and Tradition," *Voices op. cit.* 30. David Rudolph and Joel Willitts, eds., *Introduction to Messianic Judaism: Its Ecclesial Context and Biblical Foundations* (Kindle Locations 1799–1802), Zondervan.

[6] Rudolph, David J.; Willitts, Joel (2013-02-05). *Introduction to Messianic Judaism: Its Ecclesial Context and Biblical Foundations* (Kindle Locations 1594–1596). Zondervan. Kindle Edition.

Over many years, Messianic Judaism has developed and matured toward common practice based on the authority of Scripture as informed by both historic Jewish and Christian interpretations. While one can observe this in all expression of Messianic Judaism, it is most noticeable through the faith and practice of congregational Messianic Judaism. Even with differing levels of interaction with Jewish and Christian interpretation of Scripture, there has formed a core and common Messianic Jewish expression of faith articulated through Jewish life-cycles, liturgy, holidays and synagogue and family life.

Synagogues and Congregations

Historically, the modern congregational movement has always found a connection to the synagogue and Jewish life. David Rudolph writes:

> A synagogue is above all a sacred community of Jewish people who gather for worship, prayer, study, benevolence, social justice, lifecycle events, outreach, and other Jewish community activities. What distinguishes Messianic synagogues from mainstream synagogues is the centrality of Yeshua, the prominent place of the New Testament, and the presence of Gentile followers of Yeshua who come alongside Messianic Jews to build a congregation for Yeshua within the house of Israel."[7]

Well before the rise of the late-1960s congregational movement in the U.S., Jewish believers who were part of the Hebrew-Christian movement were exploring and recovering Jewish lifestyles and practices in their congregational events. While Jewish Identity within the Body of Messiah at times has been diminished in history, it has always been a part of the lives of Jewish believers within their particular contexts. The community context for Jewish believers has principally been with the mainstream Church; but even there, a noticeable desire for some sort of Jewish expression of faith and connection to the rest of the Jewish world has always been present, if subtly.

As noted in the previous chapter, as early as the first century Jewish believers defined themselves in terms of their connection with the

---

[7] Rudolph, *Introduction, op. cit.*, Kindle Locations 815–819).

Temple and to Judaism itself.[8] In its infancy, the modern Messianic movement revived and wrestled with similar relational concepts, and established Messianic communities and organizations as places for Jewish believers to have an autonomous community in which to feel at home and reach out to other Jewish people. Yaacov Ariel writes:

> Between 1850 and the 1870's, there were a number of attempts in America to create Hebrew Christian Brotherhoods. These organizations were designed to serve both as centers for carrying out missionary work among Jews and as congregations in which Jews who converted to Christianity could feel at home. Jewish converts established their own organization in Great Britain as early as 1860 and in the United States in 1915.[9]

For example, when Jacob Freshman, the founder of the first Hebrew-Christian church in America, started his congregation, he included Isaiah 56:7, "For my house shall be called a church of prayer for all nations," in Hebrew *and* English on the side of the building. Hebrew-Christians often gave accounts of their faith from their standpoint as Jewish believers.[10] They preached in multiple languages (German, Hebrew, Yiddish, English) and debated friends in the Orthodox community in public forums. While early Hebrew-Christians were squarely within Christian denominations, many had rabbinical Jewish training, ordination, a Jewish approach to Scripture and a desire to create Jewish communal space for Jewish believers.[11] The term *Messianic* was used as early as the late 19th century to distinguish Jewish believers within the overall church. Arno Gaebelein's magazine *Our Hope* briefly even was subtitled *A Monthly [Magazine] Devoted to the Study of Prophecy and*

---

[8] See the early chapters in the book of Acts, Acts 22:3, Philippians 3:5–6; Bruce, F. F. *Paul Apostle of the Heart Set Free*. Carlisle, Cumbria, UK: Grand Rapids: Wm. B. Eerdmans Publishing Company, 2000; Chilton, Bruce. *Rabbi Paul: An Intellectual Biography*. Reprint edition. New York: Image, 2005.

[9] Ariel, Yaakov. *Evangelizing the Chosen People: Missions to the Jews in America, 1880–2000*. 1st ed. Chapel Hill: The University of North Carolina Press, 2000, 220.

[10] Charles F. Deems and others, "Christian Thought," *Christian Thought* 4 (1886): 236.

[11] See Rosenberg, Jacob. "The Perfect Storm of Jewish Evangelism: How Jewish Immigration, the Russian Pogroms, Dispensationalism, Pre-Millennialism, Zionism, and Hebrew Christianity Coalesced Into the Foundation for Modern Jewish Missions in New York City Between 1880–1920," 2012. Ariel. *Evangelizing, op.cit.,* Cohn-Sherbok, Dan. *Messianic Judaism*. London; New York: Continuum, 2000. Harris-Shapiro, Carol. *Messianic Judaism: A Rabbi's Journey Through Religious Change in America*. Boston: Beacon Press, 1999.

to Messianic Judaism.[12] He pushed further by exploring the historic restriction on Jews from continuing to follow Torah. When Hope of Israel established its core values in 1896, *they focused on Jewish believers' right to observe Jewish practices and the theological understanding that Jews did not need to convert to Christianity to follow the Jewish Messiah.*[13] Ariel says, "This was an outstanding experiment because the mission's directors, [Gaebelein and Stroeter], advocated for … years the idea that Jews who had accepted Christianity had the right to observe the Jewish Law."[14]

In the late 19th century, Jewish believers in Yeshua worshiped primarily in Lutheran, Presbyterian and Anglican churches. But by the 1880s, groups such as "Israelites of the New Covenant," formed by Joseph Rabinowitz, and The First Hebrew Christian Church of New York, were forming independent congregations and Hebrew-Christian churches that focused on Jewish identity as a core value. [15] Rich Robinson points out, "[T]hat a mainline Christian denomination began these congregations tells us this was not a splinter move made in opposition to the Church, but done out of positive motives—to see Jews remain as Jews within the Body of Christ."[16] Early attempts of Jewish missions and congregations to rediscover and re-employ core values of Jewish identity for Jews became the foundation for modern Messianic Judaism. Though the early Hebrew Christian organizations and churches strove to establish Jewish spaces and places of worship that allowed for the observance of Jewish law, it was not until the mid-20th century this idea truly became a reality.

Starting in the mid-20th century, there was a much larger and distinct rise in desire for Messianic congregations and synagogues. These congregations and organizations continued to grow into the movement we have today. Rudolph writes:

---

[12] Arno C. Gaebelein and Ernst F. Stroeter, *Our Hope: A Christian Monthly Devoted to the Study of Prophecy and to Messianic Judaism* 1, no. 9 (1895). This subheading only lasted for six months.

[13] Gaebelein and Stroeter, "The Principles of the Hope of Israel Movement" *Our Hope, op. cit.* 3, no. 5 & 6 (1896): 149.

[14] Yaakov Ariel, On Behalf of Israel: American Fundamentalist Attitudes Toward Jews, Judaism, and Zionism, 1865–1945 (Brooklyn: Carlson, 1991), 99–108; Ariel, Evangelizing op. cit.; David A. Rausch, Arno C. Gaebelein, 1861–1945: Irenic Fundamentalist and Scholar: Including Conversations With Dr. Frank E. Gaebelein (Lewiston: Mellen, 1983), 19–52.

[15] See Kjaer-Hansen, Kai. Joseph Rabinowitz and the Messianic Movement: The Herzl of Jewish Christianity. Handsel Press, 1995; Rosenberg, "The Perfect Storm," op. cit.; and Rich Robinson and Naomi Rothstein, The Messianic Movement: A Field Guide for Evangelical Christians. Jews for Jesus, 2005.

[16] Robinson, *Field Guide, op. cit.*, 22–23.

There are presently over 500 Messianic synagogues in the world today. These congregations are committed to Jewish continuity and work hard to pass on Jewish identity to the next generation of Jewish followers of Yeshua. They provide a weekly Messianic Jewish community experience that focuses on the Lord, follows the rhythm of Jewish life, and fosters a connection with the wider Jewish world.[17]

In many ways, Messianic Judaism has run the same cycle as modern American Christianity and Judaism. Late 19th-century Jewish believers tended to mimic methods conventional, mainline mission groups perfected. During the 1960s and '70s Jesus movement, though, many Messianic believers in the U.S. started to forge communities out of revivals, based on revival fervor and what they construed as a move of the Holy Spirit. Not content to be just another revival movement, near the end of the 20th century and into the early 21st, Messianic leaders and communities started to wrestle more seriously with the question of what it meant to be Jewish believers. Believers in Jesus they were; but what is a *Jewish* believer?

The modern Messianic Movement has developed and matured, and has manufactured a robust understanding of Jewish life and practice in light of New Testament principles and understandings. Rudolph and Klayman write:

> Messianic Jewish services commonly incorporate song, dance, and instrumental music, along with Hebrew liturgy from the siddur (prayer book). Although the average Messianic synagogue service includes instrumental music and dancing, some Messianic Jewish congregations follow a more classic synagogue model. High Holy Day services in Messianic synagogues tend to be more traditional and [come] replete with Hebrew liturgy.[18]

In addition to instruction on New Testament Scripture, Messianic congregations have Torah-based education for children and adults. Messianic congregations and ministries incorporate varying degrees of music, dance and Hebrew liturgy into services and outreaches. Most

---

[17] "What Are Messianic Synagogues?" *MessianicJudaism.net*. MessianicJudaism.net, n.d. Web. 9 Dec. 2014. www.messianicjudaism.net/synagogues.html.
[18] Rudolph and Willitts, *Introduction, op. cit.*, 37.

Messianic congregations' services include reading from the Torah, the prophets and the writings, in both Hebrew and English. Every congregation has some incorporation of modern and worship music with Hebrew and English liturgy based on siddurs, based on traditional Jewish services. [19] Shoshanah Feher writes: "For Jews, Messianic Judaism allows a personal relationship with God; it permits them to integrate their faith in Jesus with their Jewish identities... these people have found something that resonates with their childhood experiences and allows them to hold on to their Jewishness, an important aspect of their identity."[20] This is an important point: Messianic Judaism is always discovering, expanding and reclaiming its identity, as more and more Jewish people worship the God of their fathers in light of New Testament truth.

Messianic identity is centered on Yeshua, but expressed in traditional Jewish ways, using symbols, rituals and objects recognizable to our non-believing Jewish friends who participate in modern mainstream Judaism. Men often wear prayer shawls and *kippot*; the services often come replete with a Torah, Ark, and a Ner Tamid (eternal light). Services are often led now by an ordained Messianic Rabbi. Rudolph and Klayman write:

> Synagogues are above all sacred communities of Jewish people who gather for worship and prayer, fellowship, study, simchas (celebrations), outreach, and other Jewish community activities. Messianic synagogues have a special calling to be a place where Jews who follow the Jewish Messiah can remain Jews and become better Jews in keeping with the eternal purposes of the God of Israel. This includes conveying Jewish identity to their children and being a visible testimony of Yeshua from within the Jewish community. Messianic Jews, Jewish visitors who are not Messianic, intermarried couples, Messianic Gentiles, Gentile Christian visitors, and family and friends of all the above, together form the unique amalgam of

---

[19] See Barry Budoff, *Siddur Prayers for Messianic Jews* (Skokie, IL.: Devar Emet Messianic Jewish Publications, 2006); John Fischer, *Siddur for Messianic Jews* (Palm Harbor, Fla.: Menorah Ministries, 2002); Jeremiah Greenberg, *Messianic Shabbat Siddur: A Messianic Prayer Book for Use in Sabbath Services and at Home* (Gaithersburg, MD.: Messianic Liturgical Resources, 2004).

[20] Shoshanah Feher, Passing Over Easter: Constructing the Boundaries of Messianic Judaism (Walnut Creek, CA.: Altamira, 1998), 139.

people found in a healthy and vibrant Messianic Jewish congregation.[21]

The Union of Messianic Jewish Congregations defines the Messianic congregation as "a movement of Jewish congregations and groups committed to Yeshua the Messiah that embrace the covenantal responsibility of Jewish life and identity rooted in Torah, expressed in tradition, and renewed and applied in the context of the New Covenant."[22] The International Association of Messianic Congregations and Synagogues' purpose is to see Jewish revival, unify Messianic congregations, strengthen and establish new congregations. Their stated vision reads: "The spiritual vision of the IAMCS is to see the outpouring of G-d's Spirit upon our Jewish people through Messianic congregations."[23] Messianic Judaism in all its expressions recognizes the need for congregational life and Jewish expression of faith. However, some feel this expression of Jewish life is better found in conventional churches rather than messianic synagogues. This said, every group allows for and understands the goal of the modern Messianic believer is to find a balance between culture and scriptural interpretation. Jewish believers who attend conventional churches often still celebrate Jewish life cycle events. Similarly, they very often celebrate traditional expressions of Jewish life, including Jewish holidays and festivals, together with those in the congregational movement.

Holidays and Festivals

While synagogue life is not a universal among Messianic Jews, believers share a common belief in the current and continued celebration of biblical holidays and festivals, as well as many traditional Jewish holidays that have developed over the years. Those who do not attend a synagogue or congregation share a priority and desire to celebrate holidays with those whose faith commitments are rooted more directly and frequently in Messianic congregations. Often, as is the case in the Jewish mainstream, Messianic synagogues swell in numbers and have large celebrations around major Jewish holidays. Seth Klayman notes:

---

[21] Rudolph and Willitts, *Introduction, op. cit.*, Kindle Location 1008.

[22] The Union of Messianic Jewish Congregations "UMJC – Defining Messianic Judaism." Accessed Nov. 31, 2014. https://www.umjc.org/defining-messianic-judaism.

[23] The International Association of Messianic Congregations and Synagogues. Accessed Dec. 1, 2014. http://iamcs.org/about-us/vision

"Messianic Jewish worship and prayer in the home and synagogue generally follows the cycle of the Jewish calendar, highlighting the fullness of each holy day's meaning in light of the past and future work of Messiah Yeshua."[24] While Messianic Jews often celebrate important events from Jewish history like Chanukah, Purim, the death and resurrection of Yeshua, and memorializing the loss of our people in the Holocaust, the primary and universal core value for all Messianic believers are God's appointed times as described in Torah.

Messianic Jewish believers have historically honored and observed the Sabbath as a day of rest and worship. In the late 19th and early 20th centuries, Hebrew-Christian congregations, like Jacob Freshman's first Hebrew-Christian Church of New York, held prayer meetings on Friday nights and special services on Saturdays. [25] In addition, Hebrew Christians were a part of a renewal movement to reestablish the importance of the Sabbath.[26] As the Messianic movement developed and matured, there has been a decisive stance that while God can be worshiped on any day and His rest entered at any moment, Friday night into Saturday is accepted as the biblical Sabbath, not Sunday. Klayman writes: "The cycle commences with the weekly celebration of Shabbat, a day of rest, remembrance of creation and the Exodus, and, for Messianic Jews, a day of exalting Yeshua, mediator of creation and redemption, in whom is found eternal rest."[27]

For Messianic believers, the Sabbath is foundational for understanding all of God's appointed times and festivals. On Friday night there is often a Sabbath meal, challah, Sabbath prayers and blessings, all common to the Jewish experience. On Saturday, there are Torah services, reading from the Tanakh and the New Covenant, a sermon and times of fellowship. For Messianic believers these celebrations and observances are made even more meaningful by the

---

[24] Rudolph and Willitts, *Introduction, op. cit.*, Kindle Locations 1301–1303. See Also See Barney Kasdan, *God's Appointed Times: A Practical Guide for Understanding and Celebrating the Biblical Holidays* (Clarksville, MD.: Messianic Jewish Publishers, 1993).

[25] "Homiletic Review: An International Magazine of Religion, Theology and Philosophy." *Homiletic Review: An international magazine of religion, theology and philosophy* 11 (1886): 331.

[26] Wilbur F. Crafts, The Sabbath for Man: A Study of the Origin, Obligation, History, Advantages and Present State of Sabbath Observance, With Special Reference to the Rights of Workingmen, Based on Scripture, Literature, and Especially on a Symposium of Correspondence With Persons of All Nations and Denominations (New York: Funk & Wagnalls, 1885).

[27] Rudolph and Willitts, *Introduction, op. cit.*, 54.

work of Yeshua, in light of the rest He provides through His life and sacrifice.

In fall, messianic believers also celebrate the high holy days in Scripture and Jewish tradition. In Rosh Hashanah, Yom Kippur, and Sukkot there is meaning and depth, as the shofar blasts a signal calling our people to return to the God of our fathers through Yeshua. While many congregations follow a traditional service order and sing customary Jewish prayers on Rosh Hashanah and Yom Kippur, the expectation that God is judge and mankind is in need of redemption is articulated with an understanding that brings the sacrifice of Yeshua to center-stage. There is a consistent idea throughout all of Scripture that God has written the names of His remnant of His people in the book of life. Both Rosh Hashanah and Yom Kippur celebrate that through Yeshua's perfect sacrifice, Man is written in the book and reconciled to God, and we now can celebrate our place in His Kingdom. In addition, the holiday teaches the need for repentance and turning back to God. On Sukkot, we celebrate that God makes His place among His people. Traditionally for Messianic believers, Sukkot is celebrated with the building of a *sukkah*, not only to remind us of the story of the Exodus in the wilderness, when we made our way to the Promised Land, but also so we may recall the present journey and, along the way, taste the promise of His Messianic Kingdom. Klayman: "For Messianic Jews, Yom Teruah points toward the eschatological great trumpet blast, Yom Kippur points to Yeshua's sacrifice on our behalf as well as the fountain of cleansing to come at his return, and Sukkot points to the fullness of the kingdom of Messiah on this earth."[28]

In spring, Messianic believers often celebrate Purim, Passover, counting of the Omer, and Shavuot. For Messianic believers, the most significant of these holidays are Passover and Shavuot. Most celebrate Passover in their home and/or congregation by celebrating a seder and using a holiday storybook *haggadah*. As noted elsewhere, and as particularly important here, it has been common practice since the start of the modern Messianic movement to incorporate Jewish tradition in light of New Testament understanding and theology. Modern Jewish believers have always found it important to not only celebrate Passover but also share the fullness of the story and background in light of Yeshua with Gentile believers. This trend is seen as early as the late 19th

---

[28] Rudolph and Willitts, *Introduction, op. cit.*, 55.

century, and was so common that it has become for many the cornerstone of modern Messianic missions outreach and fundraising to churches. Passover is a natural connection between the Gentile church and the Messianic synagogue because it is a central expectation of the Tanakh fulfilled and expounded upon in the New Covenant. And while there are varying beliefs concerning the frequency of Communion, most congregations and Messianic believers find Passover the natural time to participate in Communion, in remembrance of what Yeshua did and accomplished on Passover. This symbolic act connects Messianic Judaism to both the Jewish world and the larger Christian community.

The period of counting the Omer starts after Passover and ends with Shavuot.[29] In the same way that Communion and Passover bridge the gap between the Christian and Jewish communities, Shavuot naturally connects Messianic Judaism with both mainstream Judaism and the Christian Church. Though a harvest holiday initially, traditionally for Jews Shavuot commemorates the giving of the law. The prophetic promise of the Old Covenant is that one day God will make a New Covenant with the house of Israel, and in that day He will put the law on and in Jewish hearts.[30] The New Covenant Scriptures state this happened on Shavuot. Fifty days after Yeshua was sacrificed as our Passover Lamb, His Spirit was poured out, fulfilling many prophecies and putting the Law in our hearts.[31] Commonly in Christian circles this event is called Pentecost (meaning "50 days"), but for Jewish believers this not only unifies us as the body of Messiah, but also validates our Jewish understanding and expression of our faith and practice. God did not establish and then replace or destroy Shavuot; He both fulfilled and expanded the meaning. It is a historic common core value for Messianic believers that the biblical holidays improve an understanding of God's plan for His people and enrich the communities experience through Yeshua. In conjunction with these appointed times, the common values of Messianic believers extend to life-cycle events, despite whether the person attends a Messianic congregation or synagogue on a regular basis.

---

[29] Leviticus 23:9–14.
[30] Jeremiah 31:33, Romans 2:15, Hebrews 10:16.
[31] Acts 2ff.

Jewish Life-cycle

It is only natural that corporate congregational life and practice lead to a common private life cycle experiences for Messianic believers. For that matter, Jewish believers not bounded to synagogue life still engage Jewish life-cycle events as a profound expression of personal and communal faith. Messianic Jewish boys, for example, are circumcised on the 8th day. Some employ a *mohel* and have a party for family and friends.[32] Similarly, Messianic believers often participate in Bar/Bat Mitzvahs. These ceremonies traditionally occur when a child turns 13. The young person often reads Scripture in both Hebrew and English. They offer a public telling of the week's Torah and *haftorah* portions and give a formal message on it. They don't just participate in a Torah service; they are central to it.[33] When they grow up, Stuart Dauermann writes: "Consistent with traditional Judaism, Messianic Jews marry under a *huppah* (wedding canopy), sign a *ketubah* (marriage contract), and break a glass at the conclusion of the wedding ceremony to shouts of "Mazel Tov!"[34] All these life-cycle events often occur with celebration and parties. It is also common that Messianic believers follow traditional Judaism's form concerning death, mourning and funerals. These, of course, are embellished by the consistent interweaving of teaching from the New Testament, and punctuated by the words of Yeshua concerning life and death. Messianic believers often sit *shiva*, chant the *Kaddish* and light *Yahrzeit* candles.[35] Overall, as the movement has developed and matured, so has its understanding and employment of traditional Jewish life and practice, both of which are articulated in light of faith in Yeshua as Israel's Messiah.

---

[32] Cohn-Sherbok, Messianic Judaism op. cit., 142–145; Kasdan, God's Appointed Customs: A Messianic Jewish Guide to the Biblical Lifecycle and Lifestyle (Clarksville, MD.: Messianic Jewish Publishers, 1993), 9–26; Kasdan, Barney. Appointed Times, op. cit., 9–26.

[33] See also Elliot Klayman, "The Bar/ Bat Mitzvah: A Liturgy," *Kesher: A Journal of Messianic Judaism* 1 (1994): 122–35.

[34] Stuart Dauermann, Michael Rudolph, and Paul L. Saal, "The Wedding Ceremony: Viable Models for Diverse Unions: Three Messianic Jewish Wedding Ceremonies," *Kesher: A Journal of Messianic Judaism* 9 (1999): 89–115.

[35] Rudolph and Willitts, *Introduction, op. cit.*, Kindle Locations 881–882. "David J. Rudolph, *Growing Your Olive Tree Marriage: A Guide for Couples From Two Traditions* (Clarksville, MD: Lederer, 2003), 127. See Cohn-Sherbok, *Messianic Judaism, op. cit.*, 153–55; Kasdan, *Customs, op. cit.*, 71–85.

Conclusion

Over time, the Messianic movement has galvanized, become more and more consistent, and moved closer to common core practices and theology. A distinctive now is how Messianic Judaism "refuses to partition Judaism and Christianity into two mutually exclusive theological systems." [36] Consistent with the evangelical mainstream, Messianic believers believe in God, the divine nature of Yeshua the Messiah, and the work of the Holy Spirit. The Hebrew language is more oft employed, Old and New Covenant Scriptures are forever connected, synagogue-style worship abounds, Jewish life-cycle events are celebrated, as are the biblically based holidays and festivals. While distinctions do exist in how Messianic believers interpret some Scriptures, maintain Jewish traditions and identity, utilize Jewish literature and develop congregational affiliation, historically, as noted, at the core there is more we share in common than that may keep us apart.

---

[36] Harvey, Richard. *Mapping, op. cit.*

The Revival of Messianic Jewish Worship

(All scripture quotations in this article are from the *TLV*)

Dr. Greg Silverman and Paul Wilbur

Moving beyond the theological matters that speak to the head, we will here look at theological issues that move the heart. This chapter starts with a consideration of the modern confluence of decidedly Jewish forms of worship and Christian praise. Dr. Greg Silverman gives theological voice to that emergence, looking at worship with his biblically informed Jewish lens; Paul Wilbur goes on to tell the story of the emergence of Messianic Jewish praise and worship music that's often employed within the congregational life described in the previous chapter.

Ancient Jewish experience and modern Christian experience have found each other. It is only natural that the new offspring would emerge from the long-lost lost lovers' embrace. One such child is a new form of worship.

Worship is at the heart of Messianic Judaism. In fact, the word "Jewish" literally comes from the Hebrew root *yadah*, "to worship with the hands." Just think, an entire people group has actually been named "worshipers." If you were to name a child "Grace," you'd think she would be *gracious*. If you named your dog "Barking," you would expect a loud dog. Names are significant. Thus it is noteworthy that a whole nation is named "Jewish," meaning "worship."

The literal meaning of the adjective "Messianic" also enlightens our understanding. "Messianic" translates "anointed." In biblical times, priests and others were *anointed* with oil. It would be poured out upon them to designate their position and qualifications to minister. Placing the words side-by-side, the phrase "Messianic Judaism" expresses the idea of "anointed worship," and "Messianic Jews" are to thus be "anointed worshipers." A distinct form of anointed praise and worship of Yeshua is central within the terms Messianic Judaism, much as it's central to the experience of Messianic Judaism.

The First Tabernacle of David

Dr. Greg Silverman

To provide an appropriate framework for modern Messianic worship, we will first alight upon and reintroduce the model and worship environment King David established nearly 3000 years ago. Not only a worshiper himself, he also laid an important foundation for what became the worship patterns for the nation of Israel. David took pains to ensure Israel was praising and worshiping the King of kings: twenty-four hours a day, seven days a week. Before the building of the temple, worship occurred in a tabernacle or large tent, hence the *Tabernacle of David*.

Before discussing this Tabernacle of David, let us investigate King David's qualifications to lead such a worship movement. What does it take to lead others in worship? Primary answer: to be a worshiper yourself. David praised God both in public and in private, in his prayer room. This private characteristic qualified him to publicly lead the nation in blessing and glorifying God. Of King David, Scripture says, "But Adonai said to Samuel, 'Do not look at his appearance or his stature, because I have already refused him. For He does not see a man as man sees, for man looks at the outward appearance, but Adonai looks into the heart'" (1 Samuel 16:7). David had a heart after God's own, and, with that inclination, he is remembered as one of our greatest models of a true worshiper. In the book of Psalms alone, we have access to the inner desires and motivations of David's heart. He was thankful to God because God is good (Psalm 100:5); he came to God because of His awesome might and strength (Psalm 24:8); David knew he could turn to Adonai for mercy, forgiveness and even physical healing (Psalm 103); and David's last words included acknowledgement of the Lord's omnipotence:

> David blessed Adonai before the whole congregation saying, "Blessed are You, Adonai, God of Israel our father, from eternity to eternity! Yours, Adonai, is the greatness, the power and the splendor, and the victory and the majesty, indeed everything in heaven and earth. Yours is the kingdom, Adonai and You are exalted above all. (1 Chronicles 29:10-11)

After maturing from a shepherd boy to the King of Israel, David knew, loved and worshiped his God. David, the king, viewed God as his King and Head of all heaven and earth. David thought his Lord had very high *worth*, and in its most literal sense, the word *worship* means to ascribe worth. Our English word worship is itself cut from the word "worth."

Not only did David worship, he also established organization and patterns for the entire nation of Israel to follow. As part of the Tabernacle, David appointed priests and leaders to be in charge of the daily music and offerings. Among the top music directors were Asaph, Heman and Juduthum. 1 Chronicles 25:1 says, "Moreover, David and the commanders of the army, set apart for *avodah* [service] the sons of Asaph, Heman, and Jeduthun who prophesied with lyres, harps and cymbals" (). They were the chief musicians. As is frequently the case in Scripture, their names had significance: Asaph, "gatherer"; Heman, "faithful"; and Jeduthun, "praising." These men were *faithful* to *gather together* the Jews ("worshipers") and bring *praise* to God. Another top music leader in the Tabernacle of David was Chenaniah. He was a very notable choir director as expressed in 1 Chronicles 15:22, "Chenaniah, leader of the Levites in music, was to direct the music because he was a master." Under these leaders' supervision, there were multiple worship teams and groups of priests who brought sacrifices and praised the Lord. Each team would be assigned particular shifts, and ultimately worship would occur all twenty-four hours a day, seven days a week. During biblical feasts (such as Passover, Shavuot/Pentecost, and Sukkot/Feast of Tabernacles), multitudes of priests were assigned to serve in Jerusalem at the Tabernacle at once. This was the basic pattern of the Old Testament Tabernacle of David.

Another special characteristic of these worship teams was they were composed of teammates from the same families. Worship leaders served together with their kinsmen: "David ordered the leaders of the Levites to appoint their kinsmen, the singers, with musical instruments, harps, lyres, and cymbals, to joyfully make their voices heard" (1 Chronicles 15:16). Sons, daughters and relatives served in King David's Tabernacle *together*. 1 Chronicles 25 details this:

> Moreover, David and the commanders of the army, set apart for *avodah* the sons of Asaph, Heman, and Jeduthun who prophesied with lyres, harps and cymbals... The sons of Asaph were under the supervision of Asaph, who prophesied under the hand of the king. As for Jeduthun, from Jeduthun's sons...

> six, under the charge of their father Jeduthun—who prophesied
> with the harp, giving thanks and praise to Adonai. As for
> Heman, from Heman's sons... All these were the sons of
> Heman the king's seer according to the promise of God to lift
> up a horn. God gave Heman 14 sons and three daughters. All
> these were under the direction of their father for singing in the
> House of Adonai with cymbals, harps and lyres for the *avodah*
> of the House of God under the hand of the king. Asaph,
> Jeduthun, and Heman along with their kinsmen all trained and
> skillful singers of Adonai. (1 Chronicles 25:1–7).

Within the Tabernacle of David, the assigned chief musicians led
worship to Adonai together with their sons, daughters and family
members. Interestingly in the modern Messianic movement, much of the
initial worship music was birthed through a few particular families, and
since then their children and grandchildren have continued to carry the
torch together with the overall worldwide community of Messianic
worship leaders.

Hopefully the above has served as a reasonable, initial introduction
to the *first* tabernacle of David. Why the *first*? Is there also a *second*
tabernacle of David? Yes. The prophet Amos speaks of the raising up or
restoration of the Tabernacle of David, during the end of days. Looking
many generations past the time of King David, the Scriptures prophecy
that something like the Tabernacle of David would exist again, even
after being seemingly extinct for thousands of years. This tabernacle is a
"resurrection," so to speak. In ca. 750 B.C., Amos communicated: "In
that day *I will raise up David's fallen sukkah [tabernacle]*. I will restore
its breaches, raise up its ruins, and rebuild it as in days of old" (Amos
9:11). He referred to a future time when the worship patterns established
by King David would reemerge among the Jewish people. It could be
said the time is now.

We are living in intriguing prophetic times. In this past century,
much of the modern Messianic Jewish movement emerged, and with it a
new type of Davidic worship. On the one hand, Messianic worship is
still a relatively recent phenomenon. Yet it is a renaissance, or
reemergence, of impassioned Jewish worship from ancient times.
Therefore, this new music has deep roots and a strong impact. As we
shall see, modern Messianic worship *is* in some ways this end-time
prophetic restoration of the Tabernacle of David as spoken by the
prophet Amos.

The Second Tabernacle of David

Paul Wilbur, M.M.

Music, they say, is the language of the soul and/or the heart of man. It's an international language, one that has the power to calm the rage of the savage beast, woo the heart of an intended love, and much, much more. In fact, there has never been a culture uncovered, modern or ancient, where music has not played a significant role in its day-to-day life and expression. With regard to music and worship, I have heard it expressed that every move of the Spirit of God needs both someone to preach it, and… yes, someone to sing it.

In the previous pages, my esteemed colleague Dr. Greg Silverman has set us up by directing our attention to the Tabernacle of David and the promise to raise it back up again in the last of days. He defines Messianic Jewish music as a movement of prophetic, anointed worship, and I couldn't agree more. My task now is to fill in the gap and connect the dots that have led us to this place and time in history. So without further ado…

Music is well-documented in the Scriptures, beginning with the mention of Jubal in Genesis 4:21. Jubal was the pioneer of all who played skillfully on the stringed instruments and the wind instruments, noted in Genesis and with the opening of the heavens and the courts of Adonai in Revelation. One might argue it was anointed, prophetic worship that brought down the mighty walls of Jericho, even though only one instrument was used. It was the singers who were sent out ahead of the armies of Jehoshaphat that won the day in II Chronicles 20 against a "great multitude" of Moabites and Ammonites. Verse 22 records these words: *"As they began singing and praising, Adonai set ambushes against the children of Ammon, Moab, and Mount Seir who had come against Judah, and they were defeated."*

If you read on to the end of the story, you discover that not only were the enemies of Israel defeated then, but their enemies turned on each other and slaughtered themselves, to the man! This suggests to me that the force that unified Israel's enemies against her was not natural or carnal, but an unseen enemy with great power to persuade—a demonic force, to be exact. The lesson here of course is quite obvious, even back in the time of Jehoshaphat: *"[O]ur struggle is not against flesh and blood, but against the rulers, against the powers, against the worldly forces of this darkness, and against the spiritual forces of wickedness in the heavenly places."*

The first Temple in Jerusalem, built and dedicated by Solomon, son of King David and Batsheva, also comes to mind as a place where Messianic worship played a significant role. II Chronicles 5:13–14, *"Then it came to pass that when the trumpeters and singers joined as one to extol and praise Adonai, and when the sound of the trumpets, cymbals and musical instruments and the praise of Adonai—"For He is good, for His mercy endures forever"—grew louder, the Temple, the House of Adonai, was filled with a cloud. The kohanim [priests] could not stand to minister because of the cloud, for the glory of Adonai filled the House of God."*

One more reference sticks out in my mind in this regard, so let me refer you to a heavenly scene as recorded for us in Revelation chapter 15. In verses 2 and 3 we read: *"And I saw something like a sea of glass mixed with fire, and those who had overcome the beast and his image and the number of his name standing by the sea of glass, holding the harps of God. And they are singing the song of Moses, the servant of God and the song of the Lamb... And the Temple was filled with smoke from the glory of God and from His power."*

It is impossible, in my estimation, to read the Hebrew Scriptures and not see the foundational role that music, as a partner with praise and worship, has played in the life of Israel—and can play in the lives of worshipers today. Let me point out one of the wonderful themes in this passage, since we are looking at power and presence in praise. A theme that resonates with me derives from an observation that in heaven there is perfect harmony and cohesion between the "song of Moses" the Law Giver, and the "song of the Lamb," the Covenant Maker. For me, this passage begs the query: Why do we continue to build walls of doctrine on Earth that separate us, when Heaven sings a song of perfect unity? After all, Yeshua broke down the middle wall of partition, did he not? I really do love the way true worship invokes the presence of Heaven, where revelation and understanding seem to flow like a river. In fact, it is this unique attribute of Messianic worship that continues to motivate and stimulate me after nearly four decades of worship ministry. It could be said that worship leaders stand in the gap, and unite Heaven and Earth in the process.

This last statement also leads me to this thought about worship in Spirit and in truth (John 4). Messianic worship music has always taken its cue directly from the Scriptures; there it gets its lyrical content and spiritual inspiration. Several years ago there was a wave of this kind of writing. Songs hit the church from companies like Maranatha Music, Zondervan, Vineyard Music, Benson Company and Integrity Music. Simple Scripture choruses seemed an excellent way to memorize the Scriptures in a meaningful way. From the very start, this was the logical way for Messianic worship to develop. Much material came directly from the Psalms, Prophets and New Covenant, along with appropriate passages from the *Siddur*, the Hebrew Prayer Book and other Jewish sources. The *Siddur* (pronounced *sih-dooor*) is a collection of Jewish prayer used for worship. Its material is taken largely from the Hebrew Scriptures, rabbinic prayers, hymns and blessings. The earliest material is extracted from the Torah, such as Deuteronomy 6:4, "Hear O Israel, the Lord our God is One…" and Numbers 6:24–26, "May the Lord bless you and keep you… and also from the Prophets. The famous *Amidah* or "standing prayers" are attributed to the Great Assembly at the time of Ezra, but there seems to be no real standardization of daily prayer until after the destruction of the Second Temple and the Council at Yavne, under the direction of Rabbi Gamaliel II. At any rate, the Siddur is a wonderful source of inspiration I find very compelling. Much of the church world overlooks this; Messianic artists don't.

We discovered early on that worship derived from holy writ had a very powerful influence on both the atmosphere in the sanctuary and the heart of the worshiper that was turning Godward in the sanctuary. Since we found this to be absolutely true, we also discovered the Spirit of prophecy, as well as all the other gifts of the *Ruach* (Spirit) were powerfully present in corporate praise and worship. When we fill our hearts and mouths with the Word of the Living God and the praises of Adonai, we reasoned, He inhabits those praises, with the result that even the very air we breathe is changed! Where He abides, ALL that He is becomes available by the *Ruach HaKodesh* (the Holy Spirit). The upshot is one can minister with great confidence, and almost prophesy at will. Worship can even go on all night, if folk desire. People seem to forget their watches and are particularly predisposed then to reset their spiritual time clocks.

Why is worship so fundamental, so powerful? It is all easily explained by Melech (King) David in one verse of Psalm 22. Verse 4 (3 in some translations): *"Yet You are holy, enthroned on the praises of*

Israel." Another translation: "You inhabit the praises of your people Israel" (KJV). Yet another: "You are the praise of your people Israel" (NIV). The reason for these discrepancies is the Hebrew verb *yoshe*, "sit, dwell, inhabit." The translation hangs on this word. so translations depend on where translators place it. So the same verse can be rendered two different ways, giving a slightly different emphasis on the text: (1) You are enthroned as holy; (You are) the praise of Israel. (2) You are holy; inhabiting / enthroned upon the praises of Israel.

Irrespective of how one settles on the reading of this verse, it is impossible to separate His Name, His power and His presence. And so when we call upon the Name of Adonai in holiness, He inhabits the praises of His people; and where His presence abides, there is His glory, His power, His throne, His Kingdom. All that He is, is present. HE inhabits our praises, our worship, and all that we need is in Him!

When I speak about the power of Messianic praise and worship, linked with the vehicle of music, I see a supernatural progression I think is very relevant. Since God inhabits, or is enthroned upon, the praises of His people, what then is the effect of those praises and that presence on the worshiper? Psalm 16:11 says: *"Abundance of joys are in Your presence, eternal pleasures at Your right hand."* To finish this train of thought, let's hear from the prophet Nehemiah, who tells us in chapter 8 verse 10b; *"...for the joy of Adonai is your strength."* My point here is simple: Our praises provoke His presence, His pleasures and joy, and that joy becomes our strength. If you want to be strong in the Lord and the power of His might, you need to be a worshiper whose mouth is full of praise!

Psalm 118:15–16 declares, "Shouts of joy and victory are in the tents of the righteous: Adonai's right hand is mighty! Adonai's right hand is lifted high! Adonai's right hand is mighty!" I love these verses and sing them frequently. I refer to these verses quite often when asked about all the "noise" and movement in Messianic praise. They have become a very practical example of the outworking of corporate praise and worship. What do I mean by that? I like to answer a question with a question, so I ask, "Where is there no singing, no shouting, no rejoicing?" The answer: in the tents of the defeated. In a lifeless, godless graveyard, there is no victory and no presence of Adonai! This is not our space. Messianic worship has always been a platform for dance, banners, the waving of flags, sounding shofars and tambourines, shouts of joy and more. Where there is true worship, there is life, His presence; and where His presence dwells—there is the fullness of joy. Nehemiah tells us joy begets strength, and round and round we go from praise to presence, to joy to strength, and so forth until an Amen! is sounded.

The history of modern Messianic praise, in my estimation, is about one generation old— around 40 years. In the late sixties the world experienced an amazing outpouring from heaven we now call the Jesus Movement. During these special years, many souls were swept into the Kingdom of God, including many Jewish people who are currently leaders of the modern Messianic Jewish Movement worldwide. There are many wonderful stories of hippies living in communes from San Francisco to New York, to mountain outposts in New Mexico, young men and women who also experienced the manifest presence of God during these years, and gave their lives wholeheartedly to Yeshua the Messiah. I recall one such story of a personal friend, Andrew Shishkoff, a young Jewish man living with an entire tribe of Jewish social outsiders in a commune. Their collective salvation comes to mind.

Along with the spiritual revival among our Jewish people came a unique, special revival in praise and worship. While the rest of the world was also experiencing a renewal in spirit and worship with names like Amy Grant, Second Chapter of Acts, Love Song, Keith Green, Chuck Gerard and so many more leading the way with new sounds, the revival in worship had visited the new Jewish believers as well. Probably the most outstanding sound of this revival came from a young Jewish man from Cincinnati, Joel Chernoff. In the early '70s he teamed up with another young believer, Rick Coghill, and together they formed the very popular well-known Messianic singing group "Lamb." Their fresh new sound caught on very quickly with its minor keys and Jewish dance rhythms. Not only did it resonate within newly forming Messianic synagogues and congregations, their music was enjoyed for many years on the largest Christian radio stations as well. Joel's iconic song, "Sacrifice Lamb," became wildly popular and led to recording contracts and record tours that lasted well into the early '90s. Joel is now the General Secretary of the largest gathering of Messianic Jewish believers in the world known as the *Messianic Jewish Alliance of America*. He is also the founder of the *Joseph Project*, a ministry that funnels hundreds of millions of dollars worth of aid into the nation of Israel.

Another force to be reckoned with during the early '70s was an evangelistic association that has become world-renown—"Jews for Jesus." The leader of this band of young, enthusiastic Jewish believers was a man by the name of Moishe Rosen. He began to gather a troupe of young, eager, talented people, who would become infamous in time for their unashamed dispositions and voices that spoke out on the streets of L.A., Miami, New York City, virtually anywhere major Jewish populations existed. Names like Mitch Glazer, Bob Mendelssohn, Steffi Rubin and Jhan Moskowitz come to mind at the tip of that spear. One of their number, however, became the musical voice of the ministry. Do you recall the song "Trees of the Field"? Of course you do. It became another iconic melody sung every week in Messianic congregations and churches alike. Christian radio stations continually played the music of the "Liberated Wailing Wall," the musical outreach of Jews for Jesus. Their premiere songwriter, Stuart Dauermann, continues to write and lead. He is a champion for the recovery and propagation of Jewish liturgical music today. As a side note, the scope and influence of Jews for Jesus has been so broad and great, the Orthodox Jewish community felt the need to raise up its own voice to the world they call "Jews for Judaism." But my point is, they made their point with their music, not just their speeches.

Also appearing during those early years of the revival amongst the Jewish people came husband-and-wife duo Merv and Merla Watson. Their songs and lively, upbeat presentation made them easy to enjoy while getting their message through the music that simply drew you in. Merla is the principal writer who has produced many popular songs such as "Jehovah Jireh," "Awake O Israel" and many, many more. Originally from Canada, they moved their family and ministry to Jerusalem, Israel in 1976, where they helped spearhead the International Christian Embassy and the world-renown Christian Celebration of the Feast of Tabernacles. This organization in the heart of Jerusalem hosts more than 7000 Christian pilgrims each fall from over 100 nations. Enthusiasts gather to honor Israel and celebrate the Feast of Tabernacles. The work of the Watsons and the ICEJ have done much to foster an appreciation among the Gentile Church worldwide with a love for Israel, the Jewish people, and the "Jewish roots" of the faith. I have personally recorded three major projects with the ICEJ over the years as a part of this great festive and musical celebration to the King of Israel.

In 1981 my wife Luanne and I left a thriving contemporary Christian singing group in Bloomington, Indiana called "Harvest." This was where I had been "born again," set into a fabulous and anointed ministry with friends, met my wife, and received the Baptism of the Holy Spirit, and it was then and there that my first son was born. Something else was born there, too. I was trained up in music ministry there—and my world would never be the same again.

As a Jewish kid from Boston I had a lot to learn! But the draw of a Messianic congregation in Rockville, Maryland, where the Gospel would go "to the Jew first," proved too much of a temptation for my heart to resist. Within a very short timeframe, two other Jewish brothers were added to the small worship team at Beth Messiah Congregation, and the group "Israel's Hope" was born. I and Marc Chopinsky were the group's primary writers, although Marc's compositions like "He Shall Reign" and "Come Let Us Go Up" quickly became well-loved around the movement. René Bloch brought his smooth saxophone playing to the band of brothers, along with clarinet and flute. Before long, several recordings were produced with Maranatha Records and we were traveling full-time as a Messianic worship team. The songs were conceived and recorded with the sole purpose of fostering congregational worship. The bulk of our work caught on and was used widely in worship circles in both the Messianic movement, and the greater church at large. The lyrics were lifted directly from Scripture, so the "shelf life" of these songs has continued even to this day. We are humbled and thankful.

During those early years, I was made aware of yet another man and his wife writing scriptural songs from Jerusalem. David and Lisa Loden penned dozens and dozens of simple faith-based Hebraic songs. Like ours, theirs were taken directly from the Hebrew Scriptures and set to Jewish music. Their brightly colored plastic albums became important resource materials for me as a worship leader in a local Messianic congregation in those early years. In particular, I recall two songs of theirs: "Adon HaKavod" and "Roni, Roni Bat Zion." Both are still classics. The latter remained mostly in the Messianic and Christian Zionist community until I recorded it in English and Hebrew on my first live recording from Israel in 1995, "Shalom Jerusalem." I would use that song again for another medley during another live recording in Israel called "Jerusalem Arise!" in 1998. The song has remained very popular to this day and has been a mainstay in my personal repertoire. The pioneering Lodens live in Jerusalem, where David continues to compose and perform new music.

From the Land of Israel came yet another team: Barry and Batya Segal. Over several decades of international ministry, based out of Jerusalem, this husband-and-wife duo has produced many popular recordings. Batya's song "Kumi Ori" (Arise and Shine) is sung and loved all over the world. Batya is a *sabra*, or native-born Israeli, while Barry has his roots in Cleveland. We discovered years later that Barry and I had both attended The Temple, a Reform synagogue in downtown Cleveland, and at the very same time. We did not know each other then, however. It's a small world after all! Barry and Batya continue to travel and sing as well. They also sponsor a warehouse from which they give to the poor of Israel and do much, much more.

There are other names from Israel who have also carried the Messianic message through music. My dear friend Avner Boskey, an American Jew who made *aliya* many years ago with his young family, is one. Karen Davis and her husband David pastor a large congregation outside Haifa called The Carmel Congregation, and theirs is another. Karen writes and travels to minister as well as being the worship leader of their home *kehilah* (congregation). Elisheva Shomron wrote the very popular setting of "Kadosh." It has been recorded by many people, including me—in my case, I did it in Jerusalem in 1998.

Marty Goetz is a name that deserves mentioning here. His composition "For Zion's Sake" is known and loved widely. He continues to write and perform. He gained wide recognition as a professional musician, as the keyboard player for Debby Boone; but it didn't take long for his gifting to carry him into a solo career that continues today.

There are other names that should be mentioned here, for they too carry the message and music of the modern Messianic Movement— though some may not be known for their writing as much as their presentation. "Kol Simcha" ("Sounds of Joy"), under the direction of leader Joseph Finkelstein, was founded out of Beth Yeshua Messianic Synagogue in Philadelphia in the late '70s. This group of 12–15 talented, committed volunteers sang, danced, played instruments and engaged audiences internationally with the best of Messianic music. They carried the music, message and ministry of the Messianic revival for nearly three decades.

Jonathan Settel is a very talented singer with a smooth, resonant bass-baritone voice. He is a Jewish believer. I met him years ago while he was transitioning as a professional singer at Disney World in Orlando to a full-time traveling ministry in the States. He is bilingual in English and Spanish, and continues to be widely received around the world. Another bilingual writer/worship leader I enjoy is Debbie Kline-Iantorno. She has ministered with me in Havana, Cuba, and has led worship at a thriving congregation in southern California for many years.

There are a few new names on the scene these days I should mention. Joshua Aaron is a very talented, passionate singer/songwriter who continues to grow in scope and influence. Sharon Wilbur—yes, my own daughter-in-law and the firstborn of Joel Chernoff, mentioned above as the "voice" of modern Messianic music—is worthy of mention. She is a very gifted artist/singer and songwriter who appeared with me on several of my Integrity Music recordings both in Israel and the U.S. She appeared on *American Idol* back in 2006 and continues to pursue a career in broadcast television while living in L.A.

Ted Pearce, though not Jewish by birth, has had a long and powerful impact on modern Messianic music. His songs "Zealous Over Zion" and "Hallelu Et Adonai" are known and loved all over the world. Ted continues to write, minister and travel extensively, and is often seen leading a "March of Remembrance" somewhere in the world, to combat anti-Semitism and commemorate those lost in the Holocaust.

Sue Samuel is another name that deserves to be mentioned as one who has spent many years as a writer and worship leader. Her quiet, intimate style, along with her songs, has made her a very popular voice of worship and praise for decades that will continue well into the future.

It is always risky when you begin to mention names and single out individuals for their contribution to the cause, because someone who deserves inclusion will inadvertently be omitted.

The writings of the artists mentioned above take on a character all their own as they write new songs of praise and worship from texts that are thousands of years old. To illustrate the timelessness of biblical songs, Psalm 150 is not only one of the best-known of David's works, but it may also embody the heart and soul of Messianic praise in its few lines.

Halleluyah! Praise God in His sanctuary!
Praise Him in His mighty expanse.
Praise Him for His acts of Power.
Praise Him for His enormous greatness.
Praise Him with the blast of the shofar.
Praise Him with harp and lyre.
Praise Him with tambourine and dance.
Praise Him with string instruments and flute.
Praise Him with clash of cymbals.
Praise Him with resounding cymbals.
Let everything that has breath
praise Adonai. Halleluyah!

This Psalm, taken directly from the new *Tree of Life Version*, sounds like a man overwhelmed with love for God. This song was set several years ago by my friend Ted Pearce. I re-recorded it with an added verse of my own at Ein Gedi, Israel during the Feast of Tabernacles in 2009. Worship music like the above is the only vehicle I know that stimulates us in every area of our human experience, all at the same time, body, soul and spirit. Our bodies are enthusiastically involved as the dance rhythms and percussive instruments tempt us to get stand up and join in the celebration. Our souls (mind, will and emotions) are engaged as we think about what we are singing and get caught up in the emotion of His presence filling the sanctuary. Our spirits soar as deep begins to speak to deep in the worship of our King who is enthroned on our praises, and shouts of joy and victory (Ps. 118) begin to echo through the congregation.

Wrapping all this up, Messianic worship music strikes me as a unique expression. I have come to love it, not only for its Scriptural content, but also for its focus and intent. *Where much of today's contemporary Christian music focuses on the worshiper and his or her needs, Messianic worship focuses on the One we worship, who is our source and strength.* For me, it is a matter of pronouns. Instead of "I need" or "We are..." In the Messianic genre, the pronouns often change to "You alone are holy...", and "Yeshua, You are Lord..." The difference is both subtle and profound. Praise and worship that is directed toward the throne and the One who sits there is how I characterize our worship. Direct quotes from Scripture are often great opening lines for our material. "Lord God of Abraham, Isaac and Israel, let it be known today that You are God" (I Kings 18:36) is a quote from Elijah's famous showdown with the Priests of Baal on Mount Carmel, and the opening line of the song that leads my "Watchman" recording from 2006. The very next song says, "Adonai, You alone are God, every tongue will cry, Adonai" (from Romans 14:11). I think you get the picture.

Messianic worship music is very direct, even masculine to my way of thinking. It is strong, Bible-based, as it is, it is also tender and sensitive—as a loving father would be with his child. It is poignant and instructive, never compromising for a cultural expression. Messianic worship is unashamed of its roots and unafraid of what others might think who don't appreciate its roots in Jewish sediment and sentiment.

Its intention is always to bow down before a King and to provoke His presence with passion and love.

To me, and returning now to Dr. Greg Silverman's opening, Messianic music is the heart of King David through the New Covenant lens of hearing, seeing and understanding. The propagating and ministering of this worship, message and ministry have become my life's passion and focus for the past 35 years. It will continue to challenge and engage me for the rest of my life. It is not a particularly easy ministry, I might add, as our message and music are resisted worldwide. Bad doctrinal teachings like Replacement Theology, and growing violent anti-Semitism, prompt way too many to resist our message. Some churchmen misunderstand the reason for our passion and purpose, saying we desire to re-erect the middle wall of partition that Messiah destroyed by the cross. Nothing could be further from the truth! Our goal is the unity and peace that only comes by the presence of the Prince of Peace. We want to see all Israel saved, much as we want to help all believers be appreciative of the Jewish roots of their Christian understanding. May the God of Abraham, Isaac and Israel give us enough grace and love to finish our race with strength, till we hear those blessed words, "Well done, good and faithful servant..." Who knows, we may even hear them in Hebrew.

Not Rejected or Forgotten:
God's Plan and Purposes for Israel

Mitch Glaser, Ph.D.
President, Chosen People Ministries

The purpose of this essay is to develop an overview of God's purposes and plan for the Jewish people as revealed in the Bible. We will focus primarily on three sources: the Scriptures, both Old and New Testaments; traditional Jewish thought; and Christian theology.

There are major differences between the way in which Messianic Jews and the mainstream Jewish community arrive at an understanding of Israel's role in God's plan. First of all, we believe in the inspiration of the New Testament as well as the Hebrew Scriptures. Secondly, we rely far more on the Bible than Jewish tradition, and lastly, we include the use of Christian commentaries and resources to inform our understanding of the role God has given to Israel and the Jewish people in His plan and purposes. The following is therefore written with this perspective in mind.

The Chosen People in Jewish Tradition

As one would imagine, there is an abundance of rabbinic material discussing the choosing of the Jewish people and how this affects Jewish life and community. There is also a diversity of opinion within the historic and global Jewish community regarding what it means to be chosen and how this theological understanding influences the lives of Jewish individuals and communities.

Perhaps the following traditional prayer best expresses a common thread held by Jewish people who take the Jewish religion seriously and are convinced the Lord of the universe has chosen the Jewish people for

a special purpose. The prayer is a call to worship and recited just prior to
the reading of the Torah in the Synagogue service.

בָּרוּךְ אַתָּה ה' אֱלֹהֵינוּ מֶלֶךְ הָעוֹלָם, אֲשֶׁר בָּחַר-בָּנוּ מִכָּל הָעַמִּים וְנָתַן לָנוּ

אֶת תּוֹרָתוֹ. בָּרוּךְ אַתָּה ה' נוֹתֵן הַתּוֹרָה

*Baruch atah Adonai, eloheinu melech ha-olam, asher ba-
char-banu mi-kol ha-a-mim, v'natan lanu et torato.*

Baruch atah Adonai, notein hatorah.

Translated into English, the prayer means:

Blessed are You, L-rd our G-d, King of the universe, who
has chosen us from among all the nations and given us
His Torah. Blessed are You L-rd, who gives the Torah.[1]

Traditionally, we view ourselves as chosen by God, yet *being chosen* is
understood as a privilege, with humility, not arrogance, being the
intended response.

"Chosenness" in Jewish tradition speaks far more about our
obligation to God and His Torah than our selection for special privilege.
For example, in the blessing above chanted prior to the reading of the
Torah, we articulate, as a community, the sense of calling God has
placed upon our lives as Jews with wonder and thanksgiving.[2]

Notice the prayer is not only focused on the relationship of the Jewish
people to the God of the Jews, but on our relationship as a people to the
Torah. It is therefore in the "living out" of the Torah that Jewish people
find the meaning of being chosen. The Jewish understanding of what it
means to be chosen is worked out practically by keeping the Torah. We
are chosen to know God and serve Him by keeping His commandments.

It is also critical to understand that for a religious Jew, the Torah
goes beyond the five books of Moses and usually includes the entirety of
the Holy Scriptures (the Old Testament canon) as well as the long
history of traditional commentaries on the Bible found in the Talmud
and a host of other Jewish sacred texts.

---

[1]   Dovid   Zaklikowski,   comp.,   "Blessings   and   Instructions   for   Getting   an   Aliyah,"
www.chabad.org/library/howto/wizard_cdo/aid/382001/jewish/Blessings-and-Instructions.htm

[2] Jewish philosopher of religion Michael Wyschogrod says, "By sanctifying the nationhood of Israel, God
confirms the national orders of all peoples and expresses his love for the individual in his national setting and
for the nations in their corporate personalities." Michael Wyschogrod, *The Body of Faith: God in the People
Israel* (Northvale, NJ: Jason Aronson, 1996), 68.

For most observant Jews, obedience to the Torah and all it entails has historically shaped the community and caused the Jewish people to live separately from non-Jews or more-secular Jewish people. Religious practices such as keeping kosher, observing the Sabbath, wearing distinctive clothing, etc. marked Jewish communities as distinct and separate from non-Jewish citizens. This has been particularly true in the Diaspora (the "dispersion" of Jewish people living outside the Land of Israel), though this is true among the more religious communities in Israel as well.

The Pharisaic party, prominently mentioned in the New Testament, developed a form of religious "separatism" that influenced Jewish tradition for many years to come.[3] Deep piety leading to separatism became the usual outcome for Jewish communities who recognized themselves as chosen by God for the Torah.

This general perspective on equating chosenness with "living separately" often contributed to anti-Semitism and persecution of Jews by the surrounding non-Jewish communities. To a greater degree, this "separateness" was not sought voluntarily but forced upon Jewish communities through the creation of Medieval ghettos and later reflected in the Pale of Settlement in Russia, the designated areas where Jews were allowed to reside, encompassing thousands of miles and millions of Jewish people in Russia, Poland, Romania and Ukraine.

I mention this because the idea that God chose the Jewish people for a special purpose has shaped the very core of Jewish community life. The Jewish understanding of chosenness led to the cultivation of a theological system and lifestyle that had both positive and negative results for the Jewish people. This "ghettoization" became a rallying cry throughout the *Haskalah* (the Jewish Enlightenment of the 1700s) as Jewish people in Europe preferred assimilation in one form or another to the separateness that led to limitations upon Jews within Gentile societies.

It can also be argued that Jewish community cohesion throughout the years has been a direct result of maintaining this separateness (both coerced and voluntary) and enduring the resulting persecution in the various countries where Jews have lived.

---

[3] The New Testament mentions the Pharisees about 100 times, mostly in the Gospels. According to Joseph Thayer, the Greek term φαρισαῖος, *pharisaios*, denotes "a Pharisee, a member of the sect or party of the Pharisees." *Thayer's Expanded Greek Definition*, Electronic Database (Seattle, WA: Biblesoft, 2011), https://www.studylight.org/lexicons/greek/5330.html.

To try and come to this question of God's plan and purposes for Israel and the Jewish people with a degree of objectivity, I feel our best course is to found our answers upon Scripture—both Testaments—as the Bible is the ultimate spiritual authority for Messianic Jews. Therefore, as Messianic Jews, to build a future for our movement, we must develop a deeper biblical understanding of what it means to be chosen. We need a Messianic Jewish theology that is informed and does not ignore the thinking of traditional Judaism yet is consistent with both the Hebrew Bible and New Covenant Scriptures.[4]

In some areas, we might arrive at the same conclusions as our fellow Jews who do not believe Jesus is the Messiah and do not accept the New Covenant Scriptures. Yet, for example, our relationship alone to non-Jewish believers in Jesus will demand we blaze a new trail that will be different than our fellow Jews. There is really no other solution within mainstream Judaism for regular Gentile engagement with the Jewish community outside of conversion. This would not work for Messianic Jews who attend a local evangelical church; conversion would likely not be the average pastor's solution for Jewish-Gentile unity. Messianic Jews solve problems as biblically as possible, and oftentimes a Messianic congregation provides a solution for mixed, Jewish-Gentile couples who love Jesus and want to remain part of the Jewish community and the church.

Messianic Jews do understand Jews and Gentiles are "one in the Messiah" and that in some fashion God has created "one new man" as taught by the New Testament. Though we cannot develop this further in this essay, this issue is far more challenging for Messianic Jews than for the mainstream Jewish community, as our community must include Gentiles based upon the teaching and authority found in the New Testament.

That we see Yeshua as the fulfillment or goal or consummation of the Torah (Romans 10:4; Matthew 5:17–19) calls upon us to see our chosenness and future participation in God's plan and purposes for the Jews as intertwined with our faith in Jesus the Messiah. We would not expect the mainstream Jewish community to think along these same lines, though we pray and hope many of our fellow Jewish people will come to know the Lord.

---

[4] The New Testament

The very idea that we believe that Yeshua is the Messiah and G-d incarnate, two cardinal doctrines our mainstream Jewish community rejects, moves us along a very different path than the mainstream Jewish community. This has profound implications for our understanding of God's plan and purposes for His chosen people.

A Messianic Jewish theology that wrestles with Israel's chosenness will be quite different than that of mainstream Judaism as we ask a different set of questions of Scripture and live with historic pressures most Christians have not endured. These pressures have also shaped the attitude of the Jewish community toward Jesus and caused the Jewish community to strive for separateness from Christianity, and for the more Orthodox, from Gentiles in general.[5]

These are just a few reasons why a Messianic Jewish theology is necessary and will differ from traditional Jewish thinking on these issues, though we are not suggesting traditional Jewish thinking is monolithic. Therefore, let us begin our journey by examining the biblical narrative in Genesis.

The Promise: Genesis 12:1–2

The existence of the Jewish people is based upon a covenant God made with Abram many, many years ago! We can only begin to understand God's plan and purposes for the Jewish people by understanding the nature of this covenant.

God's plan and purposes for the Jewish people begin after the Bible's first eleven chapters, which narrate the record of God's creation of the world, the fall and corruption of mankind, and God's deliverance of Noah through the judgment of the flood. Subsequently, God confused the language of the people building the Tower of Babel, which resulted in the division and scattering of world's people into language-based groups. Then, while still tracing the family line back to Adam, the reader

---

[5] In his magnum opus *The Body of Faith: God in the People Israel*, dean of Orthodox Jewish theologians Michael Wyschogrod elaborates the difficult relationship between Judaism and Christianity in the Middle Ages that reinforced social exclusion of the Jews. He writes, "Behind them, as Jews, was a long history of exclusion from European civilization. Once Europe had been Christianized, the Jews were the only non-Christians tolerated in the Christian world. The attitude toward them was ambivalent. Having previously rejected the savior, Jews had to be punished for their obduracy. But because the second coming of the Christian savior was somehow thought to be connected with the conversion of the Jews, Christendom generally also thought it necessary not to eradicate the Jewish presence completely but to tolerate it, though as an inferior position" (p. 44).

is introduced in Genesis 12 to Abram, a man living in Ur of the Chaldees.

> *Now the LORD said to Abram,*
> *"Go forth from your country,*
> *and from your relatives*
> *and from your father's house,*
> *to the land which I will show you;*
> *and I will make you a great nation,*
> *and I will bless you,*
> *and make your name great;*
> *and so you shall be a blessing."* (Genesis 12:1–2)

The covenant assures Abram of five distinct promises: two national and three personal. God tells Abram he will be given a land and become a great nation; He also tells him he will be personally blessed, his name will be made great, and he will be a blessing to others. We will take a look shortly at three additional promises made in verse 3. But a question that should be addressed first is, "Why did God choose Abram?" What was so unique about this man that God would select him to be such an important personage in the development of His plan for humankind?

Why Did God Choose Abram?

Essentially, why God chose Abram is one of the great mysteries. The Scriptures do not tell us. We know Abram was a descendant of Noah's son Shem, who according to Genesis 9 was the progenitor of the Messianic line of redemption instituted after the flood. Although the narrative clearly indicates Noah was a righteous man who faithfully walked with God, even while living in a severely corrupted generation (6:8–9), he was not sinless. On one occasion after the flood, Noah "drank of the wine [from his vineyard] and became drunk and lay uncovered in his tent." His son Ham, the father of Canaan, saw this and somehow used it to dishonor and humiliate his father. He tried to involve his brothers Shem and Japheth, but they refused to look and instead covered their father (9:21–23).

> *When Noah awoke from his wine, he knew what his youngest son had done*
> *to him. So he said,*
> *"Cursed be Canaan;*
> *a servant of servants*
> *he shall be to his brothers."*

He also said,
   "Blessed be the LORD,
   the God of Shem;
   and let Canaan be his servant.
   May God enlarge Japheth,
   and let him dwell in the tents of Shem;
   and let Canaan be his servant." (Genesis 9:24–27)

Shem is chosen above his siblings to continue the line of blessing that was established through the cryptic *protoevangelium* (the first gospel) prophecy in the Garden of Eden where we read about God's judgment of Adam and Eve and the serpent. In pronouncing judgment on the serpent, God, as one may recall, makes a promise that a future son of the woman will undo what has been destroyed by sin.

And I will put enmity
between you and the woman,
and between your seed and her seed;
He shall bruise you on the head,
and you shall bruise him on the heel. (Genesis 3:15)

Abram is a descendant from the line of Shem through his father, Terah.

These are the records of the generations of Shem. Shem was one hundred years old, and became the father of Arpachshad two years after the flood. (Genesis 11:10)
Terah took Abram his son, and Lot the son of Haran, his grandson, and Sarai his daughter-in-law, his son Abram's wife; and they went out together from Ur of the Chaldeans in order to enter the land of Canaan; and they went as far as Haran, and settled there. (Genesis 11:31)

There is a famous *midrash* (Jewish homiletical story) found in Genesis Rabbah (called *B'reshith Rabba* in Hebrew), a collection of rabbinic comments on the book of Genesis from the Classical period, that recognizes the election of Abram and the Jewish people as a sovereign act of God, rather than a deserved choice of man. In this story, Abram's father, Terah, leaves their idol-making shop, and while his father is away Abram smashes all of the idols except one. Upon Terah's return and wondering what happened, Abram suggests the one idol left intact was responsible for the destruction.

In my estimation, the story is written to describe Abram's youthful godliness, vindicating God's choice of this one particular descendant of Shem to become the father of a new nation created and called for His holy purposes (Genesis Rabbah 38, *Tanna Debei Eliyahu*). This story simply shows Israel's sages also struggled with God's sovereign choice of Abram and developed various traditions to explain God's choice, assuring the Jewish people God had chosen wisely! Even so, the most important spiritual figure in religious history, outside of Moses and Jesus, remains a mystery.

Blessings and Curses: Genesis 12:3

The promise given by God to Abram continues with additional details in verse 3. It is at this point that God reveals the nature of the relationship the Jewish people will have with the nations of the world.

And I will bless those who bless you,
and the one who curses you I will curse.
And in you all the families of the earth will be blessed.
(Genesis 12:3)

Just as Genesis 12:1–2 includes three personal promises to Abram, there are also three parts to this promise in verse 3. First, those who bless Abram and his descendants will experience God's blessing. Second, those who curse Abram's descendants will themselves be cursed. Note the Hebrew word used for "curses" in line two literally means "to make light." The second word translated "curse" in line three is the usual term for judgment that is often used in both Deuteronomy 28 and Leviticus 26. The play on words should not be missed. Those who devalue or make light of Israel's role in the plan of God or demean the role of the Jewish people could actually experience the very same curses God promised the Jews were to receive for disobedience of the Torah.

This elevates the importance of properly understanding what it means for the Jews to be chosen by God for His purposes. It is a serious issue for Jewish people who are themselves chosen, but also important for non-Jews as this passage describes the ongoing benefits and repercussions regarding how Gentile people treat the Jewish people.

Space precludes discussing the many interpretive discussions of Genesis 12:3 and the preceding verses. However, one of these issues—the unconditional nature of this covenant—should be mentioned. There is a debate as to whether any stipulations or conditions are attached to this covenantal agreement between God and Abram. Clearly, this is not the case in this recounting of the covenant. Since it is the foundational expression of God's relationship to Abram and His descendants, it should be understood plainly. This and the later retelling of the covenant in Scripture, in both the Old and New Testaments, should be viewed in light of this initial formulation.

This is why I believe the covenant has no stipulations. It does not depend upon the obedience of Abram or his descendants. There are no time parameters to this covenantal relationship. In effect, every aspect of this agreement between God and Abram remains unencumbered by further stipulations throughout the ages. *There will never be a time when Abram's descendants will become "un-chosen" nor will there come a moment when the Promised Land will not belong to the Jewish people through divine deed.*

This latter point is reiterated in Genesis 15 and 17, and throughout the Hebrew Scriptures. The Abrahamic covenant as stated in Genesis 12 should be viewed as the foundation stone for understanding God's plan and purposes for the Jewish people according to the Scriptures. As I see it, the Abrahamic is unconditional, which simply means God Himself assures us the obligations of the covenant will be fulfilled.

This does not mean the Jewish people will receive all of God's ultimate blessings while disobedient, but rather suggests that God will one day cause the Jewish people to be obedient in order to experience the promised blessings.

Third, the personal promise of God to Abram involves the ways in which He will use the Jewish people to bless the nations of the world. This will be further explained in our discussion of the Jewish people's mission in relation to the nations of the world.

A *Different* Approach to Understanding the Role of Israel in the Plan of God

At the heart of this presentation is a new way to understand the role of Israel and the Jewish people in God's plan. In Christian and somewhat in Messianic Jewish circles, the two primary theological systems used to answer this question are Dispensationalism and Covenant theology.[6] Theological systems always fall short in detailing all God has to say to humans through His Word, but they are useful for understanding varying perspectives.

As much as I appreciate these traditional schools of theological thought and personally identify closely with Dispensationalism, *I believe it is time to rethink our traditional categories and approach the role of Israel in God's plan by looking at the broad sweep of Scripture rather through a set theological system.*

We began our journey in Genesis 1–11 and continue with the basic theological truths found in the promises of God to Abram in Genesis 12:1–3 and in the reiteration of these promises throughout Genesis. We will further explore the Old Testament Scriptures and conclude with a summary of what is taught in the New Testament regarding the role of Israel and the Jewish people according to God's Word.

I believe we can boil down the Abrahamic covenant to a fourfold promise, which leads to four distinct relationships. This promise includes a promise of a people, a land, a king and a mission. The relationships that grow out of these promises call upon Israel and the Jewish people to engage in a relationship with one another (a community), with the Land (the physical land of Israel), with God, and finally with the nations of the world.

Let's focus on each of these promises and relationships.

---

[6] Many variations exist within Dispensationalism and Covenant theology for understanding the role of Israel and the Jews in God's plan. As this note is provided by way of background and introduction to the methodology in this essay, we will not further develop these differences. For key works representing different approaches see: D. Jeffrey Bingham and Glenn R. Kreider, ed., *Dispensationalism and the History of Redemption: A Developing and Diverse Tradition* (Chicago: Moody Publishers, 2015); Craig Blaising and Darrell Bock, *Progressive Dispensationalism* (1993; repr., Grand Rapids: Baker Academic, 2000); Craig Blaising, Kenneth Gentry Jr., Robert Strimple, *Three Views on the Millennium and Beyond: Premillennialism, Postmillennialism, Amillennialism*, ed. Darrell Bock (Grand Rapids: Zondervan, 1999); Darrell Bock and Mitch Glaser, eds., *To the Jew First: The Case for Jewish Evangelism in Scripture and History* (Grand Rapids: Kregel, 2009); Charles Feinberg, *Premillennialism or Amillennialism?: The Premillennial and Amillennial Systems of Biblical Interpretation Analyzed and Compared*, 2nd ed. (New York: American Board of Missions to the Jews, 1961); and Gerald McDermott, *The New Christian Zionism: Fresh Perspectives on Israel and the Land* (Downers Grove, IL: InterVarsity Press, 2016).

1. The First Promise: A People

The first of God's promises to Abram involves the promise of a people.

> *Now the LORD said to Abram,*
> *"Go forth from your country,*
> *and from your relatives*
> *and from your father's house,*
> *to the land which I will show you;*
> *and I will make you a great nation,*
> *and I will bless you,*
> *and make your name great;*
> *and so you shall be a blessing."* (Genesis 12:1–2)

God miraculously creates a people from the aged loins of Abraham and Sarah. This results in the first of the key relationships outlined in the Abrahamic covenant—the relationship the Jewish people have to one another.

Assuming now that God created the Jewish people for His holy purposes, what are these purposes? Why do we exist as a people? Why were we chosen? These questions are answered and once again have their foundations in the Abrahamic covenant.

This passage provides the theological and historical foundation for Jewish national existence. *If Israel is anything at its core, it is a people or community bound by ethnicity and covenantal purpose.* God called Abram, and through father Abraham and mother Sarah, God created the people of Israel. You cannot have a nation without the people who are part of it. It was God's intention from the start that the Jewish people be fruitful and multiply and live in the Promised Land in peace.

If anyone asks "What does it mean to be Jewish?", we need to ask is being Jewish a race or religion? The answer is simple—*to be Jewish is to be part of a people that God created for His holy purposes.* We are a community—created by God for Him and for one another. The great American humorist Mark Twain describes this well:

> If statistics are right, the Jews constitute but one percent of the human race. It suggests a nebulous dim puff of stardust lost in the blaze of the Milky Way. Properly—the Jew ought hardly to be heard of, but he is heard of, has always been heard of. He is as prominent on the planet as any other people, and his commercial importance is extravagantly out of proportion to the smallness of his bulk. His contributions to the world's list

of great names in literature, science, art, music, finance, medicine, and abstruse learning are also away out of proportion to the weakness of his numbers. He has made a marvelous fight in this world, in all the ages; and had done it with his hands tied behind him. He could be vain of himself and be excused for it.

The Egyptian, the Babylonian, and the Persian rose, filled the planet with sound and splendor, then faded to dream-stuff and passed away; the Greek and the Roman followed; and made a vast noise, and they are gone; other people have sprung up and held their torch high for a time, but it burned out, and they sit in twilight now or have vanished. The Jew saw them all, beat them all, and is now what he always was, exhibiting no decadence, no infirmities of age, no weakening of his parts, no slowing of his energies, no dulling of his alert and aggressive mind. All things are mortal but the Jew; all other forces pass, but he remains. What is the secret of his immortality?[7]

The secret to Jewish "immortality" is God who promised to create a people for His purposes, and until those purposes are completed, the people must continue. It is because of God that the Jewish people have not been destroyed.

The Chosen People

What does it mean to be chosen? As stated at the start of our journey, understanding ourselves as chosen by God within Jewish tradition must never lead to arrogance but to humility. In some sense, Israel was married to God, thus chosen. God called forth the Jewish people to be a bride and a community that serves His purposes, and when we do not serve His purposes, we lose our national purpose for existence.

Biblical Terms for God Choosing the Jewish People

Our understanding of the Jewish people as the chosen people is foundational to understanding God's plan and purposes for the Jewish people throughout the ages. There are a few key passages and terms, both in the Old Testament and the New, that when understood give us a

---

[7] Mark Twain, "Concerning the Jews," *Harper's Magazine*, September 1899, https://harpers.org/archive/1899/09/concerning-the-jews

clear and multidimensional understanding of what we commonly mean by "the chosen people."

There are also many good articles and books on the subject of God's election of or choosing Israel, so allow me to distill some of this information that can be discovered on this topic and present some ideas I believe are necessary to help us understand them. So in this section, we will examine four key terms used to describe God choosing the Jewish people: בָּחַר, *bachar*, סְגֻלָּה, *segullah*, סְגֻלָּה, *nachalah*, and ἐκλογή, *eklogē*.

בָּחַר, *Bachar, "Choose"*

The Hebrew word בָּחַר, *bachar*, "choose," is most often used in Scripture to express the idea that the Jewish people are God's chosen people.[8] Two key instances of the term occur in Deuteronomy 7 and 14.

> *For you are a holy people to the LORD your God; the LORD your God has **chosen you** to be a people for His own possession out of all the peoples who are on the face of the earth.*

> *The LORD did not set **His love** on you **nor choose you** because you were more in number than any of the peoples, for you were the fewest of all peoples, but because **the LORD loved you and kept the oath which He swore to your forefathers**, the LORD brought you out by a mighty hand and redeemed you from the house of slavery, from the hand of Pharaoh king of Egypt.* (Deuteronomy 7:6–8, emphasis added)

> *For you are a holy people to the LORD your God, and **the LORD has chosen you** to be **a people for His own possession** out of all the peoples who are on the face of the earth.* (Deuteronomy 14:2, emphasis added)

---

[8] The key Hebrew term בָּחַר, *bachar*, "to choose," occurs 172 times in 164 verses in the Old Testament. Strangely, H. Wildberger only identifies 146 occurrences: 32 times in non-theological contexts, 83 times in theological contexts of which 67 had God as the subject of *bachar*, "to choose." *Theological Lexicon of the Old Testament*, ed. Ernst Jenni and Claus Westermann, trans. Mark Biddle (Peabody, MA: Hendrickson Publishers, 1997), 1:211. The most significant cognate, *bachir*, occurs 13 times, always modifying an object of God's choice (2 Sam. 21:6; 1 Chron. 16:13; Ps. 89:3; 105:6, 43; 106:5, 23; Isa. 42:1; 43:20; 45:4; 65:9, 15, 22). *Eklegomai, eklektos* and *haireomai* are the words used to translate *bachar* in the LXX. The words *barar* (*qal*—1 Chron. 7:40; 9:22; 16:41; Neh. 5:18; Isa. 49:2) and *barah* II (1 Sam. 17:8) also mean "to choose, select." (*Lexicon*, 2:75). See also Emile Nicole, "bachar," *New International Dictionary of Old Testament Theology and Exegesis*, ed. Willem VanGemeren (Grand Rapids: Zondervan, 1997), 1:638.

The verb *bachar* is used in the Hebrew Scriptures in both secular and sacred ways. For example, in Genesis 6:2 we read about the sons of God taking wives for themselves, "whomever they *chose*" (emphasis added). This is the same term. It is also used in 1 Samuel 17:40 to describe how David "*chose* for himself five smooth stones" (emphasis added). The word, in itself, is easy to understand. It speaks of a discriminating selection amidst available options.

Throughout the Bible we see the term *bachar* used with *places* that were chosen, such as Jerusalem (1 Kings 8:44, 48; 2 Kings 23:27), as well as with *individuals* such as Abram (Nehemiah 9:7) and corporately of the nation of Israel (Isaiah 43:10).

The people God chooses seem to have some type of innate worthiness, which is the condition for His choice. However, others are chosen unconditionally, having no merit. This choice is made solely by the will of God and not the worthiness of man. *God's choosing of Israel is an unconditional choice and serves as the basis for the unconditional covenant He made with Abraham.*

Those chosen by God, such as judges, prophets, Gentile national leaders, etc., were selected for service. The older theologians use the term *vocational choosing.* In other words, most were chosen to do some kind of work for God. Although the term *bachar* is not always present, there are clear examples of those who were chosen for blessing, either for salvation or to be a blessing to others, such as Isaiah 43:10, 12; 44:1; 49:5, 6–8, and 9. All of these are good illustrations of the way in which God chose Israel to be both blessed and to be a blessing to the nations as per Genesis 12:1–3.

Election also carries with it both privileges and responsibilities. This is illustrated in many different ways in the Bible, but especially in God's choosing Israel. In his letter to the believers living in Rome, Rabbi Saul describes the benefits and blessings received by Israel because of God's choice.[9]

> *For I could wish that I myself were accursed, separated from Christ for the sake of my brethren, my kinsmen according to the flesh, who are Israelites, to whom*

---

[9] The Apostle Paul's writings reflect his understanding of the Old Testament Scriptures regarding the benefits of God's choice of Israel. For instance, God gave the Law to Israel (Deuteronomy 4:8) and viewed Israel as His inheritance (Deuteronomy 4:20; 32:9). In addition, Israel received a measure of the presence of God beyond that of other nations (Exodus 40:34–38; Deuteronomy 4:7).

belongs the adoption as sons, and the glory and the covenants and the giving of the Law and the temple service and the promises, whose are the fathers, and from whom is the Christ according to the flesh, who is over all, God blessed forever. Amen. (Romans 9:3–5)

Israel also received responsibilities that came along with privilege. If Israel did not keep up "its end of the bargain," then the nation will be judged and penalties will be brought upon the nation for their disobedience. Certainly, Leviticus 26 and Deuteronomy 28 clearly reveal the penalties for Israel's disobedience.

The Scriptures never say that Israel's disobedience will outlast God's grace, nor do they say that anything can stop God's intervention when He wants the nation to repent and once again receive His blessings and turn the nation back to Him. If anything, the book of Hosea proclaims the message to Israel that God is not going to reject them but will wait for their repentance. Once chosen, always chosen!

סְגֻלָּה, *Segullah, "Treasured Possession"*

The Hebrew word סְגֻלָּה, *segullah,* "treasured possession," is mainly used in the Bible to express the idea that the Jewish people are God's special inheritance. Israel is God's *segullah*—His own treasured possession. Through His servant Moses, the Lord says to His people from Mount Sinai,

> *"Now then, if you will indeed obey My voice and keep My covenant, then you shall **be My own possession** among all the peoples, for all the earth is Mine; and you shall be to Me a kingdom of priests and a holy nation."* These are the words that you shall speak to the sons of Israel. (Exodus 19:5–6, emphasis added)

An article in *Dispatch From Jerusalem* magazine says, "*Segullah* is used eight times in the Hebrew Scriptures. Six of those times, it refers to Israel (Exod. 19:5; Deut. 7:6; 14:2; 26:18; Ps. 135:4; Mal. 3:17). It is translated in various Bible versions as peculiar treasure, special treasure, or treasured possession. One commentator defined it as 'property in the special sense of a private possession that one personally acquired and carefully preserves.'"[10] Later in the article, Charleeda Sprinkle says, "In ancient times, it referred to the special treasure that a conquering king chose for himself among all the spoils of war. This is implied in Ecclesiastes 2:8, where King Solomon records, 'I also gathered for myself silver and gold and the special treasures of kings and of the provinces.' David also used *segullah* to describe the gold and silver that he gave to build the Temple (1 Chron. 29:3)."[11]

In his commentary on the Torah, Rabbi Samson Raphael Hirsch says *segullah* "denotes an exclusive possession ... to which no one else except its owner is entitled, and which has no relationship to anyone except its owner."[12] Similarly, Rashi says, "*Segullah* means a cherished treasure, the same as (Ecclesiastes 2:8), 'and treasures of kings' costly vessels and precious stones which kings store up. In the same manner shall you be unto Me a cherished treasure more than other peoples."[13] Rabbi Tony Arroyo of Kol Simcha Messianic Congregation suggests it is really God's "term of endearment for His would-be bride, Israel," and writes, "Accordingly, the King of Kings possesses all of the earth, as stated in *Shemot* [Exodus] 19:5, but chooses Israel to be His special, valued and beloved possession—His *am segullah*."[14] Allusions in the New Testament to this kind of special and treasured devotion of God's heart toward His people are evident in verses such as Titus 2:14 and 1 Peter 2:9.

The root word *sagal* has also been translated as "purple." The term is commonly used this way in modern Hebrew as purple was a rare color dye, and anything dyed purple in the ancient world was considered very valuable. *Segullah* speaks of an object that has great value to its owner, a possession that is treasured.

---

[10] Quoted from article summary for Charleeda Sprinkle, "A Particular Treasure—Segulah," *Dispatch From Jerusalem*, Oct. 26, 2008. www.bridgesforpeace.com/category/insights-from-the-hebrew-language/page/5.

[11] Charleeda Sprinkle, "A Particular Treasure—Segulah," *Dispatch From Jerusalem* magazine, Oct. 26, 2008, archived on Bridges for Peace, www.bridgesforpeace.com/article/peculiar-treasure-segulah.

[12] Quoted from translation and commentary on Exodus 19:5 by Rav Samson Raphael Hirsch, *The Hirsch Chumash: The Five Books of the Torah*, vol. 2, *Sefer Shemos*, trans. Daniel Haberman (1962; Jerusalem: Feldheim Publishers; New York: Judaica Press, 2005), 317.

[13] Rashi, *The Torah With Rashi's Commentary*, vol. 2, *Sefer Shemot* (Exodus), trans. Yisrael Isser Zvi Herczeg, ArtScroll (Brooklyn, NY: Mesorah Publications, 1999), 98. Rashi is an abbreviation of Rabbi Shlomo Yitzchaki (1040–1105 C.E.), a medieval French rabbi who wrote extensive authoritative commentaries on the Bible and the Talmud.

[14] Tony Arroyo, "*Am Segullah*—The Biblical Status of the Bride: Commentary on Parashat Yitro (Exodus 18:1–20:23)," Shabbat Teaching, Kol Simcha Messianic Congregation, Gainesville, FL, Feb. 14, 2009, www.kolsimcha.org/messages/2009/021409M.pdf, p. 2.

Segullah is sometimes used with *bachar*. Both words are used in Deuteronomy 7 and 14. For instance, in 7:6, *"For you are a holy people to the LORD your God; the LORD your God has **chosen you [bachar]** to be a people for **His own possession [segullah]** out of all the peoples who are on the face of the earth"* (emphasis added). God called Israel to be *holy*—set apart for His purposes. The Jewish people were *chosen* for this unique status out of (or "above," per some texts' translation) all other nations. The Jewish people are His *segullah*, a unique, treasured possession. Israel is chosen to be God's possession. He is the true owner of Israel and is committed to the stewardship of His treasure.

Further, the basis for God's choice has nothing to do with Israel's merits, as we read in the Torah itself:

> The LORD did not set **His love** on you **nor choose you** because you were more in number than any of the peoples, for you were the fewest of all peoples, but because **the LORD loved you and kept the oath which He swore to your forefathers**, the LORD brought you out by a mighty hand and redeemed you from the house of slavery, from the hand of Pharaoh king of Egypt. (Deuteronomy 7:7–8, emphasis added)

The above passage demonstrates two critical observations:

- The choosing of the Israelites as God's chosen people was God's idea, not man's.
- The basis for God's choice of the people of Israel has nothing to do with the merits—past, present, or future—of the Jewish people, but rather is founded upon the will and character of God.

Further, the passage indicates God chose Israel according to these three bases:

- because of His love
- because of His grace
- because of His holy purposes

Israel was not chosen because of who they were, what they have done or even who they will become or what they will do, but simply because God decided to love them into existence and use them to accomplish His purposes in the world. Israel did not merit God's love or grace nor deserve to be entrusted with His holy purposes. This divine choosing or election does not apply to any other nation on the face of the earth, past or present, either. God simply chose Israel, and Israel alone.

Denying that the Jewish people are still the chosen people or that they are chosen for specific purposes that will result in blessing the nations makes the immutable God appear fickle and subjects His plans and purposes to the will of the created rather than the other way around.

This also includes the giving of the land to the Jewish people. Israel did not earn the right to the deed or title of the Promised Land but was rather given the land as a gift from God. Therefore, *there is no time when the Jewish people are unable to rightfully claim a "divinely sanctioned," ownership of the land.* All charges against Israel, including the modern Israel of being a usurper and taking what does not belong to them, is wrong when measured against the promises of God.

נַחֲלָה, *Nachalah, "Inheritance"*

The Hebrew word נַחֲלָה, *nachalah,* frequently translated in the Scripture as "inheritance" but sometimes "possession" or "heritage," is similar to yet different from *segullah,* which is also translated "inheritance." The term *nachalah* refers to what is inherited, usually land, and conveys the fact that the deed has passed to new owners.[15] Moses says to God's people from Mount Sinai,

> But the LORD *has taken you and brought you out of the iron furnace, from Egypt, to be a people for His own* **possession** *[or inheritance], as today.* (Deuteronomy 4:20, emphasis added)

God chose the Jewish people as His inheritance, His portion and His possession amongst all the peoples of the earth. The word *nachalah* is used this way with reference to Israel in Deuteronomy 4:20; 9:26; 32:9; 1 Kings 8:51, 53; Psalm 33:12; 78:71; Jeremiah 10:16; and in many other passages. The phrase "Israel My inheritance" is also used in Isaiah 19:25 and Joel 3:2 (4:2 in the Hebrew text).

This term *nachalah* is built on the Hebrew root נָחַל, *nachal,* which refers to property that is inherited and divided between the heirs. *Nachalah* is sometimes translated as "possess," since naturally once we inherit something, we possess it.

---

[15] The idea is paralleled in the New Testament as Peter and Paul view the saints in Messiah to have inherited the kingdom of God—an inheritance that cannot be taken away (Ephesians 1:11; 1 Peter 1:4).

The Jewish people are God's inheritance: *Both the Land and the people are God's inheritance—they are His special possessions*, and He does not want His Land to be inherited by another people whose names are not written in the deed, namely, the Abrahamic covenant. The Land of Israel itself is specifically noted as the inheritance of God and of the Jewish people (Psalm 136:21–22).

Ἐκλογή, *Eklogē, "Selection, Choice, Election"*

The handful of times it occurs in the Bible, the Greek word ἐκλογή, *eklogē*, is usually translated "choice," or possibly "selection" or "election." The Apostle Paul says of the Jewish people,

> *From the standpoint of the gospel they are enemies for your sake, but from the standpoint of God's **choice** they are beloved for the sake of the fathers; for the gifts and the calling of God are irrevocable.* (Romans 11:28–29, emphasis added)

Paul describes his fellow Jews as acting as if they are enemies of the Gospel, but though some may reject the message and the Messiah, they are still beloved by God. So *eklogē* may simply refer to the divine choice exercised in selecting the Jewish people to be His bridge of redemption to a broken world. The reference is not to the Jewish people in and of themselves, but to the election of the Jewish people as the nation from whom the Messiah will come. As Jesus himself says, "salvation is of[16] the Jews" (John 4:22). The Greek grammar implies the Jews are the source of salvation, which suggests the Abrahamic covenant and its promise of universal blessings to the nations will come through the descendants of Israel and primarily through the Jewish Savior himself.[17]

As Paul confirms in Romans 11:29, the Jewish people cannot possibly be destroyed or the covenants annulled, for God's holy purposes for the physical descendants of Abraham, Isaac and Jacob must be fulfilled. And His choice cannot be undone by mere human disobedience.

---

[16] Grammatically, this is a genitive of source. Thus, many translations render this phrase "salvation is from the Jews."

[17] John 4:22 says, ὅτι ἡ σωτηρία ἐκ τῶν Ἰουδαίων ἐστίν, *hoti hē sōtēria ek tōn Ioudaiōn estin*, "for salvation is of the Jews." The genitive of source is used, indicating the Jewish people are indeed the source of salvation for the world.

2. The Second Promise: The Land

The second of God's promises to Abram involves the promise of the land.

> *On that day the LORD made a covenant with Abram, saying, "To your descendants I have given this land, from the river of Egypt as far as the great river, the river Euphrates: the Kenite and the Kenizzite and the Kadmonite and the Hittite and the Perizzite and the Rephaim and the Amorite and the Canaanite and the Girgashite and the Jebusite."* (Genesis 15:18–21)

Clearly, the Jewish people are not the only group of people that has been dispersed from its national boundaries. But *the Jewish people may be the only people created as a nation prior to receiving their national boundaries.*

It is important to understand God chose Israel before they emerged as a nation on the international scene. In fact, Israel had no prior existence to the Abrahamic covenant and would have had no existence but for the direct intervention of the One who created the heavens and the earth, determined the appointed times and boundaries of nations, and holds the hearts of the kings of nations in His powerful hand (Deuteronomy 32:8–9; Proverbs 21:1; Acts 17: 24–27). So, in the midst of creating the Jewish people as a nation and all the unique, special revelation this included, we should not think it at all odd that God would also literally determine the specific boundaries of Israel's national existence.

Let's rehearse for a moment what we have covered:

- God created the people of Israel.
- God created the people of Israel for a purpose.
- God created the national boundaries of the people of Israel.

The Promises of the Land Pass Through His Physical Descendants

The scope of God's promises regarding the land include all four phases being discussed here: first the people and then the land, followed by the king and the mission, which we will discuss below. God's promise of the land passes from Abram to his sons, Isaac and Jacob.

The Promise of the Land in General

In terms of the broad brushstrokes of biblical theology, God first promises the following to Abram and his descendants:

> Abram said, "O Lord GOD, what will You give me, since I am childless, and the heir of my house is Eliezer of Damascus?" And Abram said, "Since You have given no offspring to me, one born in my house is my heir." Then behold, the word of the LORD came to him, saying, "This man will not be your heir; but one who will come forth from your own body, he shall be your heir." And He took him outside and said, "Now look toward the heavens, and count the stars, if you are able to count them." And He said to him, "So shall your descendants be." (Genesis 15:2–5)

> I will establish My covenant between Me and you and your descendants after you throughout their generations for an everlasting covenant, to be God to you and to your descendants after you. (Genesis 17:7)

> Indeed, I will greatly bless you, and I will greatly multiply your seed as the stars of the heavens and as the sand which is on the seashore; and your seed shall possess the gate of their enemies. (Genesis 22:17)

The Promise of the Land Through Isaac

These same promises of God then pass through Abram's son, Isaac:

> But God said, "No, but Sarah your wife will bear you a son, and you shall call his name Isaac; and I will establish My covenant with him for an everlasting covenant for his descendants after him. As for Ishmael, I have heard you; behold, I will bless him, and will make him fruitful and will multiply him exceedingly. He shall become the father of twelve princes, and I will make him a great nation. But My covenant I will establish with Isaac, whom Sarah will bear to you at this season next year." (Genesis 17:19–21)

The Promise of the Land Through Jacob

God then makes these promises of the land made to Abraham and Isaac pass through Jacob:

> God said to him,
>   "Your name is Jacob;
>   you shall no longer be called Jacob,
>   but Israel shall be your name."
> Thus, He called him Israel. God also said to him,
>   "I am God Almighty;
>   be fruitful and multiply;
>   a nation and a company of nations shall come from you,
>   and kings shall come forth from you.
>   "The land which I gave to Abraham and Isaac,
>   I will give it to you,
>   and I will give the land to your descendants after you." (Genesis
>   35:10–12)

Let us again summarize these promises of God to Abraham, Isaac and Jacob, whose name God changed to Israel at this point in the narrative, after a great struggle:

- God created the people of Israel from "nothing."

- God Himself gave birth to the nation and set its spiritual and national boundaries.

- God established Israel's principles of government, directly revealed its constitution, legal system, worship structures and even the design of its sanctuary, originally the portable tabernacle or "tent of meeting" and later the Temple.

The unconditional gift of the land was passed from father to sons and then to the physical descendants of Abraham, Isaac and Jacob.

3. The Third Promise: The King

The third of God's promises to Abraham involves the promise of the king. This promise was part of the Abrahamic covenant according to Genesis 17:6,

> I will make you exceedingly fruitful, and I will make nations of
> you, and kings will come forth from you.

And again in Genesis 17:16,

> *I will bless her, and indeed I will give you a son by her. Then I will bless her, and she shall be a mother of nations; kings of peoples will come from her.*

The sad story of Israel's demand for a human king is well-known (1 Samuel 8). For some sovereign reason, God accommodates the people's demand and chooses Saul to be Israel's king. But in wanting a king over them like all the nations, they were really rejecting God from being their king (1 Samuel 8:7). Saul was not a good king for Israel. After God rejects Saul, He chooses as king a man after His own heart, and establishes the House of David as an everlasting dynasty (2 Samuel 7:16). Until the Babylonian captivity, the Old Testament story focuses on the good and bad descendants of David, while at the same time prophetically preparing the way for the very king He always wanted to rule His chosen people. This king will be God Himself, through the person of the incarnate Son of God, whom according to Isaiah 9:6–7 will rule His chosen people forever.

> *For a child will be born to us, a son will be given to us; and the government will rest on His shoulders; and His name will be called Wonderful Counselor, Mighty God, Eternal Father, Prince of Peace.*

> *There will be no end to the increase of His government or of peace, on the throne of David and over his kingdom, to establish it and to uphold it with justice and righteousness from then on and forevermore.*

> *The zeal of the LORD of hosts will accomplish this.*

The Abrahamic covenant promises Abram's descendants they will become a people and also inherit a land, but implicit within the covenant as well is their eventual submission to their rightful king. One of the most important stories within the narrative of the Bible is this slow march to the fullness of redemption when the Jewish people will enjoy the Land in sync with their relationship to their king.

In summary, the Jewish people were promised their descendants will become a nation—a people, a community bound by ethnicity and covenant. Second, this nation will have a land with specific boundaries outlined by God. And as stated above, the descendants of Abram will also eventually be in a "right" relationship with the God who created them. Those who believe the present, secular, modern state of Israel is the fulfillment of God's promises to the Jewish people have a case. There is, however, so much more to come when Israel embraces Jesus as Lord and King (Romans 11:25–27).

4. The Fourth Promise: The Mission

The fourth aspect of God's promises to Abraham focuses on the mission of Israel. This answers the question that is sometimes asked regarding God's plan for the nation of Israel: "Chosen for what?" Was Israel chosen for a purpose, and if so, what is it?

The answer is found within the terms of the covenant as God said to Abram,

> *And I will bless those who bless you,*
> *and the one who curses you I will curse.*
> *And in you all the families of the earth will be blessed.*
> (Genesis 12:3)

God created and purposed the nation of Israel to bring blessings to the world. In effect, God chose Israel for the sake of the Gentiles to be His bridge of redemption to the pagan world.

The Scriptures describe three ways Israel will bring blessings to the nations as promised in Genesis 12:3.

Israel Will Be a Kingdom of Priests

In the book of Exodus, God describes Israel as a kingdom of priests.

> *Moses went up to God, and the LORD called to him from the mountain, saying, "Thus you shall say to the house of Jacob and tell the sons of Israel: 'You yourselves have seen what I did to the Egyptians, and how I bore you on eagles' wings, and brought you to Myself. Now then, if you will indeed obey My voice and keep My covenant, then you shall be My own possession among all the peoples, for all the earth is Mine; and you shall be to Me a kingdom of priests and a holy nation.' These are the words that you shall speak to the sons of Israel." (Exodus 19:3–6)*

As priests, the nation of Israel is to serve as intermediaries between the nations of the world and the God of the nations. Another passage of Scripture in the book of Zechariah indicates the nations will eventually come up to Jerusalem during the Feast of Tabernacles, presumably during a future time when the Messiah returns to reign as King.

> *Then it will come about that any who are left of all the nations that went against Jerusalem will go up from year to year to worship the King, the LORD of hosts, and to celebrate the Feast of Booths.* (Zechariah 14:16)

Here Israel takes on a priestly role, receiving religious participation and adoration from the nations of the world. Is this more-literal understanding of Israel's priesthood on behalf of the nations what God had in mind? Time will tell. Some say we cannot be sure. But we do know that God mediated His blessings of revelation through His Word (Romans 9:4–5), and that the Messianic King came through the Jewish people.

We're told great blessings came to the Gentiles as a result of Israel's spiritual failures. Paul speaks to this in Romans 11:12–15. Eventually, we're also told, Israel's spiritual transformation will bring about even greater blessings and the fulfillment of its mission. For instance, in describing this blessing, Paul in verse 15 uses the phrase ζωὴ ἐκ νεκρῶν, *zōē ek nekrōn*, "life from the dead." Ultimately, Israel's turning to Jesus brings the fullness of blessings God promised to the nations of the world (Romans 11:25–29). In effect, *when the Jewish remnant turns to Jesus* (Romans 11:25), *Jesus returns to reign as King*, in literal fulfillment of the Abrahamic, Davidic and New covenants.

God assured the continuity of the Jewish people, the receiving of the Land promises, the spiritual regeneration of the entire nation, and now the divine ability to fulfill the mission of blessing the world. However, the enacting of the fourfold covenantal promise rests upon the God who is faithful to His promises and powerful enough to do what He said.

Covenantal Convergence: When Will the Promise Be Fulfilled?

The existence of the Jewish people depends upon God's unconditional promise outlined in the Abrahamic covenant. [18] The covenant's unconditional nature is depicted in Genesis 15, when Abram falls into a "deep sleep" and sees "a smoking oven and a flaming torch which passed between these pieces" (Genesis 15:17). The cutting of the animals in half describes an unbreakable covenant, and the imagery of the oven and the torch speak of God Himself taking on the obligation to effectuate the covenant agreement. At the conclusion of this dream, the land boundaries are delineated for Abram, which forever binds the covenant and the giving of the land to Abram and his descendants.

Thankfully, the fulfillment of the promises God made to Abraham and his descendants depends on God Himself and is not subject to the will and whims of man. But when will God fulfill His promise made so many thousands of years ago to His chosen people, the Jews? Christians and Jews alike are mindful that we live in a sin-soaked world, and both long for the dawning of a material Messianic era.

When Will the Jewish People Repent and Return to the Land and the Lord?

According to the Scriptures, the Jewish people will repent and return to the land and to the Lord in the end of days. The way in which Israel ultimately receives the blessings promised to the nation will be through their repentance and their faith in Messiah, by turning and becoming obedient to the God of Abraham, Isaac and Jacob.

This end-time repentance and turning of the Jewish people to the Messiah is fundamental to our once again being more fully blessed by God and being engaged by God to fulfill the purposes and blessings for which Israel was created and chosen. Furthermore, this repentance and return were anticipated, even predicted, in the Torah by the Prophet Moses before the children of Israel ever set foot in the Promised Land.

---

[18] Scholars disagree on whether the Abrahamic covenant is unconditional or conditional. In my view, as discussed earlier ("Blessings and Curses: Genesis 12:3"), God's covenant with Abraham is unconditional, and God Himself is the one who takes responsibility for the performance of the covenant requirements.

> *When you become the father of children and children's children and have remained long in the land, and act corruptly, and make an idol in the form of anything, and do that which is evil in the sight of the* LORD *your God so as to provoke Him to anger, I call heaven and earth to witness against you today, that you will surely perish quickly from the land where you are going over the Jordan to possess it. You shall not live long on it, but will be utterly destroyed. The* LORD *will scatter you among the peoples, and you will be left few in number among the nations where the* LORD *drives you. There you will serve gods, the work of man's hands, wood and stone, which neither see nor hear nor eat nor smell. But from there you will seek the* LORD *your God, and you will find Him if you search for Him with all your heart and all your soul. When you are in distress and all these things have come upon you, in the latter days you will return to the* LORD *your God and listen to His voice. For the* LORD *your God is a compassionate God; He will not fail you nor destroy you nor forget the covenant with your fathers which He swore to them.*
> (Deuteronomy 4:25–31)

If we turn the prophetic clock ahead to one minute before twelve, then we have the proper context for this end-time turning of the Jewish remnant to Jesus as described by the Prophet Zechariah. Israel will repent and return to the Lord through the one and only Yeshua the Messiah.

> *I will pour out on the house of David and on the inhabitants of Jerusalem, the Spirit of grace and of supplication, so that they will look on Me whom they have pierced; and they will mourn for* **him**, *as one mourns for an only son, and they will weep bitterly over him like the bitter weeping over a firstborn.*
> (Zechariah 12:10, emphasis added)

At that time, the Jewish people will become what God always intended, and they will receive the fullness of the covenantal blessings promised to our forefather Abraham. The Jewish people will:

- become a *holy people*—a spiritual nation,
- live in a *holy land*—peace in the land,
- worship a *holy God*—a right relationship with God, and
- fulfill a *holy purpose*—the nations will be blessed.

The Apostle Paul confirms these covenantal expectations in the book of Romans where he writes,

> *If their transgression is riches for the world and their failure is riches for the Gentiles, how much more will their fulfillment be!* (Romans 11:12)

And further,

> *For if their rejection is the reconciliation of the world, what will their acceptance be but life from the dead?* (Romans 11:15)

Israel can never be all God intended the nation to be without this convergence. All four elements—a people, a land, a king and a mission—must be fulfilled because these elements are still part of the foundational Abrahamic covenant, and the God who makes promises always keeps them.

This convergence is evidently future to our present day. Yet we do see the telltale signs that give us hope that God will complete what He started. Israel has held together as a community even after thousands of years of dispersion and persecution. Though the Jewish people are "left few in number," through time and circumstance, the nation still exists and remains an identifiable community, even in the dispersion. Happily, the Land of Israel is currently in Jewish hands, even though the full boundaries God described in Genesis 15 are not yet in Israel's possession.

Yet frankly, at this point in history, there is little evidence all these elements of the Abrahamic promise are in the process of fulfillment. Many aspects of this process of convergence appear to be incremental. The return to the Land is still partial, and the promised Messianic blessings of peace in the Land (Isaiah 9:6–7; 19:23) are presently out of reach. Israel is, in many respects, irreligious. And clearly, the Messiah, the Son of David, is not currently reigning on a literal throne in Jerusalem. We're not there yet, but happily, momentum is moving in the right direction.

We see enough to fuel our hope, but we still look to a future day of covenantal convergence when God will restore the Jewish people fully though the Messiah.

Our Response to the Plan and Purposes of God for Israel

I would like to briefly conclude this chapter by applying what we've learned throughout our journey in three different areas. First of all, what are the implications of the plan and purposes of God as outlined here for the Jewish community in general? Secondly, what significance does this have for the Messianic Jewish community? And finally, knowing God's plan for Israel, what should the believers do with this knowledge? What actions should be taken?

Regarding the Mainstream Jewish Community

The mainstream Jewish community has the same blessed hope of a future covenantal convergence as those who believe in Jesus of Nazareth. The mainstream Jewish community, with some exception, believes in the coming of the Messiah, the establishment of His Kingdom, and His bringing true, lasting peace to the land of Israel that will be a great blessing to the nations of the world. We're on the same page here.

Again, the key to this covenantal convergence is the Messiah. Yet we also know this convergence cannot come until Israel turns to the One who fulfilled countless Messianic prophecies in the Scriptures. He was born in Bethlehem and was of the tribe of Judah and house of David. He is a prophet, priest, king and redeemer, fulfilling the detailed predictions of Isaiah 53, which says the Messiah will come as a humble servant who will die for the sins of the Jewish people and the nations of the world. Only by believing in the Messiah will Jewish people have a share in the messianic age to come.

This is why reaching Jews with the message of the Messiah today is so critical. We cannot remain silent and watch our people follow false messiahs, whether a Rebbe from Crown Heights, Brooklyn, or a depersonalized messianic age embraced by some forms of Judaism. *It is because we have so much in common with our Jewish community that we must speak to our wider Jewish community of the mercy and grace revealed to us through "the Lamb of God who takes away the sin of the world"* (John 1:29)!

We Jewish believers are still part of the Jewish community. We love our people but cannot allow that love to drive us to silence. We must speak of the true Messiah to our people. We are not the only Messianic Jews within the greater Jewish community; other movements exist. *We are the Messianic Jews who believe the Messiah is Yeshua of Nazareth who came once and will come again* (John 1:1–18, 45; 14:3; Acts 1:11).

It is not enough to share the same covenantal destiny as the rest of the Jewish community or to identify with the same concerns for our Jewish people. Keeping Shabbat, keeping kosher, worshiping on Friday and Saturday, and finding great value in being part of the Jewish community does not set us apart within the Jewish community. We must make the Messiah we love and worship known by lifting His name high, or we will simply blend into the Jewish community and lose our testimony for Yeshua.

Regarding the Messianic Jewish Community

As Messianic Jews, we understand the Bible promises a bright and glorious future for the Jewish people. God will preserve our people, and when the Messiah returns we will finally live in peace in our Promised Land. We will have a new and restored relationship with the God who chose us to be His people and fulfill our divinely appointed destiny as a light among the nations (Isaiah 42:6; 49:6). The Lord will transform the curses of the past into blessings. This is our hope and sure expectation founded upon God's purpose and plan for Israel revealed in the Bible.

And though there is tremendous pressure on the Messianic Jewish community to live on the margins of the wider Jewish community, we cannot be content to stay there. The people of Israel are our people, the land of Israel is our land, the God of Israel is our God, and the mandate of Israel to shine His light among the nations is our commission. We cannot accept an outsider's position, for we are insiders by virtue of God's covenant. We share these covenant promises with our people. Therefore, knowing the truth of God's Word, we must embrace who we are as Jews, and in spite of the pressure, we must remain part of the Jewish community, show love to all Israel, and show loyalty to the land of Israel as we serve the God of Abraham, Isaac, and Jacob among the nations.

Regarding the Church

The Church in general, and especially Gentile believers, should understand the significant role non-Jews have in God's plan as founded on the Abrahamic promises. Gentiles are participants in the Abrahamic covenant in that they are spiritual descendants of Abraham (Galatians 3:6–9). This does not mean Gentiles become Jews upon receiving Yeshua as this is passed through physical lineage beginning with the patriarchs. However, Gentiles may now become the spiritual sons and daughters of Abraham by faith as God's blessings have come to "those far off" through the mediation of the Jewish Messiah.

The Church has a twofold duty and obligation to the Jewish community.

First of all, the Church, knowing God's covenantal faithfulness, must support the Jewish people and pray for them. This does not mean the Church must totally agree with the nation of Israel's politics or policy decisions, but we must all support God's plan and purposes for the Jews. Gentiles in the Church must also affirm the Jewish identity of the Messianic Jewish community. We must find ways as part of the Church to encourage the Messianic Jewish community to identify itself with the mainstream Jewish community.

The Church should also support Messianic Jewish efforts to remain part of the Jewish community. This may mean affirming Messianic Jewish congregations, encouraging Messianic Jews to make *aliyah* (immigrate) to Israel or at least celebrate the Jewish holidays, especially with families and friends who might not yet know the Messiah. The Church also needs to encourage Messianic Jews to remain a faithful part of the Jewish community. The Abrahamic covenant has not been rescinded, and Messianic Jews are still part of this ancient agreement between God and our forefather Abraham.

Second, the Church must accept the mandate in Romans 1:16 and 11:11 and bring the Gospel to the Jew first, thereby making the Jewish people jealous. Jewish outreach can never become the great omission of the Great Commission. Gentiles must draw close enough to the Jewish people in order to make the remnant jealous. Gentile Christians need to lead the charge in denouncing the evils of the past such as the Holocaust so that Jews will now see the Church as God intended and become jealous of the Jewish Messiah living in the hearts of the true and authentic, faith-filled members of His Body.

It is to the fulfillment of this magnificent future covenantal convergence that this chapter is dedicated.

> *For I do not want you, brethren, to be uninformed of this mystery—so that you will not be wise in your own estimation—that a partial hardening has happened to Israel until the fullness of the Gentiles has come in; and so all Israel will be saved.* (Romans 11:25–26)

Together, then, Messianic Jews and Gentile followers of Yeshua, bound together through the Messiah and Abrahamic covenant, must work together as partners with God in progressing towards this great day of covenantal convergence. In that day the Jewish people will be all God intended, as the Messiah will establish His rightful throne in a literal and renewed Jerusalem. Both Jews and Gentiles will then rejoice in the knowledge of the Lord that fills the earth as the waters fill the sea (Isaiah 11:9–12).

An Evangelical Theologian Interacts with Messianic Jewish Theology: A Providential Journey Toward a Professional "Take"

A. Boyd Luter, Ph.D.

Before proceeding further, I wish to thank Dr. Jeffrey Seif, my associate at King's University and project editor, for his gracious invitation to contribute this chapter. If nothing else is accomplished, this wonderful opportunity has allowed me to: (1) look back and track a personal journey the Lord has providentially led me through for the past four and a half decades, to the point of being somewhat prepared to (2) share a reasonably informed opinion on what has been presented earlier in this book regarding the present status of Messianic Jewish Theology. Those two points provide the "shape" (i.e., outline) for the remainder of what appears below.

My Providential Guided Tour of the Context for Messianic Jewish Theology

Sometimes, occurrences in life that seem small at the time turn out, in retrospect, to have great significance. For example, it appeared that Ruth "just so happened"[1] (Ruth 2:3) to choose to glean in the field of Boaz, but it led to the birth of King David (4:22). Similarly, the casting of the lot (Heb. *pur*) in Esther 2:7 allowed enough time to pass during the year in question for the people of Israel to be spared from genocide, which is commemorated annually by the Jewish in the feast of Purim (9:23–26). Finally, it was the insomnia of King Ahasuerus (Esther 6:1–

---

[1] The Hebrew noun *miqreh* here in Ruth 2:3 may be rendered as "accident, chance" (BDB, 900), but it is clear in this context that the wording is tongue-in-cheek and is intended to make it clear that "...[D]ivine providence is the cause" (TWOT, 814).

3) that led to the king honoring Mordecai and him later becoming authority-wise in Persia "second only to King Ahasuerus" (10:3). Sooner or later, the astute believer comes to realize that such occurrences are the providence of God—what I call "God behind the seen."[2]

Prior to the invitation to contribute the present chapter, I had never seriously reflected on the possibility that the chain of events I am about to describe could be the Lord guiding me toward a deeper interest in— and to some extent, a closer relationship to—Messianic Judaism. Because there was much more to the Lord's "guided tour" than I would have ever thought, though, it has proven to be both an intriguing and eye-opening experience. And, apparently, I have not been a particularly astute believer (see the paragraph above), because it has taken me this long to perceive "God behind the seen" in all of the following far-more-than-ongoing-coincidence events and influences.

As far as I am aware, next to nothing in my background as a child would have prompted me toward a personal interest in Messianic Jews or their theology. I grew up in a very liberal United Methodist congregation, had only a general knowledge of the Holocaust and was completely unaware that there was such a thing as Jewish Christians.

First Inklings of Messianic Jews

My conversion to Christ occurred in 1970, at the beginning of my senior year at Mississippi State University. That timing was roughly in the middle of the Jesus Movement, the last real culture-wide revival in the United States. At that time, however, I was completely unaware that the Movement was stirring to faith in Jesus a number of Jews who would later become prominent leaders within Messianic Judaism.

Because I came to faith through the ministry of Campus Crusade for Christ, I went to a Crusade Christmas Conference in December 1970 in Atlanta, where I was initially exposed to the music of the Jews for Jesus musical group, "The Liberated Wailing Wall."[3] Next summer, I attended a Campus Crusade Institute for Biblical Studies held on the campus of Southern Methodist University in Dallas, where I met Hebrew Christian Zola Levitt (1938–2006), who was at that time just about to begin his ministry.

---

[2] Note the subtitle of the commentary volume on Ruth and Esther I co-authored with Barry Davis: *Ruth and Esther: God Behind the Seen*, 2nd Ed. (Fearn, Ross-shire, Scotland: Christian Focus Publications, 2003).

[3] This exposure to Messianic Jewish music was quickly broadened in the summer of 1972, when I attended Campus Crusade's Explo '72 conference in Dallas.

Initial Exposures to Messianic Jewish Theology

In the fall of 1972—partly as a result of the Campus Crusade influence mentioned above—I began ministry training at Dallas Theological Seminary. In my first semester at DTS, as part of a field education course, I attended a Messianic service at Beth Sar Shalom in Dallas that made a huge impression that stuck with me. In the summer of 1974, I was part of a study trip to the Holy Land through DTS, which marked me deeply.

In my first pastorate, in the early 1980s, (now Dr.[4]) Arnold Fruchtenbaum came to the church and presented his excellent "Christ in the Passover" demonstration in an Easter service, which I found fascinating. Later, Arnold invited me to take part in a Passover *Seder* meal in San Antonio, hosted by Ariel Ministries, which he had recently founded.[5] While each of these exposures whetted my thirst to learn more about Jewish Christianity and its theological beliefs, I did not yet comprehend the factors leading to the gradual emergence of the full-blown Messianic Jewish movement.

Opportunities for In-Depth Study of Scriptural Issues Related to Messianic Judaism

In 1988, I became Chair of the Bible Exposition Department at Talbot School of Theology. As part of that position, I inherited the offering the Daniel-Revelation course required for M.Div. and M.A. students. That (initially daunting!) teaching responsibility forced me to come face-to-face with biblical and theological factors I had missed (or skirted) in my previous top-heavily New Testament teaching repertoire.

Specifically, I was now confronted with numerous ideas and passages that had vast ramifications for how to view the Jewish people in God's plan, including Messianic believers. Alongside that challenge, there were several invitations to speak in Messianic Jewish congregations in Southern California in which Talbot students were serving as rabbis, which greatly piqued my interest!

In 1997, Dr. Paul Feinberg, himself a Jewish Christian, suffered a sudden illness, and Dr. Wayne House asked me to step in and quickly write a book chapter for a volume commemorating the 50th anniversary

---

[4] He received his Ph.D. from New York University in 1989.
[5] Arnold's previous ministry was with the American Board of Missions to the Jews (now Chosen People Ministries).

of the modern State of Israel.[6] Among the joyful and unanticipated consequences of that unexpected opportunity was a period of intense study on what the Lord has long been, and is, doing in and through Messianic Jews.[7]

In Summer 1998, I was a co-leader for a group of students from Cedarville University going to Israel to take a study course at Jerusalem University College.[8] To try to guarantee the students' course credits would transfer back to Cedarville, I became the "tutor" who clarified the material presented in class by the instructor, re-presenting it in simplified form the next morning before the next class session. Surprisingly, everybody in the class ended up attending my tutoring. Still, nobody learned as much as I did, doing all the extra daily preparation. And, the material being covered burned into me a deep love for the Land of Israel—and also began to open my eyes to the spiritual blindness of the Jewish population of Israel, much of which is very secular and irreligious.

Moving forward, in 1999, after arriving at Criswell College in Dallas, I became friends with (now Dr.[9]) Jim Sibley, a former missionary to Israel, who was then serving as the Coordinator of Jewish Ministries for the North American Mission Board of the Southern Baptist Convention but had an office at Criswell. Over the next four and a half years that I was at Criswell, Jim and I had numerous discussions that pushed forward my understanding of Messianic Jews and their theology.[10] (At that point, neither of us had any idea we would both take part in the Messianic Jewish Theology Summit[11] held at The King's

---

[6] Actually, the book was made up of papers presented—except mine—at a conference in Jerusalem in 1997 sponsored by Jews for Jesus. I could not attend and present because the conference budget did not allow for another plane ticket to Jerusalem, and Dr. Feinberg's advance-purchase ticket was non-refundable.

[7] That chapter was published as A.B. Luter, "Israel and the Nations in God's Redemptive Plan," in H.W. House, gen. ed., *Israel, The Land and the People* (Grand Rapids: Kregel, 1998), 283–97. However, the first edition is now out of print. The second edition is available as *Israel, The Land and the People: An Evangelical Affirmation of God's Promises* (San Francisco: Jews for Jesus, 1998/2012).

[8] This is the current name for what was long called the Institute for Holy Land Studies, located on the slope of Mount Zion in Jerusalem.

[9] He received his Ph.D. from Southwestern Baptist Theological Seminary in 2012.

[10] Dr. Sibley is currently a Professor of Biblical Studies at Israel College of the Bible, Netanya, Israel.

[11] The occasion for the August 2016 Messianic Jewish Theology Summit and Bible Conference was the announcement that Baker Books was taking over the publication of the Tree of Life Version () of the Scriptures, which was produced by a predominantly Messianic Jewish translation team.

University campus in Southlake, TX, in August 2015—or that both of us would be involved, in different ways, in the present volume.)

How Messianic Jews / Messianic Jewish Theology Became "Personal" to Me

Up to this point in my Divinely guided journey, I now realize that, while I was strongly interested in emerging Messianic Judaism and its theology, I did not really—as they say in my native Deep South—"have a dog in that hunt" (*i.e.*, a personal stake in what was going on). Although I fully realized that "total objectivity" is impossible, [12] I apparently was still strongly attempting to maintain an objective distance from the wider complex of issues related to Messianic Judaism and its theology.

In 2011, though, things quickly changed. The issue that brought that about doesn't matter nearly so much as that it succeeded in making Messianic Judaism and Messianic Jewish Theology "up-close and personal" for me. What happened was that a book review I published led quickly to a scholarly paper, which, in astoundingly short order (providentially?), was published as a journal article. What I had written prompted a rejoinder from the author of the book I'd reviewed in the same journal in which my article was published. Finally, the rejoinder's weak content and *ad hominem* tone led to me being allowed to have the final word in a surrejoinder. This entire whirlwind of words was compressed into a period of a year and a half[13]—and I didn't even mention that my wife and I took a trip to Israel—her first, my third—in March 2011.

Before my theological response to the material in this book, I should mention two people, a paper and a publication regarding the most recent steps in God taking me on His guided tour of Messianic

---

[12] This is a point made frequently in recent years. An accessible recent example in regard to interpreting the Bible is J.S. Duvall and J.D. Hays, *Grasping God's Word: A Hands-on Approach to Reading, Interpreting and Applying the Bible,* 3rd Ed. (Grand Rapids: Zondervan, 2012), 146.

[13] The book was Gary Burge, *Jesus and the Land: The New Testament Challenge to "Holy Land" Theology* (Grand Rapids: Baker, 2010). My review was in the *Journal of the Evangelical Theological Society* 54 no. 1 (March 2011), 217–21. My article was A.B. Luter, "The Land as Covenant Backdrop: A Modest Response to Burge and Waltke," *Criswell Theological Review* New Series 9/1 (Fall 2011), 59–73. The reply was G. Burge, "Rejoinder to Boyd Luter—*Jesus and the Land,*" *CTR* N.S. 9/2 (Spring 2012), 76–78. My "last word" was A.B. Luter, "Surrejoinder to Gary Burge—"The Land as Covenant Backdrop," *CTR* N.S. 10/1 (Fall 2012), 107–108.

Judaism/theology. First, Jeff Seif (mentioned above) invited me to do a paper at the Messianic Jewish Theology Summit in August 2015.[14] It turned out to be a wonderful experience, as I was privileged to present alongside the brilliant Messianic Jewish polymath Dr. Michael Brown. Also, the Fall 2015 issue of the *Criswell Theological Review* contained my review of the volume of papers originally given at a conference focusing on Israel sponsored by Chosen People Ministries, which was held in New York City in October 2013. That book was edited by well-known Jewish Christians Darrell Bock and Mitch Glaser—also a contributor to the present volume—and contained a foreword by well-known author and Jewish believer Joel Rosenberg.[15]

Last but certainly not least, one of my newest colleagues at The King's University is Dr. David Rudolph, a highly respected Messianic Jewish leader and scholar.[16] When David was being interviewed last year, I called to introduce myself, and he said he had a journal article of mine sitting on his desk. I was both flattered and humbled that a scholar of Dr. Rudolph's stature would consult something I had researched and composed.

Also, I would be remiss if I did not acknowledge up-front that several aspects of what follows are directly informed by material in the excellent volume David Rudolph co-edited with Dr. Joel Willits, *An Introduction to Messianic Judaism*.[17] Although that book does not deal with Messianic Jewish Theology in much depth, it certainly filled in many gaps in my understanding of the development of, and, in numerous cases, the variety within, wider Messianic Judaism.

Bottom line: In the earlier periods I described above, I became *intellectually engaged* with Messianic Judaism and its theology. But only in the last two periods did I become *both intellectually engaged with and emotionally passionate* about Messianic Judaism/theology. Why? Because I finally "closed the distance": I no longer thought of Messianic Judaism as some broad, faceless movement and accompanying theology. What I now thought of—and felt—was, and is, Messianic Jewish believers with individual faces ... and hearts that fuel their theology and theology-based practice.

---

[14] My presentation was titled "What If the *First* Council of Nicea Had Proceeded Like a *Second* Council of Jerusalem?"

[15] A.B. Luter, Review of The People, the Land and the Future of Israel: Israel and the Jewish People in the Plan of God, CTR N.S. 13/1 (Fall 2015), 136–139.

[16] M.A., Gordon-Conwell Theological Seminary; Ph.D., Cambridge University.

[17] D. Rudolph and J. Willits, gen. eds., Introduction to Messianic Judaism: Its Ecclesial Context and Biblical Foundations (Grand Rapids: Zondervan, 2013).

A Somewhat-Informed Personal "Take" on Messianic Jewish Theology

From a "helicopter view," the preceding chapters in this volume strike me as similar to the terrain over which the Tour de France bicycle race is contested annually. Some of it is flat, and the cyclists can proceed with great speed. However, a good bit of the course is mountainous and full of sharp curves, requiring cyclists to work much harder and watch the terrain more carefully. As a result, the Tour stages that are in the mountains take much longer to complete and usually are far more demanding and depleting to the rider.

This analogy makes the point nicely that several of the chapters I am reviewing are a "steep climb," so to speak, while others are written at a simpler (or, at least, more readily understood by non-specialists) level and are thus quicker to read and digest. It is also true that several of the chapters are quite lengthy, while the remaining chapters, though not what I would call "short," certainly are brief by comparison.

Initial "Big Picture" Points Worth Noting

In general, it is a tenuous undertaking to attempt to discern much from *the number of footnotes* authors utilize in their essays. Yet, on some occasions, the sheer contrast in numbers is simply too much to ignore.

Consider the following: In the eight previous chapters in this volume, there are 450 footnotes. That is an average of just over 56 footnotes per chapter. However, only three of the chapters contain approximately that average (of about 56 footnotes): (1) Daniel Juster's "Theology the Jewish Way: Remembering the Lord Who Brought Us Out of Egypt," with 54 footnotes; (2) Vered Hillel's "Messianism in Jewish Literature Beyond the Hebrew Bible," with 58 footnotes; and (3) Jeffrey Seif's "The Way We Were: The Truth About So-Called 'Christian' Origins," with 61 footnotes. The remaining chapters range from a high of 136 footnotes in Seth Postell's "Messianism in the Hebrew Bible" to a low of *zero(!)* in Paul Wilbur's and Greg Silverman's "The Revival of Messianic Jewish Worship." Hence, because these numbers are so strikingly different, it is evident that the depth of research behind the various essays varied greatly.

A similar observation jumps out when comparing the *lengths* of the different chapters. The average chapter length in this volume is about 35 pages. However, only one chapter (Mitch Glaser's "Not Forgotten or Forsaken: God's Plan and Purpose for Israel and the Jewish People") is in that general page range. The remaining seven chapters vary from some 80 pages for Seth Postell's essay to around 15 pages for Jacob Rosenberg's "Core Practices in Messianic Judaism."

Certainly, every chapter in an edited, multi-authored work should not be "homogenized" size-wise (*i.e.*, nearly identical in length). However, from my editorial experience, it is definitely more common for an editor (or editors) to emphasize expected length parameters for chapters up-front and to attempt to enforce them so that the chapters, as the parts of a whole, will "fit together" reasonably well due to the more-or-less comparable lengths of the contributions.

In this case, two plausible explanations could lie behind these observed apparent major discrepancies in the research depth and length of the preceding chapters:

1. Some chapters' topics may have a much longer and stronger "research trail" than others. *(This may largely explain why, e.g., Wilbur and Silverman's chapter has no footnotes: They are essentially recounting from memory the relatively short history of the development of distinctively Messianic Jewish music and worship. It also explains why in Rosenberg's chapter, the "Core Practices in Messianic Judaism" are only relatively sketchily developed: Messianic Jews are still, in many cases, feeling their way along toward establishing contemporary movement "traditions" that properly honor their Jewish forebears while also being sensitive to New Covenant theological realities and the moving of the Holy Spirit.)*

2. It may have been necessary to lay a much more detailed, scholarly foundation for some crucial theological issues than for others. *(This could go a long way toward explaining why Postell's and Juster's chapters are significantly longer. After all, this book is about Messianic Jewish Theology, and these two chapters focus on those two central terms: Postell deals with "Messianism in the Hebrew Bible," the very basis of what Jewish believers affirm about Yeshua as their Messiah; Juster deals with the most foundational of all the loci of systematic theology—the doctrine of God (i.e., "In the beginning God..." [Gen. 1:1a,]).*

3. Also, it is of course quite possible that *both* of these explanations are true.

Beyond such initial observations, I would characterize all the chapters in this volume as delightful reading and quite informative for a *Goy* (Gentile) reader such as myself. That is true even for one who is somewhat conversant with many of the theological and practical issues up for discussion in Messianic Judaism today.

As will be seen below, "the whole is greater than the sum of its parts," because while each chapter makes its own unique contribution, it is also a "building block" in the overall presentation and its cumulative impact. In making those unique contributions, the meaning of the term "theology" as usually employed in evangelical Christian circles is expanded to its fullest extent, while at the same time missing its most common evangelical expression: systematic (or doctrinal) theology.[18]

That does not mean, however, that the preceding chapters are lacking in doctrinal reasoning or perspective. Both Postell's lengthy study of Messianism throughout the Hebrew Bible and Juster's assembling of what the Hebrew Bible teaches about God are indeed serious contributions utilizing the methodology of biblical theology. In addition, Glaser and Johnson skillfully extrapolate the wider theological ramifications of the Abrahamic Covenant. And Hillel's excellent essay extends a type of biblical theology methodology to exacting analysis of the Jewish extra-biblical literature.

Three of the four remaining chapters, one way or another, fit best within the dated (but in this case accurate) category of practical theology: Bjoraker's contribution asks and answers the question as to the most appropriate way to communicate the Scriptures for Jews. Wilbur's and Silverman's reflections have much to say about the practical area of worship. Then, Rosenberg's chapter on the "core practices" of Messianic Judaism deals with "where the rubber meets the road" in the ongoing rhythms of Messianic Jewish life.

The remaining chapter is Seif's contribution. Among standard evangelical theological categories, it is closest to church history/historical theology, focusing on the period traditionally known as

---

[18] This reviewer does not know whether the absence of a chapter developing a systematic theology perspective, in a volume focused on Messianic Jewish Theology, was purposeful or not. Though Dr. Bjoraker states this is a volume of systematic theology, it would be the most unusual "systematic theology" work I have ever read. However, the perception among some Messianic Jews—including at least twice earlier in this volume—that the approach of typical evangelical systematic theology is captive to Greek categories may well be a factor in the theologizing of the wider Messianic Jewish movement in the time ahead. Until what approximates an up-to-date Messianic Jewish systematic theology appears—if it does—the spadework done is such works as Richard Harvey's *Mapping Messianic Jewish Theology* (Carlisle: Paternoster, 2009), remains valuable guides.

the early Church Fathers, immediately after the New Testament Era. As his chapter subtitle ("The Truth about So-Called 'Christian' Origins") crystallizes and, as the content of his chapter makes clear, though, nothing approaching a balanced telling of the story of the early Patristic Era regarding Messianic Jews has become common knowledge in evangelical Christian circles to this point in time.

Review of Chapter One

William Bjoraker (Ph.D., Fuller Theological Seminary) is Faculty in Biblical Studies, William Carey International University. In my considered opinion, his chapter, "The Place of Story and Storytelling in a Jewish and Messianic Jewish Theology: Rediscovering the Lost Treasures of Hebraic Narrative Epistemology," is at once the most *creative*—and potentially most *controversial*—essay in this volume to at least a segment of evangelical Christianity.

The *creative* aspects of Bjoraker's contribution are far greater than the comparatively small part that may be *controversial*. His essay is organized around ten "narratives" that have to do with story/storytelling. In order, they are:

Narrative 1:   Hebraic Theology Is Based on Story

Narrative 2:   The Hebraic and Jewish Roots of Story and Storytelling

Narrative 3:   "Hear O Israel": Orality Is Fundamental to Human Communication

Narrative 4:   European Enlightenment Epistemology

Narrative 5:   Hebraic Epistemology

Narrative 6:   Jewish *Midrash* and Story

Narrative 7:   The Power of Story

Narrative 8:   Yeshua the Messiah and Story

Narrative 9:   The Postmodern Moment and Its Prospects for Story

Narrative 10: Storytelling in Contemporary Jewish Ministry

I am in near-complete agreement with eight of these: (1) Bjoraker makes his case well that "Hebraic theology is based on story"; (2) story/storytelling indeed has very deep Hebraic/Jewish "roots"; (3) orality is indeed "fundamental to human communication" and the entirety of Scripture (the Hebrew Bible and New Testament) came into being in oral cultures[19]; (4) and 5) the stark contrast drawn between Hebraic and Enlightenment epistemology is, to the best of my knowledge, on-target and a most-helpful analysis; 6) Bjoraker describes Hebraic *midrash* accurately (*i.e.*, as narrative commentary that fills in the gaps), though I'd have preferred he call for more caution in such "imaginative reconstruction"; and (7) and (9). Without question, story/storytelling is powerful—*when communicated well!* —and, also without question, the postmodern mindset is far more accessible ("open") to story/storytelling than to traditional evangelism or apologetics.

It is Narrative 8 ("Yeshua the Messiah and Story") that, in my respectful opinion, goes "beyond what is written" (1 Corinthians 4:6,). Dr. Bjoraker even begins with an accurate proportioning between the part of Scripture that is narrative and that which is not (about 70% narrative, 30% non-narrative). The problem arises—in regard to Narratives 8 and 10—when Bjoraker extrapolates from the above correct proportioning of Scripture genre-wise to both the way Jesus taught and the way the communication of Scripture should take place in Messianic Jewish ministry today, claiming Jesus primarily taught by story (*i.e.*, parable) and metaphor, then asserting Messianic Jewish ministries today should ideally follow that same 70% narrative/parable proportion.

To utilize the most Jewish of the Gospels (Matthew) as a counterpoint of sorts, by my admittedly unscientific count, the First Gospel includes about 60% narrative and 18% parable and metaphor. However, three important points need to be made here:

1. Matthew *also* contains about 20% standard didactic instruction by Yeshua;

---

[19] Not only do I agree with Dr. Bjoraker, but I co-authored, with Dr. Richard Wells, *Inspired Preaching* (Nashville: Broadman & Holman, 2002), a volume which explores the orality factor and its rhetorical/literary ramifications in regard to all of the New Testament books.

2. The very chapter in which Yeshua begins His ministry of parables (Matthew 13) is 63.8% parable and 36.2% regular teaching—including the primary reason He spoke in parables: "because seeing they do not see, and hearing they do not hear nor do they understand" (13:13,). In other words, according to Matthew 13, Yeshua's ministry in parables had more to do with withholding spiritual truth from "blind" unbelievers than communicating with believers;

3. Though containing considerable parabolic material, both of the remaining major discourses in Matthew after chapter 13—chapter 18 and chapters 24-25—begin with standard instruction (i.e., 18:1-9; 24:1-31) before the parables are added for illustrative/application purposes.

To be clear: Dr. Bjoraker's chapter is an outstanding contribution! His "diagnosis" is right on target. However, his "prescribed treatment" is overstated according to what is actually seen in Matthew and thus requires further discussion to arrive at a balanced position in regard to narrative/storying in preaching ministry today.

Review of Chapter Two

Daniel Juster (M.Div., McCormick Seminary; Th.D., New Covenant International Seminary) is Founder and Executive Director of Tikkun Ministries International and an Adjunct Professor for The King's University. His chapter is titled "Theology the Jewish Way: Remembering the Lord Who Brought Us Out of Egypt."

After initially discussing arguments for the existence of God, Juster picks up what he considers the major passages dealing with the character and Person of God from the foundational chapters of all the Scriptures—Genesis 1–3—all the way through to Revelation. Overall, it is an excellent biblical theology survey and that includes his six wider "Conclusions About the Doctrine of God from Scripture." However, this reviewer feels further comments should be made in two areas:

1. Juster's earlier discussion on whether God is a singular or a "uni-plural" Being and his later brief comments on the Christian doctrine of the Trinity are well-considered. Christians—including evangelicals—must be aware that presenting *first* the three Persons of the Godhead *before* the unity of God is contrary to both the order of the revelation in the biblical text (*i.e.*, Deuteronomy 6:4 before

Matthew 28:19–20) and to the priority of monotheism to both Jews and, in this case especially, Messianic Jews.[20]

2. I commend Juster's bringing up Open Theism. It is true that the Openness of God viewpoint made noise about some important questions about the nature of God a decade and a half ago. But to my knowledge, none of the answers original to Open Theism were ever biblically valid[21]—I say that after spending most of my research time from 2001 to 2003 on Open Theism.[22] Actually considerably closer in thought patterns to Process Theology/Philosophy than to evangelical Arminianism, Open Theism portrays God as vulnerable to failure (*i.e.*, not omnipotent) and sometimes mistaken about what will happen in the future (*i.e.*, not omniscient)[23]—both very serious assertions and both completely contrary to the detailed description of God's attributes in Psalm 139.[24]

Review of Chapter Three

Seth Postell (Ph.D., Golden Gate Baptist Theological Seminary) is Faculty in Biblical Studies, Israel College of the Bible. His lengthy contribution, "Messianism in the Hebrew Bible," echoes works by his doctoral supervisor, John Sailhamer, of which this reviewer is aware[25] at certain points. Apparently, a number of aspects of this long essay are

---

[20] I made very similar remarks in the paper I presented at the Messianic Theology Summit: "What If the *First* Council of Nicea Had Proceeded Like a *Second* Council of Jerusalem?"

[21] Before claims arise that Open Theists raised the issue of the need to revise the previous understanding of God's immutability, it should be understood that the shift on immutability had begun in earnest in the 1980s but was a "quiet revolution." How do I know? Because I am one of those who changed my view on Greek-based immutability in the early '80s. So I was quite surprised when Open Theists brought up immutability as "their issue," when I knew full well that the Openness types were only popularizers, not original theological thinkers/innovators at all.

[22] e.g., Review of C. Pinnock, *Most Moved Mover: A Theology of God's Openness* (Grand Rapids: Baker, 2001), in *JETS* 45/4 (2002), 720–722; Review of G. Boyd, *Satan and the Problem of Evil: Constructing a Trinitarian Warfare Theodicy* (Downers Grove: IVP, 2001), in *JETS* 46/1 (2003), 158–160; and A.B. Luter and E.H. McGowin, "From Bad to Worse: A Portrait of Open Theism as a Theological System," *CTR* N.S. 1/2 (Spring 2004), 147–165.

[23] R.E. Picirilli, "An Arminian Response to John Sanders' *The God Who Risks*," *JETS* 44 (Sept. 2000), 483.

[24] Particularly troubling has been Open Theism's very odd—and *very* distorting—tendency in biblical exegesis, *i.e.*, claiming their presumed exegetical positions *correct* simply because they are *possible*, though hardly probable.

[25] Notably, J.H. Sailhamer, The Pentateuch as Narrative: A Biblical-Theological Commentary (Grand Rapids: Zondervan, 1992) and J.H. Sailhamer, The Meaning of the Pentateuch: Revelation, Composition and Interpretation (Downers Grove: IVP, 2009).

adapted from his dissertation, which is now published as *Adam as Israel*.[26]

To this reviewer, it is striking that the proportion of the chapter expounding the messianic material in the Torah (5 books) is far longer than the discussion for the rest of the Hebrew Bible (19 books in the HB, 34 books in the Bible read by most evangelicals). The primary reason for the focus on the early chapters of Genesis has to do with the failure of Adam in Genesis 1–3. Postell's thesis that Israel is given the task at which Adam failed is, with few exceptions, convincingly made throughout his chapter.

In the end, Postell recaps and well states that Messianic prophecy in the Hebrew Bible is neither "scattered nor random." After carefully reading Sailhamer's related works, I commend Postell for clarifying some aspects of Sailhamer's views I did not previously understand completely. And, it all points forward to the ultimate fulfillment in the Messiah, Yeshua, "the last Adam" (1 Corinthians 15:45,).

Review of Chapter Four

Vered Hillel (Ph.D., Hebrew University, Jerusalem) is Provost, Messianic Jewish Theological Institute. Her meticulously documented chapter, "Messianism in Jewish Literature Beyond the Bible," deals with Second Temple Jewish literature that evangelical Christians, other than a relative handful of evangelical specialists, have never heard of beyond the categories Apocrypha, Pseudepigrapha and Dead Sea Scrolls (*i.e.*, Qumran writings), as well as the traditional Jewish rabbinic writings. Even this reviewer had only done spotty previous study related to these documents.

Hillel's study of Jewish Messianism in this Second Temple literature begins with three scriptural ideas that appear again and again in connection with the Messianic conception in this literature: the scepter of Judah (Genesis 49:10); the star out of Jacob (Numbers 24:17); and the seed of David who was to be established forever (2 Samuel 7:12–16). Hillel also develops two "messianic typologies" with eschatological overtones: Davidic Rule (*restorative* messianism) and the Day of the Lord (*utopian* messianism).

---

[26] Seth D. Postell, *Adam as Israel* (Eugene: Pickwick, 2011).

Significantly, the major early Jewish rabbinical writings picked up more or less whole the perspectives of the Second Temple Era Jewish writings mentioned above. This demonstrates the strong impact of the Second Temple extra-biblical writings on Jewish exegesis of Messianic scriptural texts. It also underlines why Messianic Jews today need to be more conversant with Second Temple Jewish writings outside the Hebrew Bible and why evangelical Christians seeking to understand either Jewish eschatology of the New Testament Era or Messianic Jewish eschatology today do well to follow suit.

Review of Chapter Five

Jeffrey Seif (D.Min., Southern Methodist University) is University Distinguished Professor of Bible, The King's University. His chapter, "The Way We Were: The Truth About So-Called 'Christian' Origins," offers close documentation of a conflict, which I'd never even heard of, that greatly impacted early Messianic Jews, though it occurred in a historical context I considered myself fairly conversant in. It also contains an interpretive perspective on the Gospel of Matthew that is well worth considering[27] and a unique window on Messianic Jews of the era from the Odes of Solomon.

Most Gentile evangelical Christians are at least generally aware of the Jewish revolt against the Romans in AD 66–73, which resulted in the utter destruction of Jerusalem, including the Second Temple, in AD 70. Many—but fewer—Gentile evangelicals have some passing awareness of the Bar Kochba Revolt in AD 132–135. But another, if somewhat smaller, Temple, like the one in Jerusalem—in Egypt? Unthinkable to me … *until now!* And that the Roman authorities had the Jewish population in North Africa (150,000 in Alexandria alone) effectively annihilated—several hundred thousand in all? Incredible, I thought! Apparently, I had not taken into account the Romans' desire of to get on top of any further possible revolts by the Jews in that region.

But that warfare may not be the saddest part of Seif's chapter. To this reviewer, the way the leadership of both traditional Judaism and the by-now strongly Gentile church viewed and treated Messianic Jews was

---

[27] A recent accessible contribution in regard the Jewishness of Matthew is D.J. Harrington, "Matthew's Christian-Jewish Community," in Rudolph and Willitts, *Introduction to Messianic Judaism*, 159–167.

absolutely tragic.[28] They were caught in a most-painful and difficult crossfire, being too Christian for their fellow Jews and too Jewish for church leaders to accept. The content of the citations Seif produces from church leaders of the Patristic Era are, in fact, not notably different from the kinds of anti-Semitic attitudes that emerged in Hitler's Germany in the later 1920s and early '30s.

Review of Chapter Six

Jacob Rosenberg (Ph.D., Trinity Evangelical Divinity School) is Spiritual Leader, Adat Hatikvah Messianic Congregation, Deerfield, IL. Dr. Rosenberg also is head of the Theology Committee for the Union of Messianic Jewish Congregations.

Rosenberg's chapter, "Core Practices in Messianic Judaism," is a succinct survey of what he considers the "common core that unites the movement." Those factors are: (1) belief in Yeshua as the "promised divine Messiah of Israel; (2) a "high view of Scripture"; (3) Messianic congregations and synagogues; (4) the keeping of Jewish holidays (*i.e.*, holy days) and festivals; and (5) traditional life-cycle events, covering the life spectrum from birth to death (i.e., circumcision, Bar/Bat Mitzvah ceremonies, Messianic Jewish weddings and funerals, and more. Over the past decades, the Messianic Jewish movement has only become more consistent in keeping these core practices.[29]

At both the beginning and end of his chapter, Rosenberg echoes Richard Harvey's contention that Messianic Judaism "…refuses to partition Judaism and Christianity into two mutually exclusive theological systems."[30] With the entirety of the Hebrew Bible as inspired "common ground," this is a tightrope that is worth Messianic Jews walking, carefully but confidently.

---

[28] This is quite a different vantage point than that described by D. Rudolph, in "Messianic Judaism in Antiquity and in the Modern Era," in Rudoph and Willitts, *Introduction to Messianic Judaism*, 21–36.

[29] Natural supplementary discussions to the content in Rosenberg's chapter are D. Rudolph and S. Klayman, "Messianic Jewish Synagogues"; C. Kinbar, "Messianic Jews and Scripture"; and Kinbar, "Messianic Jews and Jewish Tradition," all in *Introduction to Messianic Judaism*, 37–50, 61–71, 72–81.

[30] Harvey, Mapping Messianic Jewish Theology, 96.

Review of Chapter Seven

Paul Wilbur (M.M., Indiana University) is a well-known Messianic Jewish musician and President, Wilbur Ministries. Greg Silverman (D.M.A., University of Arizona) is President of Greg Silverman Ministries and Faculty in Choral Music, Eastern University. Together they author "The Revival of Messianic Jewish Worship." Silverman writes the first, and shorter, part of the chapter, explaining the meaning of worship in Hebrew, what made David a model worshiper and how he developed the musical part of Israel's worship related to the Tabernacle during his reign. As Silverman completes this description, he also offers his conviction that, in contemporary Messianic Jewish worship, the Lord is putting into place the worship aspect of the fulfillment of raising up David's fallen tabernacle, as predicted in Amos 9:11. While this perspective does not obviously cohere with the apparent understanding of Amos 9:11–12 by Jacob/James at the Jerusalem Council in Acts 15:15–18, it is certainly worth pondering.

Without question, Wilbur's part of the chapter contains the most autobiographical material in any of the chapters in this volume. Having been converted in 1977, with his first Christian album released in 1979,[31] Paul Wilbur transitioned to recording—often significant Messianic Jewish music in the mid-1980s and, over the years, has come to serve as a sort of unofficial ambassador for Messianic worship/music internationally.[32]

Wilbur begins his portion of the chapter with further reflection on biblical material related to worship. He helpfully points out to the reader that music first appears in Scripture in Genesis 4 and is seen in relation to the heavenly throne room in Revelation several times, as well as that the worshipers God seeks must worship in "spirit and truth" (John 4:24,).[33] The rest of the chapter is an extraordinary "walk down memory lane" in regard to the Messianic Jewish organizations, leaders and artists who, in Wilbur's estimation, have made significant contributions to Messianic Jewish music and worship in the past generation—which he defines as 40 years (*i.e.*, roughly 1975–2015 [when this chapter was written]).

---

[31] Wilbur was then part of a Christian singing group called "Harvest," which, interestingly, included my present colleague at The King's University, Professor Ed Kerr, Director of the TKU Associate of Worship Leadership program.

[32] The biographical information included here was taken from the Biography section of the Wilbur Ministries website and may be accessed easily at *http://www.last.fm/music/Paul+Wilbur/+wiki.*

[33] The weakness of Wilbur and Silverman's chapter is what is not included. There is no focus on Messianic Jewish worship in the congregational/synagogue setting. However, Seth Klayman's "Messianic Worship and Prayer," in Rudolph and Willitts, *Introduction to Messianic Judaism*, 51–60.

Review of Chapter Eight

Mitch Glaser (Ph.D., Fuller Theological Seminary) is President, Chosen People Ministries. His chapter, "Not Rejected or Forgotten: God's Plan and Purpose for Israel and the Jewish People," was especially enjoyable for me to read because I have worked directly in this theological area off and on for almost 20 years.[34] And, for the most part, I agreed down to the smallest details with what Dr. Glaser set forth. Yet there are two related areas that deserve a little further discussion:

1. It is my considered opinion that adding "King" as a fourth separate aspect of the Abrahamic Covenant (*i.e.*, beyond Land, Seed and Blessing) muddies the water, given that the development of the Covenant is already far along before the first whiff of a Messianic King is encountered in Genesis 49:10. It is better to develop the idea of a dual concept of "Seed": (a) the plural descendants of Abraham (*i.e.*, Israel); and (b) the singular "Seed" (*i.e.*, Messiah).

2. While the Abrahamic Covenant is without question ultimately unconditional [35] at its "bedrock," given the covenant cutting ceremony portrayed in Abram's vision in Genesis 15:9–21, those with dispensational sympathies—which would include Mitch Glaser and me—still must pay attention to the one apparently conditional aspect found anywhere in the Abraham corpus (Genesis 12–25): After Abram was obedient, the Angel of the Lord says to him, "*Because* you have done this thing, and you did not withhold your son, your only son, I will richly bless you…" (Genesis 22:15, 18,), including most of the features of the Abrahamic Covenant going all the way back to Genesis 12:1–3. The word "because" here communicates the idea of conditionality. Interestingly, though, that puff of conditionality immediately vanishes from that point forward. In the repeating of the Covenant to Isaac after Abraham's death in Genesis 26:5, the wording is "because *Abraham* listened to My voice" (, emphasis mine) and obeyed…", and the conditionality angle never comes up again in regard to the Abrahamic Covenant. The theological point here would seem to be that God was testing

---

[34] *i.e.*, to Wayne House's invitation to write "Israel and the Nations in God's Redemptive Plan" for the Jerusalem conference and *Israel, the Land and the People.*

[35] *i.e.*, *unilateral*, depending on only one of the two parties to the covenant for it to continue in force.

Abraham in some unique way—on behalf of all his future descendants—in Genesis 22, and Abraham passed the test with flying colors![36]

---

[36] The discussion under (2) above reflects my long-considered interpretation of the "way too much to be mere coincidence" spread chiasm in Genesis (which I have been tweaking since 1997, when I wrote "Israel and the Nations in God's Redemptive Plan" [see p. 292]) found on the following page:

What's a Nice Gentile Boy Doing in a World That Embraces Messianic Jewish Theology?
A Response to A. Boyd Luter's
An Evangelical Theologian Interacts With Messianic Jewish Theology:
by Barri Cae Seif, Ph.D.

As I read through Dr. Luter's chapter, I could not help but feel grateful for his faith in Jesus. I enjoyed his initial reflection about his salvation experience, which occurred over 44 years ago. As I came to faith in Jesus/Yeshua in 1980, 10 years after Dr. Luter, many of the places Dr. Luter alighted upon intersected with me, as well. For me, reading him was, itself, a walk down memory lane.

Professor Luter shared about his association with many Messianic Jewish pioneers, one of whom was Zola Levitt. He also made note about Dallas Theological Seminary, Dr. Arnold Fruchtenbaum and Ariel Ministries, Beth Sar Shalom and so on. As a new Jewish believer who had just come to know Yeshua/Jesus, the first place I went after I came to faith in a Jewish delicatessen was Beth Sar Shalom, Dallas, on a Thursday afternoon, after which I made my way into Arnold's world, Dallas Seminary folk and the like.

Luter went on to reflect: "While each of these exposures whetted my thirst to learn more about Jewish Christianity and its theological beliefs, I did not yet comprehend the factors leading to the gradual emergence of the full-blown Messianic Jewish movement." He continues on to relate to how a set of circumstances, divinely guided, set him on a journey in which he became a major contributor to Messianic Jewish Theology before it was a popular subject. Luter lovingly reflected on his first journey to the land of Israel, noting it was there that God truly opened his eyes about replacement theology and the spiritual blindness of the Jews. Luter writes about a serendipitous encounter with Dr. Jim Sibley—a friend and mentor of mine. I knew Jim years ago when he and his wife Kathy served faithfully in Israel. Jim became a forceful figure within the Messianic movement. God strategically placed him at an influential and dynamic church, First Baptist Church of Dallas. There he thrived and honed his talents and skills, making him one of Christianity's more able theologians and Messianic Jewish friends. Little did Dr. Luter know how God used that friendship for good, years later.

Luter flashes forward to the year 2010. He says: "In the earlier periods ... I became *intellectually engaged* with Messianic Judaism and its theology. But, only in the last two periods did I become *both intellectually engaged with, and emotionally passionate in regard to,* Messianic Judaism/theology. ... Because I finally 'closed the distance' I no longer thought of Messianic Judaism as some broad faceless movement and accompanying theology. What I now thought of— and felt—was, and is, Messianic Jewish believers with individual faces... and hearts that fuel their theology and theology-based practice." Personally, as a Jewish believer, this is so important in bringing Jew and Gentile believers together. The church is a picture of Ruth and Naomi. Your people shall be my people and your God my God. (Ruth 1:16) Professor Luter got it; not only did Luter now have head knowledge, he had heart knowledge.

Luter's next section made me wonder if he has an affinity for the Tour de France. He likened Messianic Judaism to the famous bicycle competition. As an individual who also enjoys footnotes, this reviewer found it almost amusing to note his interest in the many numerical facets of this book. He first reflects on the number of pages per chapter, possibly because he was a contributor and wanted to make sure his own contribution was in the page range of the others. He also had great interest in the number of footnotes, or lack thereof, in this book. This reviewer appreciated Luter's CliffsNotes summary of the various chapters. He objectively addressed the highlights of each one and said it was a delight to him, a *Goy* (Gentile). Of particular interest was his taking a position contrary to one of Dr. Bjoraker's reflections on Yeshua. As Dr. Bjoraker is a storyteller, I gave him great latitude in his reflection. This reviewer has observed that storytellers can truly take a passage of Scripture and bring forth revelations never before seen. Systematic theologians like Dr. Luter, however, seem more inclined to place a premium on the disciplines of theological inquiry and are less inclined to abide narrative stories.

This reviewer appreciated the content Dr. Luter included from Dr. Juster and Dr. Postell—both of whom great storytellers. He gave a cursory reflection of Dr. Hillel's contribution, spending most of his energies on Dr. Seif's exposition. Luter seemed noticeably shaken at the sorrow Dr. Seif shared about the church's

Conclusion

If the previous chapters of this book are a fair indication, Messianic Judaism is in good stead as far as both its theological thinkers and practitioners are concerned. Also, I come away from this stimulating task as a reviewer with the gnawing awareness that most evangelical Christians do not have anything close to a "good read" on what is going on within the Messianic Jewish movement. If nothing else, it is hoped that this volume, and others like Rudolph's and Willitt's *Introduction to Messianic Judaism*, will begin to bridge that unfortunate gap.

---

treatment of the Messianic Jewish people: "They were caught in a most-painful and difficult crossfire," said he, "being too Christian for their fellow Jews and too Jewish for church leaders to accept." He observed the "content of the citations Seif produces from church leaders of the Patristic Era are, in fact, not notably different from the kinds of anti-Semitic attitudes that emerged in Hitler's Germany in the later 1920s and early '30s." Luter enjoyed the contributions of Paul Wilbur and Dr. Silverman. Messianic music has gained popularity, and it was a joy to see these gentlemen's contributions in this book. He concluded with reflection from Dr. Rosenberg and Dr. Glaser. This reviewer appreciated his conclusion.

Luter left me feeling good. He cared about our story. He listened to it. He got it! I thank God for this man who is a true Jew (Romans 2:28–29). He noted there remains much work in bridging the gap between evangelical Christians and Messianic Jews. In that regard, Professor Luter himself reminds me of the book you just read: He, like the volume, is a bridge-builder; he, like the book, is a pioneer. He may not see himself in the same light this reviewer sees him in, as a pioneer both within and outside the Messianic Jewish movement, but we often don't see ourselves and our stories as others do.

The New Testament is understood as the greatest story *ever* told; the Jewish connection to it is similarly understood as the greatest story *never* told. Having listened to it with Dr. Luter, with me, and with all on board in this seminal volume, and having considered what the Christian story looks like when seen through Jewish eyes, I hope you, like Dr. Luter, will walk away with a deeper appreciation for the ancient Jewish connection to Jesus' story, and a deeper connection to the modern Jewish people as we experience it in our own unique ways.

A (17:5-8 [to Abram]) **5** No longer will your name be Abram, but your name will be Abraham, because I make you the father of a multitude of nations. **6** Yes, I will make you exceedingly fruitful, and I will make you into nations, and kings will come forth from you. **7** Yes, I will establish My covenant between Me and you and your seed after you throughout their generations for an everlasting covenant, in order to be your God and your seed's God after you. **8** I will give to you and to your seed after you the land where you are an outsider—the whole land of Canaan—as an everlasting possession, and I will be their God."

B (22:16-18 [to Abraham]) **16** and said, "[B]ecause you have done this thing, and you did not withhold your son, your only son, [a] **17** I will richly bless you and bountifully multiply your seed like the stars of heaven, and like the sand that is on the seashore, and your seed will possess the gate of his enemies. **18** In your seed all the nations of the earth will be blessed—because *you* obeyed My voice."

B' (26:3-5 [to Yitzhak]) Live as an outsider in this land and I will be with you and bless you—for to you and to your seed I give all these lands—and I will confirm my pledge that I swore to Abraham your father. **4** I will multiply your seed like the stars of the sky and I will give your seed all these lands. And in your seed all the nations of the earth will continually be blessed, **5** because *Abraham* listened to My voice and kept My charge, My *mitzvot*, My decrees, and My instructions."

A' (35:10-12 [to Jacob]) **10** God said to him: "No longer will your name be Jacob, for your name will be Israel." So, He named him Israel. **11** God also said to him:"I am *El Shaddai*. Be fruitful and multiply. A nation and an assembly of nations will come from you. From your loins will come forth kings.**12** The land that I gave to Abraham and to Isaac—I give it to you, and to your seed after you I will give the land."

(All citations are from the ; emphasis mine)

First Time in History!

General Editor: Rabbi Barry Rubin
Theological Editor: Dr. John Fischer

The Complete Jewish Study Bible

Insights for Jews and Christians
—Dr. David H. Stern

A One-of-a-Kind Study Bible that illuminates the Jewish background and context of God's word so it is more fully understandable. Uses the updated *Complete Jewish Bible* text by David H. Stern, including notes from the *Jewish New Testament Commentary* and contributions from Scholars listed below. 1990 pages.

Hardback	978-1619708679	$49.95
Flexisoft	978-1619708693	$79.95
Leather	978-1619708709	$139.95

< Hardcover Edition

Leather Edition w/color gift box   Flexisoft Edition w/color sleeve

CONTRIBUTORS & SCHOLARS				QUOTES BY JEWISH SCHOLARS & SAGES
Rabbi Dr. Glenn Blank	Forbes	Rabbi Barney Kasdan	Rosenberg	Dr. Daniel Boyarin
Dr. Michael Brown	Rabbi Dr. David	Dr. Craig S. Keener	Rabbi Isaac Roussel	Dr. Amy-Jill Levine
Rabbi Steven Bernstein	Friedman	Rabbi Elliot Klayman	Dr. Michael Rydelnik	Rabbi Jonathan Sacks
Rabbi Joshua	Dr. Arnold	Jordan Gayle Levy	Dr. Jeffrey Seif	Rabbi Gamaliel
Brumbach	Fruchtenbaum	Dr. Ronald Moseley	Rabbi Tzahi Shapira	Rabbi Hillel
Rabbi Ron Corbett	Dr. John Garr	Rabbi Dr. Rich Nichol	Dr. David H. Stern	Rabbi Shammai
Pastor Ralph Finley	Pastor David Harris	Rabbi Mark J. Rantz	Dr. Bruce Stokes	Rabbi Akiva
Rabbi Dr. John Fischer	Benjamin Juster	Rabbi Russ Resnik	Dr. Tom Tribelhorn	Maimonides
Dr. Patrice Fischer	Rabbi Dr. Daniel Juster	Dr. Richard Robinson	Dr. Forrest Weiland	and many more
Rebbitzen Malkah	Dr. Walter C. Kaiser	Rabbi Dr. Jacob	Dr. Marvin Wilson	

Complete Jewish Bible: *An English Version*
—Dr. David H. Stern (Available March 2017)

Now, the most widely used Messianic Jewish Bible around the world, has updated text with introductions added to each book, written from a biblically Jewish perspective. The CJB is a unified Jewish book, a version for Jews and non-Jews alike; to connect Jews with the Jewishness of the Messiah, and non-Jews with their Jewish roots. Names and terms are returned to their original Hebrew and presented in easy-to-understand transliterations, enabling the reader to say them the way *Yeshua* (Jesus) did! 1728 pages.

Paperback	978-1936716845	$29.95
Hardcover	978-1936716852	$34.95
Flexisoft Cover	978-1936716869	$49.95

Jewish New Testament
—Dr. David H. Stern

The New Testament is a Jewish book, written by Jews, initially for Jews. Its central figure was a Jew. His followers were all Jews; yet no other version really communicates its original, essential Jewishness. Uses neutral terms and Hebrew names. Highlights Jewish references and corrects mistranslations. Freshly translated into English from Greek, this is a must read to learn about first-century faith. 436 pages

Hardback	978-9653590069	**JB02**	$19.99
Paperback	978-9653590038	**JB01**	$14.99
Spanish	978-1936716272	**JB17**	$24.99

Also available in French, German, Polish, Portuguese and Russian.

Jewish New Testament Commentary
—Dr. David H. Stern

This companion to the *Jewish New Testament* enhances Bible study. Passages and expressions are explained in their original cultural context. 15 years of research. 960 pages.

Hardback	978-9653590083	**JB06**	$34.99
Paperback	978-9653590113	**JB10**	$29.99

Is Christ *Really* The "End of The Law"?
Another Look at *Telos* in Romans 10:4
—Drs. Jeffrey and Barri Cae Seif

"There are few Pauline statements more controversial than Romans 10:4, specifically the meaning of the word τέλος, telos.

τέλος γὰρ νόμου Χριστὸς εἰς δικαιοσύνην παντὶ τῷ πιστεύοντι.

The verse has traditionally been rendered, "For Christ is the *end* of the Law for righteousness to everyone who believes." Some say, "For the *goal* at which the Torah aims is the Messiah" while others prefer *new beginning*. Still others offer, "For Messiah is the *end* of the Torah, that everyone who has faith may be justified" or "Messiah is the *culmination* of the Torah so that there may be righteousness for everyone believes." 179 Pages

Paperback	978-1733935418	$21.99

Messianic Jewish Orthodoxy
The Essence of Our Faith, History and Best Practices
–Dr. Jeffrey Seif, General Editor

A work from the moderate, conservative center of the Messianic Jewish revival. This book speaks to the interests that group and the Church have in Jews, Israel and eschatology, with a need for a more-balanced consideration of faith, theology and practice—from Jewish perspectives.

This is vital for the many tens of thousands of Jews who have come to faith and who participate in Messianic Jewish experience and also those who frequent churches. Our non-Jewish friends who associate with the Messianic Jewish movement will find this book beneficial as well. It represents some of our best thinking and practice. 314 pages

Paperback	978-1733935425	$26.99

Demonstrating the Wonderful Power and Word of God in
The Life and Ministry of ELIJAH and ELISHA
—Dr. Walter C. Kaiser, Jr.

It's no wonder Old Testament professor Walt Kaiser is one of America's most beloved Bible expositors. This series of studies on Elijah and Elisha is vintage Kaiser, interspersed with his trademark humor. Organized in outline format, it offers an easy-to-follow look at the lives of two of the most famous and lively prophets ever to grace the pages of the Old Testament. Highly recommended to enhance anyone's study of the Scriptures! 208 pages

Paperback	978-1733935449	$17.99

Social Justice The Bible and Application for Our Times
—Daniel C. Juster

In this work, addressing many of the social justice issues of today, one of the more seasoned Messianic Jewish leaders and scholars, Dr. Dan Juster, offers his thoughts. Not an academic book, we read what this well-known pioneer of Messianic Judaism, director of Tikkun International, founding president of the Union of Messianic Jewish Congregations and senior pastor of Beth Messiah Congregation from 1978-2012, thinks about the way our world is today. You will find his thoughts challenging and surprising. 124 pages

Paperback	978-1733935456	$12.99

The Book of Ruth
This delightful version of *The Book of Ruth* includes the full text from the *Complete Jewish Bible* on the left page of the two-page spread. On the right are artful illustrations with brief story summaries that can be read to young children. Can be read any time during the year, but especially on *Shavuot* (Pentecost), the anniversary of the giving of the Torah on Mount Sinai and when the Holy Spirit was poured out on Yeshua's disciples (Acts 2). *The Book of Ruth* points to Yeshua as the ultimate Kinsman Redeemer.
6 x 9 inches, 26 pages with full color illustrations.

Paperback	978-1-936716-94-4	$ 9.99

The Book of Esther
This delightful version of *The Book of Esther* includes the full text from the *Complete Jewish Bible* on the left page of the two-page spread. On the right are artful illustrations with brief story summaries that can be read to young children. Can be read any time during the year, but especially during *Purim*, the festival that celebrates how Queen Esther risked her life and became a vessel for the deliverance of her people Israel. Though God is not mentioned, Mordecai and Esther humbled themselves before God by fasting and praying, which showed dependence upon him. God answered and delivered his people while bringing the proud Haman to justice.
6 x 9 inches, 34 pages with full color illustrations.

Paperback	978-1-936716-95-1	$ 9.99

Dear You
Letters of Identity in Yeshua ~ for Women ~
—Victoria Humphrey

Dear You is about discovering the truth of who you are as a beloved and courageous daughter of the King. It is an invitation to uncover what Elohim says about you through Scripture, silencing all other noise that vies to define you. While weaving together personal testimonies from other women, along with an opportunity to unearth your own unique story, it presents the challenge to leave a shallow life behind by taking a leap into the abundant life Yeshua offers. 232 Pages

| Paperback | 978-1-7339354-0-1 | $19.99 |

A Life of Favor
A Family Therapist Examines the Story of Joseph and His Brothers
—Rabbi Russell Resnik, MA, LPCC

Favor is an inherent part of God's reality as Father, and properly understood, is a source of blessing to those who want to know him. The story of Jacob's sons points to a life of favor that can make a difference in our lives today. Excellent insight—judgments in exegesis are matched by skillful use of counseling principles and creative applications to contemporary situations in life and in the family. —Walter C. Kaiser, Jr. President Emeritus, Gordon-Conwell Theological Seminary, Hamilton, Mass. 212 Pages

| Paperback | 978-1936716913 | $19.99 |

Will the Nazi Eagle Rise Again?
What the Church Needs to Know about BDS and Other Forces of Anti-Semitism
–David Friedman, Ph.D.

This is the right book at the right time. exposing the roots of Anti-Semitism being resurrected in our days, especially in our Christian Church.
—Dr. Hans-Jörg Kagi, Teacher, Theologian, Basle, Switzerland
Timely and important response to the dangerous hatred of the State of Israel that is growing in society and in the Church. 256 pages

| Paperback | 978-1936716876 | $19.99 |

The Day Jesus Did Tikkun Olam
—Richard A. Robinson, Ph.D.

Easy-to-read, yet scholarly, explores ancient Jewish and Christian scriptures, relevant stories and biblical parallels, to explain the most significant Jewish value—*tikkun olam*—making this world a better place. This is a tenet of both religions, central to the person of Jesus himself. 146 pages
—Murray Tilles, Director, Light of Messiah Ministries; M.Div.
A wealth of scholarship and contemporary relevance with great insight into Jewish ethics and the teachings of Jesus.
—Dr. Richard Harvey, Senior Researcher, Jews for Jesus

| Paperback | 978-1-936716-98-2 | $ 18.99 |

Jewish Giftedness & World Redemption
The Calling of Israel
—Jim Melnick

All things are mortal but the Jew; all other forces pass, but he remains.
What is the secret of his immortality?

—Mark Twain, Concerning the Jews, *Harper's Magazine*, September, 1899.

The most comprehensive research of the unique achievements of the Jewish people. The author comes up with the only reason that makes sense of this mystery.

—Daniel C. Juster, Th.D., Restoration from Zion of Tikkun International

Paperback (280 Pages)   978-1-936716-88-3 $24.99

Messianic Judaism *A Modern Movement With an Ancient Past*
—David H. Stern

An updated discussion of the history, ideology, theology and program for Messianic Judaism. A challenge to both Jews and non-Jews who honor Yeshua to catch the vision of Messianic Judaism. 312 pages

Paperback   978-1880226339   **LB62** $17.99

Restoring the Jewishness of the Gospel
A Message for Christians
—David H. Stern

Introduces Christians to the Jewish roots of their faith, challenges some conventional ideas, and raises some neglected questions: How are both the Jews and "the Church" God's people? Is the Law of Moses in force today? Filled with insight! Endorsed by Dr. Darrell L. Bock. 110 pages

English - Paperback   978-1880226667   **LB70** $9.99
Spanish - Paperback   978-9653590175   **JB14** $9.99

The Return of the Kosher Pig *The Divine Messiah in Jewish Thought*
—Rabbi Tzahi Shapira

The subject of Messiah fills many pages of rabbinic writings. Hidden in those pages is a little known concept that the Messiah has the same authority given to God. Based on the Scriptures and traditional rabbinic writings, this book shows the deity of Yeshua from a new perspective. You will see that the rabbis of old expected the Messiah to be divine. Softcover, 352 pages.

"One of the most interesting and learned tomes I have ever read. Contained within its pages is much with which I agree, some with which I disagree, and much about which I never thought. Rabbi Shapria's remarkable book cannot be ignored."

—Dr. Paige Patterson, President, Southwest Baptist Theological Seminary

Paperback   978-1936716456   **LB81** $ 39.99

Messianic Jewish Commentary Series

Matthew Presents Yeshua, King Messiah
—Rabbi Barney Kasdan

Few commentators are able to truly present Yeshua in his Jewish context of his background, his family, even his religion. This commentator is well versed with first-century Jewish practices and thought, as well as the historical and cultural setting of the day, and the 'traditions of the Elders' that Yeshua so often spoke about. 448 pages

| Paperback | 978-1936716265 | **LB76** | $29.99 |

Rabbi Paul Enlightens the Ephesians on Walking with Messiah Yeshua
—Rabbi Barney Kasdan

The Ephesian were a diverse group of Jews and Gentiles, united together in Messiah. They definitely had an impact on the first century world in which they lived. But the Rabbi was not just writing to that local group. What is Paul saying to us? 160 pages.

| Paperback | 978-11936716821 | **LB99** | $17.99 |

Paul Presents to the Philippians Unity in the Messianic Community
—R. Sean Emslie

A worthy read and an appropriate study for any Messianic Jewish *talmid* or Christian disciple of Yeshua wanting to fairly and faithfully examine apostolic teaching. Emslie's investigation offers a keenly diligent analysis and faithfully responsible apostolic viewpoint. 165 pages

| Paperback | 978-1733935432 - Coming by June 30, 2020 | $18.99 |

James the Just Presents Application of Torah
—Dr. David Friedman

James (Jacob) one of the Epistles written to first century Jewish followers of Yeshua. Dr. David Friedman, a former Professor of the Israel Bible Institute has shed new light for Christians from this very important letter. 133 pages

| Paperback | 978-1936716449 | **LB82** | $14.99 |

John's Three Letters on Hope, Love and Covenant Fidelity
—Rabbi Joshua Brumbach

The Letters of John include some of the most beloved and often-quoted portions of scripture. Most people – scholars included – are confident they already have John's letters figured out. But do they really? There is a need for a fresh, post-supersessionist reading of John's letters that challenges common presuppositions regarding their purpose, message and relevance. 168 pages

| Paperback | 978-1-7339354-6-3 Coming by June 30, 2020 | $19.99 |

Jude On Faith and the Destructive Influence of Heresy
—Rabbi Joshua Brumbach

Almost no other canonical book has been as neglected and overlooked as the Epistle of Jude. This little book may be small, but it has a big message that is even more relevant today as when it was originally written. 100 pages

| Paperback | 978-1-936716-78-4 | **LB97** | $14.99 |

Yochanan (John) Presents the Revelation of Yeshua the Messiah
—Rabbi Gavriel Lumbroso

The Book of Revelation is perhaps the most mysterious, difficult-to-understand book in all of the Bible. Scholar after scholar, theologian after theologian have wrestled with all the strange visions, images and messages given by Yochanan (John), one of Yeshua's apostles. 206 pages

| Paperback | 978-1-936716-93-7 | $19.99 |

Psalms & Proverbs *Tehillim* תְּהִלִּים-*Mishlei* מִשְׁלֵי
—Translated by Dr. David Stern

Contemplate the power in these words anytime, anywhere: Psalms-*Tehillim* offers uplifting words of praise and gratitude, keeping us focused with the right attitude; Proverbs-*Mishlei* gives us the wisdom for daily living, renewing our minds by leading us to examine our actions, to discern good from evil, and to decide freely to do the good. Makes a wonderful and meaningful gift. 224 pages.

Paperback	978-1936716692	**LB90**	$9.99

At the Feet of Rabbi Gamaliel
Rabbinic Influence in Paul's Teachings
—David Friedman, Ph.D.

Paul (Shaul) was on the "fast track" to becoming a sage and Sanhedrin judge, describing himself as passionate for the Torah and the traditions of the fathers, typical for an aspiring Pharisee: "…trained at the feet of Gamaliel in every detail of the Torah of our forefathers. I was a zealot for God, as all of you are today" (Acts 22.3, CJB). Did Shaul's teachings reflect Rabbi Gamaliel's instructions? Did Paul continue to value the Torah and Pharisaic tradition? Did Paul create a 'New' Theology? The results of the research within these pages and its conclusion may surprise you. 100 pages.

Paperback	978-1936716753	**LB95**	$8.99

Debranding God *Revealing His True Essence*
—Eduardo Stein

The process of 'debranding' God is to remove all the labels and fads that prompt us to understand him as a supplier and ourselves as the most demanding of customers. Changing our perception of God also changes our perception of ourselves. In knowing who we are in relationship to God, we discover his, and our, true essence. 252 pages.

Paperback	978-1936716708	**LB91**	$16.99

Under the Fig Tree *Messianic Thought Through the Hebrew Calendar*
—Patrick Gabriel Lumbroso

Take a daily devotional journey into the Word of God through the Hebrew Calendar and the Biblical Feasts. Learn deeper meaning of the Scriptures through Hebraic thought. Beautifully written and a source for inspiration to draw closer to Adonai every day. 407 pages.

Paperback	978-1936716760	**LB96**	$25.99

Under the Vine *Messianic Thought Through the Hebrew Calendar*
—Patrick Gabriel Lumbroso

Journey daily through the Hebrew Calendar and Biblical Feasts into the B'rit Hadashah (New Testament) Scriptures as they are put in their rightful context, bringing Judaism alive in it's full beauty. Messianic faith was the motor and what gave substance to Abraham's new beliefs, hope to Job, trust to Isaac, vision to Jacob, resilience to Joseph, courage to David, wisdom to Solomon, knowledge to Daniel, and divine Messianic authority to Yeshua. 412 pages.

Paperback	978-1936716654	**LB87**	$25.99

Come and Worship *Ways to Worship from the Hebrew Scriptures*
—Compiled by Barbara D. Malda

We were created to worship. God has graciously given us many ways to express our praise to him. Each way fits a different situation or moment in life, yet all are intended to bring honor and glory to him. When we believe that he is who he says he is [see *His Names are Wonderful!*] and that his Word is true, worship flows naturally from our hearts to his. 128 pages.

Paperback	978-1936716678	**LB88**	$9.99

His Names Are Wonderful
Getting to Know God Through His Hebrew Names
—Elizabeth L. Vander Meulen and Barbara D. Malda

In Hebrew thought, names did more than identify people; they revealed their nature. God's identity is expressed not in one name, but in many. This book will help readers know God better as they uncover the truths in his Hebrew names. 160 pages.

Paperback	978-1880226308	**LB58**	$9.99

The Revolt of Rabbi Morris Cohen
Exploring the Passion & Piety of a Modern-day Pharisee
—Anthony Cardinale

A brilliant school psychologist, Rabbi Morris Cohen went on a one-man strike to protest the systematic mislabeling of slow learning pupils as "Learning Disabled" (to extract special education money from the state). His disciplinary hearing, based on the transcript, is a hilarious read! This effusive, garrulous man with an irresistible sense of humor lost his job, but achieved a major historic victory causing the reform of the billion-dollar special education program. Enter into the mind of an eighth-generation Orthodox rabbi to see how he deals spiritually with the loss of everything, even the love of his children. This modern-day Pharisee discovered a trusted friend in the author (a born again believer in Jesus) with whom he could openly struggle over Rabbinic Judaism as well as the concept of Jesus (Yeshua) as Messiah. 320 pages.

Paperback	978-1936716722	**LB92**	$19.99

Stories of Yeshua
—Jim Reimann, Illustrator Julia Filipone-Erez

Children's Bible Storybook with four stories about Yeshua (Jesus).
Yeshua is Born: The Bethlehem Story based on Lk 1:26-35 & 2:1-20; *Yeshua and Nicodemus in Jerusalem* based on Jn 3:1-16; *Yeshua Loves the Little Children of the World* based on Matthew 18:1–6 & 19:13–15; *Yeshua is Alive-The Empty Tomb in Jerusalem* based on Matthew 26:17-56, Jn 19:16-20:18, Lk 24:50-53. Ages 3-7, 48 pages.

Paperback	978-1936716685	**LB89**	$14.99

To the Ends of the Earth – How the First Jewish Followers of Yeshua Transformed the Ancient World
— Dr. Jeffrey Seif

Everyone knows that the first followers of Yeshua were Jews, and that Christianity was very Jewish for the first 50 to 100 years. It's a known fact that there were many congregations made up mostly of Jews, although the false perception today is, that in the second century they disappeared. Dr. Seif reveals the truth of what happened to them and how these early Messianic Jews influenced and transformed the behavior of the known world at that time. 171 pages

Paperback	978-1936716463	**LB83**	$17.99

Jewish Roots and Foundations of the Scriptures I & II
—John Fischer, Th.D, Ph.D.

An outstanding evangelical leader once said: "There is something shallow about a Christianity that has lost its Jewish roots." A beautiful painting is a careful interweaving of a number of elements. Among other things, there are the background, the foreground and the subject. Discovering the roots of your faith is a little like appreciating the various parts of a painting. In the background is the panorama of preparation and pictures found in the Old Testament. In the foreground is the landscape and light of the first century Jewish setting. All of this is intricately connected with and highlights the subject—which becomes the flowering of all these aspects—the coming of God to earth and what that means for us. Discovering and appreciating your roots in this way broadens, deepens and enriches your faith and your understanding of Scripture. This audio is 32 hours of live class instruction - audio is clear and easy to understand.

9781936716623   **LCD03 / LCD04** $49.99 each

The Gospels in their Jewish Context
—John Fischer, Th.D, Ph.D.

An examination of the Jewish background and nature of the Gospels in their contemporary political, cultural and historical settings, emphasizing each gospel's special literary presentation of Yeshua, and highlighting the cultural and religious contexts necessary for understanding each of the gospels. 32 hours of audio/video instruction on MP3-DVD and pdf of syllabus.

978-1936716241   **LCD01** $49.99

The Epistles from a Jewish Perspective
—John Fischer, Th.D, Ph.D.

An examination of the relationship of Rabbi Shaul (the Apostle Paul) and the Apostles to their Jewish contemporaries and environment; surveys their Jewish practices, teaching, controversy with the religious leaders, and many critical passages, with emphasis on the Jewish nature, content, and background of these letters. 32 hours of audio/video instruction on MP3-DVD and pdf of syllabus.

978-1936716258   **LCD02** $49.99

The Red Heifer *A Jewish Cry for Messiah*
—Anthony Cardinale

Award-winning journalist and playwright Anthony Cardinale has traveled extensively in Israel, and recounts here his interviews with Orthodox rabbis, secular Israelis, and Palestinian Arabs about the current search for a red heifer by Jewish radicals wishing to rebuild the Temple and bring the Messiah. These real-life interviews are interwoven within an engaging and dramatic fictional portrayal of the diverse people of Israel and how they would react should that red heifer be found. Readers will find themselves in the Land, where they can hear learned rabbis and ordinary Israelis talking about the red heifer and dealing with all the related issues and the imminent coming and identity of Messiah. 341 pages

Paperback   978-1936716470   **LB79** $19.99

The Borough Park Papers
—Multiple Authors

As you read the New Testament, you "overhear" debates first-century Messianic Jews had about critical issues, e.g. Gentiles being "allowed" into the Messianic kingdom (Acts 15). Similarly, you're now invited to "listen in" as leading twenty-first century Messianic Jewish theologians discuss critical issues facing us today. Some ideas may not fit into your previously held pre-suppositions or pre-conceptions. Indeed, you may find some paradigm shifting in your thinking. We want to share the thoughts of these thinkers with you, our family in the Messiah.

Symposium I:
The Gospel and the Jewish People
   248 pages, Paperback   978-1936716593   **LB84** $39.95

Symposium II:
The Deity of Messiah and the Mystery of God
   211 pages, Paperback   978-1936716609   **LB85** $39.95

Symposium III:
How Jewish Should the Messianic Community Be?
   Paperback   978-1936716616   **LB86** $39.95

Passion for Israel: *A Short History of the Evangelical Church's Support of Israel and the Jewish People*
—Dan Juster

History reveals a special commitment of Christians to the Jews as God's still elect people, but the terrible atrocities committed against the Jews by so-called Christians have overshadowed the many good deeds that have been performed. This important history needs to be told to help heal the wounds and to inspire more Christians to stand together in support of Israel. 84 pages

   Paperback   978-1936716401   **LB78** $9.99

On The Way to Emmaus: *Searching the Messianic Prophecies*
—Dr. Jacques Doukhan

An outstanding compilation of the most critical Messianic prophecies by a renowned conservative Christian Scholar, drawing on material from the Bible, Rabbinic sources, Dead Sea Scrolls, and more. 217 pages

   Paperback   978-1936716432   **LB80** $14.99

Yeshua *A Guide to the Real Jesus and the Original Church*
—Dr. Ron Moseley

Opens up the history of the Jewish roots of the Christian faith. Illuminates the Jewish background of Yeshua and the Church and never flinches from showing "Jesus was a Jew, who was born, lived, and died, within first century Judaism." Explains idioms in the New Testament. Endorsed by Dr. Brad Young and Dr. Marvin Wilson. 213 pages.

   Paperback   978-1880226681   **LB29** $12.99

Gateways to Torah *Joining the Ancient Conversation on the Weekly Portion*
—Rabbi Russell Resnik

From before the days of Messiah until today, Jewish people have read from and discussed a prescribed portion of the Pentateuch each week. Now, a Messianic Jewish Rabbi, Russell Resnik, brings another perspective on the Torah, that of a Messianic Jew. 246 pages.

Paperback	978-1880226889	**LB42**	$15.99

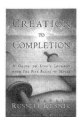

Creation to Completion *A Guide to Life's Journey from the Five Books of Moses*
—Rabbi Russell Resnik

Endorsed by Coach Bill McCartney, Founder of Promise Keepers & Road to Jerusalem: "Paul urged Timothy to study the Scriptures (2 Tim. 3:16), advising him to apply its teachings to all aspects of his life. Since there was no New Testament then, this rabbi/apostle was convinced that his disciple would profit from studying the Torah, the Five Books of Moses, and the Old Testament. Now, Rabbi Resnik has written a warm devotional commentary that will help you understand and apply the Law of Moses to your life in a practical way." 256 pages

Paperback	978-1880226322	**LB61**	$14.99

Walk Genesis! Walk Exodus! Walk Leviticus! Walk Numbers! Walk Deuteronomy!
Messianic Jewish Devotional Commentaries
—Jeffrey Enoch Feinberg, Ph.D.

Using the weekly synagogue readings, Dr. Jeffrey Feinberg has put together some very valuable material in his "Walk" series. Each section includes a short Hebrew lesson (for the non-Hebrew speaker), key concepts, an excellent overview of the portion, and some practical applications. Can be used as a daily devotional as well as a Bible study tool. Paperback.

Walk Genesis!	238 pages	978-1880226759	**LB34**	$12.99
Walk Exodus!	224 pages	978-1880226872	**LB40**	$12.99
Walk Leviticus!	208 pages	978-1880226926	**LB45**	$12.99
Walk Numbers!	211 pages	978-1880226995	**LB48**	$12.99
Walk Deuteronomy!	231 pages	978-1880226186	**LB51**	$12.99
SPECIAL! Five-book Walk!		5 Book Set **Save $10**	**LK28**	$54.99

Good News According To Matthew
—Dr. Henry Einspruch

English translation with quotations from the Tanakh (Old Testament) capitalized and printed in Hebrew. Helpful notations are included. Lovely black and white illustrations throughout the book. 86 pages.

Paperback	978-1880226025	**LB03**	$4.99
Also available in Yiddish.		**LB02**	$4.99

They Loved the Torah *What Yeshua's First Followers Really Thought About the Law*
—Dr. David Friedman

Although many Jews believe that Paul taught against the Law, this book disproves that notion. An excellent case for his premise that all the first followers of the Messiah were not only Torah-observant, but also desired to spread their love for God's entire Word to the gentiles to whom they preached. 144 pages. Endorsed by Dr. David Stern, Ariel Berkowitz, Rabbi Dr. Stuart Dauermann & Dr. John Fischer.

Paperback	978-1880226940	**LB47**	$9.99

The Distortion *2000 Years of Misrepresenting the Relationship Between Jesus the Messiah and the Jewish People*
—Dr. John Fischer & Dr. Patrice Fischer

Did the Jews kill Jesus? Did they really reject him? With the rise of global anti–Semitism, it is important to understand what the Gospels teach about the relationship between Jewish people and their Messiah. 2000 years of distortion have made this difficult. Learn how the distortion began and continues to this day and what you can do to change it. 126 pages. Endorsed by Dr. Ruth Fleischer, Rabbi Russell Resnik, Dr. Daniel C. Juster, Dr. Michael Rydelnik.

Paperback	978-1880226254	**LB54**	$11.99

God's Appointed Times *A Practical Guide to Understanding and Celebrating the Biblical Holidays* – **New Edition.**

—Rabbi Barney Kasdan

The Biblical Holy Days teach us about the nature of God and his plan for mankind, and can be a source of God's blessing for all believers–Jews and Gentiles–today. Includes historical background, traditional Jewish observance, New Testament relevance, and prophetic significance, plus music, crafts and holiday recipes. 145 pages.

English - Paperback	978-1880226353	**LB63**	$12.99
Spanish - Paperback	978-1880226391	**LB59**	$12.99

God's Appointed Customs *A Messianic Jewish Guide to the Biblical Lifecycle and Lifestyle*

— Rabbi Barney Kasdan

Explains how biblical customs are often the missing key to unlocking the depths of Scripture. Discusses circumcision, the Jewish wedding, and many more customs mentioned in the New Testament. Companion to *God's Appointed Times*. 170 pages.

English - Paperback	978-1880226636	**LB26**	$12.99
Spanish - Paperback	978-1880226551	**LB60**	$12.99

Celebrations of the Bible *A Messianic Children's Curriculum*

Did you know that each Old Testament feast or festival finds its fulfillment in the New? They enrich the lives of people who experience and enjoy them. Our popular curriculum for children is in a brand new, user-friendly format. The lay-flat at binding allows you to easily reproduce handouts and worksheets. Celebrations of the Bible has been used by congregations, Sunday schools, ministries, homeschoolers, and individuals to teach children about the biblical festivals. Each of these holidays are presented for Preschool (2-K), Primary (Grades 1-3), Junior (Grades 4-6), and Children's Worship/Special Services. 208 pages.

Paperback	978-1880226261	**LB55**	$24.99

Passover: *The Key That Unlocks the Book of Revelation*

—Daniel C. Juster, Th.D.

Is there any more enigmatic book of the Bible than Revelation? Controversy concerning its meaning has surrounded it back to the first century. Today, the arguments continue. Yet, Dan Juster has given us the key that unlocks the entire book—the events and circumstances of the Passover/Exodus. By interpreting Revelation through the lens of Exodus, Dan Juster provides a unified overview that helps us read Revelation as it was always meant to be read, as a drama of spiritual conflict, deliverance, and above all, worship. He also shows how this final drama, fulfilled in Messiah, resonates with the Torah and all of God's Word. — Russ Resnik, Executive Director, Union of Messianic Jewish Congregations.

Paperback	978-1936716210	**LB74**	$10.99

The Messianic Passover Haggadah
Revised and Updated
—Rabbi Barry Rubin and Steffi Rubin.

Guides you through the traditional Passover seder dinner, step-by-step. Not only does this observance remind us of our rescue from Egyptian bondage, but, we remember Messiah's last supper, a Passover seder. The theme of redemption is seen throughout the evening. What's so unique about our Haggadah is the focus on Yeshua (Jesus) the Messiah and his teaching, especially on his last night in the upper room. 36 pages.

English - Paperback	978-1880226292	**LB57**	$4.99
Spanish - Paperback	978-1880226599	**LBSP01**	$4.99

The Messianic Passover Seder Preparation Guide
Includes recipes, blessings and songs. 19 pages.

English - Paperback	978-1880226247	**LB10**	$2.99
Spanish - Paperback	978-1880226728	**LBSP02**	$2.99

The Sabbath *Entering God's Rest*
—Barry Rubin & Steffi Rubin

Even if you've never celebrated Shabbat before, this book will guide you into the rest God has for all who would enter in—Jews and non-Jews. Contains prayers, music, recipes; in short, everything you need to enjoy the Sabbath, even how to observe havdalah, the closing ceremony of the Sabbath. Also discusses the Saturday or Sunday controversy. 48 pages.

Paperback	978-1880226742	**LB32**	$6.99

Havdalah *The Ceremony that Completes the Sabbath*
—Dr. Neal & Jamie Lash

The Sabbath ends with this short, yet equally sweet ceremony called havdalah (separation). This ceremony reminds us to be a light and a sweet fragrance in this world of darkness as we carry the peace, rest, joy and love of the Sabbath into the work week. 28 pages.

Paperback	978-1880226605	**LB69**	$4.99

Dedicate and Celebrate!
A Messianic Jewish Guide to Hanukkah
—Barry Rubin & Family

Hanukkah means "dedication" — a theme of significance for Jews and Christians. Discussing its historical background, its modern-day customs, deep meaning for all of God's people, this little book covers all the how-tos! Recipes, music, and prayers for lighting the menorah, all included! 32 pages.

Paperback	978-1880226834	**LB36**	$4.99

The Conversation
An Intimate Journal of the Emmaus Encounter
—Judy Salisbury

"Then beginning with Moses and with all the prophets, He explained to them the things concerning Himself in all the Scriptures." Luke 24:27
If you've ever wondered what that conversation must have been like, this captivating book takes you there.

"The Conversation brings to life that famous encounter between the two disciples and our Lord Jesus on the road to Emmaus. While it is based in part on an imaginative reconstruction, it is filled with the throbbing pulse of the excitement of the sensational impact that our Lord's resurrection should have on all of our lives." ~ Dr. Walter Kaiser President Emeritus Gordon-Conwell Theological Seminary. Hardcover 120 pages.

Hardcover	978-1936716173	**LB73**	$14.99
Paperback	978-1936716364	**LB77**	$9.99

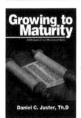

Growing to Maturity
A Messianic Jewish Discipleship Guide
—Daniel C. Juster, Th.D.

This discipleship series presents first steps of understanding and spiritual practice, tailored for the Jewish believer. It's purpose is to aid the believer in living according to Yeshua's will as a disciple, one who has learned the example of his teacher. The course is structured according to recent advances in individualized educational instruction. Discipleship is serious business and the material is geared for serious study and reflection. Each chapter is divided into short sections followed by study questions. 256 pages.

Paperback	978-1936716227	**LB75**	$19.99

Growing to Maturity Primer: *A Messianic Jewish Discipleship Workbook*
—Daniel C. Juster, Th.D.

A basic book of material in question and answer form. Usable by everyone. 60 pages.

Paperback	978-0961455507	**TB16**	$7.99

Conveying Our Heritage A Messianic Jewish Guide to Home Practice
—Daniel C. Juster, Th.D. Patricia A. Juster

Throughout history the heritage of faith has been conveyed within the family and the congregation. The first institution in the Bible is the family and only the family can raise children with an adequate appreciation of our faith and heritage. This guide exists to help families learn how to pass on the heritage of spiritual Messianic Jewish life. Softcover, 86 pages

Paperback	978-1936716739	**LB93**	$8.99

That They May Be One *A Brief Review of Church Restoration Movements and Their Connection to the Jewish People*
—Daniel Juster, Th.D

Something prophetic and momentous is happening. The Church is finally fully grasping its relationship to Israel and the Jewish people. Author describes the restoration movements in Church history and how they connected to Israel and the Jewish people. Each one contributed in some way—some more, some less—toward the ultimate unity between Jews and Gentiles. Predicted in the Old Testament and fulfilled in the New, Juster believes this plan of God finds its full expression in Messianic Judaism. He may be right. See what you think as you read *That They May Be One*. 100 pages.

Paperback	978-1880226711	**LB71**	$9.99

The Greatest Commandment
How the Sh'ma Leads to More Love in Your Life
—Irene Lipson

"What is the greatest commandment?" Yeshua was asked. His reply—"Hear, O Israel, the Lord our God, the Lord is one, and you are to love Adonai your God with all your heart, with all your soul, with all your understanding, and all your strength." A superb book explaining each word so the meaning can be fully grasped and lived. Endorsed by Elliot Klayman, Susan Perlman, & Robert Stearns. 175 pages.

Paperback	978-1880226360	**LB65**	$12.99

Blessing the King of the Universe
Transforming Your Life Through the Practice of Biblical Praise
—Irene Lipson

Insights into the ancient biblical practice of blessing God are offered clearly and practically. With examples from Scripture and Jewish tradition, this book teaches the biblical formula used by men and women of the Bible, including the Messiah; points to new ways and reasons to praise the Lord; and explains more about the Jewish roots of the faith. Endorsed by Rabbi Barney Kasdan, Dr. Mitch Glaser, & Rabbi Dr. Dan Cohn-Sherbok. 144 pages.

Paperback	978-1880226797	**LB53**	$11.99

You Bring the Bagels, I'll Bring the Gospel
Sharing the Messiah with Your Jewish Neighbor
Revised Edition—Now with Study Questions
—Rabbi Barry Rubin

This "how-to-witness-to-Jewish-people" book is an orderly presentation of everything you need to share the Messiah with a Jewish friend. Includes Messianic prophecies, Jewish objections to believing, sensitivities in your witness, words to avoid. A "must read" for all who care about the Jewish people. Good for individual or group study. Used in Bible schools. Endorsed by Harold A. Sevener, Dr. Walter C. Kaiser, Dr. Erwin J. Kolb and Dr. Arthur F. Glasser. 253 pages, Paperback.

English	978-1880226650	**LB13**	$12.99
Te Tengo Buenas Noticias	978-0829724103	**OBSP02**	$14.99

Making Eye Contact With God
A Weekly Devotional for Women
—Terri Gillespie

What kind of eyes do you have? Are they downcast and sad? Are they full of God's joy and passion? See yourself through the eyes of God. Using real life anecdotes, combined with scripture, the author reveals God's heart for women everywhere, as she softly speaks of the ways in which women see God. Endorsed by prominent authors: Dr. Angela Hunt, Wanda Dyson and Kathryn Mackel. 247 pages.

Hardcover	978-1880226513	**LB68**	$19.99

Divine Reversal
The Transforming Ethics of Jesus
—Rabbi Russell Resnik

In the Old Testament, God often reversed the plans of man. Yeshua's ethics continue this theme. Following his path transforms one's life from within, revealing the source of true happiness, forgiveness, reconciliation, fidelity and love. From the introduction, "As a Jewish teacher, Jesus doesn't separate matters of theology from practice. His teaching is consistently practical, ethical, and applicable to real life, even two thousand years after it was originally given." Endorsed by Jonathan Bernis, Dr. Daniel C. Juster, Dr. Jeffrey L. Seif, and Dr Darrell Bock. 206 pages

Paperback	978-1880226803	**LB72**	$12.99

Praying Like the Jew, Jesus
Recovering the Ancient Roots of New Testament Prayer
—Dr. Timothy P. Jones

This eye-opening book reveals the Jewish background of many of Yeshua's prayers. Historical vignettes "transport" you to the times of Yeshua so you can grasp the full meaning of Messiah's prayers. Unique devotional thoughts and meditations, presented in down-to-earth language, provide inspiration for a more meaningful prayer life and help you draw closer to God. Endorsed by Mark Galli, James W. Goll, Rev. Robert Stearns, James F. Strange, and Dr. John Fischer. 144 pages.

Paperback	978-1880226285	**LB56**	$9.99

Growing Your Olive Tree Marriage *A Guide for Couples*
from Two Traditions
—David J. Rudolph

One partner is Jewish; the other is Christian. Do they celebrate Hanukkah, Christmas or both? Do they worship in a church or a synagogue? How will the children be raised? This is the first book from a biblical perspective that addresses the concerns of intermarried couples, offering a godly solution. Includes highlights of interviews with intermarried couples. Endorsed by Walter C. Kaiser, Jr., Rabbi Dan Cohn-Sherbok, Jonathan Settel, Dr. Mitchell Glaser & Natalie Sirota. 224 pages.

Paperback	978-1880226179	**LB50**	$12.99

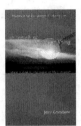

In Search of the Silver Lining *Where is God in the Midst of Life's Storms?*
—Jerry Gramckow

When faced with suffering, what are your choices? Storms have always raged. And people have either perished in their wake or risen above the tempests, shaping history by their responses...new storms are on the horizon. How will we deal with them? How will we shape history or those who follow us? The answer lies in how we view God in the midst of the storms. Endorsed by Joseph C. Aldrich, Ray Beeson, Dr. Daniel Juster. 176 pages.

| Paperback | 978-1880226865 | **LB39** | $10.99 |

The Voice of the Lord *Messianic Jewish Daily Devotional*
—Edited by David J. Rudolph

Brings insight into the Jewish Scriptures—both Old and New Testaments. Twenty-two prominent Messianic contributors provide practical ways to apply biblical truth. Start your day with this unique resource. Explanatory notes. Perfect companion to the Complete Jewish Bible (see page 2). Endorsed by Edith Schaeffer, Dr. Arthur F. Glaser, Dr. Michael L. Brown, Mitch Glaser and Moishe Rosen. 416 pages.

| Paperback | 9781880226704 | **LB31** | $19.99 |

Kingdom Relationships *God's Laws for the Community of Faith*
—Dr. Ron Moseley

Dr. Ron Moseley`s Yeshua: A Guide to the Real Jesus and the Original Church has taught thousands of people about the Jewishness of not only Yeshua, but of the first followers of the Messiah.
In this work, Moseley focuses on the teaching of Torah -- the Five Books of Moses -- tapping into truths that greatly help modern-day members of the community of faith. 64 pages.

| Paperback | 978-1880226841 | **LB37** | $8.99 |

Mutual Blessing *Discovering the Ultimate Destiny of Creation*
—Daniel C. Juster

To truly love as God loves is to see the wonder and richness of the distinct differences in all of creation and his natural order of interdependence. This is the way to mutual blessing and the discovery of the ultimate destiny of creation. Learn how to become enriched and blessed as you enrich and bless others and all that is around you! Softcover, 135 pages.

| Paperback | 978-1936716746 | **LB94** | $9.99 |

Train Up A Child *Successful Parenting For The Next Generation*
—Dr. Daniel L. Switzer

The author, former principal of Ets Chaiyim Messianic Jewish Day School, and father of four, combines solid biblical teaching with Jewish sources on child raising, focusing on the biblical holy days, giving fresh insight into fulfilling the role of parent. 188 pages. Endorsed by Dr. David J. Rudolph, Paul Lieberman, and Dr. David H. Stern.

| Paperback | 978-1880226377 | **LB64** | $12.99 |

Fire on the Mountain - *Past Renewals, Present Revivals and the Coming Return of Israel*
—Dr. Louis Goldberg

The term "revival" is often used to describe a person or congregation turning to God. Is this something that "just happens," or can it be brought about? Dr. Louis Goldberg, author and former professor of Hebrew and Jewish Studies at Moody Bible Institute, examines real revivals that took place in Bible times and applies them to today. 268 pages.

| Paperback | 978-1880226858 | **LB38** | $15.99 |

Voices of Messianic Judaism *Confronting Critical Issues Facing a Maturing Movement*
—General Editor Rabbi Dan Cohn-Sherbok

Many of the best minds of the Messianic Jewish movement contributed their thoughts to this collection of 29 substantive articles. Challenging questions are debated: The involvement of Gentiles in Messianic Judaism? How should outreach be accomplished? Liturgy or not? Intermarriage? 256 pages.

| Paperback | 978-1880226933 | **LB46** | $15.99 |

The Enduring Paradox *Exploratory Essays in Messianic Judaism*
—General Editor Dr. John Fischer

Yeshua and his Jewish followers began a new movement—Messianic Judaism—2,000 years ago. In the 20th century, it was reborn. Now, at the beginning of the 21st century, it is maturing. Twelve essays from top contributors to the theology of this vital movement of God, including: Dr. Walter C. Kaiser, Dr. David H. Stern, and Dr. John Fischer. 196 pages.

| Paperback | 978-1880226902 | **LB43** | $13.99 |

The World To Come *A Portal to Heaven on Earth*
—Derek Leman

An insightful book, exposing fallacies and false teachings surrounding this extremely important subject... paints a hopeful picture of the future and dispels many non-biblical notions. Intriguing chapters: Magic and Desire, The Vision of the Prophets, Hints of Heaven, Horrors of Hell, The Drama of the Coming Ages. Offers a fresh, but old, perspective on the world to come, as it interacts with the prophets of Israel and the Bible. 110 pages.

| Paperback | 978-1880226049 | **LB67** | $9.99 |

Hebrews Through a Hebrew's Eyes
—Dr. Stuart Sacks

Written to first-century Messianic Jews, this epistle, understood through Jewish eyes, edifies and encourages all. 119 pages. Endorsed by Dr. R.C. Sproul and James M. Boice.

| Paperback | 978-1880226612 | **LB23** | $10.99 |

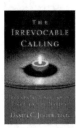

The Irrevocable Calling *Israel's Role As A Light To The Nations*
—Daniel C. Juster, Th.D.

Referring to the chosen-ness of the Jewish people, Paul, the Apostle, wrote "For God's free gifts and his calling are irrevocable" (Rom. 11:29). This messenger to the Gentiles understood the unique calling of his people, Israel. So does Dr. Daniel Juster, President of Tikkun Ministries Int'l. In *The Irrevocable Calling*, he expands Paul's words, showing how Israel was uniquely chosen to bless the world and how these blessings can be enjoyed today. Endorsed by Dr. Jack Hayford, Mike Bickle and Don Finto. 64 pages.

Paperback	978-1880226346	**LB66**	$8.99

Are There Two Ways of Atonement?
—Dr. Louis Goldberg

Here Dr. Louis Goldberg, long-time professor of Jewish Studies at Moody Bible Institute, exposes the dangerous doctrine of Two-Covenant Theology. 32 pages.

Paperback	978-1880226056	**LB12**	$ 4.99

Awakening *Articles and Stories About Jews and Yeshua*
—Arranged by Anna Portnov

Articles, testimonies, and stories about Jewish people and their relationship with God, Israel, and the Messiah. Includes the effective tract, "The Most Famous Jew of All." One of our best anthologies for witnessing to Jewish people. Let this book witness for you! Russian version also available. 110 pages.

English - Paperback	978-1880226094	**LB15**	$ 6.99
Russian - Paperback	978-1880226018	**LB14**	$ 6.99

The Unpromised Land *The Struggle of Messianic Jews Gary and Shirley Beresford*
—Linda Alexander

They felt God calling them to live in Israel, the Promised Land. Wanting nothing more than to live quietly and grow old together in the country of refuge for all Jewish people, little did they suspect what events would follow to try their faith. The fight to make *aliyah*, to claim their rightful inheritance in the Promised Land, became a battle waged not only for themselves, but also for Messianic Jews all over the world that wish to return to the Jewish homeland. Here is the true saga of the Beresford's journey to the land of their forefathers. 216 pages.

Paperback	978-1880226568	**LB19**	$ 9.99

Death of Messiah *Twenty fascinating articles that address a subject of grief, hope, and ultimate triumph.*

—Edited by Kai Kjaer-Hansen

This compilation, written by well-known Jewish believers, addresses the issue of Messiah and offers proof that Yeshua—the true Messiah—not only died, but also was resurrected! 160 pages.

| Paperback | 978-1880226582 | **LB20** | $ 8.99 |

Beloved Dissident *(A Novel)*

—Laurel West

A gripping story of human relationships, passionate love, faith, and spiritual testing. Set in the world of high finance, intrigue, and international terrorism, the lives of David, Jonathan, and Leah intermingle on many levels--especially their relationships with one another and with God. As the two men tangle with each other in a rising whirlwind of excitement and danger, each hopes to win the fight for Leah's love. One of these rivals will move Leah to a level of commitment and love she has never imagined--or dared to dream. Whom will she choose? 256 pages.

| Paperback | 978-1880226766 | **LB33** | $ 9.99 |

Sudden Terror

—Dr. David Friedman

Exposes the hidden agenda of militant Islam. The author, a former member of the Israel Defense Forces, provides eye-opening information needed in today's dangerous world.

Dr. David Friedman recounts his experiences confronting terrorism; analyzes the biblical roots of the conflict between Israel and Islam; provides an overview of early Islam; demonstrates how the United States and Israel are bound together by a common enemy; and shows how to cope with terrorism and conquer fear. The culmination of many years of research and personal experiences. This expose will prepare you for what's to come! 160 pages.

| Paperback | 978-1880226155 | **LB49** | $ 9.99 |

It is Good! *Growing Up in a Messianic Family*

—Steffi Rubin

Growing up in a Messianic Jewish family. Meet Tovah! Tovah (Hebrew for "Good") is growing up in a Messianic Jewish home, learning the meaning of God's special days. Ideal for young children, it teaches the biblical holidays and celebrates faith in Yeshua. 32 pages to read & color.

| Paperback | 978-1880226063 | **LB11** | $ 4.99 |